# FINANCIAL SERVICES IN INDIA

(for MBA (Finance), M.Com, CA, ICWA, PGDFM, PGDBM, CFA etc..)

**By the Same Author**

Financial Markets and Institutions

---

**About the Author**

**G. Ramesh Babu** obtained his Ph.D. from Kakatiya University, Warangal, Andhra Pradesh. He joined the S.S.R. Jyothi Arts and Science College, Khammam in 1987 as a faculty in Commerce. He has vast teaching experience both at UG and PG levels, his area of specialisation being Finance. He has published six research papers in journals of repute. He is member of All India Management Association; Associate Member of Society for Capital Market Research and Indian Institute of Public Administration, New Delhi.

# FINANCIAL SERVICES
# IN
# INDIA

Dr. G. RAMESH BABU
M.Com., Ph.D., MIAM.,
Department of Commerce,
S.S.R. Jyothi College, Khammam
E-mail: ramesh-238712@rediffmail.com

CONCEPT PUBLISHING COMPANY, NEW DELHI-110059

**Cataloging in Publication Data—DK**
*Courtesy:* D.K. Agencies (P) Ltd. <docinfo@dkagencies.com>

**Ramesh Babu, G. (Gunda),** 1963-
Financial services in India / G. Ramesh Babu.
p. cm.
Includes bibliographical references.
Includes index.
ISBN 8180692183

1. Financial services industry—India. I. Title.

DDC 332.109 54 21



ISBN 81-8069-219-1 (P.B.)

First Published 2005



*Published and Printed by*
Ashok Kumar Mittal
**Concept Publishing Company**
A/15-16, Commercial Block, Mohan Garden
New Delhi-110059 (INDIA)

*Phones* : 25351460, 25351794
*Fax* : 091-11-25357103
*Email* : publishing@conceptpub.com

*Dedicated*
*to*
*Lord Balaji*

The most powerful man in the Universe.

my father Laxminarayana
my mother Kasturi

# PREFACE

"Money is like an arm or a leg use it or lose it"

*—Henry Ford*

Finance is a subject of growing importance and interest. The economics of the world continue to integrate and there is now Unwavering Commitment to the principles and practices of a free market economy. The structural reforms necessary to promote free markets, such as privatisation, trade liberalisation tax reforms, strengthening of capital markets and financial intermediation systems are taking place. The Indian Industry to become globally competitive, has to make optimal use of its resources reduce its costs and improvement in quality aspects. Financial services sector represents a significant proportion in the financial market activity in the country. The liberalisation and deregulation have provided a new era for the capital market. Financial services are the important components of the financial system. The financial system can create wonders in the economic development of a country. The financial system is a weapon to counter the poverty. The financial system is a set of complex and closely connected with various aspects i.e. Financial Instruments, Financial Institutions, Financial Markets and Financial Services.

In this book an attempt is made to give a comprehensive coverage of financial services aspects. This book has been written as per the syllabus prescribed for the MBA (Finance) M.Com, C.A., C.S., MFA, PGDBF, PGDBM, PGDFM, CFA, MFC and MFM. I am confident that this book will help the students, faculty members, executives in finance area, stock brokers, registrars, fund managers of mutual funds and Non-banking financial institutions as well as to those individuals who desire to up grade their knowledge on financial services.

This book is divided into Four Units. All the parts are organised into related chapters which should usually be read in the order presented. But these parts are fairly independent of each other

Unit I: Consists of 5 chapters and provides a broad view of the Indian financial system. i.e. Financial Institutions, Financial Markets, Financial Services.

Unit II: Contains 4 chapters deals with Mutual funds, Venture capital, Leasing and credit rating services.

Unit III: Contains 9 chapters such as Underwriting Registrars, SEBI, NSE, OTC and Depository system etc.

Unit IV: This unit consists of latest trends in financial services sector such as factoring insurance, credit cards, housing finance, hire purchase and E-commerce.

Since the book is synthesis, I am indebited to all authors who have contributed to the world of finance. I hope that I have interpreted their views correctly. I have made acknowledgements of every idea whose sources have been identified. I am indebted to my colleagues both academic and professionals and countless students. It would be impossible to list them all. Any how for evincing personal interest in undertaking a project of this magnitude and making invaluable suggestions from time to time. It is my pleasure to express grateful thanks to Sri K. Ram Mohan, President, Jyothi Education Society, Sri P. Raghu Rama Rao, Treasurer, Dr. D. Ramachandra Bose, Principal SSR Jyothi College, Khammam. I am also thankful to my professors, Prof. P. Madhusudan Rao, Prof. V. Gangadhar, Prof. Narasimha Murthy, Prof. Sudarshan, Prof. A. Shankaraiah, Prof. Krishna Reddy, Prof. Rajeswar Rao whose elderly advice has been of immense use to me. I must also place on record my sincere thanks to my teachers Sri K.V. Kameswar Rao, Sri P.V. Anjaneyulu, Sri G. Satyanarayana and Dr. K. Srinivas Rao. I am also thankful to Sri K.V. Kamaraj Parthulu for improving the language contents of this book.

I owe my gratitude to S.P. Sinha and Ashok Mittal of Concept Publishing Company for giving their personal attention in expediting printing of the book.

**G. Ramesh Babu**

# CONTENTS

## UNIT I

## UNIT II

## UNIT III

# UNIT I

- Financial Services in India
- Financial Institutions
- Financial Markets
- Financial Instruments
- Financial Services

# 1

# FINANCIAL SERVICES IN INDIA

## Introduction

The increasing and diverse needs of the growing corporate sector encourages the steady growth of financial services market. After the implementation of 1991 reforms, the financial sector has grown tremendously. Financial services organisations are increasing their role through designing the innovative product mix. The financial sector represents a significant proportion in the financial market activity in the country. Financial services organisations plays a major role in the operation of economic system. The industrial liberalisation and deregulations have provided a new era for the capital market. India's liberalisation policy has gained importance in the context of global business scene. India ranked 7th on the Confidence Index of the foreign investors who perceived India as possessing the highest potential for improving its attractions over the next 10 years. India ranked[1] quite high in terms of being an attractive destination. A large market, skilled labour force, competitive wages, easy availability of finance and political stability made India an attractive destination for the Foreign Direct Investment, but was constrained somewhat by slow pace of government reforms poor infrastructure, **cultural barriers** and **bureaucracy**. Services, industries and industrial product firms had found the opportunity for investment in India. The government cleared **640 FDI** proposals, involving **Rs. 11,910** crores during January–April, 2001, the actual inflow was only **Rs. 5,596** crores during this period. The realisation rate of the **FDI** approvals slipped to **52 per cent** in **2000**. We cannot increase our business unless we are more helpful to the global investors.

The number of intermediaries operating in the capital market have grown exponentially. The financial industry has been growing at a very fast rate. **Mumbai** is the leading financial service industry in

India. It has become more expensive on par with **Tokyo** in terms of costs. **The National Stock Exchange** is the first financial service centre in India which has completely computerised its working. Financial services are the important components of the financial system. Financial services caters the needs of financial institutions, financial market and instruments. The development of financial services will depend upon the investment climate of a country. India has recently improved its position to attract the flow of capital in global market. India has been a more powerful nation and has high potential capabilities. Recently the **Japan Bank for International Cooperation[2] (JBIC)** conducted a study of **792** manufacturing companies that have 3 or more foreign affiliates including at least one manufacturing base abroad as of **October, 2000**. The survey was conducted from July to August, 2001 and is the 13th of **annual series.**

**China** continues to be the top investment destination in **Japanese** industry. **India** has reached to **5th position** in their priority list. As per the survey the top **4 ranking** countries are **China, U.S., Thailand** and **Indonesia** respectively. The survey reveals the **China** is the only one country with high expectations of growth potential of its market. It also pointed out that there are a number of problems in that country like lack of transparency in the application of law, frequent and abrupt changes in law and regulations and the like. On the other hand, the reasons for considering **India** as a promising investment destination have not changed significantly over the years. Though its ranking has improved, the factors in favour of **India** are potentiality of future market growth **(76%)**, cheap labour force **(46%)**, excellent human resources **(22%)** and present market size **(20%)**. But the negatives in the case of India are lack of infrastructure and transportation **(42%)**, local government and social conditions **(34%)**, complicated administrative procedures **(23%)** and other small problems.

Another feature of the latest survey is that as many as **52 Japanese** manufacturers, as compared to **37** in the last year's survey cited. India as one of the top **five** promising countries for the overseas business operations over the medium term. Besides this **3 companies** actually chose India to be the top most promising country for the overseas business operations.

The survey is significant because the **Japanese** investors took considerable time in approaching the Indian market with investments despite the liberalisation and opening up of the economy in **1991**. In fact, even as the most of the top industrialised countries like the **U.S.,**

**the U.K.** and **Germany** came in with their investments in the early years of liberalisation. The **Japanese** undertook various surveys and assessment trips to India before deciding on making investment commitments here. A rigid bureaucracy and lack of infrastructural facilities are the major concerns of the potential **Japanese** investors.

## Indian Financial System

Finance is the provision of money. It is exclusively concerned with the procurement of funds. It is concerned with cash and everything that takes place for smooth functioning of a business concern. Finance is not only involved in procurement of funds but also in their effective utilisation in business. Capital formation will depend on the finance which is made available in time, quantity and terms on which it is made available. Modern economics are influenced by expansion, diversification, attitudes of the savers and risk aversion of investors. The level of economic activity is the barometre of a nation's development. The supply and volume of money and credit enhances the worth of a nation. The process of capital formation in an economy is called financial system. The financial system can create wonders in the economic development of a country. The financial system is a **weapon** to counter the poverty. It is a tool to construct a good and strong economy. The financial system can make investment dreams into realities. The wealth of a nation can only be constructed through a better financial system. The financial system directly helps to increase the savings by offering better returns to the savers. The system will convert the savers, into investors successfully. It not only encourages the investment but also makes efficient allocation of resources in different investment channels. The system enhances the efficiency of a business concern which is reflected in the economic development. The relationship between economic development and financial development is mutually reinforcing. The financial development is a part of the economic development. Development creates and nourishes the economy. The financial system is a set of complex and closely connected with various aspects, i.e., financial instruments, financial institutions markets, financial services, financial practices etc. Financial system occupies a crucial role in the function of the economy. It includes all those activities dealing in finance and are organised into a system. The growth of the Indian financial system accompanied by diversification and financial innovation. India has witnessed all types of financial innovation. Financial innovation can be defined as **"The introduction of financial instrument or service or practice or introducing new uses of funds or finding out new sources of funds or introducing new process or techniques to handle the day to day operations or carrying out a new organisation"**. At present the Indian economy has a highly diversified structure of financial institutions. Similarly a large number of new financial instruments have to be introduced to fulfil the needs of dynamic corporate sector. The innovative instruments can leverage the corporate financial muscle. The financial development of a nation can be observed through the following powerful indicators:

1. **Finance ratio**
2. **Financial interrelation ratio**
3. **New issue ratio**
4. **Intermediation ratio**

### *1. Finance Ratio*

It is a macro analysis of an economy. It measures the total analysis of primary and secondary claims of national income. National income is an important component of an economy.

### *2. Financial Interrelation Ratio*

Financial interrelation ratio reveals about the relationship between financial assets and physical assets. It is a ratio which measures the ratio between financial structure and real assets structure of the economy.

### *3. New Issue Ratio*

New issues means the shares that are offered by newly promoted companies to the public for the first time. The new issues are also called public issues. Public issues consists of the following methods:

(a) *Initial issues*: The first time issue of shares to the public by a new company.
(b) *Further issues*: Shares are issued by the existing companies.
(c) *New money issues*: Newly created securities are issued by existing companies.

(d) *No new money issues*: The shares are sold in the market by underwriters.
(e) *Bonus issue*: Shares are offered to the existing shareholders freely.
(f) *Exchange issue*: The process of exchanging securities between the companies.

The contribution of new issues reflects the industrial growth of a country. New issues facilitate the transfer of funds from the savers to the entrepreneurs. New issue ratio indicates the relationship between primary issues and physical capital formation in the country.

### *4. Intermediation Ratio*

Intermediary ratio means the relationship between primary and secondary issues. It is the ratio of secondary issues to primary issues. It reveals the importance of middlemen as mobilisers of funds relative to real sectors. The intermediaries are more important persons in mobilisation of savings. They mobilise the funds of savings made by the households towards the industrialisation of a nation.

The financial system has become much more integrated than ever before. The financial system can be classified as organised and unorganised sectors. The financial integration of the country has been influenced by—

(a) The government entry in a very big way in trading of commodities.
(b) Expansion of network of rural bank branches.
(c) Financial institutions have been transformed.
(d) Evolution of financial institutions.
(e) Increasing of the activities of financial intermediaries.
(f) Introduction of innovative financial instruments.

The financial system consists of **financial institutions, financial markets, financial instruments and financial services**. The role of financial system is to accelerate the growth rate of economic development. The development of an economy enhances the general standard of living and social welfare. It can be achieved through the mobilisation and increase of savings and investment. The Indian financial system has been presented in the following diagram:

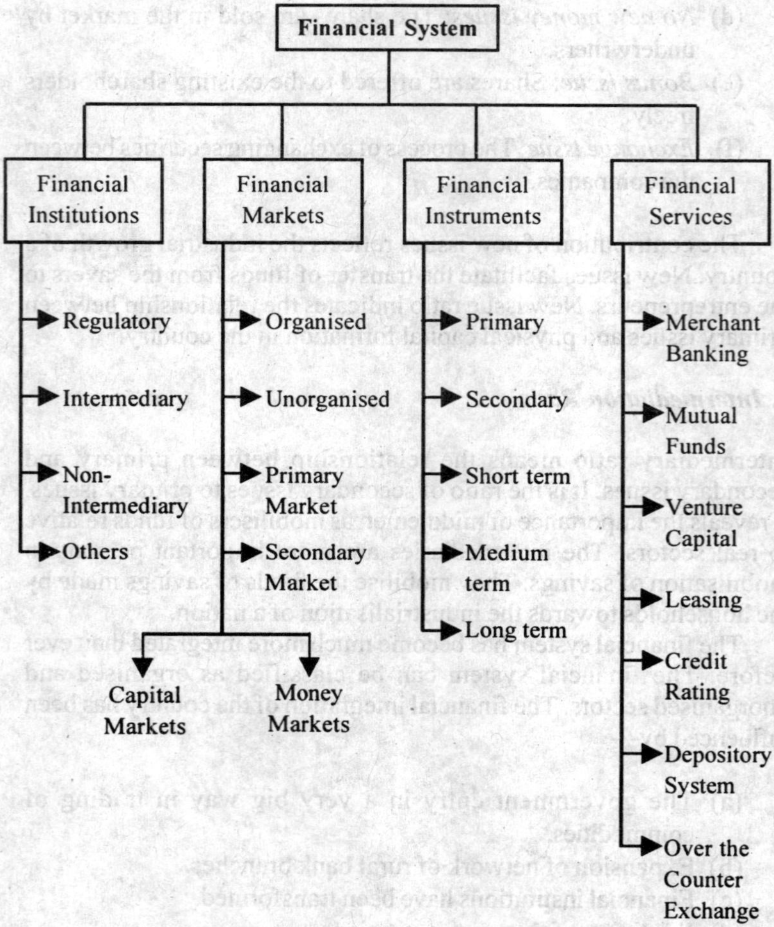


*Source*: L.M. Bhole, *Financial Institutions and Markets*, p. 4, 1998, Tata McGraw Hill, Delhi.

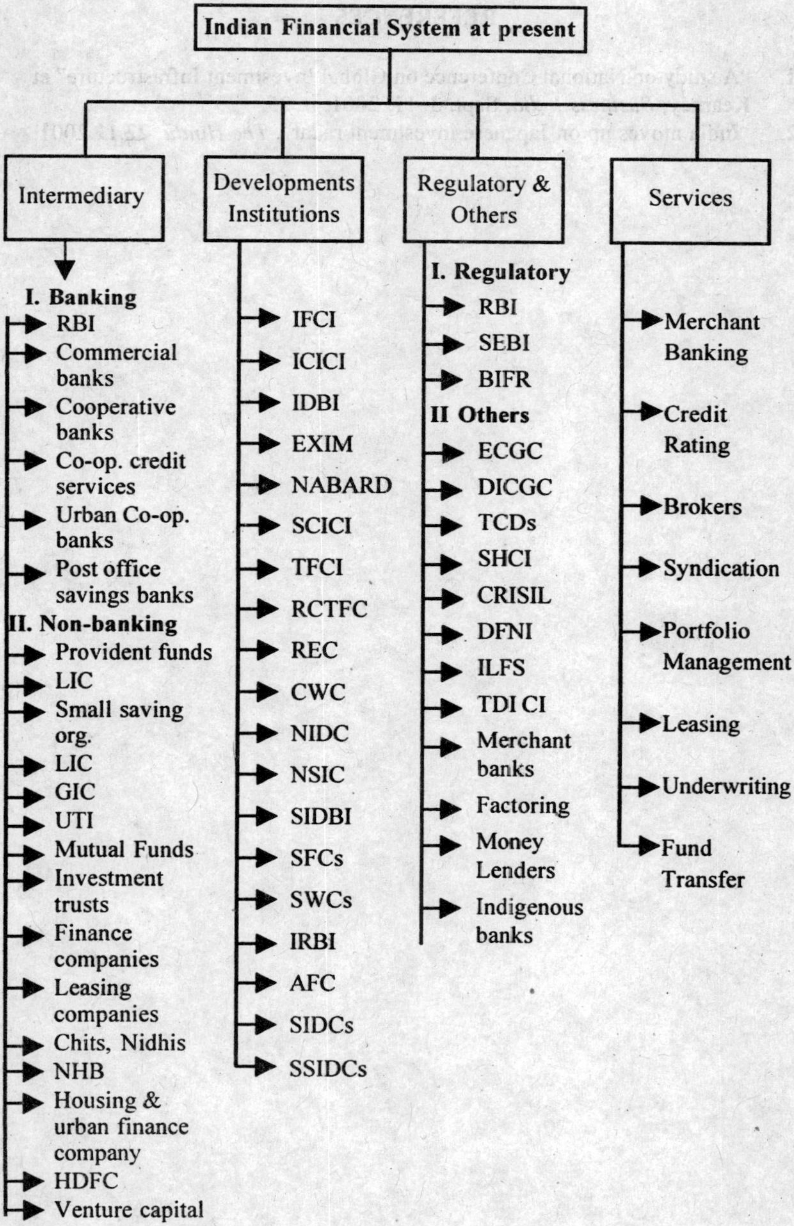


*Source*: L.M. Bhole, *Financial Institutions and Markets*, p. 35, 1998, Tata McGraw Hill, Delhi.

## REFERENCES

1. "A study on National Conference on Global Investment Infrastructure" at Kearney, *Business India*, Sept. 3–11, 2001, p. 25.
2. "India moves up on Japanese investment radar", *The Hindu*, 22.11.2001.

# 2

# FINANCIAL INSTITUTIONS

## Introduction

Beginning from 1991, India's financial system took a radically new turn towards the market model. This envisaged an increased role for the capital market, along with a fundamental restructuring of banks and financial institutions. Such restructuring has been rather slow. The bulk of the banking system and major financial institutions are still largely owned and controlled by the government.

The corporate sector desiring long-term funds can raise it by issuing shares and debentures to the members of the public. The corporate sector can also approach financial institutions for satisfying their long-term financial needs. The financial institutions are concerned with mobilising resources from different sections of society for their channelisation in productive way. The financial institutions provide a convenient and effective link between savings and investment. They pool the savings of the society and are used by them to cater to the needs of the corporate sector.

In India, we have a battery of financial institutions operating in capital market and rendering financial assistance to needy enterprises. These financial institutions can be categorised into three major groups.

(A) Commercial Banks.
(B) Development Banks.
(C) Investing Institutions.

## (A) COMMERCIAL BANKS

The Commercial Banks are the oldest institutions having a wide network of branches commanding utmost public confidence and having the lion's share in the total banking operations. The Commercial Banks operating in India fall under a number of sub-categories on the basis of ownership and control of management. They constitute a vital role in Indian financial system. These financial institutions have been major suppliers of working capital finance to the corporate sector.

The Commercial Banks assist enterprises by granting term loans and various kinds of financial modes. They render help to the corporate sector in raising long-term funds from capital market through merchant banking activity. Let us discuss the nature of long-term financing of business by the commercial banks.

**(1) Term Lending.**
**(2) Underwriting.**
**(3) Direct subscription.**
**(4) Merchant banking activity.**

### *(1) Term Lending*

Term lending by Commercial Banks is a recent phenomenon. This facility is dispensed by Commercial Banks under refinancing schemes. The Government of India had formulated a scheme in 1958. A formal scheme under which the banks were to be provided refinancing facilities through Refinance Corporation of India. The RCI was set up in June 1958 for the purpose. The RBI urged the Commercial Banks to set up their term lending divisions for providing finance to the following areas:

(a) Deferred export payments.
(b) New potential for export business.
(c) Agriculture sector.
(d) Industries in backward areas.
(e) Capital goods industries.
(f) Deferred payment arrangements for purchase of capital goods in the domestic market.

Under the refinance scheme, a Commercial Bank can grant term loan to an enterprise. Under the refinance scheme gets priority to road transport organisation. Units in backward areas and specified categories. The refinance could be upto 90 per cent of the loan to these categories. Banks are not expected to insist on security and personal guarantee particularly in the case of priority sector applicants. The role of the banks is very likely to assume significant properties in view of the latest measure taken by the RBI.

### *(2) Underwriting*

Commercial Bank in India were engaged in underwriting business since 1935. The corporate sector can raise funds through a Commercial Bank by getting its security issue underwritten by the bank. The banks did underwriting work on an *adhoc* basis, to take advantage of boom conditions in the market. The banks have been engaged in underwriting work on a continuous basis. The banks give an assurance depending upon the financial strength and reputation of the company. The banks are not interested in acquiring the securities underwritten by them.

### *(3) Direct Subscription*

Commercial Banks render financial support to industrial undertakings by investing directly in their shares and debentures.

### *(4) Merchant Banking Activity*

Commercial Banks in India are now assisting the firms in raising desired funds from capital market by performing merchant banking functions. Commercial Banks in India sponsor the security issue as a merchant banker. They also undertake credit syndication activity. For sponsoring issues. The bank should obtain consent from the SEBI. They help in preparation of the prospectus, arrangements for underwriting appointment of brokers, and bankers to the issue, press publicity, compliance with stock exchange listing requirements. They also render service in the preparation of project profiles and loan application for assistance from various terms financing institutions. A number of nationalised banks have launched subsidiaries to take up the merchant banking activities as full scale. The following institutions are providing these services:

(a) SBI Capital Markets Ltd.
(b) Canbank Financial Service Ltd.
(c) PNB Financial Services Ltd.

## (B) DEVELOPMENT BANKS

The Development Banks are also known as Industrial Banks. The development banks supply capital, knowledge and enterprise. They meet the requirements of industries. They provide long-term investments. They are able to finance the long-term investments. They employ financial experts to render the services to the prospecting projects. These banks acquire funds by issuing their own shares and debentures and obtain loans from the Central Government and international agencies. They are performing important functions for rapid industrialisation of the country. They inquire and investigate the prospects of the industry and feasibility and utilities of the various schemes. They advise the industries in financial and non-financial matters of the corporate sector. They have been specialised in investment and financial aspects of the various sectors. These banks have assisted in the development of developed countries like **USA, Japan and Germany**. These development banks have also contributed a lot to the economic development of India.

*Functions*

The functions of industrial banks can be categorised into three parts:

(a) Accepting of long-term deposits.
(b) Permitting of long-term investments.
(c) Consultancy services.

The deposits are mobilised by these banks by giving higher rate of interest to the depositors. These banks grant direct financial aids to the industries. Long-term loans are sanctioned usually on the mortgage of land, machine and other fixed assets. The companies require short-term funds for purchase of raw materials and other payments. The short-term credit is provided by Commercial Banks. The important industrial banks in India are:

**(1) IDBI**
**(2) ICICI**
**(3) IFCI**

## (1) Industrial Development Bank of India (IDBI)

***Introduction***

The Industrial Development Bank of India was established in 1964. It has been empowered to finance all types of industrial concerns. It provides direct and indirect finance to the corporate sector. As direct financier, it renders assistance to the corporate sector in the following ways:

(a) sanctioning term loans and advances,
(b) underwriting the issue of shares and debentures of the companies, and
(c) sanctioning third party loans to business community.

The direct financial assistance is usually granted for purchase of fixed assets, for expansion and modernisation of existing units. The direct financial assistance is the most useful to the large scale manufacturing units. As an indirect financier, it assist in the following ways:

(1) Refinancing of industrial loans provided by Commercial Banks and SFCs.
(2) Providing financial assistance to the financial institutions by subscribing the shares and debentures of them.
(3) Rediscounting of bills.
(4) Refinancing of export credit sanctioned by Commercial Banks to exporters.
(5) Renders consultancy services to the corporate sector.

The bank provides loans which are normally repayable over a period of 10 years. The authorised capital of the IDBI was **Rs. 2,000 crores**. It can be further increased to Rs. 5,000 crores. The main sources of the funds for the IDBI are:

(i) Borrowing from Central Government and RBI.
(ii) Issue of shares and bonds.
(iii) Grant and loans from World Bank.

***Management***

The IDBI is managed by the Board of Directors. The Board of Directors consisting of 22 persons including Chairman and Managing Director. The Chairman and Managing Director is appointed by the Central Government. The other members of the board comprise of a representative of the RBI, a representative each of the All India Financial Institutions, two officials of the Central Government, 3 representatives from each public sector bank and SFCs, 5 members having special knowledge and experience of industry. The Board of Directors has constituted an Executive Committee consisting of 10 members.

### *Role*

IDBI was set up as the principal financial institution for industrial development in the country. Now it is playing an important role in the capital market. The role of IDBI for the purpose of exposure can be categorised into three phases:

- **(a) First phase.**
- **(b) Second phase.**
- **(c) Third phase.**

#### *First Phase (1964–75)*

The IDBI was set up as a statutory corporation in July, 1964. It is a wholly owned subsidiary of the RBI. The ownership of the IDBI was transferred to the Government. In 1995, the IDBI act was amended to provide greaters operational flexibility. The Amendment of the Act was made during the dynamic phase of the bank. The life cycle of the IDBI starts from 1964 to 1975, as first phase. The transformation of the IDBI takes more than 35 years. The first phase was the most important stage in the life of the IDBI. The first phase have been concentrated towards industrialisation of the nation. The bank had focussed on establishing the core industries such as **textiles, fertilisers, chemical products, basic metals and machinery**. The industrialisation strategy also required to encourage the small ancillary industries to create more employment opportunities in the country. At this point of time SFCs, SIDCs were already in place to promote and encourage these segments of the industry. The IDBI took over the activities of the Refinance Corporation in 1964. Therefore, it started providing financial support to the SFCs and other primary lending institutions in the country by refinancing facility. The IDBI had introduced the rediscounting of machinery bills scheme to encourage the capital goods industry. Hence the IDBI is fully involved in direct project loans, refinance and bill rediscounting schemes to the industries.

The IDBI played an important role for the development of exports sector, balanced regional development and coordination between financial institutions. The IDBI started a scheme during this phase for financing projects export and export of capital goods on deferred payment basis. It actively participated in the formation of Export and Import Bank of India. The IDBI played an important role in achieving the balance regional development strategy. It initiated steps to conduct surveys for identify industrial potential in backward areas and other specific locations. It played an important role in setting up of technical consultancy organisations in collaboration with other financial institutions. The Central Government provided long-term loans to the IDBI at concessional rate of interest. The RBI created a separate National Industrial Credit Fund to meet the long-term operations of the corporate sector. The IDBI received loans from this fund at concessional rate of interest. The Government had exempted from income tax, which were issued by IDBI due to its recognition of developmental role. It also focussed on developing linkages with other financial institutions.

### *Second Phase (1976–85)*

The second phase starts from 1976 to 1985. Because the IDBI was delinked from the RBI on 16.02.1976. It was accorded as principal Financial Institution, wholly owned by the Government of India. This period was the most important in the life of the IDBI. The RBI had transmitted its all responsibilities to the IDBI. It also transferred the initial capital of the IFCI and the UTI. The share capital of the SFCs was also transferred to the IDBI by the RBI. It became an autonomous institution. During this period, it actively involved in the process of industrialisation of the country. It focussed on widening of the entrepreneurial base in the country, modernisation and upgradation of technology. It had achieved a certain degree of maturity during the second phase. The IDBI introduced a soft loan scheme involving loans at concessional rates of interest during this phase. The scheme was designed to meet the modernisation programme in industries such as jute, cotton, textiles, sugar, cement and engineering goods. Later a revised modernisation package was introduced for all industries. The Central Government created a special Technical Development Fund for modernisation of industries to boost the process of technology upgradation. According to this scheme, the IDBI provided concessional assistance for the import of balancing equipment, acquiring technical know-how and consultancy services for upgrading existing technology of the approved units. It also actively participated to provide assistance to the sick units. It had taken various measures during this period to meet the requirements of small, village and cottage industry. It initiated package of refinance to small and medium sectors towards meeting the modernisation requirements. The technology upgradation required a higher amount of foreign currency. It diversified its resources base and borrowed the foreign currency from the global markets.

The term lending is an important aspect of industrial financing system. It is the oxygen for promotion of industrial growth. The term lending widens the entrepreneurial base and the related infrastructure, services etc. The industrial activities will be increased only when the entrepreneurial base widens. Therefore, the IDBI took initiative to educate the entrepreneurs by setting up a number of institutes for entrepreneurship development in association with other financial institutions. It encouraged the entrepreneurs by introduced a scheme, which is known as **seed capital scheme**.

*Third Phase (1986...)*

The third phase was one of tremendous growth in activities of the IDBI. It provided several new challenges due to economic restructuring programme initiated by the Government. During this period, the IDBI introduced new products to meet the growing needs of entrepreneurs. It also focussed on balanced regional development of the country, sectoral growth of the industries and capital market in India. The Central Government announced the Technology Upgradation Scheme in 1987 to upgrade the technology of select capital goods industries. It was assigned to formulate the system for this scheme. It also established in 1986 a Textile Modernisation Fund to provide a point for modernisation efforts in the industry. The World Bank helped the IDBI to modernisation of cement industry.

The IDBI introduced an Export Incentive Scheme in 1986. It encouraged the export units by providing incentives in the form of rebate of interest on rupee loans. The IDBI established a Venture Capital Fund in 1986 to provide financial assistance for industrial concerns. It was also giving top priority to energy conservation sector and environmental audit aspects. The World Bank provided a special assistance to pollution control projects.

The IDBI played a major role in the development of the Capital Market in India. It took initiative steps to set up several subsidiaries and associate concerns. These concerns offer a wide range of products and services. It set up the Stock Holding Corporation of India in 1987. It provides depository services to financial institutions. The Central Government had also assigned the responsibility of setting up the SEBI. The NSE was also established by the IDBI with the instructions from the Central Government. The NSE provide nation-wide screen based trading system. It became the India's premier stock exchange. It had thrown a challenge to the Bombay Stock Exchange. The BSE is the Competitor of the NSE. The IDBI promoted/established the following institutions with the directions from the Government:

(a) National Securities Depository Ltd.
(b) Credit Analysis and Research Ltd.
(c) IDBI Capital Market Securities Ltd.
(d) IDBI Investment Management Company Ltd.
(e) IDBI Bank Ltd.
(f) North Eastern Development Finance Corporation Ltd.
(g) Infrastructure Development Finance Company Ltd.
(h) Over the Counter Exchange of India (with others)
(i) Tourism Finance Corporation of India (with others)
(j) Shipping Credit and Investment Corporation of India (with others)
(k) Bio Tech Consortium of India Ltd.

The IDBI decentralised its offices and processing of projects to meet the competition from the market. It devised a host of new products to meet the needs of modern corporate sector. It also empowered to manage its own foreign currency borrowings.

## (2) Industrial Credit and Investment Corporation of India (ICICI)

### *Introduction*

The Industrial Credit and Investment Corporation was incorporated on 5.1.1955. It was founded by the Government of India, World Bank and others. It was promoted as a Public Limited Company. It has been established for the purpose of assisting industries in the private sector. The aim of setting up of ICICI was to provide foreign currency finance to industrial projects and promote industries in private sector. It provides financial packages for R&D, commercialisation of technology, venture capital, pollution control and environment protection. It has diversified into a number of other activities. It has also been managing United States Agency for international development and World Bank funds through its technological financing programmes.

ICICI principal business was to provide medium and long-term project financing, underwriting to shares, guarantees to suppliers of equipment and foreign lenders. It has entered into new areas of business like commercial banking, investment banking, non-banking finance, broking, investor servicing, venture capital financing and infrastructure financing. It operates in general in accordance with the guidelines of RBI/SEBI. It has the status as a public financial institution. This status is useful in getting the benefits of taxation. Its bonds are treated as public securities for investment by trusts.

### *Financial Resources*

The resources of the ICICI comprise two kinds:

(a) Foreign currency resource.
(b) Rupee resources.

The resources of the ICICI consisted with interest free loan from the GOI and an advance in foreign currency from the World Bank.

The rupee resources of the ICICI comprise the following components:

**(a) Share Capital.**
**(b) Reserves.**
**(c) Borrowings.**
**(d) Public Deposits.**

#### *(a) Share Capital*

It started with initial resources of about Rs.17.5 crores. At the end of the March 1996 paid up capital amounted to **Rs. 376.3 crores** and reserves and surplus amounted to **Rs. 2,059.4 crores**. A large part of the capital is held by public sector institutions such as banks, LIC, GIC and its subsidiaries, IDBI, UTI etc. It issued ADRs and GDRs and a significant change is resulted its share ownership structure.

*(b) Reserves*

It has been consistently building up a large chunk of reserves. Reserves are the most important element for the financial companies. The higher amount of reserves is the financial strength of the company. The reserves are consists of capital reserve, capital redemption reserve, share premium account, general reserve and special reserve.

*(c) Borrowings*

It mobilises the funds from domestic and foreign markets. The domestic borrowings by the ICICI are from—

1. the Government of India,
2. Institutional borrowings,
3. Government backed bonds,
4. Public issue of bonds, and
5. Miscellaneous

The foreign currency resources consists of the following borrowings:

1. Multilateral borrowings.
2. Commercial borrowings.

The multilateral borrowings have been from the multilateral institutions. The World Bank played an important role in setting up of the bank. It has been providing financial assistance on regular lines of credit. It also received financial assistance from ADB, Commonwealth Development Corporation, UK. It has also getting assistance from the Government export credit agencies. All of these lines of credit are guaranteed by the Government of India. It has received assistance from the **Overseas Development Administration** of the UK through the Government of India. It has been receiving financial assistance from various foreign agencies.

Commercial borrowings played an important role of the financial architecture of the ICICI. It has diversified its resources base with a view to establish in the global market. It raised a public issue of SF 8 million bonds in the Swiss markets in 1973. It depends upon the commercial borrowings has increased. The commercial borrowings from various countries made it a financial stability to survive in the global market. It borrowed the commercial borrowings in the following ways:

(a) Euro credits and other loans.
(b) Bond issues in Switzerland.
(c) Private placements in Japan.
(d) Euro convertible debt market.

It received strong support from the international banking and financial community. It also achieved its objectives of interest and currency diversification by borrowing in various markets in dollar, Swiss franc, yen, pound, sterling. It constantly searching for financial assistance in the international markets. It launched a Global Medium-Term Note Programme in 1996–97 to facilitate borrowing in small amounts at competitive rates.

*(d) Public Deposits*

It started accepting public deposits from 1979. It is only a marginal source of funds. It also invites public deposits from the public by offering competitive rates of interest.

***Business Operations***

The business operations of the ICICI can be categorised into 5 kinds:

**(a) Lending operations.**
**(b) Capital market operations.**
**(c) Advisory services.**
**(d) Sponsorship.**
**(e) Subsidiaries.**

*(a) Lending Operations*

Lending is the basic operation of any financial institution. This activity refer to the provision of funds for asset creation to the business concerns.

The lending operations generate income to the ICICI by charging different rates of interest from the corporate sector. The lending operations of the ICICI consist the following activities:

(1) Project finance.
(2) Technology finance.
(3) Non-project finance.

**Project finance** is the most important activity of the bank. It grants the loan to business concerns in the form of Rupee and foreign currency loans, underwriting and direct subscription to issue of shares and debentures. It also provide financial assistance for the modernisation, expansion of manufacturing and processing units. The Rupee project loans are involved in financing the purchase of equipment and machinery. It also finance under this scheme towards cost of land, construction of factory and preliminary expenses etc. The Rupee currency loans dominated the portfolio of loans disbursed by ICICI. The share of Rupee loans in the total financial assistance provided by the Bank increased substantially. **Foreign currency project loans** are provided to finance the purchase of imported capital goods. The World Bank to channelise foreign currency resources for the private industry through ICICI. It did not sanction any foreign loans during the commencement of its operations. It started financing the foreign currency loans from 1958 with the emergence of foreign exchange crisis. After 1971, the component of foreign currency loan was declined substantially. This was due to the recessionary state of the economy. At present the Indian companies are directly accessing international capital markets through the issue of GDRs.

It started guaranteeing loans from the private investment sources. It charges 1 per cent P.A. as the outstanding balances of guarantee issued in rupees and 1.8 per cent in case of foreign currencies. It also offers assistance to corporate sector by underwriting the issue of shares and debentures. Now it has been following a policy of direct subscription of shares to the extent of **Rs. 1 crore**.

**Technology financing** has emerged as one of the sources of finance. The ICICI is the largest financiers of technology in India. This source of finance is run with the help of United States Agency of International Development and World Bank. They are providing funds for various schemes of financing. It offers a wide variety of financial packages for R&D, commercialisation of technology. It also offers package relating to pollution control and environmental protection. The following schemes are offered by the ICICI:

**(1) SPREAD.**
**(2) ACE.**
**(3) TEST.**
**(4) PACT.**
**(5) PACER.**

**Sponsored Research and Development Programme** (SPREAD) is one of the schemes which are offered by ICICI. It encourages Indian corporate sector to set up their R&D activities. It link up the technology and industry. The package offers for the projects which are involved in development of new product or process. The product modification will also be considered by this package. The package allows activities like preparation of feasibility studies, laboratory trials and pilot plant operations. The project under this scheme should have feasible and quantifiable objectives. The project should not take larger than two years to be completed. The Company should bear 50 per cent of the total cost of the project. The remaining amount will be granted as eligible project specific expenses which are included equipment, facilities, materials, payment to consultant, fee payable to technology institutions, project related travel and overhead expenses. The financial assistance provided by the ICICI will be charged with an interest rate of **6** per cent during the implementation period of the R&D project. The repayment period is upto 10 years. At the final stage of the project, the rate of interest will be increased to **15** per cent.

The **Agricultural Commercialisation Enterprise** (ACE) is the another programme which is funded by the ICICI. This scheme is formulated for the development of agri-business in India. It provides financial assistance for setting up innovative projects in horticulture, floriculture, mushrooms, fruits, essential oils, herbal products, enzymes, etc. This project activities involves, loans to private sector, providing technical assistance and conducting travels. It conducts field trips to members of industry for observing and knowing of technical aspects.

The ICICI is conducting another research based programme which is related to commercialisation of energy. It provides funds for development of the technology in India towards energy sector. The financial assistance is provided for the technology development of energy such as renewable sources of energy, energy conservation, fossils, etc.

The ICICI is also financing Indo-US Joint Ventures in R&D for the development of technology process in specified areas. The scheme is applicable to agriculture, health and other areas. It aims at improving the availability of quality products and services in the segments of child health, AIDS and reproductive health. It also finances for the technology development of the environmental and pollution control.

The ICICI is also providing non-project finance to the industry with medium and long-term maturity period. It provides short-term loans to the corporate sector to meet working capital needs. It provides assistance to the corporate sector by a number of schemes.

*(b) Capital Market Operations*

The ICICI mobilises funds through debt and equity. It actively involved in capital market operations. It encourages entrepreneurs by making investments in their companies by direct subscription to public issues. It participates in capital market operations by taking up **Rights issues** of the companies, conversion option of loan assisted companies, participating in private placement of the corporate sector and provide rehabilitation package for the sick industries. It does not acquire securities in the secondary market. The investment operations of the ICICI have been increasing at present. It also offers fee based services to its clients. These activities are advisory in nature provide consultancy services. It has been offering project advisory services since 1991 to PSUs, and private sector companies. It acts as a trustee for the holders of convertible and non-convertible debenture issues. These financial instruments are issued by the companies to the public in the form of Rights issue, Private placement etc. It offers comprehensive custodial services since 1992. Its clients include FIIs, overseas depository banks.

The ICICI has been actively involving in promoting a number of institutions which are strengthening the institution structure of the money and capital market. The Credit Rating Information Services of India Ltd., had been established in association with UTI in 1987. It provides a variety of consultancy services to the corporate sector. CRISIL is involved in rating various types of financial instruments offered to the investing public. It also instrumental in promoting the following institutions:

1. Technology Development and Information Company of India Ltd. (TDCI).
2. Over the Counter Exchange of India Ltd. (OTC).
3. Stock Holding Corporation of India Ltd. (SHCI).
4. Discount and Finance House of India (DFHI).
5. Management Development Institute (MDI).

After the liberalisation, privatisation and globalisation, the ICICI entered new areas of business like investment banking, asset management, commercial banking etc. It has set up specialised subsidiaries which are presented below:

1. ISEC Ltd.
2. ICICI brokerage.
3. ICICI banking.
4. ICICI Infotech.
5. ICICI Personal Financial Services Ltd.
6. ICICI Capital Services Ltd.
7. ICICI Venture Ltd.
8. ICICI International.
9. ICICI Properties.

***Merger of ICICI with ICICI Bank***

The ICICI have been merged with ICICI Bank on 28.03.2002. The Universal Bank plans major thrusts on the retail and international fronts. The ICICI and ICICI Bank have been moving towards a merger for over two years now. The formal announcement was made on 25.10.2001. There has been frenetic activity in the ICICI group to conform to the statutory obligations on the way to turning into a Universal Bank. The merger process required the ICICI to show **Rs. 23,000 crores** by way of SLR for the combined entity. The ICICI Bank already having **Rs. 5,000 crores**[1] in its SLR portfolio, an additional Rs.18,000 crore was required from ICICI. Then the ICICI have been mobilised the fund through a combination of retail deposits and asset swaps. The remaining Rs. 10,000 crores was brought in by way of retail deposits. The merger regulations did not allow merged entity to have any subsidiary that was involved in non-banking activities. The swap ratio has been fixed at **one share of ICICI Bank** for every two shares of **ICICI**. Therefore, the final 2:1 ratio falls within the ambit of all the valuation norms. The aim of the post-merger was: **aggressive capital management, optimal size technology-intensive multi-channel delivery architecture world class skill bases, and enduring customer relationship**. The post-merger will bring several advantages. ICICI itself gets access to cheaper retail funds. The merged entity is focussing on the new avenues. They are fee income, trade finance, forex remittances, cash management services, dividend management, agri-business, small and medium enterprises, consumer finance, auto loans, credit and debit cards, housing finance, personal loans, internet banking, retail business, third party products, mutual funds, insurance, pension products, smart cards and fund transfer.

Recently it introduced **"e-cheque"** system in fund transfer process. According to the scheme, the customer can transfer money to any account in any bank in any of **14 cities** is becoming very popular. Another service has been launched in Delhi, any cell phone owner can tap up with the ICICI ATM. It also focussing on cross selling instead of individual marketing. The major advantage of cross selling is that the customer acquisition cost comes down massively, customer loyalty and satisfaction is reflected in cross selling. The another major thrust area is the international division. The international business is to provide 10-15 per cent of ICICI Bank's turnover and profits in the forthcoming 5 years but zero today. It identified four geographies setting up representative offices in the US, UK, Dubai, Singapore and London. The international division will be setting up a consultancy to provide services to banks and other financial sector players internationally.

The Indian economy requires large banks to cater its requirements. The ICICI merger will create a significant player. The merger is clearly a reflection of the overdue consolidation the banking industry needs.

The expressions by the analysts and experts is that the new merged entity may be sitting on mountain of Non-performing Assets that may come home to roost. Their conclusion is that its loan portfolio cannot be too different from that of IDBI or IFCI. All of them were lending to the same sectors and companies with similar profiles. ICICI comes with net NPAs at around Rs. 3,000 crores or 5.3 per cent. The ICICI Bank has net NPAs at 1.36 per cent.

**A Merger Snapshot**

*(Rs. in crores)*

| | | As on September, 2001 | | | March 31, 2002 |
|---|---|---|---|---|---|
| | | ICICI | Bank | Merged | |
| | **Assets** | | | | |
| 1. | Total Credits | 61235 | 11660 | 72895 | 65000 |
| 2. | SLR Investments | 489 | 5400 | 5889 | 23500 |
| 3. | Cash Reserves | – | 1450 | 4500 | 4500 |
| 4. | Other assets | 12650 | 2290 | 14940 | 15000 |
| 5. | Total assets | 74374 | 20800 | 95174 | 108000 |
| | **Liabilities** | | | | |
| 1. | Equity capital | 796 | 220 | 613 | 600 |
| 2. | Reserves | 7996 | 1224 | 9612 | 9600 |
| 3. | Borrowings | 59668 | 685 | 60353 | 60000 |
| 4. | Deposits | – | 17515 | 17515 | 32000 |
| 5. | Other liabilities | 74374 | 20800 | 95174 | 108000 |

## (3) Industrial Finance Corporation of India (IFCI)

### *Introduction*

The Industrial Finance Corporation of India was set up in July 1948 by the Government of India. It was established under the IFCI Act, 1948 with the basic objective of providing finance to the industries in private sector. At prèsent it also providing financial assistance to cooperative, joint, public sector units. It provides loans for expansion, diversification and modernisation of existing units. It also underwrites and directly subscribes to industrial securities, merchant banking services and lease finance. It renders financial assistance both in rupees and foreign currencies to the corporate sector.

The small scale industries, proprietary and partnership concerns were not eligible for financial assistance from the IFCI. It did not grant assistance for the purpose of working capital. It did not provide assistance for the acquisition of capital goods for commercial or trading purposes. It did not grant loans in foreign currencies for purchasing of raw materials, imports or payments of royalties, interest and dividends. The IFCI Act was amended in 1986, the authorised business of the IFCI was presented in the following:

(a) It acts as agent to World Bank.

(b) It provides technical, administrative assistance, legal and marketing assistance to any industrial concern.

(c) It provides consultancy services in and outside India.
(d) Appointed as administrator.

### *Financial Resources*

The sources of the funds are: share capital, retained earnings, by the issue of bonds, borrowings from the Government, repayment of past loans and sale of investments, borrowings from IDBI, borrowings from foreign lending institutions, foreign capital markets and public deposits.

The paid up capital of the IFCI was held directly by the Central Government and the RBI. The holdings of the two concerns were transferred to the IDBI. The balance of the paid up capital contributed by the Commercial Banks, Insurance Organisations and Cooperative banks. It made a first public issue of equity shares in December 1993. The authorised capital has now been increased to **Rs. 339.1 crores.** It had consistently increased and built up sizeable reserves. The reserves of the IFCI consists of the following elements:

**(a) General reserves**
**(b) Reserve fund**
**(c) Benevolent reserve**
**(d) Special reserve**
**(e) Specific grant from the GOI**
**(f) Share premium account**

It mobilises funds from the sale of bonds. It grants Rupee Currency and Foreign Currency loans. The Rupee Currency loans are met from the domestic market and foreign market respectively. The IFCI policy is to reduce its dependence on government. It focussed on market borrowing by issue of bonds. The bonds are guaranteed by the Government and redeemable at par at coupon rates ranging from 8.75 per cent and 13.5 per cent. It depends on bonds which are privately placed and issued to public. The issued bonds to the public carry a maturity of 7 to 30 years. The privately placed bonds have a maturity of one to 27 years. It offered a variety of innovative bonds targeting different segments. It also issued deep discount bonds, education bonds, gift bonds, retirement bonds, floating millionaire bonds etc.

It was authorised in 1952 to borrow in foreign currency. It has been borrowing from foreign agencies/financial institutions. It was allowed to borrow from global market. It obtain financial assistance from USA, Germany, France and UK. The borrowings from international capital markets are from–

(a) Euro currency market,
(b) Germany markets, and
(c) Japanese capital market.

It diversified its resources base by raising short-term funds through certificate of deposits and commercial papers. It reduced its dependence on GOI and RBI. Its main funding source is market borrowings through a variety of innovative family bonds.

***Business Activities***

IFCI was actively participated in industrialisation of the country. It provides financial assistance to corporate sector through different schemes. The industrial financing activities consists of two segments. They are:

**(a) Project Finance.**
**(b) Financial Services.**

**Project Finance** covers the entire funding new projects, expansion, diversification and modernisation in the form of foreign currency and rupee term loans. The project finance is the main activity of the IFCI. The projects will be financed through term loans. The IDBI directly subscribes to equity shares of smaller new companies to encourage the new breed of entrepreneurs.

It also involved in capital market operations. Its investment portfolio consists of acquisition of shares for underwriting obligations, direct subscription to shares, bonus issues, subscriptions to right shares, convertion of convertible debentures proportion, conversion of dues into shares or debentures. It also guarantees to finance the amount to the industry. IFCI now also provides indirect finance for leasing companies. It has started providing short-term loans to corporates for meeting working capital financing.

**Financial Services** is the secondary activity of the IFCI in order to improve its profitability. The financial services include fund based, fee based, project counselling, issue management, loan syndication, financial restructuring, mergers and acquisitions, debentures trusteeship, equipment leasing, etc. It provides financial assistance to enterprise in the private corporate sector, public sector and joint sector. It actively participated in sugar cooperative the Government directed the IFCI to continue the support to textile industry also. The assistance given to industrial cooperative has in all cases been in the form of loans only. The financial assistance to the cooperative sector has substantially declined over the years. The IFCI sanctioned loans to the private sector. Its assistance to the private sector projects has increased substantially over the years. It was providing financial assistance to PSUs, Government Companies since 1969. These financial assistances were provided for expansion, diversification, provided satisfying the following clauses:

(a) public limited companies,
(b) had declared a maiden dividend,
(c) had built up sufficient internal resources, and
(d) should not have approached for budgetary support.

It provides financial assistance to a wide variety of industries. The sanctioning of loans depend upon changing conditions of national priorities. Initially it was given preference to sugar and textile projects. It also diversified its investment strategy and concentrated in power generation, telecom services, textiles, electronics, synthetic resins, plastics, fertilisers, basic chemicals, petroleum refining and cement. It provides finance to industrial enterprises is spread over to A.P., Gujarat, Maharashtra, Tamil Nadu, M.P. and W.B. It is also providing assistance to enterprises in the backward regions. It initiated measures to achieve the balanced regional development.

It actively involved in promotional activities like project identification, formulation, implementation and operations. It provides consultancy fee subsidy scheme and interest subsidy scheme and assistance schemes. The consultancy fee subsidy scheme is providing services to industrial units which are identified to the small, tiny and ancillary units. The scheme is applicable to small entrepreneurs in rural, cottage, tiny and small scale sectors, to new entrepreneurs for meeting the cost of market survey. Interest subsidy scheme is to provide encouragement to the unemployed youth and women entrepreneurs. This scheme is implemented through SFCs. It also providing assistance scheme to the existing industrial projects in the medium and small scale sector.

It encourages professionalism in management to improve the quality in day to day management. The IFCI sponsored in 1973, the Management Development Institute to provide training and research in the field of banking. It established in 1977 a Development Banking Centre as its autonomous wing. The MDI and DBC have been continuously working for the development of managerial manpower in public, private, joint and cooperative sectors in the industry. It diversified its business activities into the following areas:

**(1) Merchant banking.**
**(2) Project counselling.**
**(3) Credit syndication.**
**(4) Consultancy to sick industrial units.**
**(5) Sponsoring of financial institutions.**

## REFERENCE

1. The big picture, *Business India*, p. 51, April 1–14, 2002.

# 3

# FINANCIAL MARKETS

## Introduction

Each and every business unit must operate within the financial system. The financial system is consisted by a number of organisations and institutions and markets serving the needs of consumers, firms and governments. If a firm invests temporarily idle funds in marketable securities, then it has to approach the financial markets. Most firms use financial markets to help finance their investments in assets. Financial Markets can be defined as "All institutions and procedures for bringing buyers and sellers of financial instruments together".[1] Financial Markets provide the better facilities for buying and selling of all financial claims and services. All the participants trade in financial products in these markets either directly or through brokers. Financial institutions, agents, brokers, dealers, borrowers, lenders, savers are the participants both as the demand and supply sides of the financial markets. The demand for capital will be influenced by business expectations regarding the future state of the economy. The demand for goods is highly influenced by **prices, government policies, profitability, availability of internal funds, cost of funds and technological changes.** On the other hand, the supply of funds depends upon its level of savings by the household sector, business sector and the government sector in a given economy. The savings of all the participants in the market is determined by a number of factors. The factors will depend upon the level of current and expected income, cyclical changes in incomes, age-wise variations in income, distribution of income in the economy, degree of certainty in income, wealth, inflation, provision for old age, family members, contingencies, rate of interest, availability of savings media with required investment characteristics etc. The development banks and financial institutions can also influence the supply of funds. The Government will determine the volume of supply of funds, allocation of funds and the cost of funds and many other factors. Financial markets are usually determined by the supply and demand of funds. Financial markets are said to be perfect when—

(a) a large number of savers and investors operate in the markets,
(b) the participants are rational,
(c) all players in the market are well informed and the information is freely available to all of them,
(d) there are no taxes,
(e) there are no transactions costs, and
(f) the financial assets are infinitely divisible.

The financial markets can perform proximate functions such as—

(i) enhancing liquidity of financial assets,
(ii) transformation of financial claims to suit the needs of the participants,
(iii) enabling the business concerns to exercise their time preference,
(iv) diversification, distribution and reduction of risk, and
(v) better mode of operation of the payment mechanism.

Financial markets are characterised by many imperfections, restrictive practices, existence of transaction costs, lack of information, limited number of operators, direct and indirect intervention by the authorities and so on.

Financial markets may be categorised as primary and secondary markets. The primary market is also called as direct market. The secondary market can be called as indirect markets. Further, the direct market is called "**New Issue Market**". The NIM deal with the new securities offered by the newly established concerns or the existing enterprises. On the other hand, secondary market deals with the securities that are already issued by the Companies. The primary market creates a capital formation in the Country. It channelises the savings in a productive way. The secondary markets do not contribute directly to the supply of the additional capital but it will provide liquidity to the primary market. Therefore, the NIM and secondary markets will have impact on each other.

Financial markets have also been classified as:

(a) Organised and unorganised.
(b) Formal and informal.
(c) Official and parallel.
(d) Domestic and foreign.

The financial transactions which arises in a systematic manner in a organised system is called "organised market". The financial transactions which takes place outside the well established exchange constitute the unorganised markets. The unorganised markets refers to the markets in rural areas. The informal markets constitute, the financial transactions which arise between individuals and small families.

Financial Markets are further classified as:

**(A) Money Market.**
**(B) Capital Market.**

There is no difference between these two markets. Both of them perform same functions in transferring of financial assets. They provide a mechanism to sell a financial asset.

## (A) MONEY MARKET

### *Introduction*

Money market is a market for short-term funds. It provides the funds for less than a period of one year. It is dominated by the Central Bank. The RBI is the watchdog of the monetary system. It provides a channel for the exchange of financial assets for money. Money market is of very great help in financing industry and commerce for their working capital requirements. Money market includes money, capital and bill markets. Market consists of both money and capital market. In money market, the fund is being sold and purchased at a certain price. Money market is like the commodity market. It refers to lending and borrowing activities of banking, financial institutions and individuals.

### *Definition of Money Market*

The money market is defined by **A. Crowther,** "The money market is the collective name given to various firms and institutions that deal with the various grades of near money".[2] Money market deals with trade bills, promissory notes and treasury bills for short period. **The RBI** defined the money market, "the money market which is a market for short-term financial assets that are close substitutes for money, facilitates the exchange of money for new financial claims in the primary market as also for financial claims, already issued in the secondary market".[3]

The Central Bank acts as a promotional and development banker in money market. Money market can be organised as organised sector and unorganised sector. Unorganised sector consists of indigenous bankers and village money lenders. The organised sector consists of RBI, SBI, Mutual Funds, Companies, Cooperative Societies and Financial Institutions. Geographically money market may be located or associated with a particular place, like Indian Money Market, New York Money Market, Bombay Market, etc. In the Bombay money market, the short-term loanable fund is available for the whole India. London money market on the other hand is the market for international importance. It is known as international money market. It attracts short-term funds from all over the world for redistribution among the borrowers. The demand for short period comes primarily from the Government, business concerns and private individuals. The Government has become probably the biggest borrowers, everywhere money being required to meet the current deficits. Industrial and commercial concerns borrow funds for working capital needs. Sometimes they borrow to enable them to carry additional inventories. The other important private borrowers include stock exchange brokers, dealers in government and other security merchants, manufacturers, farmers and others. Banks themselves may require additional funds and may borrow from the Central Bank or from each other. The supply of loanable funds in the money market comes mostly from the Central Bank of the country, the Commercial Banks and other finance companies. The Central Bank is the source of credit to Commercial Banks while the latter constitute the most important source of short-term credit to both individual and business houses and the brokers.

### ***Characteristics of Money Market***

The following are the characteristics of money market:

1. It involves in arrangement of short-term funds.
2. It is a tool for preparation of monetary policy and fiscal management.
3. It deals in high liquid instruments.
4. The players in this market are RBI and Commercial Banks and Companies.
5. It is subject to RBI regulations.
6. It tells about the trends in liquidity and interest rates.
7. It provides funds at low transaction cost.
8. It suits the requirements of borrowers for the short-term funds.
9. It encourages open market operations.

Different sub-markets of a developed money market help in the proper functioning of the Central Bank. The money market and short-term rates of interest which prevail there, serves as a good barometer of monetary and banking conditioning in the country and thus provide a valuable guide to the determination of the central banking policy. The developed money market being a highly integrated structure, enables the Central Bank to deal with the most sensitive sub-markets also.

The main borrowers of short-term funds in the money market are:

(1) Commercial Banks.
(2) Central Government.
(3) State Government.
(4) Corporate Sector.
(5) Local Bodies.

The money market is viable to meet the long-term requirements of the industries. Money market consists of Central Banks, Commercial Banks, Cooperative Banks, Saving Banks, Discount houses, Acceptance houses, Bill market, Bullion market etc. The existence of a well developed money market ensures that the market instruments can be converted into money without incurring much losses.

The following chart shows the structure of the Indian Money Market:

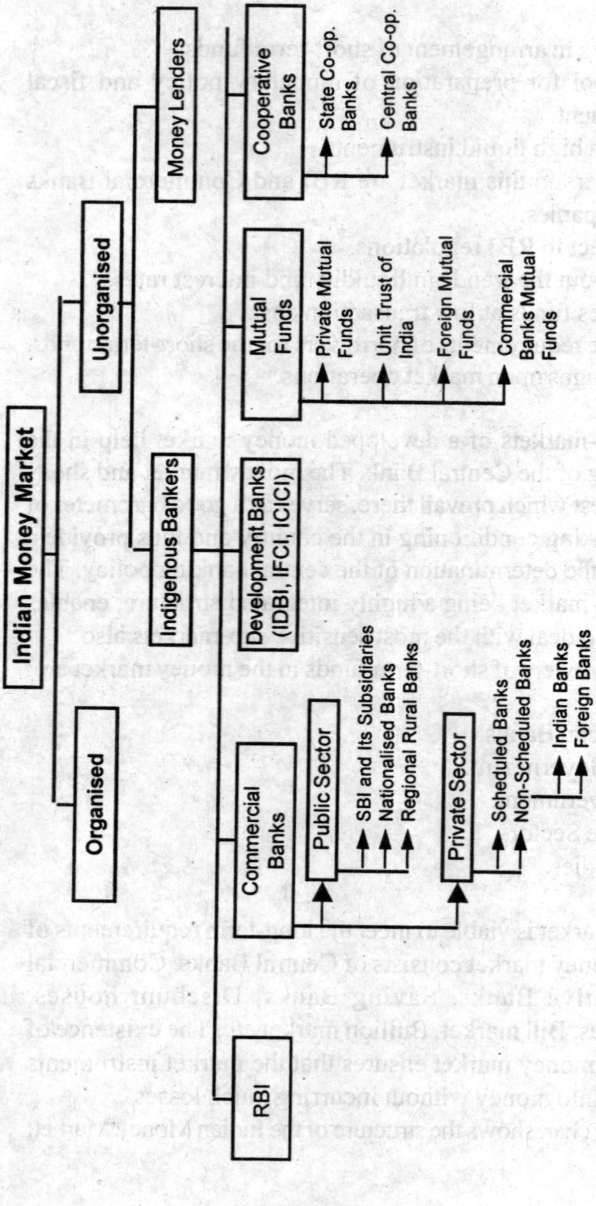
Indian Money Market
Organised
Unorganised
RBI
Commercial Banks
Development Banks (IDBI, IFCI, ICICI)
Mutual Funds
Cooperative Banks
Indigenous Bankers
Money Lenders
Public Sector
SBI and Its Subsidiaries
Nationalised Banks
Regional Rural Banks
Private Sector
Scheduled Banks
Non-Scheduled Banks
Indian Banks
Foreign Banks
Private Mutual Funds
Unit Trust of India
Foreign Mutual Funds
Commercial Banks Mutual Funds
State Co-op. Banks
Central Co-op. Banks

### *The Need for Money Market*

1. The money market is a coordinator between borrowers and lenders of short-term funds.
2. It provides transmission of funds from surplus concerns to shortage funds concern.
3. Money market is a device to the government to balance its cash inflows and outflows.
4. Money market is a weapon to business firms to meet their short-term funds.
5. Money market creates a minimum rate of return on idle fund lying at the disposal of corporate and banking sectors.
6. Money market is a tool to the finance managers in order to more utilisation of funds to enhance the shareholders wealth.

### *The Goals of Money Market Investor*

1. The main objective of the investors in money market is about the safety and liquidity of the principal amount. They also think of some gains along with their amount.
2. Money market is a parking place of idle fund.
3. The investors will escape wisely from long-term market risks.
4. Money market instruments generally offer more protection against political risk and inflation risk.

The money market is entirely dominated by the RBI. All the policy matters of the sector will be finalised by the India's Central Bank. The SEBI and other statutory organisations are also playing an important role for smooth functioning of the money market. The money market is a powerful weapon in the hands of the Central Government and it should be handled skilfully by the Ministry of Finance. Crores of Rupees are available in the market at the disposal of various large organisations within few hours. Therefore, the development of money market can boost the wealth of a nation and also encourages the capital market.

### *Recent Developments in Money Market*

The annual statement of monetary and credit policy released on April 19, 2001 projected a GDP growth of 6 to 6.5 per cent for 2000–2001. These projections are based on the assumptions of a reasonable monsoon, good performance of exports and a revival of the industrial sector.

The annual policy statement also indicated that under normal circumstances and baring emergence of any adverse and unexpected developments in domestic or external sectors, the overall stance of monetary policy for 2001–2002 will be:

(a) The average call money rate come down sharply from 8.6 per cent in early April to 7 per cent in mid-October 2001. During this period, the repo rate also came down from 7 per cent to 6.5 per cent. The CRR was reduced by 50 basis points to 7.5 per cent in May 19, 2001, augmenting lendable resources of the banking system by Rs. 4,500 crores. Responding to these operations, the interest rates in other money market instruments also showed a declining trend. The primary yield on 91 days treasury bills were declined by 150 basis points from 8.5 per cent to 7 per cent between April and mid-October 2001. During the same period, primary yield on 364 days treasury bills fell by 168 basis points from 8.85 per cent to 7.17 per cent. The discount rates on the CP also showed a similar trend. At the long end of the market, the secondary market yields on government paper in the range of 10–20 years have softened from 10.08 per cent to 10.70 per cent in April to 9.12 per cent to 9.92 per cent by mid-October, 2001.

(b) The RBI issued fresh guidelines for issuance of commercial paper on October 10, 2000 relaxing the terms and conditions and streamlining the procedures. As indicated in the annual policy statement of April 2001, Banks, FIs, PDs, Satellite Dealers (SDs) are now permitted to make fresh investments and hold the CPs only in decentralised form, effective from June 30, 2001. In this context Fixed Income Money Market and Derivatives Association of India circulated a report of FIMMADA working group on, primarily relating to market conventions and guidelines for CPs. FIMMADA along with market participants, depositories and RBI prepared the related guidelines and made them public on October 3, 2001. These guidelines seem to be working reasonably well, and no changes are being proposed at present.

(c) As announced in the annual policy statement, 14-day and 182-day Treasury Bills (TBs) have been withdrawn from the week beginning May 14, 2001. The notified amount of 91-day TBs have been simultaneously increased to Rs. 250 crores. It has also been ensured that both the 91-day and 364-day TBs mature on the same day in order to facilitate the availability of adequate fungible stocks of TBs varying maturities in the secondary market. Increased attractions of TBs is evident from the fact that no development of the RBI has taken place in TB auctions and the bid-coverge ratio, particularly in respect to 364-day TBs, has also improved.

(d) A Negotiable Dealing System (NDS) is being introduced with a view of facilitating electronic bidding in auctions and secondary market transactions in government securities and dissemination of information as trades on a real time basic. The technology infrastructure related to NDS has been tested with the involvement of all market participants in LAN and WAN environments parallel runs are expected in November 2001.

(e) The Clearing Corporation of India Ltd. (CCIL) was registered on April 30, 2001 under the Companies Act, 1956 with the SBI as the chief promoter. Initially, the CCIL would clear all the transactions and repos reported on the NDS of the RBI and also US/rupee/dollar forex spot and forward deals. The operationalisation of CCIL linked to the NDS is expected to commerce with a test run in November 2001. The necessary amendments to the notification was issued by the Government for the introduction of the uniform price auction format for the auctions of dated securities. With the approval of the government, the new auction format will be introduced on an experimental basis.

(f) A scheme of retail participation including the middle segment encompassing PF's, Trusts in the primary market for the government securities on non-competitive basis has been finalised after consulting the market participation and the technical advisory committee on Money Market and government securities market. The details of the scheme is yet to be finalised by RBI.

(g) The **Satellite Dealer** system was introduced in 1996 to serve as a second tier to PDs in the government securities market with the particular objective of promoting retail segment. The experience of Satellite Dealers confirms that in practice, Satellite Dealers role in government securities has remained very limited. Even as complementary service, the Satellite Dealers system is perceived to result in higher transaction costs to retail investors.

As many of them are broker firms because of the limited capital strength and because of under presence in non-government securities business also raised some supervisory concerns.

(h) On overall review of the present environment in the market. The RBI has decided to undertake a review of the Satellite Dealer system along with SDs, PDs and TAC. The review will consider the role covered out for SDs in the development of retail market, particularly in the context of the expanding role of PDs, emerging alternative mechanism of retailing government securities on the screen based trading in exchange and the supervisory concerns in monitoring Satellite Dealer's operations. The review will examine the scope for establishing a better linkage between SDs and PDs and thereby improving the SD system as an effective distribution channel at a retail level for government securities.

(i) The satellite system dealership was launched in 1996 to serve as a second tier to primary dealers in retailing of G-secs. The RBI in its mid-term monetary and credit policy has tacitly accepted that the concept of satellite dealers has not taken off as an efficient medium for retailing the government securities. The Central Bank has decided to review the entire system of Satellite Dealers in the fixed income market. The RBI has decided to allow players such as provident funds, trusts to participate in the government bond auctions, on a non-competitive basis. This review would consider the role carved out for Satellite Dealers in the development of retail market. The review would focus on building linkages between primary and Satellite Dealers and improving the Satellite Dealership system.

(j) Call money market with average daily gross lending has been improving to Rs. 19,600 crores during May–September, 2001 from Rs. 10,900 crores during the corresponding period of the previous year. Therefore, the Central Bank feels that the planned phasing out of non-banking participants from the call money market has not caused any strain on the market.

(k) Top rated corporates can now have the best of the both worlds. They can obtain a commitment from a bank for working capital funds by getting a cash credit limit sanctioned. Thereafter the banks can go for shopping the best sub-PLR rate available from other banks. If by any chance rates harden, they can always pull back on the cash credit limit that has already been sanctioned. Till now, the banks could not shop for funds after receiving the sanction, as 80 per cent of the sanctioned working capital funds has to be drawn immediately in the form of a loan. The remaining 20 per cent was available, now RBI has given permission to the banks that the banks can offer 100 per cent of the sanctioned limits in the form of cash credit.

ANNEXURE–I

**Average Daily Turnover in Call Money Market**

| *Fortnight Ended* | *Turnover per day (Rs. in crores)* |
|---|---|
| May 5, 2000 | 48,056 |
| May 19, 2000 | 39,214 |
| June 2, 2000 | 40,056 |
| June 16, 2000 | 38,300 |
| June 30, 2000 | 38,357 |
| July 14, 2000 | 42,465 |
| July 28, 2000 | 39,797 |
| August 11, 2000 | 39,275 |
| August 25, 2000 | 35,973 |
| September 8, 2000 | 41,797 |
| September 22, 2000 | 42,933 |
| October 6, 2000 | 44,635 |
| October 20, 2000 | 45,776 |
| November 3, 2000 | 47,321 |
| November 17, 2000 | 46,805 |
| December 1, 2000 | 47,310 |
| December 15, 2000 | 46,747 |
| December 29, 2000 | 43,568 |
| January 12, 2001 | 50,396 |
| January 26, 2001 | 49,039 |
| February 9, 2001 | 50,675 |
| February 23, 2001 | 45,987 |
| March 9, 2001 | 51,550 |
| March 23, 2001 | 50,314 |
| April 6, 2001 | 44,630 |
| April 20, 2001 | 50,957 |
| May 4, 2001 | 48,008 |
| May 18, 2001 | 41,395 |
| June 1, 2001 | 46,156 |
| June 15, 2001 | 44,790 |
| June 29, 2001 | 47,052 |
| July 13, 2001 | 47.071 |
| July 27, 2001 | 44.597 |

*Source*: *RBI Bulletin*. October 2001. p. 5997.

## ANNEXURE—II

## Daily Call Money Rates from 01.08.2001 to 12.09.2001

| As on | Range of Rates | | Weighted average rate | |
|---|---|---|---|---|
| | Borrowings | Lending | Borrowings | Lending |
| Aug. 1, 2001 | 5.47 – 7.10 | 4.92 – 7.50 | 6.90 | 6.92 |
| Aug. 2, 2001 | 5.89 – 7.10 | 4.89 – 7.40 | 6.86 | 6.88 |
| Aug. 3, 2001 | 5.85 – 7.10 | 4.85 – 7.00 | 6.92 | 6.87 |
| Aug. 4, 2001 | 6.15 – 7.05 | 5.39 – 7.05 | 6.82 | 6.96 |
| Aug. 6, 2001 | 5.80 – 7.05 | 4.80 – 7.10 | 6.78 | 6.80 |
| Aug. 7, 2001 | 5.45 – 7.20 | 4.90 – 7.10 | 6.88 | 6.89 |
| Aug. 8, 2001 | 5.70 – 7.65 | 5.10 – 7.90 | 7.11 | 7.12 |
| Aug. 9, 2001 | 5.79 – 7.60 | 5.20 – 7.60 | 7.18 | 7.26 |
| Aug. 10, 2001 | 5.94 – 7.50 | 6.25 – 7.50 | 6.93 | 6.97 |
| Aug. 11, 2001 | 5.90 – 7.25 | 5.54 – 7.25 | 6.97 | 6.97 |
| Aug. 13, 2001 | 5.21 – 7.25 | 4.97 – 7.90 | 6.92 | 6.99 |
| Aug. 14, 2001 | 6.00 – 8.30 | 5.11 – 8.30 | 7.05 | 7.06 |
| Aug. 16, 2001 | 5.59 – 7.30 | 5.09 – 7.30 | 7.04 | 7.08 |
| Aug. 17, 2001 | 5.55 – 7.30 | 5.03 – 7.30 | 7.02 | 7.01 |
| Aug. 18, 2001 | 5.96 – 7.15 | 6.50 – 7.25 | 6.97 | 7.00 |
| Aug. 20, 2001 | 5.59 – 7.34 | 5.06 – 7.90 | 7.04 | 7.04 |
| Aug. 23, 2001 | 5.61 – 7.25 | 5.06 – 7.25 | 7.04 | 7.08 |
| Aug. 24, 2001 | 6.00 – 7.50 | 5.75 – 7.25 | 7.04 | 7.05 |
| Aug. 25, 2001 | 5.86 – 7.20 | 5.42 – 7.80 | 6.86 | 6.88 |
| Aug. 27, 2001 | 5.85 – 7.05 | 4.85 – 7.05 | 6.84 | 6.85 |
| Aug. 28, 2001 | 5.30 – 7.30 | 4.75 – 7.10 | 6.74 | 6.75 |
| Aug. 29, 2001 | 5.26 – 7.30 | 4.75 – 7.80 | 6.73 | 6.78 |
| Aug. 30, 2001 | 5.44 – 7.40 | 4.89 – 7.10 | 6.90 | 6.93 |
| Aug. 31, 2001 | 5.53 – 7.55 | 4.96 – 7.55 | 6.95 | 6.98 |
| Sept. 1, 2001 | 5.92 – 7.10 | 6.10 – 7.15 | 6.91 | 6.92 |
| Sept. 3, 2001 | 5.45 – 7.45 | 4.90 – 7.50 | 6.89 | 6.91 |
| Sept. 4, 2001 | 5.85 – 7.00 | 6.00 – 7.15 | 6.85 | 6.86 |
| Sept. 5, 2001 | 5.43 – 7.25 | 4.89 – 7.25 | 6.98 | 6.90 |
| Sept. 7, 2001 | 6.00 – 7.95 | 5.89 – 7.95 | 7.14 | 7.17 |
| Sept. 8, 2001 | 6.08 – 7.40 | 6.60 – 7.40 | 7.08 | 7.08 |
| Sept. 10, 2001 | 6.05 – 7.75 | 5.05 – 7.75 | 7.02 | 7.15 |
| Sept. 11, 2001 | 6.10 – 7.80 | 5.10 – 7.50 | 7.06 | 7.06 |

*Source*: RBI Bulletin October 2001, p. 5996.

## (B) CAPITAL MARKET

### *Introduction*

Capital market deals with long-term funds. It supplies long-term and medium-term funds. It deals with shares, stocks, debentures and bonds. Securities dealt in capital market are long-term securities. The funds which flows into the capital market comes from the savers. It provides a market mechanism for those who have savings and to those who need funds for productive investments. It diverts resources from wasteful and unproductive channels to productive investments. Since 1951, the Indian capital market has been broadening slowly. There is a steady improvement in the volume of savings and investment. Many types of encouragement and tax relief exists in the country to promote savings. Many steps have been taken to protect the interest of investors. An important indicator in the growth of capital market is the growth of joint stock companies and corporate enterprises. In 1951 there were **28,500** companies with a paid up capital of nearly **Rs. 775 crores** and as on **31.3.98**. There were more than **2,00,000** companies with a paid up capital of nearly **Rs. 1,37,959 crores**. The growth of investment has been quite phenomenal in recent years in accordance with the accelerated tempo development ofthe Indian economy.

### *Definitions*

Capital market can be defined as "the market for relatively long-term financial instruments".[4] According to Arun K. Datta, the capital market may be defined as "the capital market is a complex of institutions investment and practices with established links between the demand for and supply of different types of capital gains".[5] Further **F. Livingston** defined the capital market as **"**In a developing economy, it is the business of the capital market to facilitate the main stream of command over capital to the point of the highest yield. By doing so it enables control over resources to pass into hands of those who can employ them most effectively thereby increasing productive capacity and spelling the national dividend".[6] Capital market consists of gilt edged market and the industrial securities market. The gilt edged market refers to the market for government and semi-government securities backed by the RBI. The securities traded in this market are stable in value and are much sought after by the banks and other institutions.

The industrial securities market refers to the market for equities and debentures of old and new companies. The industrial securities market is further divided by the new issue market and further capital issue market. The new issue market refers to the rising of capital by new companies in the form of shares and debentures, while further old issue capital deals with securities already issued by existing companies. Both markets are equally important. But the NIM is much more important for capital formation in the country. However, the functioning of NIM will be facilitated only when there are facilities for transfer of existing securities.

Considerable deregulation of financial markets has taken place in India favouring unbridled growth of financial services companies. Reforms undertaken have increased competitiveness within the financial sector by means of free interest rates, allowing new financial institutions and instruments. As a consequence, the scope and activities of the banks and non-banking finance companies have expanded rapidly due to liberalisation drive, more particularly since 1991. The non-banking finance companies have been competing and complementing the services of commercial banks. It has been observed that the growth of non-banking finance companies is more pronounced than banking companies.

### *Nature and Constituents*

The capital markets consists of a number of individuals and institutions. The Government is also an important player in the capital market. The players in the capital market, canalise the supply and demand for long-term capital. The constituents of the capital markets are the stock exchange, commercial banks, cooperative banks, savings banks, development banks, insurance companies, investment trusts and companies etc.

### *The Growth of the Capital Market*

The Indian financial system is both developed and integrated today. Integration has been through a participatory approach in granting of loans as well as in savings schemes. The expansion in size and number of institutions has led to a considerable degree of diversification and increase in types of financial instruments in the financial sector which are wholly owned by the Government.

The Development Banks in the Indian financial system have witnessed vast changes in the planning periods. Now the development banks constitute the backbone of the Indian capital market. The relevance of the development banks in the industrial financial system is not merely qualitative, but they have overwhelmingly qualitative dimensions in terms of their promotional and innovational functions. The growth of the capital market is determined by the following factors:

(a) Economic development.
(b) Rapid industrialisation.
(c) Level of savings and investment of the household sector.
(d) Technology advances.
(e) Corporate performance.
(f) Regulatory framework.
(g) Participation of FIIs in the capital market.
(h) Development of financial services.
(i) Liquidity factors.
(j) Political stability.
(k) Globalisation.
(l) Financial innovation.
(m) Economic and financial sector reforms.
(n) International developments.
(o) Agency costs.
(p) Emergence of financial intermediaries.
(q) Sophistication among investment managers.
(r) Tax incentives.
(s) Speed in acquiring, processing and acting upon information.
(t) NRI's investment.

### *Components of Capital Market*

In a capital market, banks and financial institutions are important components. They act as catalysts in the economic development of any country. These institutions mobilise financial savings from household, corporate and other sectors of the economy and channelise them into productive investments. They act as a reservoir of resources and form the backbone of the economic and financial systems. The banking industry has undergone a sea change during the last three decades after the modernisation of banks. They not only lend for the social and economic causes but also participate in the development programmes of the Central Government and State Government. The main components of the capital market in India are:

(1) **New-Issue Market** (Public Issue).
(2) **Secondary Market** (Stock Market).

### (1) New-Issue Market

New-Issue market is called as primary market or public issue. The NIM creates financial claims. It deals with those securities which have been made available to the public for the first time. Public issue can be defined as "**Sale of bonds or stock to the general public**".[7] The primary market may be defined as "**A market where new securities are bought and sold for the first time**".[8] The flow of new securities from the buyer of securities to the issuers of securities. Therefore, the new-issue market deals with new securities. The NIM provides the issuing company with additional funds. It facilitates transfer of funds from savers to entrepreneurs. The NIM does not have any physical existence and any administrative organisational set up. NIM facilitates the transfer of resources from savers to users. The NIM does not enjoy tangibility form, but it renders services to lenders and borrowers at the required time. New securities may be floated both by newly set up organisations or by the existing ventures. For marketing shares generally the following methods are followed:

(a) Public Issue.
(b) Rights Issue.

*Public Issue*

The role of the new issue market and stock exchange is complementary to each other in the infrastructure facilities provided for sale and purchase of securities in the market. The new issues of shares are subscribed to the corporate sector through the application forms before the date of closing of the issue. The amount of resources mobilised through **public issues** after liberalisation policy is presented in the Table 1.

**Table 1:** Capital Raised Through Public Issues 1991–2001

*(Rs. in crores)*

| Year | *Public Issues* | | *Rights Issues* | | *Grand Total* | |
|---|---|---|---|---|---|---|
| | *No. of Issues* | *Amount* | *No. of Issues* | *Amount* | *No. of Issues* | *Amount* |
| 1991–92 | 196 | 1,711 | 316 | 3,851 | 512 | 5,562 |
| 1992–93 | 527 | 6,059 | 488 | 12,630 | 1,015 | 18,689 |
| 1993–94 | 770 | 12,544 | 384 | 9,306 | 1,154 | 21,850 |
| 1994–95 | 1,342 | 2,1044 | 324 | 6,577 | 1,666 | 27,621 |
| 1995–96 | 1,426 | 14,240 | 299 | 6,564 | 1,725 | 20,804 |
| 1996–97 | 730 | 7,761 | 112 | 2,663 | 842 | 10,424 |
| 1997–98 | 62 | 2,862 | 49 | 1,708 | 111 | 4,570 |
| 1998–99 | 24 | 2,602 | 24 | 2411 | 48 | 5,013 |
| 1999–2000 | 55 | 4,028 | 24 | 1,125 | 79 | 5,153 |
| 2000–2001 | 38 | 356 | 05 | 160 | 43 | 516 |
| 2001–2002 Upto June | 02 | 410 | – | – | 02 | 410 |

*Sources*: 1. *RBI Bulletin*, March 99, p. S 277.
2. *RBI Bulletin*, July 2000, p. S 681.
3. *RBI Bulletin*, October 2001, p. S 1017.
4. Prime Annual Report 1991–94.

*Rights Issues*

The data reveals that the primary market has not been quite encouraging since 1997–98. **Rights issues** refers to raising of capital from the existing shareholders. In India, Section 81 of the Companies Act, 1956 right shares can be issued:

(a) One year after the company's first issue,
(b) Two years after its existence.

The law in India requires that the new ordinary shares must be issued to the existing shareholders on a *pro rata* basis. The SEBI has the full authority to permit the rights offered by the corporate sector.

The shareholders to whom the offer is made are not under any legal obligation to accept the offer. On the other hand, they have a right to renounce the offer in favour of any person. Rights shares are usually offered on terms beneficial to the shareholders. According to Section 81 of the Act, the following conditions are to be satisfied by a public company for issuing right shares.

**Objects of Section 81**

(a) Shares must be offered to existing shareholders on *pro rata* basis.
(b) The offer must be made by giving a notice indicating the number of shares offered.
(c) The acceptance of right shares should be informed within 15 days.
(d) Shareholders can have the right to renounce only with the consent of articles of association of the company.
(e) The board of directors may of dispose the unsubscribed shares, after the expiry of specified time.

**Exceptions to the Rule Section 81**

According to Section 81(A), such new shares may be offered by the Company to persons other than its equity shareholders. It requires the following conditions:

(a) a special resolution should be passed by the Company in general meeting,
(b) an ordinary resolution should be passed by the Company to that effect, and
(c) the approval of Central Government is necessary.

The rule laid down in Section 81 of the Act, that further shares should be offered to the existing equity shareholders does not apply:

(a) to a private company,
(b) to increase the share capital of a public company.

Provided that the terms of such issue are approved by:

(a) special resolution of the Company,
(b) the Central Government.

In India the rights issue offer can be followed in the process:

(a) Announcing of rights offer by the Company,
(b) Mailing of forms (A, B, C, D) to the existing shareholders.

### *(a) Announcement of Rights Offer*

The following situation will help to understand the rights issue process involved by the Companies.

**Example:** Let us assume that a Company announces on **2nd November, 2001** that all shareholders whose names are in the register of members as on **25th December, 2001**, will be issued rights which expire on **8th January, 2002**. The Company will mail the "Letter of rights" on **3rd February, 2002**. In the example:

(a) 2nd Nov., 2001 → Announcement date.
(b) 25th Dec., 2001 → Holder of the register of member's date.
(c) 8th Jan., 2002 → Offer of rights date.
(d) 3rd Feb., 2002 → Expiration of rights date.

It may be possible that the share may be traded a few days before the holder of the register of members date (3rd Feb., 2002) in the example and it may not be transferred and registered in the new name. The rights might then be wrongly sent to the old shareholder. If the shares are traded within the ex-rights date, it will be duly registered in the name of purchaser. The ex-rights date occurs a few days prior to the holder of the register of member date. It implies that after the ex-rights date the share sells without the rights. The price of the share before the ex-rights date is called as **"cum-rights"** while the price after this date is referred to as the **"ex-rights"** price.

### *(b) Mailing of Forms*

The letter of offering rights will be sent to all the existing shareholders of the Company. Along with the letter of rights offer 4 forms may be sent to the shareholders. They are in 4 different forms, namely i.e., **Form A, Form B, Form C and Form D**.

**Form-A** – It is intended for accepting the rights and applying for additional shares.

**Form-B** – It is meant for the purpose of foregoing the rights in favour of other person.

**Form-C** – It may be used for renunciation by the new shareholders for making the application form.

**Form-D** – It is the purpose of requesting for the split forms.

While offering the rights shares to the existing shareholders by the Company for mobilising funds, there are 3 important issues involved:

**(1) Conversion ratio.**
**(2) Conversion value of a right.**
**(3) The effect of rights on ordinary shareholders.**

### *(1) Conversion Ratio*

The conversion ratio means, the number of new shares offered to the existing shareholders in fulfilling the targeted amount by the Company. The conversion ratio can be computed by the following formula:

$$N = \frac{S_o}{S}$$

N = No. of rights.
$S_o$ = Number of existing shares.
S = New shares.

### *(2) Conversion Value of a Right*

The conversion value of a right share depends upon the two factors, i.e., the required fund by the Company, and the issue price of new share. Therefore, the value of a right can be computed by the following formula:

$$S = \frac{\text{Desired funds}}{\text{Subscription price}}$$

### *(3) The Effect of Rights on Ordinary Shareholders*

The value of a right when the share is selling ex-rights or cum-rights, it is clear that the existing shareholders does not benefit or lose from rights issue. If he receives in the form of the value of a right, he loses in the form of decline in share price. The shareholders wealth remains unaffected if he exercises his rights. He will lose if he does not exercise his rights or sells them.

#### *Advantages of Rights Issue*

There are three advantages of the right issues. They are:

(a) take over threat or financial difficulties can be eliminated,
(b) the rights issue can reduce the flotation cost for raising the funds rather than the public issue, and
(c) the profitable companies can get successful completion from rights issue.

*Disadvantages*

The main disadvantages regarding issue of rights offer:

(a) The shareholders will lose their wealth, if they fails to exercise their rights.
(b) It leads to the concentration of shareholdings in few hands, it enhances the monopoly situation.

**Recent Developments in the Market**

Fund raising activity has almost come to a standstill with a sharp and consistent decline in the number of issues over the past several months. It is not only the initial public offering market which has been affected, even the rights issue market seems to have dried up. The following table will reveal the situation of rights issues in the country:

**Statement Showing the Mobilisation of Resources through Rights Issues**

| *Year* | *No. of Rights Issues* | *Amount Mobilised (Rs. in crores)* |
|---|---|---|
| 1992–93 | 488 | 12,630 |
| 1993–94 | 384 | 9,306 |
| 1994–95 | 351 | 6,793 |
| 1995–96 | 291 | 6,520 |
| 1996–97 | 131 | 2,724 |
| 1997–98 | 49 | 1,703 |
| 1998–99 | 26 | 568 |
| 1999–2000 | 28 | 1,560 |
| 2000–2001 | 27 | 729 |
| 2001–2002 (April–Sept.) | 04 | 737 |

*Source*: *The Economic Times*, 16.11.2001.

The data reveals the market situation in the country. There were only four rights issues which hit the market during the half year that ended in September 2001 when compared with12 issues during the corresponding half of the previous year. Funds raised by the four companies, however, were substantially higher at Rs. 737 crores (compared with Rs. 350 crores by the 12 companies). The Telco alone mobilised Rs. 672 crores. There has been a sharp and almost consistent decline in the rights issues—both in terms of number and amount mobilised since the year 1992–93 which had witnessed raising of funds worth Rs.12,630 crores by 488 companies.

Telco led the pack of the issues with a Rs. 672 crores offer. The Auto Major, which had earlier announced an issue size of Rs. 1,037 crores pruned by the size by nearly **50 per cent** due to bad market conditions as well as poor corporate performance. The other issuers in the period were Alok Industries **(Rs. 51 crores)**, Dalmia Cement **(Rs. 8 crores)** and Dharamsi Morarji Chemical **(Rs. 7 crores)**.

According to Prime Database, a Delhi based research firm analysed the present situation. "The poor run of rights is primarily because of the dull conditions which have hit the market through almost the entire last two years". In fact, the steady fall in the number of companies tapping the rights route down the years can be ascribed mainly to the depressed, secondary market prices of a vast majority of companies, many due to poor fundamentals.

As an alternative to IPO and rights issues, several companies with good performance have preferred to meet their fund requirements through preferential allotments or by way of private placement to mutual funds, private equity investors and venture capital funds. Many of them mobilised funds through the private placement of Debt.

The Prime Database further reported that during the second half of the current year (2001–2002) no major trends are likely to be witnessed. Only three rights issues—Gammon India **(Rs. 19 crores)**, Arvind Mills **(Rs. 75 crores)** and SKF Bearings **(Rs. 88 crores)** have hit the market since October 2001. There are three more companies which have received the SEBI approval but are yet to come out with their issues. They are Omax Autos **(Rs. 4 crores)**, R.K. Ispat **(Rs. 3 crores)** and Tata Investment Corporation **(Rs. 33 crores)**. Few companies Mindteck **(Rs. 10 crores)** and J.K. Industries **(Rs. 47 crores)** are awaiting SEBI approval. Prime has also compiled a list of companies which announced rights issues since January of (2001) this year. Notable among them are **Essar Steel** with a planned Rs. 267 crores rights issue and Ballarpur Industries with a Rs. 250 crores offering.

**Recent Developments in NIM**

Public equity issues may be inactive at the present situation. According to the Prime Database[9], the public issues for debt and equity issues of just Rs. 1,101 crores and Rs. 6 crores respectively in the first half of the current fiscal (2001–2002) period. The first half of the current year witness 118 institutions and corporates mobilising an amount of Rs. 22,673 crores through the private placement of debt. The amount raised by the private sector recorded a 31 per cent gain to reach Rs. 6,234 crores compared to Rs. 4,812 crores raised in the first half of 2001–2002.

**Mega Issues**

During the current fiscal year 2001–2002 the leading pack of mobilisers is Reliance Petroleum Rs. 1,061 crores and it is followed by GE Capital Rs. 520 crores, TISCO Rs. 350 crores and Tata Power Rs. 300 crores. In the case of PSUs a 34 per cent improvement found with Rs. 4,816 crores being mobilised from the market. The major mobilisers are REC Rs. 869 crores, Power Grid Corporation Rs. 761 crores, SAIL Rs. 700 crores, NTPC Rs. 575 crores and BPCL Rs. 445 crores respectively. On the other hand, the mobilisation by State Level Undertakings (SLU) is by 51 per cent from Rs. 5,858 crores to Rs. 2,891 crores in the relevant periods 2000–2001 and 2001–2002 respectively.

According to the new RBI guidelines the Commercial Banks can invest in State Government papers. It is found that the most of the funds raised by SLUs have been for the infrastructure sector, mainly power, roads and water resources. The leader in mobilisation during the 6 month (2001–2002) (upto Oct. 30, 2001) was Krishna Bhagya Jal Nigam Rs. 356 crores, followed by GEB Rs 300 crores, Maharashtra Vikrikar Rs. 244 crores, JKSPDC Rs. 200 crores and GSRTC Rs. 200 crores.

Significantly a total of Rs. 12,272 crores was raised by AAA rated paper. On the other hand, Rs. 2,025 crores of paper was not rated at all during the 2000–2001 year. On an industry-wise analysis, it was found that the financial services sector including banking and term lending, continued to dominate, the market, collectively raising Rs.10,736 crores, power sector ranked second with Rs. 3,765 crores. The analysis of public issue during 2000–2001 further reveals that Maharashtra lead the resources mobilisation activity at Rs. 9,877 crores, followed by Delhi at Rs. 6,778 crores and Karnataka at Rs. 1,940 crores.

## Functions of NIM

The main function of the NIM is to facilitate the transfer of resources. The NIM can also be utilised for selling the existing concerns to the public. The NIM is a tool for the implication of privatisation policy. According to **R.F. Henderson** the functions of NIM can be categorised into two ways:

(a) Initial issues by new companies
(b) Further issues by old companies

These issues bear no relation to the age of the company. But these are based on the fact that listing of securities with stock exchange. Therefore, the classification of these issues are concerned only with the flow of new money.

Another classification of issues are concerned with the flow of funds into the market and flow of new money. Issue of shares involving in the newly created share is called as initial issue. The sale of securities which already in existence and are sold by their holders can be classified as secondary market. This classification excludes two types of issues from the category of new issues, i.e., **Bonus issues and Exchange issues**.

Therefore, the main function of the NIM is channelising the investible funds. The NIM has the following 3 functions:

(1) Origination.
(2) Underwriting.
(3) Distribution.

### *(1) Origination*

Origination is the first step in planning a public issue. It refers to the work of investigation and analysis of new proposals. In this function the specialised agencies would assess the capabilities of the issuing company. They will undertake a careful study of the technical, economic, financial and legal aspects of the issuing companies. The specialised agencies also advised the issuing company on the following matters regarding the aspects of capital issues:

(a) Investment climate.
(b) Determination of the class of security to be issued.
(c) Determination of the issue price.
(d) The timing and magnitude of issues.
(e) Method of flotation.
(f) Techniques of selling.

These functions of origination are mainly in advisory nature. The functions of origination has been taken over in India by the specialised concerns of Commercial Banks. The Commercial Banks have created a separate division called the **"Merchant Banking Division"**. Merchant Banking would advise the companies about the viability of the project. They offer the services regarding pre-and-post public issues. A detailed discussion would be available in preceding pages regarding the merchant banking.

***(2) Underwriting***

Underwriting has originated to face the uncertainities of the capital market when the company approaches the public issues. In NIM, if the issue remains unsubscribed, the directors cannot proceed to allot the shares. The directors are required to return the money to the applicants. Consequently the project would fail. To overcome the situation the companies are taking precautions about the public issue for the successful completion. Underwriting is the arrangement where the investment bankers to undertake for ensuring the full success of the issue of securities. The underwriters agrees to take a specified number of shares or debentures offered to the public in the event of non-subscription by the investors. In this situation underwriter has to contribute the share capital for his assurance part. If the company gets success in public issues, the underwriter is entitled to get a commission for this assignment. It is called as Underwriting Commission.

Generally the public financial institutions underwrite the issue of capital. The underwriting is done in addition to granting the term finance by way of loans on debentures. A detailed discussion is available in preceding chapters.

### *(3) Distribution*

Distribution is the most important aspect in the process of public issue. The sale of securities to the ultimate investors is referred to as distribution. It is a specialised job performed by brokers and dealers in securities. They maintain regular and direct contact with the ultimate investors. They know the pulse of investors and able to influence them towards the mobilisation of the share capital of the companies.

## Mechanics of Floating New Issues

The following are the methods of new issues which are placed in the market:

**(1) Public issue.**
**(2) Offer for sale.**
**(3) Private placement.**

### *(1) Public Issue*

The sale of shares and debentures through prospectus is called as public issue. It is the method of floatation of shares and debentures. The offer to the public is made directly through the intermediary at specific price. Intermediaries are not involved but they will help in mobilisation of funds. But it is an expensive method of flotation of shares, which approximately costs 10 per cent of public issue amount. The issuing company has to incur expenses on administration, advertisements, printing prospectus, paper announcements, bank's commission, underwriting commission, agents fees, legal charges, stamp duty, documents, fee, listing fees and registration charges.

### *(2) Offer for Sale*

In this method the sale of shares is made indirectly by an issuing house. It involves the sale of securities, through different steps.

In 1st step → Sale of shares by the issuing company to the issuing house or broker.

In 2nd step → The broker or issuing house will resell the shares to the public with a charged profit.

Offer for sale is not used for selling securities to the public, but to comply with certain stock exchange regulations at the time of listing the shares. This method is not used in India. But it is very popular in abroad.

### *(3) Private Placement*

Private placement refers to direct sale of newly issued securities by the issuer to a small number of investors. It is an indirect method of sale of shares. The private placement market is very popular in United States, Canada, UK, France, Sweden, Mexico and European countries. The developing countries like Korea, Indonesia, Philippines, Malaysia, Thailand and India have been accessing the private placement market in the US. The private placement market is subject to some regulations in the abroad. But in India this method is not bound by any regulatory system.

Private placement can be defined as "the sale of an entire issue of securities directly to one purchaser or a small group of purchasers".[10]

#### *Features*

The following are the important features regarding the private placement:

(a) The transactions in this method are very speed.
(b) There are no legal hurdles in this method.
(c) It can be tailored to the borrower's needs.
(d) Financing can be consummated quickly.
(e) Flexibility in borrowing/utilising of the fund.

It does not require the detailed compliance of formalities as required in public or rights issues. It is a cost and time effective way of raising funds for the corporates. In this method, for issuing the equity, companies are free to fix the quantum of placement and only follow the rule for pricing of preferential allotment as stipulated by the SEBI. These placements have no lock-in period. There is no compliance system for merchant bankers in private placement as in the case of public issues. Therefore, the method has become a favourable route for the corporates and the financial institutions in India for mobilising resources during the last few years. The private placement market to be very active in future.

### **Public Issue Process**

Public issue is essentially an exercise which involves active participation of a number of agencies. The growth of the number of public issues has become necessary to enlist the active participation and support of a number of agencies in making any issue a success. The promoter should be able to coordinate effectively the efforts of these agencies. There are different companies which approaches NIM, for every type of organisation there will be a separate legal formality that have to be fulfilled. The public issues can be made by,[11]

(a) First issue of new companies set up by the entrepreneurs without a track record.
(b) First issue of new companies set up by existing companies with a track record.
(c) First issue by existing closely held company.
(d) First public issue by unlisted companies with 3 years track record.
(e) First public issue by unlisted companies without 3 years track record.
(f) Public issue for closely held companies seeking Disinvestments.
(g) Public issue for the closely held companies seeking Disinvestment without issuing a fresh capital.
(h) Public issues by the existing listed companies.

Therefore, the public issue activities have been processed as follows:

| | | |
|---|---|---|
| I Step | — | Consent from SEBI. |
| II Step | — | Compliance with Companies Act. |
| III Step | — | Drafting of prospectus. |
| IV Step | — | Approval from the RBI. |
| V Step | — | Printing and distribution of stationery. |
| VI Step | — | Marketing and Advertising Campaign. |
| VII Step | — | Bank Coordination. |
| VIII Step | — | Stock exchange formalities. |
| IX Step | — | Post issue activities. |

Another classification of process of public issue can be found as follows:

**(A) Pre-issue activities.** **(B) Post-issue activities.**

### (A) Pre-Issue Activities

The following things should be done accordingly to make an issue as a success:

(a) Approvals and clearances for the issue.
(b) Appointment of agencies, drafting of prospectus.
(c) Permission from RBI (for issue to NRI/FII).
(d) Formalities related to banks.
(e) Pre-issue stock exchange formalities.
(f) Printing & Distribution of stationery and advertising material.
(g) Advertising and promotional campaign.
(h) Preferential offer to shareholders/promoters.
(i) Allotment formalities.
(j) Board meeting.

### (B) Post-Issue Activities

It is the next stage after the completion of public issue. After closing the issue tne following process should be involved to finalise the issues:

1. Instruction to collect the branches of bankers to the issue.
2. Receipt of applications and allotment of shares.
3. Monitoring daily collection and announcement regarding closure.
4. Feedback from collecting branches.
5. Registrars to make details about issue response.
6. Obtain certificate from the controlling branches.
7. Scrutiny of share applications by Registrar.
8. Preparation of Bank Reconciliation Statement by Registrar.
9. Allotment formalities.
10. Despatch of allotment letters with refund orders.

## (2) Secondary Market

The stock exchanges are the secondary markets. They not only serve the private sector but also the joint and public sectors by providing a forum for the transferability of shares held by the public. The stock exchanges not only effect purchase and sale of securities but also make a continuous valuation of securities traded in the market. The stock exchanges play an important role relating to the securities issued by the Central and State Governments, municipalities, investment trusts, port trusts and various other public bodies. The NIM and stock exchanges are interlinked and work together. They cannot be described as two separate markets because of the kind of functions they perform. Therefore, the stock exchange is a medium of transfer of resources for those securities which have already been issued. It also plays an important role in the transfer of securities with the companies whose shares are being dealt with as the process of registration of shares must be conducted when they are transferred. In the stock exchange, securities issued in primary markets are bought and sold. In this market the public can buy and sell securities. It does not create financial claim. In this market, funds do not flow between sellers and buyers of securities. The brokers, the investors, mutual funds, and the financial institutions are the important constituents of the secondary market. The secondary market consists of the operations associated with the primary market. The secondary market consists of regional stock exchanges, BSE, NSE, OTCEI, etc.

### *Definitions*

According to the Securities Contract (Regulation) Act of 1956, the stock exchange can be defined as "An association, organisation or body of individuals, whether incorporated or not, established for the purpose of assisting, regulating and controlling business in buying, selling and dealing in securities".

According to **Husband and Dockery** "Securities or stock exchanges are privately organised markets which are used to facilitate trading securities".

### *Functions of Stock Exchange*

The stock exchange is established with the purpose of providing a market place for the members to deal with securities under well laid down regulations and to protect the interests of the investors. Thus, the functions of the stock exchange are as follows:

1. It extends liquidity to securities.

2. It acts as clearing house of business information.
3. It brings companies and investors together.
4. It ensures wider ownership of securities.
5. It provides capital to profitable sectors.
6. It ensures safety and fair dealings to all.
7. It facilitates marketability and transparency of securities.
8. It motivates managers of well reputed companies to dominate the market.
9. It provides an orderly regulated market for securities.
10. It facilitates continuous, ready and open market for selling and buying of securities.
11. It promotes savings and capital in the economy by attracting funds from the investors.
12. It facilitates the takeovers by means of acquiring majority of shares traded on the market.
13. It allows companies to float their shares on the market.
14. It induces managers to improve performance for converting non-specified shares into specified group of shares in the exchange.

### *Classification of Securities Listed in Stock Exchange*

The securities listed for trading in Bombay Stock Exchange are grouped into the following categories:

**(1) Group–A Shares (Specified securities).**
**(2) Group–B Shares.**
**(3) Permitted Securities.**
**(4) Cleared Securities.**
**(5) Non-cleared Securities.**

#### *(1) Group–A Shares*

Listed securities are classified as cleared or specified or Group–A securities and non-cleared or unspecified or Group–B or cash securities. The securities in which forward trading is allowed are called as Group–A shares. Group–A shares are included in the cleared list of exchange after the shares have satisfied the following conditions:

(a) The Shares should be fully paid up equity shares.

(b) The Company's paid up capital should be at least **Rs. 5 crores.**
(c) The Company should have a growth potential.
(d) The Company should be a dividend paying one.
(e) The Company's shares should have market capitalisation of at least **Rs. 10 crores.**
(f) The Shares should have been actively traded on the floor.
(g) The number of Shareholders in that company must be more than 20,000.

*(2) Group–B Shares*

The shares which are traded on cash basis are called Group–B shares. They are also called as cash scrips. The carry forward facility is not available to Group–B shares.

*(3) Permitted Securities*

The securities which are listed with some of the recognised stock exchanges, when permitted to be traded by those stock exchanges where they are not listed are called as permitted securities. The permission is granted as per the rules and regulations of the stock exchange.

*(4) Cleared Securities*

The securities which are traded for fortnightly settlement. The payment and delivery will be completed in the third week following fortnightly clearing. The cleared securities are also called as specified securities. Speculation activity is permitted only for those shares which are included in the cleared securities list. The Governing Board of the Concerned Stock Exchange has the power to pass special resolutions specifying the securities which may from time to time be included in the specified securities list.

*(5) Non-cleared Securities*

The securities which are traded between the brokers are called as non-cleared securities. These securities are not cleared through the stock exchange clearing house. Therefore, the securities are not permitted to for carry over facilities.

The stock market is dominated by brokers and their role will be discussed in preceding chapters.

### *Sensex*

The equity shares of 30 companies from both the specified and non-specified groups have been selected on the basis of market activity with due representation to the major industries. The shares selected and the industrial concern to which they belong for the purpose of compiling the index are presented below:

| *S.No.* | *Name of the Company* | *Industry Group* |
|---|---|---|
| 1. | HLL | FMCG |
| 2. | Reliance Industries | Petroleum |
| 3. | I.T.C. | Cigar industry |
| 4. | Infosys Technologies | Computers |
| 5. | Reliance Petroleum | Petroleum |
| 6. | SBI | Banking |
| 7. | MTNL | Telecom |
| 8. | Ranbaxy Lab. | Pharmaceuticals |
| 9. | Dr. Reddy's Lab. | Pharmaceuticals |
| 10. | Cipla | Pharmaceuticals |
| 11. | Nestle | FMCG |
| 12. | HPCL | Petroleum |
| 13. | L&T | General Engineering |
| 14. | Hindalco Industries | Aluminium |
| 15. | ICICI | Banking |
| 16. | Satyam Computers | Computers |
| 17. | Zee Telefilms | Entertainment |
| 18. | Castrol | Lubricant |
| 19. | BHEL | Electricals |
| 20. | TISCO | Iron & Steel |
| 21. | Bajaj Auto | Automobiles |
| 22. | BSES | Electric supply |
| 23. | Grasim Industries | Misl. |
| 24. | Gujarath Ambuja Cement | Cement |
| 25. | Colgate Palmolive | FMCG |
| 26. | ACC | Cement |
| 27. | TELCO | Automobiles |
| 28. | Glaxo | Pharmaceuticals |
| 29. | MEM | Automobiles |
| 30. | NIIT | Computers |

*Source*: *The Economic Times*, Dt. 4.10.2001, p. 3.

The method of compilation of the BSE sensitive index of equity prices is the same as used by SEP, USA in construction of share price indices. The index for a day is calculated as per the percentage of the aggregate market value of the equity shares of all the companies in the sample on that day to the average market value of the equity shares of the same companies during the base period. The formula for calculation of the Sensex as follows:

$$\text{S and } P_t = \frac{\Sigma P_{it}\, \Sigma Q_{it}}{\Sigma P_{io}\, \Sigma Q_{io}} \times I_o$$

$P_{it}$ = Price of the stock $i$ in period $t$.
$Q_{it}$ = Number of shares outstanding for stock $i$ in period $t$.
$P_{io}$ = Price of stock $i$ in the base period o; and
$Q_{io}$ = No. of shares outstanding for stock $i$ in base period $o$ and the base period is 1941–43.

The Sensex has high volatile during 1995–2001 period of time the average yearly Sensex was presented below:

**Sensex**

| *Year* | *Average* | *High* | *Low* |
|---|---|---|---|
| 1995–96 | 3288.68 | 3598.37 | 2826.08 |
| 1996–97 | 3469.24 | 4096.26 | 2745.06 |
| 1997–98 | 3812.86 | 4548.02 | 3209.55 |
| 1998–99 | 3294.76 | 4280.96 | 2764.16 |
| 1999–2000 | 4658.63 | 5933.56 | 3245.27 |
| 2000–2001 | 4269.69 | 5541.54 | 3540.65 |
| 2001–2002 | | | |
| April 2001 | 3487.44 | 3605.01 | 3183.77 |
| May 2001 | 3613.84 | 3742.07 | 3494.48 |
| June 2001 | 3439.01 | 3557.64 | 3318.67 |

*Source*: *RBI Bulletin*, August 2001, p. 5796.

### *Bombay Stock Exchange (BSE)*

The Bombay Stock Exchange is the first in India under the name of **Native Share and Stock Broker's Association** in **1875**. In its 126 year history, it has seen several changes. It has been located on Dalal Street. The number of companies listed on **BSE** has grown from **197** in 1946 to **5,937** today. In **2000–2001**, the average daily volumes were **Rs. 4,775.8 crores**. The stock exchange has lost much of its former glory with the establishment of the **NSE**. The **average daily turnover** of the BSE has been presented below:

| *Year* | *Average Daily Turnover (Rs. in crores)* |
|---|---|
| 1989–90 | 134.80 |
| 1990–91 | 188.54 |
| 1991–92 | 332.30 |
| 1992–93 | 238.00 |
| 1993–94 | 387.78 |
| 1994–95 | 292.02 |
| 1995–96 | 215.79 |
| 1996–97 | 517.85 |
| 1997–98 | 851.00 |
| 1998–99 | 1283.95 |
| 1999–2000 | 2729.20 |
| 2000–2001 | 4775.70 |

*Source*: *Business Today,* Annual Issue, Jan. 20, 2002, p. 63.

**The Number of Companies Listed in BSE**

| *Year* | *No. of Companies* |
|---|---|
| 1989 (March) | 2275 |
| 1990 (March) | 2247 |
| 1991 (Dec.) | 2471 |
| 1992 (Dec.) | 2601 |
| 1993 (Dec.) | 3263 |
| 1994 (Dec.) | 4413 |
| 1995 (Dec.) | 5399 |
| 1996 (Dec.) | 5999 |
| 1997 (Dec.) | 5843 |
| 1998 (Dec.) | 5860 |
| 1999 (Dec.) | 5863 |
| 2000 (Dec.) | 5937 |

*Source*: *Business Today*, Annual Issue, Jan. 20, 2002, p. 63.

## REFERENCES

1. James. C. Van Horne, *Fundamentals of Financial Management*, p. 23, Prentice-Hall of India, 1997.
2. M.N. Mishra, *Money Banking and International Trade*, p. 340, S. Chand. and Co.
3. I.M. Pandey, *Financial Management*, Vikas Publishing House 1999, p. 964.

4. James C. Van Horne, *Fundamentals of Financial Management*, Prentice-Hall of India, p. 526, 1997.
5. Arun K. Datta, *Government, Finance and Capital Market*, P.G. Book Market, Calcutta, p. 17.
6. F. Livingston, *The English Capital Market*, Methuen, London, 1929.
7. James C. Van Horne, *Fundamentals of Financial Management*, p. 527, Prentice-Hall, 1997.
8. *Ibid.*
9. *Economic Times*, Dt. 1.10.2001, p. 13.
10. Van C. Horne, *Fundamentals of Financial Management*, p. 537, Prentice-Hall of India, 1997.
11. For a detailed discussion—*Manual of SEBI*—Nabhi Publication, New Delhi.

# 4

# FINANCIAL INSTRUMENTS

The major financial instruments in the Indian stock market are equity shares, debentures, bonds and government securities. With the growth of the capital market, new financial instruments are being introduced to suit the requirements of the companies as well as the investors. According to the investors expectation, the merchant bankers and fund managers design the new instruments. The following are the usual instruments of capital mobilisation in a capital market:

**(A) Equity shares.**
**(B) Preference shares.**
**(C) Debentures.**
**(D) Bonds.**

## (A) Equity Shares

Equity share represent the ownership position in a company. The holders of equity shares are called as shareholders or stockholders. Shareholders are real owners of the company. The shareholders bear the risk of ownership. They are the legal owners of the company. Equity shares are the permanent source of fund. The equity shares do not have a maturity date. The equity shareholders are entitled to get the dividends on their investment. If the company is wound up, they can exercise their claims as assets after all the adjustments have been made. The amount or rate of dividend is not fixed. The rate of dividend will be decided by the company's board of directors. The amount of capital contributed by the equity shares is called as share capital or equity capital. Equity shareholders have the right to attend the company's meeting and they can vote in the meeting. Equity shares has a number of features relation to the rights and claims.

### *Features*

The features of the equity shares are presented below:

1. Equity shareholders have a residual ownership claim.
2. They have a claim on the company's assets.
3. They have the legal power to elect the top level management of the company.
4. They have the voting rights in the company's meeting.
5. They have the right to buy further issue of shares.
6. They have the limited liability.

### *Advantages of Equity Shares*

Equity share capital is the most important source of the long-term finance. It offers the following advantages:

1. Equity share capital is a permanent capital.
2. The equity enhances the borrowing capacity of a company.
3. Flexibility in payment of dividend.

### *Disadvantages*

Equity share capital has some disadvantages when compared to the other sources of finance. They are as follows:

1. Flotation costs are more on equity than on debt.
2. Dividend is the highest cost sources of finance.
3. Frequent issue of shares may dilute the existing shareholder's earnings.
4. The issuance of equity shares can change the ownership.

## (B) Preference Shares

Preference shares can be defined as "preference share is often considered to be a hybrid security".[1]

Preference shares have many features of both the ordinary shares and debenture. Preference shares are similar to the equity shares in the following situations:

(a) It has no fixed maturity date.

(b) Non-payment of dividend does not effect the company.
(c) Dividends are not deductible for tax purposes.

Preference shares are also similar to debenture in the following situation:

(a) Preference shareholders usually do not have the voting rights.
(b) Preference shareholders dividend rate is fixed.
(c) They have claims an income and assets in prior to the equity shareholders.
(d) They do not share in the residual earnings.

### *Features*

Preference shares has several features. They are presented as follows:

(a) Preference share claim is honoured before that of equity share.
(b) Preference shares require a fixed rate of dividend.
(c) Preference shareholders do not have any voting rights.

### *Advantages of Preference Shares*

Preference shares has a number of advantages to the company. They are:

1. Preference shares require a fixed rate of dividend. Non-payment of dividends does not for the company into insolvency.
2. Their dividend can be postponed according to the company's convenience.
3. Preference shareholders do not participate in excess of profits as done by the equity shareholders.
4. There are no voting rights to the preference shareholders, thus the control of equity shareholders is preserved.

### *Disadvantages*

The following are the disadvantages of Preference Shares:

1. Preference dividend is not tax deductible, it is costlier than the debentures.

2. Their dividend have to be paid even in cumulative nature. It can adversely affect the image of a company.

However, the preference shares are less burden to a company. Their dividend rate is less than that of the equity. A company can redeem it when the company does not require the capital. Preference share is a senior security as compared to the equity. It has two preferences that the company must first pay

(a) The dividend before paying ordinary dividend.
(b) It also has a prior claim on the company's assets in the event of liquidation.

Preference share is called as fixed income security because it provides a constant income to the investors. The payment of dividend is not a legal obligation. Preference shares can be classified into cumulative and non-cumulative. Cumulative preference share means any unpaid preference dividend can be paid before equity dividends are paid for a particular period of time. Preference shareholders generally do not have power to force the company to pay dividends. Non-cumulative preference shares means their unpaid dividends will not be carried forward.

Preference shares may also further classified as **redeemable and irredeemable**. Irredeemable preference shares do not have a maturity date. Redeemable preference shares are redeemed after its maturity time.

## (C) Debentures

A debenture is an acknowledgement of a debt. Debenture holders are paid interests. A fixed rate of interest will be paid irrespective of profit or loss. Debenture holders are only the creditors. They have no voice in the management of the company.

### *Definition of Debentures*

According to Thomas Evelym, Debentures can be defined as "A Debenture is a document under the Company's seal which provides for the payment of a principal sum and interest thereon at regular interval, which is usually received by a fixed or floating charge as the company's property or undertaking and which acknowledges a loan to the company".

The Indian Companies Act, 1956 defines the term, "Debenture, stock, bonds and any other securities of a company whether constituting a charge of the assets of the company or not".

### *Types of Debentures*

Debentures may be classified as follows:

(1) Naked or Mortgage debentures.
(2) Redeemable or Irredeemable debentures.
(3) First and Second debentures.
(4) Bearer or Registered debentures.
(5) Convertible debentures and Non-convertible debentures.

#### *(1) Naked/Mortgage Debentures*

Naked debentures means, they do not carry any security in respect of repayment of interest or the principal. Mortgage debentures are secured by a charge on the assets or properties of the company.

#### *(2) Redeemable/Irredeemable Debentures*

Redeemable debenture means, the payment of the principal amount on the expiry of a certain period. They can be reissued even after they have been redeemed and **irredeemable debentures** are retained in the company as a part of the capital structure of the company. They are also known as perpetual debentures. They are not redeemed during the lifetime of the company.

#### *(3) First and Second Debentures*

First debentures are paid first before any payment is made to any other type of debentures. Second debentures are paid after making the payment of the first debentures.

#### *(4) Bearer/Registered Debentures*

Bearer debentures are just like bearer cheques or government currency notes. They are treated as negotiable instruments. They are transferable by mere delivery. Registered debentures are issued specifically on the name of a particular person, who is registered by the company as a holder and are transferable in the same way as shares. The interest and principal amount will be paid to the persons, those who are registered as debenture holders in the company.

*(5) Convertible and Non-convertible Debentures*

Convertible debentures means the debentures are converted into equity shares or preference with the consent of holders. These are converted at a stated rate of exchange, after a certain period. Non-convertible debentures are not convertible into equity or preference shares. Convertible debentures are very popular in India.

**(D) Bonds**

Bonds are the fixed income securities as an investment vehicle. Bonds pay a fixed interest and one can expect that their price would not be subjected to wide fluctuations. Bonds are the best sources of investment tool for the investors, those who do not wish to buy and hold. In USA the bonds are more popular and dominates the market. In USA the bonds differ from debentures. The bonds can be either secured or unsecured but the debentures are only unsecured ones. Bond holders assume risk but comparatively lower than the equity holders in the same organisation. Bonds are mostly related to the Government sector. The Governments have no choice but to borrow the funds from the market in the form of bonds to meet their expenses from the current revenue. Bonds are the cheapest sources of financing. The interest on bonds is deductible for the corporate income on tax purpose. Bonds will enhance the EPS of a company concern. The issuing concern can attract the funds from the individual investors and especially from those investing institutions which are not permitted to buy equity shares. Issue of Bonds involve three parties, **i.e. (a) issuing concern, (b) bond holders and (c) the trustee**. The first party is the debtor corporation which borrows the money, assured to pay the interest along with the principal amount. The bond holders are the second party. They lend the money for interest. The trustee is the third party with whom the bond contract is made. The trustees would give assurance on behalf of the company to repay the principal amount of bond.

***Maturity Basis***

Bonds are usually grouped by their maturity classes. The bonds are classified as follows:

(1) Short-term bonds.
(2) Medium-term bonds.
(3) Long-term bonds.

Generally short-term bonds are mature within 5 years. They may be secured or unsecured. Medium-term bonds mature ranges from **5 to 10 years**. It is backed by a fixed asset. Long-term bonds may be issued for more than **20 years**.

***Interest Payment Basis***

The bonds are further classified on the basis of interest payment. Usually the interest is paid semi-annually or annually. According to another classification bonds are of types:

**(1) Bearer bonds.**
**(2) Registered bonds.**

**Bearer bonds** are issued with a number of coupons. A coupon is the agreement of the corporation to pay a stipulated amount of money as the interest which will be due upon the bond at specified date. On the other hand, Registered debentures are issued with sequence numbers recording the name of bond holders in their ledger. The interest amount will be paid to the bond holder. **Registered bond** can be transferred only after the registration of the name of the new owner along with the trustee.

The composition of public issues in terms of equity at par, premium, and debentures is presented in for the period 1991–2001 (upto June 2001) in Table 1. During the period, the number to the issues were high in 1995–96, but in terms of amount the 1996–97 was found an overall analysis. The data reveals that debt is dominated by the average of 50 per cent, throughout the period. The data further reveals that the premium issues occupies next position.

**Table 1: Mobilisation of Resources through Public Issues**

*(Rs. in crores)*

| *Year* | *Instrument* | *No. of Issues* | *Total Public Issues* | *Percentage (%)* |
|---|---|---|---|---|
| 1991–92 | (a) equity at par | 143 | 506.05 | 29.60 |
| | (b) equity at premium | 16 | 46.72 | 2.70 |
| | (c) debentures and others | 52 | 1158.59 | 67.70 |
| | | 210 | 1711.36 | 100.00 |
| 1992–93 | (a) equity at par | 379 | 1378.32 | 22.70 |
| | (b) equity at premium | 108 | 1384.22 | 22.80 |
| | (c) debentures and others | 40 | 3296.09 | 55.50 |
| | | 527 | 6058.63 | 100.00 |
| 1993–94 | (a) equity at par | 514 | 2154.13 | 17.20 |
| | (b) equity at premium | 199 | 4033.56 | 32.20 |
| | (c) debentures | 57 | 6356.35 | 50.60 |
| | | 770 | 12544.04 | 100.00 |
| 1994–95 | (a) equity at par | 851 | 2830.00 | 21.25 |
| | (b) equity at premium | 453 | 6115.79 | 45.94 |
| | (c) debentures | 60 | 4365.81 | 32.81 |
| | | 1364 | 13311.60 | 100.00 |
| 1995–96 | (a) equity at par | 1104 | 3075.34 | 28.00 |
| | (b) equity at premium | 302 | 4679.00 | 42.60 |
| | (c) debentures | 22 | 3227.37 | 29.40 |
| | | 1428 | 10981.71 | 100.00 |
| 1996–97 | (a) equity at par | 679 | 4654.00 | 44.64 |
| | (b) equity at premium | 126 | 1462.00 | 14.02 |
| | (c) debentures and others | 37 | 4308.00 | 41.32 |
| | | 842 | 10424.00 | 100.00 |
| 1997–98 | (a) equity at par | 60 | 508.90 | 16.21 |
| | (b) equity at premium | 29 | 653.50 | 20.82 |
| | (c) debentures and others | 13 | 1975.90 | 62.94 |
| | | 102 | 3138.30 | 100.00 |
| 1998–99 | (a) equity shares | 14 | 1237.00 | 24.67 |
| | (b) equity at premium | 19 | 1326.00 | 26.45 |
| | (c) debentures and others | 15 | 2450.00 | 48.88 |
| | | 48 | 5013.00 | 100.00 |
| 1999–2000 | (a) equity at par | 21 | 583.00 | 11.31 |
| | (b) equity at premium | 48 | 2169.00 | 42.09 |
| | (c) debentures and others | 10 | 2401.00 | 46.59 |
| | | 79 | 5153.00 | 100.00 |

*(Contd.)*

***Table 1** (Contd.)*

| *Year* | *Instrument* | *No. of Issues* | *Total Public Issues* | *Percentage (%)* |
|---|---|---|---|---|
| 2000–2001 | (a) equity at par | 77 | 1399.00 | 28.26 |
| | (b) equity at premium | 57 | 1267.00 | 25.60 |
| | (c) debentures and others | 11 | 2283.00 | 46.13- |
| | | 145 | 4949.00 | 100.00 |
| 2001–2002 | (a) equity at par | 1 | 5.00 | 1.21 |
| | (b) equity at premium | 1 | 5.00 | 1.21 |
| | (c) debentures and others | 1 | 400.00 | 97.56 |
| | | 3 | 410.00 | 100.00 |

*Sources*: 1. Prime Annual Reports, 1991–95.
2. *RBI Bulletin*, Oct. 2001, p. 51017, March 99, p. 5257.

## *New Financial Instruments in the Capital Market*

The Indian capital market is very wide and large with more than 8000 companies listed, 2000 of whose scrips are actively traded. The number of investors in India are estimated about more than 25 million. The market capitalisation of equity and debt is estimated about **Rs. 5,00,000 crores** and **Rs. 10,00,000 crores** respectively. With the evolution of the capital market, new financial instruments are being introduced to suit the requirements of the companies, keeping in view, the yield expected by the investors price and credit risk, liquidity quantum of funds etc. The merchant bankers and fund managers designed the new instruments to cater the needs of the corporate sector. Some of the new financial instruments introduced in recent years are as below:

(1) Zero coupon bonds.
(2) Warrants.
(3) Secured premium notes.
(3) Stock investment instrument.
(4) Deep discount bonds.
(5) Option bonds.

### *(1) Zero Coupon Bonds*

Zero coupon bonds are debt instruments with a zero rate of interest. It has no fixed coupon rate. These bonds are introduced in the U.S. market.

carry any interest for a fixed period. The investor is not entitled to any interest on this bond. The conversion price is suitably adjusted with the consideration of the interest rate. The main advantage to the company is that there is no burden of interest on the part of the company during the gestation period of the project. These bonds are also useful to the investors in two aspects:

(a) The interest on these bonds are not subject to tax.
(b) These bonds are more useful when the interest rate declines.

*(2) Warrants*

A share warrant is an option to the investor to buy a specified number of equity shares within a specified period of time. The warrant holder has to surrender the warrant and pay some cash known as the "exercise price" on the warrant to purchase the shares. An exercise of the option, the warrant holder becomes a shareholder. Warrant is a popular means of raising the finance in developed countries. In India warrants are commonly used as a sweetener with non-convertible debentures. Gradually the trends are changing and detachable warrants are issued with convertible debentures and equity shares too. The pricing of the warrant is an important factor. However, warrant can be issued only by the existing dividend paying companies. Warrant is yet to gain popularity in India, owing to the complex nature of the instrument. Warrants are more useful to the companies, because they reduce the dependence on the financial institutions and mutual funds. It is advisable to raise additional capital to the corporate sector. This instrument is also useful to the investors, because the NCD with warrant can expect steady rate of return and capital appreciation.

*(3) Secured Premium Notes*

This type of financial instruments are issued by the Companies for the raising debt. Secured premium notes can be converted into equity after 3 to 5 years. No coupon rate of interest is fixed on these instruments. The SPNs are issued at a nominal value and do not carry any interest. They are reduced by the repayment in several instalments at a premium over the face value. The premium amount is distributed equally over the period of maturity of the instalment. The SPNs may carry a detachable warrants, which will give the holder a right to claim. They will be allotted for cash at a certain price. This right can be exercised by the holder after a certain period from the date of allotment of the secured premium notes. It is suitable for the companies with good track record and have highly capable intensive projects. They are traded on the stock exchanges and have an easy liquidity. The investor can dispose the notes on allotment at a premium when the shares of the company command a high premium in the market without even exercising the warrant option. The investor can also dispose the right from itself as a premium in a right issue of the SPNs.

### *(4) Stock Investment Instrument*

Stock investment is introduced recently in the market. It is a new financial instrument and used by the investors while applying for shares in the primary market. The stock invest is an instrument just like postal orders. The perspecting investors should deposit some amount with a bank by opening a stock invest account. According to needs and conveniences of the investor, the stock invest instruments will be issued by the Bank but the amount underlies with banker till the allotment is made and will carry interest. The share issuing company will be able to encash the instrument only when the shares are allotted to the investor. This will reduce the hardship suffered by the investors, through the loss of interest especially in the case of non-allotment of shares. This can be returned to the investors and it avoids the delay in refunds. This scheme has already been started by many public sector and private banks and it is popular in market.

### *(5) Deep Discount Bonds*

It is a new financial instrument. These bonds are sold to the investors at discount, while issuing them. The discount rate depends upon the number of years of maturity. The main advantage to the issuing company is that, there is no interest payment burden during the gestation period of the project. It is also useful to the investor, because the initial investment amount is very low as compared to other instruments. The bonds are advantageous to the investors when the long-term interest rates are expected to fall.

### *(6) Option Bonds*

Option bonds means, these bonds will be converted into equity or preference shares at the option of the investor as per the conditions stated in the prospectus. Option bonds, may cumulative or non-cumulative. In case of cumulative bonds the interest is accumulated and is payable at maturity, while in the case of non-cumulative bonds, it is payable at periodic intervals. These type of bonds are issued by the IDBI and are well received by the investors.

**Recommendations of the Pherwani Study Group on New Financial Instruments**

The Government of India constituted a study group on 27th March, 1991. Shri M.J. Pherwani was appointed as Chairman to formulate the guidelines for the issue of new financial instruments. The study group had recommended the following instruments. Some of the instruments have already been issued in the market.

1. Non-voting shares.
2. Detachable equity coupons/warrants.
3. Participating preference shares.
4. Participating debentures.
5. Zero coupon convertible bonds.
6. Debt for equity swap.
7. Convertible debentures redeemable at premium.
8. Mortgage backed securities.
9. Third party convertible debentures.
10. Convertible debentures with options.

**Recent Developments in the Market**

In the last decade since the liberalisation, Indian Industry has been exposed to the international competition. It was ill-equipped to deal with this opening up and had protested the absence of a level playing field. The Government has been attempting to make the economic regulatory environment conducive to growth.[2]

The Government has announced various amendments to the Companies Act of 1956 through the Companies Act of 2000, covering corporate governance, issuance of shares with differential rights, postal ballot.

**Shares with Differential Voting Rights**

With the simplification of take over code, the threat of lossing control over the company has loomed large over the Indian promoters, as their shareholding was historically lower. The introduction of the depository system has increased the potential threat. The promoters often feel the need to raise fresh funds without diiuting their control. Therefore, there is a demand for allowing the companies to issue the equity shares without the voting rights but carrying other benefits such as dividend (additional).

**Concept of Differential Voting Shares**

Shares with differential rights means the equity shares which have differential rights in respect to dividend, voting or otherwise. Section 86 of the Act has been amended to allow the public companies to issue shares with differential voting rights. Consequently, Section 88 of the act, which prohibited the issuance of shares with disproportionate voting rights has been omitted. The Central Gcvernment has also ratified the relevant rules in March 2001. The substantive conditions that are prescribed the 3 years profitability track record. Shares with preferential voting rights can be issued upto 25 per cent of the total share capital issued (effectively 1/3 of the share capital before such issue) ban on version of the plain vanilla equity capital into the equity shares with differential rights and *vice versa*, and no default in meeting the investor's grievances. The other conditions include the approval of shareholders by the postal ballot, authorisation by the articles of association, non-conviction of any offence under the SEBI, the FEMA and the Securities Contract Act, no default in fulfilling the annual accounts and returns, no default in the repayment of deposits, debentures and dividend repayment among others.

**Share Capital Base**

The guidelines provide that differential shares can be issued to the extent of 25 per cent of the total share capital. Thus, preference, share capital would be considered for determining the quantum.

**New Companies**

The 3 years profitability criteria would prove to be a barrier for the new public companies, as they would not be in a possible to issue shares with differential rights. These companies in their incubation period would perhaps feel the need to issue shares.

## Issuance of Non-Voting Shares

Section 86 of the Act empowers a Company to issue the shares with differential voting rights as to dividend, voting or otherwise. However, Section 87(1)(a) of the Act provides that every member should have a right to vote. The issue therefore is whether a Company can issue non-voting shares. The Companies (Amendment) Bill of 1996 specifically provided for the issuance of non-voting shares, which is conspicuously absent from the amended provisions.

However, in the rules notified for the postal ballot, the scrutiniser is required to maintain the details of the shares, irrespective of whether they have voting, differential voting or non-voting rights. Would this indicate that law contemplates the issuance of non-voting shares? It seems the issue is to be a delicated aspect.

Section 87(1)(b) of the Act states that in case of a poll, the voting rights of a shareholder would be in proportion to the paid-up capital of the company. Furthermore, Section 93 of the Act directs that dividend to shareholders should be in proportion to his share of paid up capital.

Since consequential amendments to these sections are not carried out, inherent differences *vis-à-vis* Section 86 of the Act exists. Hence, amendments are required.

## Private Limited Companies

Section 90(2) of the Act specifically exempts the Private Limited Companies from the applicability of Sections 85 to 89 of the Act. Private Companies still have unfettered leeway to exercise wide discretion in the issuance of shares, except may be, for dividend which is linked to paid up capital as per Section 93.

## Practical Application

A Company can issue different series of equity shares, carrying different rights. **For example:** a series of equity shares carries one vote per share and another series of equity shares carries five votes per share, both series have the same face value. For example, the promoter of company holds 10 per cent of the share capital of Rs.100 crores. The Company issues to the promoter, shares with higher voting rights, that is, four votes per share upto the maximum allowable limit, that is, 25 per cent of the total share capital, thereby increasing the share capital to Rs.133

crores. Now on the basis of a number of shares, the promoters hold 4.3 crore shares in a total of 13.3 crore shares which is about 32 per cent while their voting rights would have increased to 61 per cent.

Also, issue of shares carrying differential rights would help in satisfying the varying needs of a distinct set of investors. If a select group of investors place more importance on the voting rights they may invest in shares which have higher voting rights compared to the amount invested. On the other hand, small investors who generally do not attend the general meetings may find it more rewarding to have shares with a higher rate of dividend.

Shares with differential voting rights are also particularly useful to the technocrats who have low seed capital but have the high value intangible assets. It would also feasible to carry out financially innovative arrangements in joint ventures to suit the needs of the joint ventures or partners. These provisions can also provide a boost to the disinvestment process as the Government can dilute the control in the PSUs can also maintain a golden share to be used in the exceptional circumstances only. For example, disproportionate rights without the need for retaining a majority stake.

**Safeguards**

However, some promoters could misuse the provisions for increasing their stake in companies, instead of adopting creeping acquisition/open offer/buy back routes, especially since pricing guidelines have not been prescribed for the issuance of shares with differential rights.

Thus, in a listed company, equity shares carrying 4 votes per share could be issued. Today at the same SEBI-linked price (higher of the weekly average of the prices, quoted as the stock exchanges over the past 6 months or 2 weeks) for the equity shares carrying one vote per share.

This will cost the small shareholders dearly. The mergers and acquisition process would also hit the target companies and can issue the shares with differential voting rights, thereby making acquisitions all the more difficult. Therefore, appropriate precautionary regulations for the pricing etc., would have to be built in.

Companies, thus, now have wide flexibility in structuring equity instruments to suit their requirements and the demands of specific groups of investors/companies. The market for such instruments would also become wider as some investors may have specific requirements and not prefer general uniform instruments.

Till now, no major company has announced its intention of issuing such shares. The need is to popularise this concept and utilise it as a tool.

## REFERENCES

1. I.M. Pandey, *Fundamentals of Financial Management*, p. 1010, Vikas Publishing House, 8th edition.
2. *The Economic Times*, Dt. 17.11.2001, p. 7.

# 5

# FINANCIAL SERVICES

## Introduction

Financial services are an important component of the financial system. Financial services fulfil the needs of financial institutions, financial markets and financial instruments. Financial services are the part of Indian financial system. The smooth functioning of a financial system will depend upon the range of financial services extended by the providers. Financial services contribute a lot to the efforts of speeding up the process of economic growth and development. The financial services industry is growing at a very fast rate. The growth rate in **GDP** may help to increase the dominant share of the **financial services** which is associated with the ascendancy of the primary and secondary sectors. Financial services in India has witnessed remarkable changes in the recent past after the implementation of **"Liberalisation, privatisation and globalisation"**. Policies of the Government, the rapid development in information and communication technology in the financial services sector created radical changes in respect of firms, generation of innovative financial products, and financial markets. In India, the credit cult is developing very fast. The use of sophisticated and advanced technology could be reckoned as another specific feature of the global financial services industry. The global financial industry has now come out with a new instrument known as **"stored value card"**.

The following topics will be discussed in depth in this Book.

(A) Merchant Banking.
(B) Mutual Funds.
(C) Venture Capital.
(D) Credit Rating.
(E) Lease Financing.

(F) Underwriters.
(G) Registrars.
(H) Securities and Exchange Board of India.
(I) NSE, OTC, BSE.
(J) Depository System.

## Merchant Banking

### *Introduction*

Funds are tapped from the capital market to finance various **mega** industrial projects. In attracting public savings, merchant bankers play a vital role as specialised agencies. The resources raising function remains to be the primary business of a merchant banker. The primary market hold the key to rapid capital formation, growth in industrial production and exports. There has to be accountability to the end use of funds raised from the market. The trends in the NIM in India suggest, that merchant bankers have been playing a very significant role in the corporate sector's drive for mobilising funds from the public. The increase in the number of issues and amount raised the number of merchant bankers. Therefore, the field become a highly competitive market where it requires a specialised skill in handling the situation. The financial assets sold to the public should represent the genuine claims on future cash flows and viable assets. The merchant bankers have a social responsibility to in building an industrial structure in India.

### *Origin of Merchant Banking*

In the **19th Century**, a British merchant used to send an agent out to little known parts of the world. The agent took with him or had shipped with him the manufactured goods produced in the home country which he would like to sell and at the same time he would buy the products of that country and ship them home. For this trade, money had to be remitted from one country to another and the bill of exchange, an instrument which was in usage throughout the **Europe** since a long time, came to be used more and more. The bill of exchange in **London** became the means of financing the trade practically in the whole world. The well established merchant agreed to do for commission and gradually the practice of accepting the bills to finance the trade of others took the shape of accepting the bills to finance their own trade, by degrees. The merchant became a banker as acceptance credits or the accepting house. These firms in **London** are styled as **Merchant Banks**. The oldest merchant bank in **London** was **Barring Brothers**. It was very prominent in **Europe** in the 19th century. Industrial revolution had made **England** into a powerful trading nation. Rich merchant houses had made their fortunes in colonial trade diversified into banking. They involved in the acceptance of commercial bills pertaining to domestic as well as international trade. They became as **"Acceptance house, discount house and issue houses"**. A merchant banker was primarily a merchant than a banker. The merchant banker was entrusted with funds by his customers. Merchant banks in **Britain** involved in **(a) issue capital, (b) foreign loan business, (c) finance foreign trade, (d) manage individual funds and undertake, (e) foreign security business etc**. They also involved in finance sovereign governments in the form of long-term loans.

Several merchant banks were set up in **the U.S.A.** to arrange capital and enterprise to promote railways, industrial projects and trade and commerce. The investment bankers had replaced brokers and promoters in issue of securities. They actively involved in launching and organising industrial units, mergers and acquisition, transformation of private companies into public owned companies. The growth of investment bankers were facilitated by the enactment of **Federal Act of 1914** on the emergence of **U.S. dollar** as leading global currency and expansion of US banking system. The Investment bankers were involved in buying and selling of corporate bonds, securities on commission basis, dealt in municipal, state and federal securities, trading and investing in securities, originating and distributing new issues etc. After the great crash of **1929** and depression, their business considerably contracted and faced heavy financial losses. Then the federal government had enacted several laws to reform the Wallstreet practices to protect the interests of investors. The increased regulation and control made the **U.S.** banks to undertake the merchant bank functions in global capital markets. They were responsible for the development of the global capital market. Investment bankers fully involved in finding the investors for **"Initial Public Offering (IPO)"** of securities sold in the New Issue market. They brought the buyers and sellers together. They created market and made arrangements for the public issue. They also helped as a finder for the private placement of securities.

### *Definition of Merchant Banking*

Merchant Banking services are mainly related to issue house activities. *Webster dictionary* defines merchant bankers as "a bank that specialises in banker's acceptances and underwriting or syndicating equity or bond issues".[1]

According to **Rosenberg, M.J.**[2] Merchant banking means "an organisation that underwrites securities for corporations, advises such clients on mergers and is involved in the ownership of commercial ventures". The meaning of the merchant bank refers to an organisation that underwrites securities and advises such clients on issues like corporate managers in the ownership of commercial ventures. The Securities and Exchange Board of India (Merchant bankers) Rules of 1992 defined a merchant banker[3], "as any person who is engaged in the business of issue management either by making arrangements regarding selling, buying or subscribing to securities as manager, consultant, adviser or rendering corporate advisory service in relation to such issue management".

According to **Cox, D.** merchant banking is defined as, "merchant banks are the financial institutions providing specialist services which generally include the acceptance of bills of exchange, corporate finance, portfolio management and other banking services".[4]

The notification of the Ministry of Finance defines a merchant banker as, **"any person who is engaged in the business of issue management either by making arrangements regarding selling, buying or subscribing to securities as manager, consultant, adviser or rendering corporate advisory service in relation to such issue management".**[5]

Merchant banks undertake the task of new issue management, project counselling, preparation of feasibility reports, selection of underwriters/brokers and bankers to issue. They are responsible for clearing off all legal formalities from the **SEBI** for making the public issue. Merchant bankers have been handling growing number of public and rights issues. The profession of merchant banking is concerned with catering the needs of trade and industry by playing a role of intermediary, consultant, liason officer and a banker. There is a strong need for the merchant banking agencies because of a major chunk of public savings lying untapped. However, they have been playing a useful role in procuring the support of capital market for the corporate sector for financing their operations. Merchant bankers are working for the long-term end of the markets that create a niche for a specialised banker.

***Main Objects of Merchant Banking Company***

Merchant bankers render their specialised assistance in achieving the main objectives which are presented below:

1. To carry on the business of merchant banking, assist in the capital formation, manage advice, underwrite, provide standby assistance, securities and all kinds of investments issued, to be issued or guaranteed by any company, corporation, society, firm, trust, person, government, municipality, civil body, public authority established in India.
2. The main object of merchant banker is to create secondary market for bills and discount or re-discount bills and acts as an acceptance house.
3. Merchant bankers involved in assistance and promotion of economic endeavour, identification of projects, promoters, preparation of project reports, project feasibility studies, market research, pre-investment studies and investigation of industries at micro and macro level.
4. Merchant banker's another objective is to set up and provide services for the venture capital technology funds.
5. They also provide services to the finance housing schemes for the construction of houses and buying of land.
6. They render the services like foreign exchange dealer, money exchange, authorised dealer and to buy and sell foreign exchange in all lawful ways in compliance with the relevant laws of India.
7. They are involved in acquiring and holding one or more membership in stock exchange/national stock exchange, trade associations, commodity exchanges, clearing houses or associations or otherwise in India or any part of the world.
8. They will help to promote or procure incorporation, formation or setting up of concerns and undertakings whether as a company, body corporate, partnership or any other association or persons for engaging in any other association or persons

for engaging in any industrial, commercial or business activities.

9. Their objective is to perform financial services including factoring and syndication of both the loans short-term and long-term with the financial institutions, banks and others to manage mutual funds and to provide financial software programmes.
10. The objective of the merchant banking is to carry on the business of financing industrial enterprises.
11. They will invest in buying and selling of transfers, hypothecate and deal with dispose of shares, stocks, debentures, securities and properties of any other company.

***Obligations and Responsibilities***

Merchant bankers have the following obligations and responsibilities:

1. Merchant banker should maintain proper books of accounts, records and submit half yearly/annual financial statements to the SEBI within stipulated period of time.
2. No merchant banker should associate with another merchant banker who is not registered in the SEBI.
3. Merchant bankers should not enter into any transactions on the basis of unpublished information available to them in the course of their professional assignment.
4. Every merchant banker must submit himself to the inspection by SEBI when required for and submit all the records.
5. Every merchant banker must disclose information to the SEBI when it requires any information from them.
6. All merchant bankers must abide by the code of conduct prescribed for them.
7. Every merchant banker who acts as lead manager must enter into an agreement with the issuer setting out mutual rights, liabilities, obligations, relating to such issues with particular reference to disclosures allotment, refund etc.

***Code of Conduct***

According to the 13 Regulation of the SEBI of 1992 (Merchant bankers), every merchant banker should comply with following codes of conduct. They are:

(a) The merchant banker must observe high standards of integrity and fairness in all his dealings.
(b) He shall render at all times high standard of services, exercise due diligence, exercise independent professional judgement.
(c) If necessary, he must disclose to his clients the possible sources of conflict of duties and interests.
(d) The merchant banker should indulge in unfair practice or unfair competition with other merchant bankers.
(e) He should not make any exaggerated statement about his capacity or achievement.
(f) He should always endeavour to give the best possible advise and prompt efficient and cost effective service.
(g) He should maintain the secrecy of all the confidential information received during the course of service to his client.
(h) He should not engage in the creation of a false market or price rigging or manipulation.

**Merchant Banking in India**

After the termination of the managing agency system in India, a strong need of legal and financial services to the corporate sector which required an alternative agency. On such situation the emergence of merchant banking has aroused. Merchant Banking System in India was introduced by Grindlays Bank in 1967. It was the first bank which received licence from the RBI. It started with the management of a capital issues, rendering the services according to the needs of emerging new class entrepreneurs for diverse financial services ranging from production to marketing research. It also provided the services to large and medium range companies. The Citi Bank set up its merchant banking wing in 1970. Later on the Banking Commission, 1972 felt the need for setting up of merchant banking institutions to offer services like syndication or financing, promotion of projects, investment management advisory services to the corporate sector. The SBI became the First Commercial Bank in India to launch its merchant banking division in 1972. Consequent to the recommendations of Banking Commission in 1972 Indian banks were allowed to enter into this segment. Later other Commercial Banks and Financial Institutions like Indian Bank, Punjab National Bank, Indian Overseas Bank, Bank of Baroda, Syndicate Bank, Chartered Bank, LIC, GIC, UTI etc., also started merchant banking divisions. Some brokerage houses were diversified into this area like J.M. Financial and Investment Consultancy Services Pvt. Ltd., DSP Financial Consultancy Ltd., Bajaj Capital Investment Centre Pvt. Ltd., Tata Consultancy Services Ltd. Among the Development Banks ICICI started merchant banking activities in 1973 followed by IFCI in 1986 and IDBI in 1991.

***Activities/Services Rendered by Merchant Banks***

Merchant Banks are rendering diverse services and functions as organising and extending of finance for the investment in projects, acceptance house, issue of foreign currency bonds, financing of capital goods, hydropower, financing of hire purchase, purchase transactions, equipment leasing, mergers and acquisitions, valuation of assets, promotion of investment trusts. All these services are not offered by the bankers, but different bankers are specialised in different services. The Merchant Bank is a multiple service oriented agency. Merchant banking is a creative activity. In India, the Merchant Banks are engaged in the following activities:

(a) Corporate finance services (management of public issues, credit syndication).
(b) Advisory services (project counselling, financing, capital restructuring).
(c) Services to NRIs (evaluation of investment portfolio, promotion of industries).
(d) Leasing (equipment, machinary etc.).

Merchant banking activities are regulated in India by—

(1) guidelines of the SEBI,
(2) guidelines of the Ministry of Finance,
(3) Companies Act of 1956,
(4) Securities Contracts (Regulation) Act of 1956, and
(5) listing guidelines of the stock exchanges.

*(1) Guidelines of SEBI*

After the abolition of the CCI, the place was occupied by a legal organ called as **"Securities and Exchange Board of India"**. The issue of capital and pricing of issues by companies has become free of prior approval. The SEBI has issued guidelines for the issue of capital by the companies. The guidelines broadly covers the requirement of the first issue by a new or the first issue of a new company set up by the existing company, the first issue by the existing private companies and public issues by the existing listed companies. The SEBI is the most powerful organisation to control and lead both the primary market and secondary market. According to the SEBI guidelines, if any company approaches the public by issuing share capital through public issues must be kept open for three working days and it should be mentioned in the prospectus. In the case of rights issue, the subscription time should not be kept more than 60 days. The gap between rights and public issue should not exceed 30 days. The issued capital must be fully paid up within 12 months of the date of issue. The minimum amount of subscription by the investors in the public issue either at par or premium has been fixed at Rs. 5,000. The amount of issue should not exceed the amount specified in the prospectus. Over subscription amount retention by the Company is not permitted under any circumstances.

The SEBI has announced the new guidelines for the disclosures by the Companies leading to the investor protection. They are presented below:

(a) If any Company's other income exceeds 10 per cent of the total income, the details should be disclosed.

(b) The Company should disclose any adverse situation which affects the operations of the Company and occurs within one year prior to the date of filing of the offer document with the Registrar of Companies or Stock Exchange.

(c) The Company should also disclose the information regarding the capacity utilisation of the plant for the last 3 years.

(d) The Promoters of the Company must maintain their holding at least at 20 per cent of the expanded capital.

(e) The minimum application money payable should not be less than 25 per cent of the issue price.

(f) The Company should disclose the time normally taken for the disposal of various types of investor's grievances.

(g) The Company can make firm allotments in public issues as follows:
   (1) Indian mutual funds (20%),
   (2) FIIs (24%),
   (3) Regular employees of the company (10%),
   (4) Financial institution (20%).

(h) The Company should disclose the safety net scheme or buy back arrangements of the shares proposed in public issue. This scheme is applicable to a limited number of 500 shares per allottee and the offer should be valid for a period of at least 6 months from the date of despatch of securities.

(i) According to the guidelines, in case of the public issues, at least 30 mandatory collection centres should be established.

(j) According to the SEBI guidelines regarding rights issue, the Company should give advertisements in not less than two news-papers about the dispatch of letters of offer. No preferential allotment may be made along with any rights issue.

(k) The Company should also disclose about the fee agreed between the lead managers and the Company in the memorandum of understanding.

The guidelines will apply to all the issues to be made after the promulgation of the ordinance by which capital issues act has been repealed. Further, the SEBI issued guidelines for the **"disclosure and investor protection"** as presented below (issued by SEBI wide GL/IP No. 1/SEBI/PMD 92–93, dated 11.6.92).

1. **First issue of new companies.**
2. **First issue by existing private/closely held companies.**
3. **Public issue by existing listed companies.**
4. **Underwriting.**
5. **Issue of PCD/FCD/NCD.**
6. **Employee stock option scheme.**
7. **Promoter's contribution and lock in period.**
8. **Bonus shares.**
9. **Guidelines for the protection of the interest of debenture holders.**
10. **General.**

### *1. First Issue of New Companies*

According to the guidelines, a New Company will be defined as, "one which has not completed **12 months** of commercial operations and its audited operative results are not available and where it is set up by the entrepreneurs without a track record". They will be permitted to issue capital to public only at **par**. If a New Company is being set up by the Existing Companies with a **5-year** track record of consistent profitability, it will be free to price its issue provided the participation of the promoting companies would be not less than **50 per cent** of the equity of the New Company and the issue price is made applicable to all the investors, uniformly, provided that the prospectus or offer documents shall contain justification for the issue price.

A draft prospectus that contains the disclosures will be vetted by SEBI before a public issue is made. No private placement of the promoters share should be made by the solicitation of share contribution from unrelated investors through any kind of market intermediaries. The shares of the above companies can be listed on either the **OTC** or any other stock exchanges.

### *2. First Issue by Existing Private/Closely Held Companies*

According to the guidelines the first issue by the Existing Private Companies with a **3-year** track record of consistent profitability shall be permitted to **freely price** the issue and list their securities on the stock exchanges. The pricing would be determined by the issuer and the lead managers to the issue and would be on justification for the issue price.

### *3. Public Issue by Existing Listed Companies*

The SEBI permitted these companies to raise fresh capital by freely pricing their further issues. The issue price will be determined by the issuer in consultation with the lead managers. The draft prospectus will be vetted by SEBI to ensure adequacy of disclosures. The prospectus shall contain the net asset value of the company and a justification for the price of the issue. It should also disclose high and low of the shares for the last **2 years**.

### *4. Underwriting*

According to the SEBI guidelines underwriting is mandatory for the full issue and minimum requirement of **90 per cent** subscription is also mandatory for each issue of capital to public. The number of underwriters would be decided by the issuing company. If the Company does not receive **90 per cent** of issued amount from public subscription plus accepted development from underwriters within **120 days** from the date of opening of the issue, then the company should refund the amount of subscription. The Lead Managers must satisfy themselves about the networth of the underwriters and the outstanding commitments should disclose the same to the **SEBI**. The underwriting agreements may be filed with the stock exchanges.

### *5. FCD/PCD/NCD*

The SEBI issued guidelines on the convertible and the non-convertible debentures as follows:

(a) In case of issuing of Fully Convertible Debentures, the debentures may be converted after **36 months** and the conversion is made optional with put and call option. The crediting should be made if conversion period is **after 18 months**. In the prospectus, the premium, time of conversion, stages required shall be indicated. The interest rate for the debentures will be freely determined by the Issuing Company.

(b) In case of issue of debentures with maturity of **16 months** or less are exempted from the requirement of appointment of the debenture trustee. The trust deed should be executed within **6 months** of the closure of the issue. The **SEBI** may prescribe additional disclosure requirement from time to time.

### *6. Employee Stock Option Scheme*

Employee stock option is a voluntary scheme to motivate the employees to have a higher participation in the Company. A suitable percentage of reservation can be made by the Issue Company for its employees. However, the reservation amount should not exceed 5 per cent of the issue. Equal distribution of shares among the employees will contribute to the smooth working of the scheme. The Company may like to have non-transferability of shares at its discretion in the new issues. The allotted shares to employees cannot be transferable for a period of 3 years.

### *7. Promoter's Contribution and Lock in Period*

The promoters, directors, his friends, relatives and associates can contribute upto 25 per cent of the total issue of the equity capital and upto Rs.100 crores and 20 per cent for the issue above Rs.100 crores. In the case of fully convertible debentures, 1/3rd of the issue amount should be contributed by promoters, directors, friends, relatives and associates in the form of equity before the issue is made. In the case of PCDs, 1/3rd of the convertible portion should be brought in as the contribution of promoter before the issue is made. The minimum subscription by each of the friends/relatives and associates under promoters quota should not be less than Rs. 1.00 lakhs. The promoter must bring in his full subscription to issues in advance before public issue. The promoters contribution should not be diluted for a lock in period of 5 years from the date of commencement of the production or date of allotment whichever is later. Further, all the firm allotments, preferential allotments to collaborators, shareholders of promoters companies whether corporate or individual should not be transferable for 3 years from the date of the commencement of production or date of allotment whichever is later. The share certificates issued to promoter, his associates should carry the inspection "not transferable" for a period of 3–5 years as may be applicable from the date of commencement of production or date of allotment whichever is later.

### *8. Bonus Issue*

SEBI issued guidelines in case of bonus issue. The Company should ensure the following while issuing bonus shares:

(a) The bonus issue is made out of free reserves or share premium collected in cash.
(b) Reserves created by revaluation of fixed asset should not be capitalised.
(c) The investment allowance reserve is considered as free reserve for the calculation of residual reserves.
(d) All contingent liabilities should be taken into account in the calculation of residual reserves.
(e) The residual reserves after the proposed capitalisation would be at least 40 per cent of the increased paid up capital.

(f) The declaration of bonus issue, in lieu of dividend is not made.

(g) The bonus issue should be made only after full payment of share capital.

(h) There should be a provision in the articles of association for capitalising reserve.

(i) The Company should get a resolution passed in its general body meeting for the bonus issue.

(j) Before the bonus issue, the Company should not default in the payment of interest and dues to employees.

(k) The Company should implement the bonus issue within 6 months after approval of the board.

### *9. Protection of Debenture Holders*

SEBI issued guidelines to protect the interest of the debenture holders in two aspects:

(i) Servicing of debentures.

(ii) Protection of debenture holder's interest.

#### *(i) Servicing of Debentures*

Subject to the provisions of Section F, a debenture redemption reserve would be created by all the companies raising debentures on the following basis:

(a) Company may redeem the debentures in greater number of instalments.

(b) Companies may distribute dividends out of general reserves in certain years.

(c) A marotorium upto date of commercial production can be provided for creation of Debenture Redemption Reserve (DRR).

(d) Company should create DRR equivalent to 50 per cent of the amount of debenture issue before redemption commences.

(e) Drawal from DRR is permitted only after 10 per cent of the debentures, liabilities has been actually redeemed by the Company.

(f) The DRR may be created either in equal instalments or higher amounts.

(g) In case of PCDs, DRR should be created.

(h) In case of convertible issues by the New Companies, the creation of DRR should commence from the year earn profits for the remaining life of debentures.

*(ii) Protection of Debenture Holder's Interest*

(a) Debentures are issued by the Companies for the purpose of acquiring shares in other companies will not be permitted.

(b) Debenture holders have the right to appoint a nominee director on the board.

(c) The lead bank of the Company will monitor debentures raised for working capital funds.

(d) Institutional debenture holders should obtain a certificate from the Company's auditor in respect of utilisation of funds during the implementation period of projects.

**10. General**

(a) Subscription list should be kept open for at least 3 days to public issues and upto 60 days to Rights-issue.

(b) The quantum of issue, shall not exceed the amount specified in the prospectus.

(c) No retention of over subscription is permitted under any circumstances.

(d) After closing the issue the Company should submit a compliance report from Chartered Accountant and forward it to SEBI by the Lead Managers within 45 days.

(e) SEBI will have full rights to prescribe further guidelines to bring transparency in primary market.

(f) The provisions in the Companies Act, 1956 and other applicable laws shall be complied in connection with the issue of shares and debentures.

(g) Any violation of the guidelines by the issuer/intermediaries will be punishable through prosecution by the SEBI under the Act.

(h) SEBI should have the right to issue necessary clarifications to these guidelines to remove any difficulty in its implementation.

(i) According to the RBI guidelines the stock invest would now be restricted to individual investors and mutual fúnd only.

MBs irrespective of the form in which they are organised governed by the Merchant Bankers rules issued by the SEBI and Ministry of Finance.

## Companies Act, 2000

Companies can issue equity shares with differential voting rights.[6] The Government has announced various amendments to the Companies Act, 1956. Through the Act, 2000, it covers corporate governance, issuance of shares with differential rights, postal ballot. Shares with differential rights means equity shares having differential rights in respect to dividend, voting or otherwise. Section 86 of the Act has been amended to allow the public companies to issue shares with differential voting rights. The Government has notified the relevant rules in March 2001. The substantive conditions prescribed three-year profitability track record, shares with differential voting rights can be issued upto 25 per cent of the total share capital issued (i.e., effectively 33 per cent of the share capital before such issue) ban on conversion of plain vanilla equity capital into equity shares with differential rights and *vice versa* and no default in meeting investor's grievances. The other conditions include the approval of shareholders by postal ballot authorisation by the articles of association, non-conviction of any offence under the SEBI, FEMA and the SCRA no default in filing annual accounts and returns, no default in the repayment of deposits, debentures and dividend repayment among others. The rule on investor's grievances disqualification are vague. Section 87(1)(a) of the Act provides that every member shall have a right to vote.

## Registration of Merchant Bankers and Regulations

The Ministry of Finance, the Department of Economic Affairs have issued guidelines for the merchant bankers. According to the guidelines any person or body proposing to engage in the business of MB would need authorisation from SEBI. The authorised activities covers issue management, corporate advisory services relating to the issue, underwriting, portfolio management and managers, consultants or advisers to the issue. The SEBI categorised MB into four kinds. They are:

**Category I** — to carry on any activity of the issue management and also act as adviser, consultant, co-manager, underwriter, portfolio manager.

**Category II** — to act as adviser, consultant, co-manager, underwriter, portfolio manager.

**Category III**— to act as underwriter, adviser, consultant to an issue.

The minimum networth prescribed for the categories are Rs. 1 crore; Rs. 50,00,000; Rs. 20,00,000 and nil for category I, II, III and IV respectively. The general obligations and responsibilities, according to the regulations, related to their code of conduct, maintaining of books of accounts, records, submission of the half yearly results, their appointment, restriction on appointment, responsibilities as lead managers, submission of diligence certificate documents to be furnished to the board.

**Authorised Activities**

The merchant bankers will be permitted to involve in activities as per guidelines issued by the SEBI. Every activity performed by the Merchant banker should be allowed by the SEBI. Without the SEBI permission no merchant banker will act in public issues and other activities. The authorised activities of the merchant banker would include issue management and other authorised activities would be portfolio management services. The criteria for the authorisation of different activities are based on several factors such as—

(a) professional qualification in **finance, law or business management**,
(b) infrastructure like adequate office space, manpower and equipment,
(c) experienced members in merchant banking business as an employee status,
(d) capital adequacy, and
(e) past track record, experience, general reputation and fairness in all transactions. The merchant bankers should get the permission from the SEBI within **3 months**.

**Terms of Authorisation**

The following are the terms of authorisation issued by the SEBI:

(a) All the merchant bankers must have a minimum networth as prescribed.

(b) The authorisation will be for initial period of **3 years**.

(c) Merchant bankers should pay initial authorisation fee, an annual fee, and a renewal fee.

(d) All issues should be managed by at least one authorised merchant banker in issues of over **Rs. 100 crores**, the number could go upto a maximum of **four**.

(e) The responsibilities of each lead manager must be submitted to the SEBI before the public issue.

(f) Merchant bankers should verify the prospectus contents and they should submit a certificate to the SEBI for this effect.

(g) Merchant bankers should submit to all the information to the SEBI from time to time such as documents, returns and reports as prescribed and called for.

(h) The authorisation of merchant bankers can be suspended or cancelled in case of violation of the guidelines.

(i) The involvement of merchant bankers in an issue should continue at least till the completion of the essential follow up steps, i.e., listing of the instrument and despatch of certificates/ refunds.

(j) Merchant bankers have to adhere to a code of conduct prescribed by the SEBI.

(k) The guidelines should be followed by the Company and its functionaries. No exemption will be given to them if it fails any responsibility.

## Penalty System

In the interest of the investors into the affairs of the merchant banker SEBI can inspect the books of accounts, records, documents etc. If anything was found wrong the SEBI can give reasonable notice to the merchant banker. If the situation is severe the SEBI may appoint a qualified auditor to investigate the books of account. Penalties will be imposed for the defaults made by the merchant bankers. The SEBI categorised the following defaults as penalty points:

| | | | |
|---|---|---|---|
| (a) | General defaults | Penalty Points | 01 |
| (b) | Minor defaults | " | 02 |
| (c) | Major defaults | " | 03 |
| (d) | Serious defaults | " | 04 |

### *(a) General Defaults*

For the purpose of penalty point, the following activities are categorised under general defaults which attract one penalty point:

(1) Non-receipt of draft prospectus from the lead manager by the SEBI before filing with Registrar of Companies (**ROC**).
(2) Non-receipt of *inter se* allocation of responsibilities of lead manager is an issue by the SEBI prior to the opening of issue.
(3) Non-receipt of due diligence certificate in prescribed manner by the SEBI, before opening of the issue.
(4) Failure to ensure submission of certificate of minimum **90 per cent** subscription to the issue as required under the Government of India, press note number **F2/14/CCI/90**, dated 6.4.1990.
(5) Failure to ensure publishing of despatch of refund orders, shares/debenture certificates, filing of listing application by the issuer as required under Government of India Press Notification No. **2/6/CCI/89**, dated 10.1.1990.

### *(b) Minor Defaults*

The following activities are categorised under minor defaults and it attracts **two penalty** points:

(1) Advertisement, circular, brochure, press release and other issue related materials not being in conformity with contents of the prospectus.
(2) Exaggerated information to the prospectus is given by issuer or merchant banker in any manner.
(3) Delay in refund/allotment securities.
(4) Non-handling of investor grievances promptly.
(5) Failure to provide adequate and fair disclosure to the investors about the risk factors in the prospectus.
(6) Failure to exercise due diligence in verifying contents of prospectus.
(7) Violation of the Government of India, letter. No. **F1/23/SE/86**, Dt. 24.3.1986 and Government of India letter. No. **F/23/SE/86**, Dt. 24.7.1987 regarding advertisements on new capital issues.

(8) Failure to substantiate matter containing in highlights to the issue in the prospectus.

### *(c) Major Defaults*

The following activities are categorised under major defaults and it attracts **three penalty points**:

(1) Mandatory underwriting not taken up by the Lead Manager.
(2) Association of unauthorised merchant banker in an issue.
(3) If excess number of lead managers involved than permitted under the SEBI guidelines. The SEBI released a press note on 28.2.1991 in this regard.

### *(d) Serious Defaults*

The following activities are categorised under serious defaults and it attracts **four penalty points**:

(1) Unethical practice followed by the Merchant Banker and/or in violation of code of conduct.
(2) Non-cooperation with SEBI in furnishing desired information, documents, evidence as may be called for.

A merchant banker who reaches a **cumulative penalty points of 8** attracts the termination/suspension of authorisation by SEBI. The maximum penalty points awarded in a single issue managed by Merchant Bankers are restricted to **four to take the correct action**.

### Defaults in Prospectus

If highlights are provided, the following deficiencies can be treated as negative points:

(a) absence of risk factors in highlights,
(b) absence of listing in highlights, and
(c) extraneous contents to the prospectus.

The total points allotted to prospectus is **10**. A merchant banker who scored **8** or more than **8** points will be assigned **A+ grade**. The merchant banker who scored **6 or** less than **8 points** as **A** and with **4 or** less than **6 points will be B**. The banker with a score of less than **4** points will be assigned **C** category. A merchant banker on reaching the cumulative penalty points of **8** shall attract the action from the **SEBI**. It may be added that the above list is not an exhaustive one and the action could be taken by the **SEBI** for other reasons like non-fulfilment of authorisation criteria **(networth)**, carrying out business detrimental to the interest of the public, conviction in any economic offence by the Merchant Banker or any of its directors or its principal officer, violation of any other guidelines/notification which has a bearing on the functioning of merchant bankers.

In the wake of important developments in the recent times, merchant banking and financial services have become more sophisticated unlike before and therefore there is a great demand for highly specialised skill in planning, decision making and control in these areas. To cope with these challenges in the areas of merchant banking and financial services, the country now needs a large body of trained professionals. To provide the necessary institutional infrastructure for imparting specialised training, the **Institute of Chartered Financial Analyst of India (ICFAI)** has launched an innovative programme **"Merchant Banking and Financial Services (MBFS)"**. This programme needs post-graduation qualification meant for those managers who are involved in finance area. The objective of the programme is to improve the conceptual, managerial and operational skills of the managers engaged in merchant banking and financial services and to help them render the best services to their clients. The programme seeks to impart the **knowledge of basic** concepts in merchant banking and to improve the ability to rationally evaluate the alternatives in the decision making process. This programme is divided into **five groups**. Foundation group, Group A, Group B, Group C and Group D. The subjects under groups are divided as follows:

1. Foundation group (Financial and Cost accounting, Financial management, quantitative methods).
2. **Group A** (Financial services, New issue management, Asset based financing).
3. **Group B** (Security evaluation and Investment, Portfolio management and Mutual funds, V.C.).

4. **Group C** (Corporate Advisory Services, International Finance and Capital markets, MES).
5. Project work and viva.

## Project Preparation and Appraisal

Project counselling is one of the basic activities of the merchant banking. It is a part of the financial services they render to their clients for the preparation of project report and pre-investment studies. Merchant bankers are involved in feasibility studies and project reports. The appraisal of the project will be made by the merchant banker in analysing the financial soundness of an investment project. Before the preparation of project report, the merchant banker has to satisfy himself that the project is viable and it meets the requirements of the term lending institutions. The following steps are involved in project preparation and appraisal:

**(A) Project identification.**
**(B) Project selection.**
**(C) Feasibility study.**
**(D) Appraisal of project.**
**(E) Special cost benefit analysis.**

### *(A) Project Identification*

Project is a plan to do something. It is a proposal for capital expenditure items to create facilities like providing goods and services. The investment proposal can be for setting up of a new unit, expansion or diversification. Project idea is a creative activity. The idea generation is the desire of an entrepreneur. Projects can be identified on the basis of an formation about the environment and technical process evolved in the country or elsewhere. Project identification is highly influenced by **"the factors such as agricultural raw materials, forest products, fishing products, mineral resources, human skills, the needs of population, family budget, national income, GDP, NDP, per capita income, purchasing capacity, tastes and habits of consumers etc.** For this purpose of project identification, market surveys are to be conducted for assessing the demand and supply gap of a product. It must be remembered that, if you want to select a project, the demand and supply gap should be more. Import substitution product of a project is well encouraged by the Government.

### *(B) Project Selection*

Project selection is the most important task before an entrepreneur. It is followed by the project identification process. The objective at this stage is to decide whether the project can be studied in detail and what should be the scope of further studies. The findings at this stage are embodied in a pre-feasibility study. The information and findings which are available in this stage must be screened and priorities should be fixed. For the screening purpose, the project ideas are developed into pre-feasibility studies. Pre-feasibilitys studies provide a wide variety of information about the plant size, availability of raw material, plant location, availability of technical manpower, proximity to near markets, transportation, abundant power supply, availability of financial facilities, tropical environment, soil suitability and other infrastructure facilities, and government policies about the industrial sector. The project selection exercise is a commitment of the entrepreneur.

### *(C) Feasibility Study*

After the selection of project, it is mostly desirable to implement the plan. A detailed and in-depth analysis will be carried on by the experts called **"feasibility study"**. Feasibility study is the final document in the formulation of a project proposal. The amount of expenditure involved in preparation of feasibility study can be **debited** to project cost and it can be treated as promoters contribution. The feasibility study contain all technical and financial data which are essential for the evolution of the project. The feasibility study should examine public policy with respect to the industry. The study should also think about the different alternative techniques of production in terms of process choice, ecology friendliness, choice of raw material and choice of plant size. Before the presentation of financial data, market analysis has to be done to determine the economic levels of production. Financial data is another important factor in preparation of feasibility report. It should cover the preliminary assessment of **sales revenue, capital cost, operating cost, administrative cost, marketing cost, selling and distribution cost, levels of leverage** and other elements. The study should also estimate about the **fixed asset cost and working capital requirements** at different levels of production.

### *(D) Appraisal of Project*

**Appraisal of project** is the other step in confirmation of a desired project. The terms in project evaluation, appraisal and assessment are used interchangeably. They will be used in an analysis of financial soundness of an investment project. The analysis will be made on the basis of projected cash flows. The appraisal will be carried out by the promoter. This will be helpful to the merchant banker. The merchant banker is going to be involved in the management of public issue and underwriting it and ultimately financial institutions will lend the money. Project evaluation will be made in comparison with respect of various alternatives to technology, raw material, production capacity, location and local production etc. Project appraisal may involve in the following steps:

**(1) Technical appraisal.**
**(2) Economic appraisal.**
**(3) Financial appraisal.**

#### *(1) Technical Appraisal*

**Technical appraisal** of a project is primarily concerned with the selection of the best available technology, design and other infrastructure facilities. The quality of a finished product will depend upon the technology adopted by the Company. Technical appraisal will undertake the study about the project regarding **plant capacity, degree of integration, by product recovery and flexibility** of the plant. The capacity of the plant will be determined by several factors such as product mix, product specification and raw material composition. The plant capacity will depend upon several situations. While appraising the project, the flexibility of the plant should be taken into consideration. Spare capacity should be made available in the plant to maintain uninterrupted production in the event of unforeseen situations. Flexibility creates more strength to a given project. The technical appraisal also should take into consideration about **inputs, location and technology process**. The delay in implementation of the project leads to cost and time overruns implications. The planning control tools like **PERT, CPM, CAD** etc., should be used in technical appraisal of the project.

*(2) Economic Appraisal*

**Economic appraisal** of a project reflects in two ways. The first aspect of impact is on employment and foreign exchange. The proposed project may generate direct employment and indirect employment. Direct employment means, the new employment opportunities created by the project within the sphere of the unit. Indirect employment means providing employment opportunities created in projects related on both input and output sides of the project under appraisal. A project may be export oriented or import substitution unit. Therefore, the project will show an impact on balance of payments. If the project is **100 per cent export oriented unit**, then it may reflect in increase of foreign exchange and if the unit is import substitution concern the calculation of foreign exchange savings should be done. The analysis of net foreign exchange effect may be done for the entire life years.

*(3) Financial Appraisal*

**Financial appraisal** is concerned with the analysis of profitability of resources invested in the project without consideration of their sources. It is concerned with the projects benefits' after taking into consideration of market prices. Financial appraisal may be made with three popular methods. The three methods can be classified as follows:

1. Simple rate of return method.
2. Payback period.
3. Discounted cash flow method.

**Simple rate of return** is the method of calculation to arrive the ratio of net profit for a year to the initial investment with a consideration of fixed and working capital. The capacity utilisation is the barometer for expecting a return on project. The simple rate of return method is useful to the short-term projects. It helps in making a quick assessment of profitability. **Payback period** is another method for financial appraisal of a project. It measures the number of years required to recover a project total investment from the cash flow generated by it. This method is easy to calculate and in terms of liquidity it is advisable for financial appraisal of a project. The shorter the payback period, the quicker the recovery of initial investment. The **Discounted cash flow method** considers the magnitude and timing of the expected cash flows in each period of the projects' life. The discounted cash flow techniques are further classified as **"Internal rate of return and net present value method."** The internal rate of return is the discount rate that equals the present value of the expected cash outflows with the present value of the expected cash inflows. According to this method, the project is selected, if it exceeds the required rate of return. The net present value method tells us about the selection of a project if an investment proposal amount, discounts cash flows becomes **zero or more**. If it is not the project will be rejected. When the NPV is **zero**, the project would cover all expenses and has no excess returns. If a project's NPV is positive it is acceptable and if NPV is negative the project should be rejected. The two **DCF** techniques lead to the acceptance or rejection of decisions.

***Financial Analysis***

Financial analysis is the part of financial appraisal. Financial analysis takes into account financial features of the project with reference to the sources of financing. It helps to determine the smooth operation of the project for the entire lifecycle. The financial analysis contains two major aspects which are **liquidity and capital structure analysis.** For the two aspects of analysis ratios are employed to know the financial status of a project in a given period. **Liquidity** ratio reveals the projects' ability to meet its short-term obligations. The two ratios are calculated to measure the **position of liquidity, the current ratio** and **quick ratio**. The current ratio can be calculated by the following formula. The current ratio reveals the relation between current assets and current liabilities.

$$\text{Current ratio} = \frac{\text{Current Assets}}{\text{Current Liabilities}}$$

**Current assets** consists of cash, bank balance, investment insecurities account receivables, and inventories. **Current liabilities** are payable within **one accounting** period like creditors, bank O.D., advances from customers, short-term loans from banks etc. An ideal current ratio is **1.5 to 1.0**. Therefore, the project is always kept in mind to maintain the ideal current ratio. Another ratio is called **"quick ratio"**. This ratio reveals how far a firm can quickly collect the cash from the sources. The quick ratio can be calculated by the following formula:

$$\text{Quick ratio} = \frac{\text{Current Assets - Stock}}{\text{Current Liabilities}}$$

An ideal quick ratio is **1:1**. The firm should always maintain this ratio.

Long-term solvency ratio measures the projects ability to meet the long-term commitments to creditors. The creditors have the legal authority to fulfil the claims. The two long-term solvency ratios are **(a) debt utilisation ratio, (b) debt equity ratio**. Debt utilisation ratio indicates the projects' indebtedness. It is a relation between total debt and total assets of the company. It is the combination of debt and equity proportion in a project.

Debt equity ratio is also referred as debt capitalisation ratio. It is the value of total debt divided by the book value of equity share. It can be calculated by applying the following formula. Short-term obligation less than one year duration is to be excluded.

$$\text{Debt equity ratio} = \frac{\text{Long - term liabilities}}{\text{Shareholder's equity}}$$

The other ratios relating to long-term stability are mostly used by the development banking institutions. They are fixed assets coverage ratio, debt coverage ratio, interest coverage ratio etc. **Fixed assets coverage ratio** shows the number of times fixed assets to cover the loan proportion. The ratio can be calculated through the formula

$$\text{Fixed assets coverage ratio} = \frac{\text{Net fixed assets}}{\text{Term loan}}$$

**Debt coverage** ratio measures the earnings to cover the payment of interest and principal amount. It measures the degree to which the fixed payments are covered by operating profits. It emphasis the ability of the project to generate adequate cash flow to service its financial leverage. An ideal debt coverage ratio is **2**. Another ratio interest is coverage ratio, it measures the earnings to meet the interest cost. The interest coverage ratio can be computed by the following formula:

$$\text{Interest coverage ratio} = \frac{\text{PBT + Interest}}{\text{Interest}}$$

The most important tool of the financial analysis is **"Break even point"**. It is an essential aspect of financial appraisal. Break even point means the level of production and sales at which total revenues are exactly equal to the operating costs. It indicates the volume necessary for the profitable operation of the project. BEP analysis shows how much quantity of goods are to be produced at desired levels of profit. If the BEP is too high, the price of the product may be increased and it needs revision. The viability of a project can be assessed with the help of break even analysis. For the break even analysis, the income statement should be prepared and analysed. The income statement contains all the financial data regarding sales, fixed expenses, variable expenses and profit. Therefore, we cannot ignore the role of BEP in financial appraisal of a project.

### *(E) Special Cost Benefit Analysis*

Earlier, the project appraisal aspect covered only the private costs and benefits. Social cost benefit is another dimension of the project appraisal. Cost benefit analysis is meant for the evaluation of public investment. Now-a-days the mega projects are well established with the blessings of public. The public contribution in mega projects cannot be ignored. India is a vast populated country with a high potential investors to peace the industrial sector. Merchant banker's role is more important in this context, to tap the savings of Indian community cost benefit analysis is concerned with the examination of a project from the view point of maximisation of net social benefit. In this analysis, a careful observation will be made about the proposed projects in the society. The analysis will be made about the advantages and disadvantages in terms of a common monetary unit. A project which approaches this analysis has its objective function of the net benefits to the society. Social benefit will be reflected in the form of price of a commodity. The economist uses as a measure of the preference. In many situations the prices are not observable. The maximisation of net benefit should be finally equivalent to the maximisation of social utility or social welfare. Social cost and benefits and private cost and benefits are different from **market imperfections, external environment** and **redistribution**. Market imperfection means the industrial policy of the government. The speed of industrial progress will depend upon the policy of a stable government. Since markets were regulated and prices were controlled by the Government earlier in our nation, the resources used by the private sector were under priced. The recent phenomenon of deregulation has freed several resources price from the control of the government. For example, the foreign exchange rate is now determined by the market forces. This situation will be more useful to the nation. **Externalities** is the measurement of a proposed project regarding the advantages and disadvantages. A proposed project which is established, may create infrastructural facilities like roads, power, communication, transport, banking etc. The effects may benefits or costs. These benefits are however not considered if the projects have some harmful environmental effects. The environmental policy is the most important information of projects. The cure for poverty is the development and it may cure some kinds of pollution. The promoter of a project did not bother about the projects benefit to the society. But the government or society thinks about the possible benefits regarding the investment in various projects. Industrial projects are established by either private or public sector to remove the poverty and to improve the income level. All the five-year plans in India have poverty alleviation as their basic objectives. But they failed to improve the lifestyle of a poor citizen. The opportunities which were provided by industrial units cannot be availed by the poor. The poor people are unskilled and illiterate and they do not have the skills that factory type of employment demands. The poor will be benefited only by encouraging the cottage industries and rural based industries, like agro based material processing, printing, fishing, dairy, animal husbandry, poultry etc. Projects promoted by the industrialists are not suitable for integrating poor into the market oriented activity.

After the completion of project appraisal and evaluation of different alternatives are being examined, ultimately the selection of project lies in the hands of a promoter. The next step is to approach the capital market for mobilisation of funds. The approach to the public by a company for the requirement of capital is called as **"public issue"**. The public issue of securities is the main important task before a merchant banker. The main function of the merchant banker is to prepare a plan and to make arrangements for public issue for successful completion of a project construction. The availability of funds may reduce the time period of a commercial enterprises commencement. When the companies seek to raise the resources for the implementation of a new project they retain the services of a merchant banker. Merchant bankers are identified as **"issue houses"**. Merchant bankers are the issue managers to a public issue and they have to assist the company in all the stages connected with the issue. The functions of a merchant banker can be classified as:

**(I) Pre-issue management.**

**(II) Post-issue management.**

Public issue requires the fulfilment of many legal formalities and involvement of various agencies activities which have to be time by coordinated public issue may be described as a social event like a "marriage".

## (I) PRE-ISSUE MANAGEMENT

Pre-issue management involves many steps before approaching the market. Pre-issue management is concerned with issue of share and pricing of shares. The pre-issue management can be categorised as follows:

**(A) Issue of shares.**
**(B) Marketing, Coordination and underwriting of issue.**
**(C) Pricing of issues.**

### (A) Issue of Shares

Funds raised through the public is called as **"primary market"** public issue of securities, shares or debentures are made in the primary market. There is no fixed place for the issue of new securities. The household savings constitute the primary sources of capital formation in the country. The net savings ratio will encourage the capital market. It is the job of the merchant banker to help the company in mobilisation of pooled savings. The shares and debentures have to compete with other financial instruments to attract the savings. Public issues are offered through a prospectus. Prospectus is a document which invites the public to contribute the share capital to attain better returns on their investments. Wide publicity about the offer is to be made through different media like **newspapers, periodicals and television**. The merchant bankers will put their entire efforts to make it successful. The issue of equity shares are further categorised as issue of shares at the first time, further issue, of shares made by existing companies either by **public issue** or **rights issue**. Rights issue of share means the new issue of shares to the existing shareholders at a stated proportion and at a fixed price. Rights shares are issued at a premium which is freely determined by the company making issue. Issue of shares can be made as follows:

**(1) Public issue through prospectus.**
**(2) Offers for sale.**
**(3) Private placement.**

### *(1) Public Issue Through Prospectus*

This is the most common and popular method of public issues through prospectus. Shares and debentures are issued in this method. For public issue, every company has to fulfil the legal formalities with the SEBI. SEBI has the legal authority in permitting the companies to enter the capital market. A fixed number of shares at the stated price will be issued in primary market. According to SEBI guidelines, a company which has not completed **12** months of commercial operation, can issue shares only at **par** or **face value**. If a new company is set up by an **existing company** with 5 years track record, the new company is free **to determine** the price of the share. The prospectus has to be vetted by the SEBI before the public issue. The merchant banker has to draft the prospectus and get clearance from the officials. **Sections 55 to 68A** of the Companies Act deals with the issue of prospectus. The prospectus contains all the information regarding the company's activities. **Section 2(36) of the Companies Act** defines a prospectus as "any document described or issued as prospectus and includes any notice, circular, advertisement or other document inviting deposits from the public or inviting offers from the public for the subscription of purchase of any shares in or debentures of a body corporate". It is a document which invites the public to subscribe the issued capital. This invitation can be made only by a **public limited company**. The Companies Act, **Section 55** indicates that the draft prospectus has to be signed by the Directors of the Company and they would release that document at a fixed date. **Section 60** tells us about the registration of a prospectus. The registration should be done before its publication. It has to be registered with the **Registrar of Companies** by submitting a copy. The copy of registration must be accompanied by the **consent of experts, the copy of contract fixing compensation of a managing director, a copy of every material contract, consents of auditor, legal adviser, attorney, solicitor, bankers, brokers etc**. After registration of the prospectus with Registrar of Companies must be issued within **90 days**. The prospectus should contain all the information about the company as presented below:

1. The main objective of the company.
2. Particulars about the signatories to the memorandum of association.
3. Qualification shares of directors.
4. Number and classes of shares.
5. No. of redeemable preference shares.
6. Particulars about the board of directors and managing directors.
7. Minimum subscription for the shares.
8. The time and opening of subscription list.
9. The amount of application money, allotted money should be indicated.
10. Premium on shares issued.
11. Name of the underwriter, and their commission.
12. Particulars of preliminary expenses.
13. The benefits provided to promoters, if any.
14. Particulars about the contracts made by the Company.
15. Voting and dividend rights.
16. Capitalisation of profits and surplus from the revaluation of assets.

According to the Companies Act, Section 62, there will be a civil liability on the part of the promoters, directors and experts, if they submits the false information in the prospectus. Damages for mis-statements in prospectus may be claimed by any shareholder. The punishments in regard to various offences are presented below:

| | | |
|---|---|---|
| For any untrue statement in the prospectus | — | 2 years imprisonment + with a fine of Rs. 5,000. |
| For issuing of application of shares without the prospectus | — | A fine of Rs. 5,000. |
| Application in fictious names for the registration of shares | — | Imprisonment of 5 years. |
| Encouragement to invest for false information company | — | Imprisonment of 5 years or fine of Rs.10,000. |

### *(2) Offers for Sale*

The sale of shares through intermediary of issue house or firm of a stock broker is called as **"offer for sale"**. The company sells the shares or debentures to the issue house at an agreed price then the issue house resolds the shares to the public at a stated price. In this context, the company need not issue a prospectus. But a statement in lieu of prospectus should be filed with the Registrar of Companies. Three days before the allotment of shares or debentures. In this method the company can get a substantial earnings because no flotation costs are involved.

### *(3) Private Placement*

The issue of shares or debentures or preference shares by the company to the individual investors is called as **"private placement"**. The company will sell the securities directly to the genuine investors. There is no need of issue of prospectus in the private placement. In the private placement market the individual investors means **"UTI, LIC, GIC, SFCs, Pension funds, Insurance fund owners"**. The issuers could be a public limited company or private limited company. The intermediaries in this market are **rating agencies, trustees, financial advisers, merchant bankers**. In this market the investors have sufficient knowledge and well experience in evaluating the merits and demerits of the financial investment. The merchant banker will play an important in deal of private placement. His role cannot be ignored. The private placement provides a time saving channel in mobilisation of required funds. It also save the substantial amount of expenses in the form of flotation charges. It is possible to raise funds from this method within **2 or 3 months**. But public issue will take at least **6 months to one year**. In private placement market, the investors are more perfect about the assessment of their buying financial asset. The private placement is equal to the primary market which combines equity and debentures the private placement business cannot exist without the active connivance of promoters. The SEBI has put a restriction on **FIIs**, regarding the investment in shares of a particular in private placement process, they must hold the shares for 5 years.

## (B) Marketing, Coordination and Underwriting of Issues

The successful closure of public issue depends upon the efficiency of a merchant bankers to that issue. The merchant banker will have to coordinate many activities relating to issue with different agencies. Appointment of brokers, registrars, underwriters, lead managers, bankers, share transfer agents is to be done. The issue has to be groomed, publicity campaign and arrangements for printing and mailing to be made. In this context, the merchant banker should attend to the following functions of public issue:

**(a) Marketing.**
**(b) Coordination.**
**(c) Underwriting.**

### *Appointment of Bankers to Issue*

The application for the issue will be received by the bankers to issue. The applications along with which the subscription amount may be collected by the designated branches and the same will be forwarded to the registrar or merchant bankers in accordance with the instructions issued from time to time. The bankers to issue will make publicity by distributing material and application forms and prospectus with the bearing of stamp of brokers. The brokers will be paid their commission which bears the stamp on application form. The consent of banker to act as a banker to issue has to be obtained. In case of the **mega issues** adequate number of banks with offices at important places have to be appointed. The bankers will be paid a renumeration as per the agreement made by the company.

### *Appointment of Registrar to Issue*

The merchant bankers will make the arrangement for the appointment of registrars to manage the assigned works. They are specialised in their nature of work. Merchant bankers will have normally a panel of registrars and helps the issuing company. The work of registrars to issue is mainly involved in post-issue management. A detailed discussion will be made available in the preceding pages. The SEBI has drafted some rules and regulations to act as a Registrar to issue and share transfer agency. The registrars should get permission from the **SEBI** for every year. A fee has to be paid. The permission is valid for one year and has to be renewed annually. The registrar should have competence, expertise, adequacy, skilled manpower, good track record, experience, adequacy of infrastructure etc.

### *Marketing*

After the completion of drafting of the prospectus, it has to be sent to the SEBI. The SEBI will scrutinise the prospectus and will take a decision in this regard. After despatch of prospectus to the SEBI, the merchant banker will make arrangements with company representatives and advertising agents to finalise the arrangements relating to the date of opening and closing, registration of the prospectus, launching publicity campaign and fixing the date of board meeting. According to the SEBI guidelines the issue should be open for a minimum period of **3 days**. At the time of public issues, the state of the secondary market, number of other issues, tax payment time, proximity to festival time etc.

### *Coordination*

According to the Companies Act and SEBI guidelines, the merchant banker has to submit the information on behalf of the client company. They should make arrangements for drafting the prospectus with the help of the experts, legal advisers, attorney, solicitors etc. The acceptance of underwriters, brokers, bankers, solicitors, legal advisers, lead managers should be obtained and should file with other statements to the Registrar of Companies. After the preparation of prospectus, it has to be sent to the SEBI for vetting. Then it can be filed by the Registrar of Companies. The merchant banker has to coordinate with the following persons:

1. Brokers.
2. Bankers.
3. Registrars.

Brokers are the influencing persons to motivate the investors towards the subscription of issuing company. Brokers are the members of recognised stock exchange and they maintain a good relationship with the investors. They know the pulse of the investors about their regular earnings, savings, potential investment capabilities. They are able to guide the investors because the investors are regular customers to the brokers. Brokers will be appointed for the purpose of public subscription which pay brokerage. The application forms for the subscription will be supplied the brokers. Brokers to issue will participate in the canvassing of subscription by mailing the literature to the potential investors. The appointment of broker will be made by the merchant banker after consulting the client company. The appointment procedure will be same as in the case of underwriter. The broker will be appointed by the merchant banker keeping in view of the brokers reputation and coverage of wide geographical area. The reputation of the brokers can inspire the confidence among the investors. Sometimes the principal brokers may also be appointed keeping in view of the issue size and situation of the market. The principal brokers sometimes undertake centralised mailing of prospectuses, application forms and other publicity material on behalf of the merchant banker. The broker will assist the merchant bankers to devise the strategy for the success of the issue. Another factor in marketing the securities is publicity. Publicity is the most important factor for the sale of securities. The company is a high growth concern, the brand is a market leader, the product is with high quality, the price may be very low, the issue of company cannot succeed if there is no proper publicity to the issue. Therefore, the advertisement will make the issue more perfect and will get the success in the market. The advertisement in the press, radio, satellite channels, internet advertising, investors conferences will perfectly enhance the image of the issuing company. The advertisement should be in transparent and disclose all the information about the project prospects and profitability for the benefit of the investors. The merchant bankers will play an important role in the selection of media, channels of advertisement and timing of advertisements. The advertising agency is involved in printing of colourful brochures, forms, prospectus and other material. According to the stock exchange rules and regulations, every issuer must submit the material to the exchange in advance of 21 days before the issue opens for the subscription.

***Underwriting***

The public issue is the process of mobilisation of required fund by the company. Usually the companies will approach the primary market to tap the savings of small investors. A well known company, a strong brand image concern, a high growth company can easily mobilise the funds by the public issue. But sometimes they may not attract the investors and the issue may be a flop. In this situation, the third party will come into picture and gives assurance about the success of the issue. The third party is called as underwriter. The underwriter will ensure the company that, if any, unforeseen situation arises in the market. The underwriter would accept the unsubscribed portion of the issue. For this purpose he is entitled to get a commission. The commission paid to the underwriter is called as Underwriting Commission. Underwriting agreement is a contract between underwriters and issuing company. The underwriter may be a broker or a merchant banker or financial institution or a financial intermediary. The maximum liability of an underwriter is restricted to the amount underwritten by him. According to SEBI, the underwriting is a mandatory, it is not an option. The minimum requirement of 90 per cent subscription is mandatory for each issue of capital to public. The number of underwriters can be decided by the issuing company. The outstanding underwriting commitment should not exceed 5 times the networth of the underwriters. A detailed discussion will be made available later.

Pre-issue management is a time bound programme which has to be promptly attended to. A proper attention with most efficiency should be taken for the detail execution of the activities which would lead to a successful issue. The pre-issue management activities required the chronological steps. They are presented below.

**Pre-Issue Management Activities (Stepwise)**

1. Sending memorandum of association and articles of association to the concerned stock exchange.
2. Furnishing the consent letters from bankers, auditors, registrars, experts, solicitors to the prospectus.
3. Drafting the power of attorney from all the directors in favour of two directors.
4. Selection of advertising agents and printers.
5. Sending prospectus application forms to the concerned stock exchange.
6. Receipt of comments from stock exchange.
7. To discuss draft prospectus with the company.
8. Apply for the private placement with financial intermediaries.
9. Advertising strategy commencement.
10. Conducting of extraordinary general meeting for the draft resolution.

11. To collect balance sheet and audit report.
12. Company to hold meeting for approving, signing and filling prospectus.
13. To forward the prospectus to the SEBI.
14. Forwarding prospectus after vetting by the SEBI to stock exchanges.
15. To file prospectus with registrar of companies.
16. Decide the quantum of issue material that is to be printed.
17. File listing application with the concerned stock exchange.
18. Pres release and briefing.
19. Announcement of prospectus in Newspapers.
20. Registrars to issue, to prepare and send bank procedure to bankers.
21. Announcement of brief prospectus in papers.
22. Opening of subscription list, earliest closing, latest closing.
23. Company to review position in public response.
24. Closure of issue and issue of advertising.
25. Specimen of equity certificate/refund orders to be sent for approval to the stock exchange.
26. Registrars finalise the allotment process in consultation with stock exchange.
27. Board meeting for approval of allotment.
28. Payment of consolidated stamp duty.
29. Registrars to issue letters of allotment/refund orders/equity certificates.
30. Company to complete listing formalities.

## Pre-Issue Management and Pricing

According to the SEBI guidelines for capital issues a company can issue the share at its own discretion. Pricing of issues is done by the Companies themselves in consultation with the merchant banker. Pricing of the issue is a part of pre-issue management. The companies are free from pricing of their equity with some limitations with the introduction of the free pricing almost all companies have the freedom to determine the issue price. If the amount of premium is low the issue gets over subscribed and if the premium is very high it is bound to be undersubscribed and fail. The merchant banker will decide the amount of the premium taking into consideration of **EPS, book value, the average market price for the last 3 years, future**

**prospect of the company** and assess whether the market can absorb the premium on issue. The SEBI is concerned only with giving permission and checking about the facts shown in prospectus. Justification of issue price has to be stated and included in the prospectus. The equity shares offered to the existing shareholders is called **"Rights issue"**. According to **Section 81** of the Companies Act, stipulates that a company can increase subscribed capital at any time after the expiry of **2 years** or **one year** from the first allotment of shares and such further issue of shares must be offered to the existing shareholders in proportion to the share held. Sometimes the company can made rights issue and public issue at the same time. Rights issues are very popular. Rights may be issued below the market price to compensate the shareholders. Though there are no restrictions on fixation of premium but some guidelines are issued by the Ministry of Finance which are to be taken into consideration. The fair value of a share is determined by—

(1) Net asset value.
(2) Profit earning approach.
(3) Market value.

**Net asset value** is the networth after providing all the liabilities. Net asset value should be equal to equity + reserves + surplus + contingent liabilities. While calculating the NAV proper attention should be taken. **Proposal of bonus issue, excluding of intangible assets, revaluation of assets should not be taken, cash should be taken, provision of gratuity, terminal benefits to employees, arrears of preference dividend, proposed dividend, provision of depreciation etc.**

**Profit earning approach** is based on the average of the profits. It is arrived at by capitalising the average of the after tax profits for five years. The rate of capitalisation are different from sector to sector. The market price of the share reflects the track record of high and consistent dividend payments and bonus issues and reputation of management but all these factors may not be reflected in the NAV and the PE approach. The average profits are arrived at on the basis of 3 years profit in the audited accounts.

**Market value** of a share will be found, it they are listed in stock exchange. The average market value of a share in the preceding 3 years after making appropriate adjustments for bonus issue and dividend payment would be determined by high and low of the preceding two years and the high and low of each month in the preceding twelve months. The average market price is used to check the reasonableness of the average net asset value and profit earning capacity value.

The ultimate valuation is based on fair value. The fair value can be calculated in the case of listed share, the average net asset value + profit earning capacity with **15 per cent** of capitalisation rate should be less than the market price by **20 per cent**, the average is fair value. Valuation is not an arithmetic exercise. It has to be done by judicious discretion and judgement taking into account all the relevant factors. There are several other factors which may not reflect in balance sheet like **the quality and integrity of management, reputation of brand, brand image, brand loyalty, present and prospective competition, yield on securities and market sentiment.**

## (II) POST-ISSUE MANAGEMENT

After closing of public issue the next task of the merchant bankers is post-issue management. It consisting of collection of application forms from designated banks and the amount received, scrutinising of applications, deciding allotment procedure in consultation with stock exchange are discussed. This process ends with the mailing of share certificates/refund orders/allotment orders.

**Registrars to issue** occupies a key role in the post-issue management activities. They work with the association of bankers to issue. The registrars will collect the application forms from bankers, sorting them and arranging them in an order. The merchant banker will assist the company and keep in touch with the completion of process. The Registrars to issue collect the application forms on behalf of the company with the amount. They scrutinise of all forms and ensures that the applications are processed and allotment, if share certificates/refund orders are sent within 30 days of the close of the issue. The registrars should take all the precautions about the simplifications of the process.

### Listing Requirement of Stock Exchanges

Listing means admit of a scrip for trading on a stock exchange. The objective of listing is to provide liquidity and free negotiability to securities. Listing is advantageous to the company as well as shareholders. Listing is not a mandatory but it is an option. The company should indicate in the prospectus about listing. The Securities Contract Act specifies that a public limited company should list in a recognised stock exchange. Financial institutions also require listing. The **SEBI** also stipulates that companies should get their shares listed on a recognised stock exchange or OTC.

Companies entering the primary market are required to advertise in the newspapers an announcement regarding the proposed issue of capital. Until the subscription list is closed, no advertisement should be given about over subscription. Stock exchange can refuse enlistment in the case of companies which advertise oversubscription. The allotment process should be made fairly and equitably. In case of over-subscription the allotment should be made on **drawal of lots** upto certain categories of applications. If the oversubscription is marginal the allotment may be done on the basis of **pro-rata method**. The allotment should be in multiples of trading lots. The issue of shares through public issue, it may be a costly affair. The overall ceiling of the cost of public issue has been fixed. The public issue cost includes **Underwriting Commission, Brokerage Commission, Fee to the registrars, publicity cost and listing fee**.

According to the Companies Act, 1956, Section **73(1)**, every company should make an application to one or more recognised stock exchanges before public issue for listing of issue. The condition also applies to an offer for sale and is also applicable to an issue of **debentures**. The following steps are required for the enlistment of securities:

1. A board resolution approving the enlistment of the securities.
2. An application in the prescribed form for the enlistment enclosing necessary documents. The documents include prospectus, statement in lieu for subscription, advertisement, offering the new issue for subscription etc. The list also covers underwriting agreements, specimen of share certificates/ debenture certificates, letter of allotment/acceptance/ renunciation in the case of new issues, initial listing fee and other documents.
3. The standard listing agreement shall be executed on acceptance of the application for enlistment; the company should undertake to abide by the terms and conditions of the listing

agreement. The listing agreement covers various obligations like issue of letters of allotment share certificates, transfer of shares, information about supplies to the stock exchange from time to time.

## MERCHANT BANKERS AND PORTFOLIO MANAGEMENT

### Portfolio

Portfolio means a collection of different securities. It is a basket of investments held by an individual investor/foreign institutional investor/ or a corporate body. It consists of a collection of financial assets such as **equity, bonds, treasury bills, debentures**. The collection of different properties should be treated as portfolio. According to the SEBI rules of 1993, it may be defined as "the total holding of securities belonging to any person".[7] Portfolio management involves a proper investment decision making about what to buy and sell. It involves proper money management. Portfolio management reduces risk and increases returns. Portfolio management renders the service to satisfy the asset preferences of investors. Professional portfolio management is backed by a highly talented skilled research staff members. The basic objective of portfolio management is to **maximise return** and **minimise risk**. The level of risk of a portfolio depends upon many factors. Portfolio manager is an important person who holds the financial dreams of millions of investors. **Crores** of rupees and the dreams of millions of investors are at the disposal of portfolio managers. Portfolio management is a continuous process. It is a dynamic activity. After the success of mutual funds in portfolio management, a number of brokers and investment consultants who are professionally qualified have become portfolio managers. Portfolio management scheme have been floated by **finance companies**, financial institutions and money market managers. They handle funds of the investors for a fee. Any individual or organisation who can invest at least **Rs. 1,00,000** for investment in securities can approach a merchant banker. According to the SEBI guidelines, the portfolio manager should get a certificate from the SEBI for rendering the portfolio services. The guidelines also indicate that category I and II merchant bankers need not get a certificate in this respect. According to the regulations, the portfolio managers are required to enter into an agreement regarding his services with the clients. The regulations provide that the manager should independently manage the funds of the client in accordance with the needs of the client. The contract with the clients by the portfolio managers should contain the following clauses:

1. The investment objectives and the services to be provided.
2. Period of the contract.
3. Amount to be invested.
4. Fees payable to the portfolio managers.
5. Custody of securities.
6. Attendant risks involved in the management of the portfolio.
7. Procedure of settling the accounts with the clients.
8. Areas of investment and restrictions.

The portfolio manager can invest in money market or capital market instruments or both as specified in the contract with the client. But he is prohibited to invest in **Badla financing, bill discounting and lending operations**. The portfolio managers is to act in a fiduciary capacity. Portfolio management schemes are classified into two kinds: **(1) Discretionary scheme** and **(2) Non-discretionary scheme**. In discretionary schemes the portfolio manager suggests and decides the investment, but in the case of non-discretionary the investor will take all the decisions regarding buying and selling of securities. However, the profit and losses are to the account of the investor. The portfolio managers charge a lower fee in the case of non-discretionary schemes. Generally the discretionary schemes will offer a better yield and have the freedom to the managers. In this scheme, the funds are placed at the disposal of experts. Portfolio management schemes have the way for earning reasonable returns which may be preferred by the lay investors. The portfolio mangers should also make note of insider trading regulations. Insider trading is defined by the SEBI as "unpublished price sensitive information". Insider trading means misuse of confidential information and is considered as **unethical**. The following matters if published are likely to affect the price of the securities of that company in the market:

1. Bonus and Rights Issue.
2. Financial results of the company (half yearly and annual).
3. Amalgamation, mergers and takeovers.

4. Any major expansion plans or execution of new projects.
5. Any changes in policies, plans or operations of the company.
6. Interim and final dividends declaration.
7. Any other information which effects the earnings of the company.

The SEBI's intention is to curb insider trading. For the purpose of prohibiting insider trading, market manipulation, price rigging and other frauds relating to securities. The SEBI has advised **stock exchanges, banks, secondary market operators** to evolve necessary internal code of conduct. The SEBI has issued instructions to various agencies like **mutual funds, merchant bankers, other intermediaries** for maintaining the confidentiality regarding valuable information and ensure that the information should not be used for the purpose of trading in the securities to their personal again. The SEBI has recommended for the introduction of necessary checks and balances through periodic disclosures and reporting required for the securities transaction by the directors and employees of listed companies. The violation of above rules and regulations is an offence and is punishable under the SEBI Act.

## Obligation and Responsibility of Portfolio Manager

The general responsibilities of portfolio manager/merchant banker and obligations are presented below:

1. PMS (Portfolio Management Service) provided by the MB (Merchant Banker) should be in nature of investment consultancy for a fixed fee.
2. The PM (Portfolio Manager) shall give guarantee or assure either directly or indirectly any return to client.
3. Client money is to be kept in a separate account in a scheduled bank.
4. Settlement on termination of contract should be as agreed in the contract.
5. Purchase and sale of securities shall be at prevailing market prices.
6. PM should not deploy the funds in badla financing, bill discounting and lending operation.

7. PM should maintain separate clientwise accounts, it would be audited by the external auditors.
8. PM should enter into contract with the client clearly defining various terms like services to be rendered, investment areas, investment restrictions, disclosure of associated risk, amount and periodical fee to manager, custody of securities, reporting, repayment on maturity or early termination and settlement process, if any.

Penalty of cancellation of registration can be imposed if the PM involved in manipulation or price rigging or cornering activities.

**Code of Conduct of PM/MB**

According to the SEBI instructions *vide* Rule 13, Schedule III, the following conditions and rules must be followed by each and every PM and MB in the market:

1. PM shall conduct his business with high standards, integrity and fairness in all his dealings.
2. The client money should not be diverted to any other purpose.
3. The PM should render at all times high standards of service, exercise due diligence, ensure proper care and exercise independent professional judgement.
4. The portfolio manager should not create any problems to other portfolio managers while competing for any assignment.
5. A portfolio manager should not make any exaggerated statement whether oral or written to the client.
6. While making contract with client the portfolio manager should obtain in written from this client, his interest in various corporate bodies which enables him to obtain unpublished price sensitive information of the body corporate.
7. A portfolio manager should disclose to any clients or press any confidential information about his client which has come to his knowledge.
8. The portfolio manager should take necessary steps in the interest of the client. For registration of the transfer of the clients securities and for claiming and recieving dividends, interest payments and other rights accuring to the client. He

should also take necessary action for conversion of securities and subscription/renunciation of/or rights in accordance with the clients instructions.

9. A portfolio manager should not be a party for the creation of false markets in securities.
10. A portfolio manager should not be a party to those who are involving in price rigging or manipulation of securities.
11. A PM should not be a party in passing of price sensitive information to brokers, member of stock exchanges and any other intermediaries in the capital market or take any other action which is prejudicial to the interest of the investors.
12. No portfolio manager or any of its directors, partners or manager should either on their respective accounts or through their associates or family members, relatives enter into any transaction in securities of companies on the basis of unpublished price sensitive information obtained by them during the course of any professional assignment.
13. A portfolio manager shall endeavour to—

    (a) ensure that the investors are provided with true and adequate information without making any misguiding or exaggerated claims and are made aware of attendant risk before any investment decision taken by them,
    (b) render the best possible advise to the client in regard to the clients needs and the environment and his own professional skills,
    (c) ensure that all professional dealings are effected in a prompt, efficient and cost effective manner.

## Portfolio Management Procedure and Strategy

Keeping abreast of the trend in stock market is an important aspect of playing safe in the investment game. The company in whose shares or bonds the investment is made should be **fundamentally strong**. The fundamentals are related to factors like **production, market, personnel, finance, public relations** etc. The company should well above the average in respect of these factors. Production factor will show the impact on stock market prices. The factor includes the product range, the product line, the raw material supply situation, the technology adopted and related production of capacity utilisation etc. **Marketing** factor deals about market share trend, extent of competition, brand image, brand loyalty, product image, product lifecycle and the product profile should exhibit a growth trend. The image is the most important and where it is good the companies have a competitive edge over others. **Personnel** factor indicates the quality of human resources from top to bottom involved in all aspects of the business where the personnel resources are found to be versatile, resourceful and visionary particularly at the top level, results could be assured. The financial aspects and financial results are the most important factors in portfolio management. The financial standing of a business concern can be analysed in terms of **profitability, liquidity, solvency, turnover, capital structure, leverage, breakeven level** and the like past, present and future trends can be worked out and noticed that past, present and future **EPS** is important. The profitability can be measured in terms of gross profit, operating profit to the capital employed, the sòlvency measured in terms and relations of the current assets and current liabilities, liquid assets and liquid liabilities, debt to equity capital, capital gearing ratio, interest coverage ratio and debt services ratio etc., while designing and construction of portfolio, the following factors should keep in mind by the portfolio manager.

(a) **Risk** associated with certain kind of financial asset.

(b) **Return** from the financial asset expected by the portfolio manager which is based on the ultimate objective of the investor.

(c) **Correlation co-efficient** is a standardised statistical measure of the linear relationship between two securities. Its range is from **–1.0** perfect negative correlation, through **0** no correlation, to **+1.0** perfect positive correlation.

(d) **Covariance** is a statistical measure of the degree to which two securities move together. A positive value means that on average they move on the same direction.

(e) **Beta:** It is an index of systematic risk. Systematic risk is the variability of return on stocks or portfolios associated with changes in return on the market as a whole. It measures the sensitivity of a stock's returns to changes in returns on the market portfolio. The beta of a portfolio is simply a weighed average of the individual stock betas in the portfolio.

(f) **Unsystematic risk:** The variability of returns on stocks or portfolios cannot be explained by the general market movements. It is avoidable through diversification.

(g) **Total firm risk:** The variability in **EPS** is the sum of business plus financial risk.

(h) **Risk averse:** The term applied to an investor who demands a higher expected return, the higher risk.

(i) **Return:** Income received on an investment plus any change in market price, usually expressed as a per cent of the beginning market price of the investment.

(j) **Risk adjusted discount rate (RADR):** A required return (discount rate) that is increased relative to the firm's overall cost of capital for projects or groups showing greater than average risk and decreased for projects or groups showing less than average risk.

Sometimes stock prices are sensitive even unrelated factors may affect the sentiments. The investor has to concede that the activities of unsophisticated investors may also effect the market trend. Therefore, the ability to discern the causes underlying a particular trend is important. The following steps are involved in **portfolio management – procedure and strategy:**

**(1) Client's profile.**
**(2) Client's priorities.**
**(3) Portfolio construction.**
**(4) Risk-Return analysis.**
**(5) Strategy.**
**(6) Types of risk.**
**(7) Efficient portfolio.**

***(1) Client's Profile***

The portfolio manager should think about the client's profile. The construction of portfolio depends upon the client's position. The clients data should be taken into consideration. The information regarding client's income and savings decisions, asset preference profile, objectives of investment, tax brackets and time horizon etc., are to be observed and noted. The financial asset preference profile is based on the degree of risk the investor is willing to take preference for safety, need for regular income, capital appreciation, speculative gains etc.

### *(2) Client's Priorities*

The portfolio may be constructed according to the objectives of the investor. Even among specified objectives, priorities are to be decided and taken into consideration. Generally the investors would like to have capital appreciation, income, liquidity and marketability, safety and security. Tax plan is an integral part, as the investor is equally keen to reduce his tax commitments, to maximise his take home income. Then the portfolio manager should construct the portfolio on tax exempted financial assets.

### *(3) Portfolio Construction*

Portfolio construction refers to the allocation of funds among various financial assets open for the investment. The portfolio manager should fulfil the investor's desire by maximising the yield and minimising the risk and also the other objectives like regular income, appreciation of capital, marketability, liquidity, safety, minimising tax liability, etc., The investment avenues with return-risk profile tax implications, yields and other returns such as convertible options, bonus issues, rights are important and whenever possible, a ready reckoner should be maintained. An investor with growth goal would go in for a portfolio of blue chip equities and high grade convertible bonds. If the investor requires a income goal then the PM should build a portfolio of high dividend payout equities, medium grade bonds etc. Sometimes the PM may combine both the types of financial assets.

### *(4) Risk-Return Analysis*

Risk can be categorised into two kinds: **(a) Systematic risk (b) Unsystematic risk**. Systematic risk is called the market risk. It cannot be reduced. Unsystematic risk is related to company risk. It can be reduced by diversifying the portfolio of scrips upto an optimum level of **15 to 20 shares**. All these factors may influence the portfolio efficiency.

### *(5) Strategy*

The ideal investment strategy may be for a time period of **3 to 5** years.

The investment strategy consists of time bound decisions, asset allocation portfolio review, revision and selection of financial assets etc.

### *(6) Types of Risk*

The risk in the business is measured statistically by the degree of various or standard deviation of returns. The risk involvements is called the liquidity, premium, default premium, financial failure etc., the risks are to be awarded by a higher return. The portfolio manager should always think about the construction of efficient portfolio. The efficient portfolio is a well diversified portfolio which constitutes of many securities with low covariance may reduce the level of risk possible.

### *(7) Efficient Portfolio*

Once the portfolio has been designed and constructed by the portfolio manager, it requires a number of adjustments to fulfil the needs of the investor and performance of the industry and the concerned company. For this purpose the portfolio manager will have to conceptualise various combinations of investments in a basket and designate them as portfolios 1 to M. The risk involved in the business is to be estimated by measuring the standard deviation of different portfolio returns. The expected returns and standard deviation can be worked out for each individual security with a combination of securities that are represented in the Sensex Index or National Index. Portfolio monitoring requires a periodic meeting with the investors and calls for a continuous, ongoing assignment. The changes in market regarding the announcement of the companies results and performance of industry and company should be incorporate in the portfolio. The portfolio manager should always be cautious about the market movement, if any advantageous position is available, it must be incorporated in the portfolio to enhance the expected return by the investor. A well timed based decision up on the assessment of the capital market technical position leads to the construction of an efficient portfolio.

The 1991 liberalisation policies are likely to witness the major developments in the Indian stock markets which would have profound impact on the investment and portfolio strategies of individual investors and institutional investors. The structural reforms in capital market will have the impact on short, medium and long projects on the investors. A variety of factors coupled with the reforms would render the task of security analysis and would make the portfolio management more complex.

## MERCHANT BANKER—MERGERS, AMALGAMATIONS AND TAKEOVERS

Merchant Banker plays an important role in mergers, amalgamations and takeovers. Before analysing the role of the merchant banker, let us watch about the concept of **"Mergers, Amalgamation and Takeovers"**. Merger is the generic term referring to different types of combinations of the firms. A merger is an investment in a future growth opportunity to a long-term basic needs of the concern. Growth of a firm is an essential ingredient to the success and future of business. Growth can be internal or external. Internal growth means a firm acquires specific assets and finances them by the retention of earnings. **External growth** involves the acquisition of **another company**. The **merger can** be defined as "the combination of two or more companies in which only one firm survives as a legal entity".[8] A firm may grow externally through combining other firms. The fastest growth may be reflected in the form of combinations. Three forms of combinations ultimately have the objective of expansions. They are:

**(A) Mergers**
**(B) Amalgamations (Consolidations)**
**(C) Acquisitions (Takeovers)**

### (A) Mergers

The term merger refers to a situation where one company acquires the net assets of another company and the latter is dissolved. The acquired company **pays** the cash or securities to the shareholders of the merged company. The acquired company continues to operate with the resources of the merged company and its own resources. It is thus, synonymous to the term **"absorption"**. The changes in the market conditions trigger merger activity. Merger is a broad term and it denotes the combination of two or more companies. **Economics of scale** may be possible with a merger of two companies. The merger is maximisation of shareholders wealth. The objective of the merger is value creation. The factors that are **"economics of scale, financial advantage, synergy and tax**

**advantage"** are responsible for the value creation. Merger will help in achieving the operating economies. The economies will be reflected in the areas of **Marketing, accounting, purchasing and other operations**. The sales force may be reduced to avoid duplication of effort in a particular territory. The realisation of such different economies are called as **"synergy"**. Synergy can be defined as "Economies realised in a merger where the performance of the combined firm exceeds that of its previously separate parts".[9] The tax factor also motivate a merger. In the case of carry forward of losses, a sick company with cumulative tax losses might have little prospect of setting off such losses against future earnings. By merging with a profit making company the carry forward can be effectively utilised. Sometimes merger will be done by diversification. Such mergers reduce the instability of earnings.

## Types of Mergers

The mergers can be of the following types:

**(1) Horizontal Merger.**
**(2) Vertical Merger.**
**(3) Conglomerate Merger.**

### *(1) Horizontal Merger*

Horizontal merger means combining two companies in the same line of business. Two or more companies which are producing essentially the same products or providing the same services or which are in direct competition with each other join together. For example, two manufacturers of two wheelers or two hotels may merge with each other. This type of merger results in economic of scale, operating economies and elimination of duplication of facilities. This merger reduces competition and number of companies in an industry. It also tends to create the concentration of the economic power. **For example,** ***Tata Finance Ltd.*** with Tata Industrial Finance Ltd., GEC with EEC. The disadvantages are large capital requirements, reduced flexibility and less specialisation.

### *(2) Vertical Merger*

It is the joining of two or more companies in different stages of levels of the same product or services. Two or more companies which are engaged in the production of same goods or services but at different stages of production or services routes join together. For example, **An airlines company** and **a hotel company** units may merge together. Such a merger will be termed as a vertical merger. The objective of the merger ensure the sources of supply. However, this merger may lead to increase in the concentration of economic power and consequential legal and social problems.

### *(3) Conglomerate Merger*

It is the joining of two or more companies whose business is unrelated with each other vertically or horizontally. The organisations involved in the merger may be manufacturing totally different products. The objective of this type of merger is the diversification of activities. For example, a company engaged in manufacturing activities may get itself merged with a company engaged in banking business. The two businesses are totally different and therefore, such merger is called as **"Conglomerate merger"**. However, the mergers involves the following disadvantages:

(a) It eliminates the healthy competition.
(b) It leads to the concentration of the economic power.
(c) It ultimately shows adverse effect on national economy.

### (B) Amalgamations (Consolidations)

It refers to a situation where two or more existing companies are combined into a new company formed for a purpose. The old companies cease to exist and their shareholders are paid by the new company in cash or in its shares or debentures. Consolidation can be defined as "the combination of two or more firms into an entirely new firm. The old firms cease to exist. Though technically different, the terms merger and consolidation tend to be used interchangeably".[10] As a matter of fact, the term amalgamation includes merger also. According to Income Tax Act of 1961, Section 2(1A) the term amalgamation has been defined as "the merger of one or more companies with another company or merge of two or more companies to form one company in such a manner that all the assets and liabilities of the amalgamating companies before the amalgamation becomes the assets and liabilities of the amalgamated company by virtue of the amalgamation". This definition is applicable only to the companies and not to the other forms of business organisations. The shareholders holding less than **9/10th** in value of the shares in the amalgamating company or companies become shareholders of the amalgamated company by virtue of the amalgamation. Amalgamation is an arrangement whereby the assets of the two companies are vested in one which has as its shareholders all or substantially all the shareholders of the two companies. Amalgamations are governed by the Sections **390 to 394** and **396** of the Companies Act requiring the consent of shareholders and creditors. The Income Tax Act requires the fulfilment of the conditions for a valid amalgamation. A consolidation often begins with negotiations between the management of the two companies. A company may be acquired either by the purchase of its assets or its common stock. The buying company may purchase all or a portion of the assets of another company and pay them by cash or securities.

**(C) Acquisitions (Takeovers)**

The term acquisition or takeover refers to acquiring the effective working control by one company over another. The control may be acquired either through purchase of majority of shares of the other company. The acquiring company is termed as the **"Holding company"** and the company in which the shares are acquired is termed as the **"Subsidiary company"**. According to the rules for acquiring the effective control over another company it is not **necessary** to own **51 per cent** of the share capital of another company. For a widely held company ownership of **20 per cent** or as little as **10 per cent** of the share capital outstanding may constitute the effective working control. The takeover can be defined as "the acquisition of another company that may take the form of a friendly or unfriendly merger".[11]

According to the MRTP Act of 1969, takeover has been defined as "in relation to undertaking owned by a body corporate, the acquisition of not less than **25 per cent** of the voting power in relation to such body corporate; in relation to any undertaking includes, the acquisition or control of management thereof; whether by the acquisition of ownership of the undertaking or under any mortgage, lease or licence or under any agreement or other arrangement".[12]

Takeover is usually an unfriendly acquisition by the tender offer. Takeover is regulated by the Clauses **40A and 40B** of the listing agreement of stock exchange and guidelines of the SEBI with sanctions to be obtained from the SEBI in respect of offer document and from the Government under Sections **108A and 372** of the Companies Act. Holding company may be used as a devise to acquire controlling interest. The functions of the two companies are integrated to realise economies of scale.

In takeover the shares may be purchased either for cash or in exchange of shares of the acquiring company. The acquired company continues to exist. Its operational control passes into the hands of a new management. Empirical evidence is mixed in regard to the effect of merger on the shareholders of the acquiring company. Shareholders do not benefit from mergers. Mergers have no impact on the share price. Market reactions to mergers in the USA show that the shareholders gained benefits.

## Financial Implications in Mergers, Amalgamations and Acquisitions

If there is a combination of two or more companies there will be some financial consideration for the amalgamation or the acquired company. The financial consideration will be in the form of exchange of shares. In this combination the two firm's value are evaluated and a particular exchange ratio is determined. The determination of the exchange ratio is based on the value of the shares of both the merged companies. The objective of merger is to maximise the owners in the long run. A successful merger will enhance the EPS and reflects the market price of the shares of the amalgamated company. The following are the three different approaches for determining the exchange ratio:

**(1) Earning Approach.**
**(2) Market Value Approach.**
**(3) Book Value Approach.**

### *(1) Earning Approach*

Before acquisition, the acquiring firm must observe the effect on merger for the earnings of the surviving company. The effect on earnings may depend upon two factors, i.e. **PE ratio and total earnings of both the firms**. The impact on differential in price earnings ratio and the relative size of two firms as measured by the total earnings. The higher the **PE** ratio of the acquiring company than the company being acquired and the larger the earnings of the acquired company the acquiring company the greater the increase in **EPS** of the acquiring company. The company with lower earnings ratio will suffer earning dilution. Merger decision may be based on not only on the EPS basis but also on future growth in earnings.

***(2) Market Value Approach***

According to this approach, the acquisition will be made on the bargaining process on the ratio of exchange of market price per share. The market price will reflect the earnings potential of the company, as well as **dividend, risks, capital structure, asset values and other factors**. The ratio of exchange of market price is as follows:

$$\frac{\text{Market price per share of acquiring company} \times \text{Number of shares offered}}{\text{Market price per share of acquired company}}$$

The acquiring company has to offer a high price, more than market price of the share price. The premium which will pay more than the market price is called as **"Goodwill"**. The Goodwill can be defined as "the intangible assets of the acquired firm arising from the acquiring from paying more for them than their book value. Goodwill must be amortised".[13] However, the goodwill must be written off against future earnings. While acquiring the shares, an estimate must be made of the life of goodwill and it should be written off over the period which cannot exceed **40** years. The goodwill charges are not deductible for the tax purpose. When the two firms combined with each other their balance sheets are combined together. Therefore, the write ups of assets/**goodwill** are not reflected in the combination and there are no charges against future income. But the reported earnings are higher with the pooling of interests treatment than they are with the purchase treatment, many acquiring companies prefer it. Pooling of interest has been defined "A method of accounting treatment for a merger based on the net book value of the acquired company's assets. The balance sheets of the two companies are simply combined".[14] The choice of accounting treatment is governed by the circumstances of the merger and the rules of the accounting profession. Under the following conditions a merger can be treated as a pooling of interests:

1. The combined companies must be autonomous for at least two years prior to the pooling of interest. Both the companies must be owned **less than 10 per cent** of the stock of each other.
2. The combination process may be completed either in a single transaction or within one year in accordance with the plan.
3. The acquiring company can issue only common stock.
4. The surviving company must not reacquire common stock issued in connection with the combination.

### *(3) Book Value Approach*

In this approach the exchange ratio is determined according to the book value of the concerned companies shares. The book value of the share is generally determined by the following formula:

$$\text{Book value of share} = \frac{\text{Shareholder's funds}}{\text{Number of equity shares}}$$

*or*

$$\text{Book value of share} = \frac{\text{Networth}}{\text{Number of equity shares}}$$

$$\therefore \text{ The exchange ratio} = \frac{\text{Book value per share of acquired company}}{\text{Book value per share of acquiring company}}$$

The book value approach has some limitations, because the book value can easily be manipulated by the accounting practices by the company. The book value does not reflect the earnings capacity of the company. Therefore, the book value approach is generally not followed as a basis for valuation in most mergers.

There is at present on mergers and acquisitions wave sweeping the country. The benefits of taking over a company such as **ready**

**made manufacturing facilities, well entrenched brands, captive market shares, no entry delays and an entrenched distribution network** all have favoured the swelling tide in favour of takeover moves. With the recent SEBI guidelines, the legal hurdles to the mergers game has been dismantled.

## Takeover and Merchant Bankers

The acquirer must appoint a merchant banker, holding a certificate of registration as per the SEBI regulation. The merchant banker may also be required to advise the management about commercial soundness of the merger and takeover plans. The merchant banker should be given an opinion regarding legal formalities and render assistance in preparation offer document and circular to be sent to shareholder's of both companies. The merchant banker should ensure compliance of all legal formalities which may involve **listing obligations of stock exchanges, SEBI norms, Companies Act, 1956, the Securities Contract Regulation Act, 1956** etc. All of these legal procedures should be complied and he also required to guide all concerned in the context of **SEBI (Insider Trading)** Regulations, 1992. The insider trading regulations cover amalgamations, mergers and takeovers and therefore the misuse of **"unpublished price sensitive information"** should be ensured in order to get the investor's confidence.

## SEBI Regulations on Acquisitions and Takeovers

SEBI has notified the regulations pertaining to the substantial acquisition of shares and takeovers *vide* Notification No. **50800(E) dated 4.11.94** to provide greater transparency in deals through a system of **disclosure** of information. The regulations deals with **three types of** takeovers **negotiated takeovers, open market takeovers and bailout takeover**. SEBI is empowered to make investigations into the acquisition or sale of securities to ascertain whether any person has violated the provisions of the regulations. According to SEBI Act, the Section 24 indicates that any malpractice will be treated as criminal case and initiative will be taken for prosecution. Under **negotiated takeover** an acquirer shall not acquire an aggregate shareholdings of more than **10 per cent** of the shares of the company unless he makes a public announcement of his intention to acquire at least another **20 per cent** shares in the company at a price not lower than the negotiated acquisition price or the average market price in the preceding

**6 months** whichever is higher. **In case of** an open market takeover, an acquirer shall not acquire an aggregate shareholding of more than **10 per cent** of the company's shares unless he makes a public announcement of his intention to acquire at least another **20 per cent** shares in the company at a price not lower than the highest open market price or the average of the stock exchange in the preceding **6 months** whichever is higher. Such offers would provide an option to existing shareholders to sell their shares, if they do not have confidence in the likely new management of the company. In case of **bailout takeovers** there is no need of making public announcement as above situations. Under this provision it is applicable, when a promoter is taking over a financially weak company in pursuance of a rehabilitation scheme approved by a **public financial institution or scheduled bank**. Further, the provisions would not apply to sick industrial companies which will be governed by the Sick Industrial Companies Act. Prior to the issue of recent **SEBI** regulations, certain other guidelines as detailed below were also issued and these sought to protect the interest of companies and/or shareholders.

(a) Guidelines on preferential allotment of shares/warrants/ debentures issued by **SEBI** vide press note dated 4.8.1994. The guidelines governed the issue of shares or warrants/fully convertible debentures or other financial instruments on a preferential basis to a select group of persons u/s 81(1A) of the Companies Act, 1956. These were issued in the wake of practice allowed by companies making preferential allotments of shares at a price unrelated to the prevailing market price of such shares/instruments. These guidelines regulated the price and also provided for a lock in period of **5 years**.

(b) Revised guidelines by the Financial Institutions on **27th July, 1994** for preferential issue of equity shares, other securities and warrants to promoters, under which promoters were not allowed to allot naked warrants to themselves and providing lock in period for shares acquired by the promoters on exercising warrants to be for a minimum period of **10 years**; the list of preferential allottees were also to be approved by the financial institutions apart from complying with the provisions of **Section 81(1A)** of the Companies Act and the applicable regulations of SEBI for preferential allotment of shares.

(c) With effect from **30th April, 1994**, the preferential allotment to **FIIs** was revised to **15 per cent** of the equity of the company subject to the condition that the aggregate **FII/NRI/OCB** investment should not exceed **24 per cent** of the equity of the company.

(d) The following legal provisions are applicable for these issues which should be complied with the situations:

- **Sec. 81(1A)** of the Companies Act, 1956 regarding further issue of capital.
- **Secs. 108–111** of the Companies Act, 1956 regarding transfer of shares and debentures.
- **Sec. 250** of the Companies Act, 1956 imposition of restrictions upon shares and debentures and prohibition of transfer of shares or debentures in certain issues.
- **Sec. 372** of the Companies Act, 1956 purchase by Company of shares etc., of other companies.
- **Sec. 22A** of the SCRA 1956 providing for free transferability and registration of transfers of listed securities of companies.
- **Secs. 23 and 24** of the **MRTP Act** relating to merger, amalgamation and takeovers.
- **Secs. 19, 26 and 29** of FERA imposing restrictions on certain securities and place of business.
- In the case of listed companies, the provisions of amendment to clauses **40A** and **40B** of Stock Exchange Listing Agreement laying down the rules in case of takeover bids; however, the sick units under the purview of **BIFR** and conversion of loans with sick companies into equity or quasi-equity by the financial institutions are **exempted** from the aforesaid listing agreement provisions.

## Approval Procedure for Merger

Amalgamation or merger requires approval of the court. Sections **390 to 396A** of the Companies Act, 1956 deal with provisions relating to merger/amalgamation. The court has wider powers in amalgamation or mergers process. The court has to sanction the amalgamation or merger scheme and can provide for all matters incidental to it. The scheme attracts so many laws which are applicable from time to time like **Income Tax Act, 1961, the Gift Tax Act, 1958, MRTP Act, 1969, FERA 1973**. In all these Acts require the approval of the authorities prescribed in the Acts applicable to a specific scheme is required. The scheme requires many series of steps as follows:

1. Formulation of scheme.
2. Verification of Articles of Association/**Memorandum of Association.**
3. Intimation to SEBI and stock exchange and notification.
4. Director's approval of the proposed scheme.
5. Shareholders resolution.
6. Application to the court.
7. Notice issued by court.
8. Petition for confirmation of amalgamation.
9. Order of the court.

At the formulation stage, the acquirer company shall make an offer document phase, then the company will appoint the **Merchant Banker** to finalise the details of proposed scheme or merger in accordance with the guidelines framed by **SEBI**. SEBI has statutory powers to enforce the guidelines. The next step is to verify the objective clause of articles of association of amalgamated company permits or not. If it permits, the process may be continued, if it does not, then suitable alteration must be made in the manner according to the Companies Act. The third step is on acquisition of **5 per cent** of voting capital the company should inform to **SEBI** and stock exchange. On acquisition of **10 per cent** of voting capital an offer should be made to other shareholders to acquire **20 per cent** of the floating stock. As soon as the offer of merger is made, the concerned stock exchange should be notified and the fact of the offer will be announced in the media. The next process involved in the schemes is that the directors of both the companies must approve to this effect. Bulk transfer of shares cannot be refused by the board. If the board has reservations it has to call an extraordinary general meeting of shareholders within 6 weeks of an application for substantial transfer of shares and seek their decision. After the approval of the board of director's the scheme will be placed before the shareholders at a meting to get their approval. Then it will be filed in the court for consideration. The court on receipt of the application convenes a meeting with the creditors and members of the company. The following legal process is involved in the finalisation of merger and amalgamation:

- The chairman of such a meeting/any other person directed by the court is required to send individual notices to the creditors and members.
- The notice should be accompanied by a copy of the proposed scheme of merger is sent by post under the certificate of posting.
- The notice should sent at least 21 days before the meeting.
- A notice of the meeting is advertised in English newspaper and another in regional language as the judge may direct.
- The chairman of the meeting should submit the notices, meeting files advertisement, an affidavit, at least 7 days before the meeting to the court.
- The proposed merge scheme is taken as approved if it is passed by a majority in number, representing **3/4th** in value of the members/creditors presented and voting in person or proxy.
- The chairman of the meeting should report the results of the meeting to the court within 7 days of the meeting or within that time as directed by the court.
- If the scheme is passed by the creditors and members, the company within 7 days has to present a petition of the filing of the report, this is only for the confirmation of the scheme and for the appropriate orders and directions as per Section 394 of the Companies Act.
- On receipt of the petition from the company, the court will fix a date for hearing the petition.
- The notice for hearing the petition must be advertised in the media before 10 days of hearing the petition.
- The notice must be served to Central Government, the Registrar, the CLR and the Official Liquidator.
- For passing an order, the court has to receive a report from the Registrar of Companies and the Official Liquidator, that the affairs of the company have been made to the interest of its members.

- The court has to receive the reports from the **CLB** (for altering A/A), the Central Government **(MRTP Act)**, the RBI **(FERA)**, the SEBI.
- The court on hearing from all the parties, satisfies itself, then passes the order sanctioning the scheme.
- Every company in relation to which the order is passed should file a certified copy of the Order with the Registrar of Companies, within **10 days** of the order.

## Summary

Finance is the provision of the money. The increasing and diverse needs of growing corporate sector encourages the steady growth of financial services market. After implementation of 1991 reforms, the financial sector has grown tremendously. The industrial liberalisation and deregulations have provided a new era for the capital market. India's liberalisation policy have gained importance in the context of global business scene. India ranked **7th** on the confidence index of foreign investors who perceived India as having the highest potential for improving its attractiveness over the next **10 years**. India ranked quite high in terms of being an attractive destination. A large market, skilled labour force, competitive wages, easy availability of finance and political stability made India an attractive destination for **FDI**, but was constrained somewhat by slow peace of government reforms, poor infrastructure, cultural barriers and bureaucracy. We cannot increase our business unless we are more helpful to the international investors.

The number of intermediaries operating the capital market have grown exponentially. The financial industry is growing at a very fast rate. **Mumbai** is the leading financial services in industry in India. It has become more expensive on par with **Tokyo** in terms of costs. The **NSE** is the first financial services centre in India which has completely computerised its working. Financial services are an important component of the financial system. Financial services caters to the needs of financial institutions, financial markets and instruments. The development of financial services will depend upon the investment climate of the country. Finance is concerned with the procurement of funds. The financial system can create wonders in economic development of a country. The financial system is a weapon to counter the **poverty**. The financial development is the part of economic development. Development creates and nourishes the economy. India has witnessed all the types of financial innovation. A large number of new financial instruments have to be introduced to fulfil the needs of dynamic corporate sector. The innovative instruments can leverage the corporate financial muscle. The financial development of a nation can be observed through the powerful indicators like **Finance ratio, Financial interrelation ratio, new issue ratio, intermediation ratio.** Finance ratio is a macro analysis of an economy. Financial interrelation ratio reveals about the relationship between financial assets to physical assets. **New issue ratio** relates to new issues offered by newly promoted companies to the public at **first time**. The new issues are also called as **public issue**. Public issues are consisting with initial issues, further issues, new money issues, no new money issues—bonus issues, exchange issues. Intermediation ratio is the relationship between primary and secondary issues. The financial integration of the nation have been influenced by many factors. Financial system can be classified into **four categories**: Financial institutions, financial markets, financial instruments, financial services. The Indian financial system at present can be categorised as **"Financial Intermediaries, Development Institutions, Regulatory Organisations, Financial Instruments and Financial Services"**. Financial institutions are just like a modern business concern. They are involved in mobilisation of funds and channelises the savings towards productive way. The institutions have to play an important role for the development of a nation. **IFCI, IDBI, ICICI** institutions are fully involved in providing of finance to the industries. With the emerging needs of industry, the financial institutions had reoriented their policies and assistance structure with much sharper customer focus by developing and introducing a variety of products and services in the post reform period. Financial markets help to finance the investment needs of business concerns. Financial markets provide the better facilities for buying and selling of all financial claims and services. Financial markets can be categorised as **Primary and secondary markets**. The primary market is called as **Direct market**. Secondary market can be called as **Indirect markets**. The secondary markets do not contribute directly to supply of the additional capital but it will provide liquidity to the primary market. Financial market can also be classified as **Money market and Capital market**. Money market is a market for short-term funds. It is dominated by **the Central Bank**. The main borrowers of short-term funds in the market are **Commercial Banks, Central**

**Government, State Government, Corporate Sector, Local Bodies.** The annual policy statement of the Government regarding money market indicated that the overall performance is quite encouraging. **Capital market** deals in long-term funds. Capital market deals in shares, stocks, debentures and bonds. Securities dealt in capital market are long-term securities. Capital markets consists of a number of individuals and institutions. The development banks in the Indian financial system have witnessed vast changes in the planning periods. The main components of the capital market in India are: **New issue market** and **Stock market**. The NIM is called as primary market. It deals with the capital formation of tangible assets in the country. For marketing shares generally in the form of **Public issue** and **Rights issue**. During the current fiscal year **2001–2002** the leading pack of mobilisers was **Reliance Petroleum** Rs.**1,061 crores**, followed by GE Capital Rs.520 crores, TISCO Rs.350 crores and Tata Power Rs.300 crores. The major mobilisers are **REC Rs. 869 crores**, Powergrid Corporation Rs.761 crores, SAIL Rs.**700 crores**, NTPC Rs.575 crores and BPCL Rs.445 crores respectively. The NIM has three functions **Originations, Underwriting and Distribution**. The methods of NIM which are placed in the market are **public issue, offer for sale, and private placement**. The issue of shares will be made indirectly through an issuing house. Private placement refers to direct sale of newly issued securities by the issuer to a small number of investors. Public issue process involves two activities: **Pre-issue** and **Post-issue**. The stock exchanges are the secondary markets. The NIM and stock exchanges are interlinked and work in conjunction with each other. The secondary markets consisting of **regional stock exchanges, BSE, NSE, OTC etc**. The securities which are listed for trading in BSE are grouped into **Group A, Group B, permitted securities, cleared securities, non-cleared securities**. The securities which are grouped in A is allowed for **forward trading**. The securities which are traded on cash basis are called as **Group B shares**. The securities which are listed with some of the recognised stock exchanges are called **permitted securities**. The securities which are traded for fortnightly settlement. The securities which are traded between brokers is called as **Non-cleared securities**. The equity shares of 30 companies from both specified and non-specified groups are called as blue chip scrips. They will be settled on market activity basis. The major financial instruments available in the markets are **equity shares, preference shares, debentures and bonds**. Equity shares represent the ownership position

0in a company. Preference shares have many features of both ordinary shares and debentures. A debenture is an acknowledgement of debt. Debentures may be classified as naked debentures, redeemable or irredeemable, first and second, bearer or registered convertible and non-convertible. The new financial instruments introduced in the markets are **ZCB , warrants, SP notes, stock investment instrument, deep discount bonds, option bonds**. Zero coupon bond has no fixed coupon rate. A share warrant is an option to the investor to buy a specified number of equity shares at a specified period of time. Secured premium notes can be converted into equity after **3 to 5 years**. Stock invest is a new financial instrument and had to be used by the investors while applying for shares in primary market. Deep discount bonds are sold to the investors at discount, while issuing them option bond will be converted into equity at the option of the investor as per the conditions stated in the prospectus. The Government has announced various amendments to the Companies Act 1956. Through the Companies Act **2000**, covering corporate governance, issuance of shares with **differential** rights, postal ballot shares with differential votings right are particularly useful to technocrats who have low **seed capital** but high value intangible assets. Till date, no major company has announced its intention of issuing such shares. **Financial services** are an important components of the Indian financial system. Financial services fulfils the needs of financial institutions, financial markets and instruments. The smooth functioning of a financial system will depend upon the quality of financial services rendered by its providers. Financial services constitutes a wide range of activities like **Merchant banking, mutual funds, venture capital, credit rating, lease financing, underwriting, registrars, SEBI, NSE, OTC, BSE and depository system**. Funds are tapped from the capital market to finance various **Mega** industrial projects. Merchant banking services are related to **issue house** activities. Merchant banks undertake the task of new issue management, **project counselling, preparation of feasibility reports, selection of underwriters/brokers** and bankers to issue. The objective of merchant banking is to carry on the business of financing industrial enterprises. Every merchant banker should comply with the professional code of conduct. The Merchant Bankers must observe high standards of integrity and fairness in their dealings. After the termination of managing agency system in India, there is a strong need of legal and financial services to the corporate sector. The SBI became the first Commercial Bank in India to launch its Merchant

Banking division in 1972. Consequent to the recommendations of Banking Commission in 1972 that **Indian Banks** were allowed to enter into this segment. Later other commercial banks and financial institutions like **Punjab Bank, Indian Overseas Bank, Bank of Baroda, Syndicate Bank, Chartered Bank, LIC, GIC, UTI** started merchant banking divisions. Merchant banking regulations operated in India by **SEBI, MOF, Companies Act, 1956, SCRA 1956, Stock Exchange** listing etc. After the abolition of **CCI** the place was occupied by a legal organ called as **"SEBI"**. SEBI has issued guidelines for the issue of capital by the companies. The guidelines covers the requirement of first issue by a new company or first issue of new company set up by existing company, first issue by existing private companies and public issues by existing listed companies. **SEBI** is the most powerful organisation to control and lead the both primary and secondary market. SEBI has announced new guidelines for disclosures by companies leading to investor protection *vide* **GL/IP No. 1/SEBI/ PMD, 92–93, dated 11.6.1992**. The Ministry of Finance, Department of Economic Affairs has issued guidelines for registration of a merchant banker. According to the guidelines any person or body proposing to engage in the business of MB would need authorisation from SEBI. The authorised activities covered **issue management, corporate advisory services, underwriting, portfolio management and managers consultants or advisers to the issue**. The SEBI categorised merchant bankers into four kinds. SEBI can inspect the books of accounts, records, documents in the interest of investors. Penalty points will be imposed by SEBI to the merchant bankers in default of the duties. Project counselling is one of the basic activities of merchant banking. Project preparation involves project identification, project selection, feasibility study, appraisal project, social cost benefit analysis. Portfolio management is another activity involved by the Merchant Bankers. Portfolio management involves a proper money management. Portfolio management reduces risk and increase returns. Merchant bankers also render the services to the corporate sector in **Mergers, Acquisition and Takeovers**. The merchant bankers play an important role in takeover process.

## Questions

1. Explain the structure of Indian financial system.
2. What are the basic components of financial system? Discuss

about the recent trends in the Indian financial system?

3. What is financial market? What are the main components?
4. Discuss the role of financial institutions of a component of financial system.
5. Explain the role of **IFCI** in industrialisation of our nation.
6. Critically evaluate the functioning of **IDBI**?
7. What are the objectives and functions of **ICICI**?
8. Define money market. Write about the structure of the Indian money market and explain the recent developments in money market.
9. What is capital market? Discuss its objectives and importance.
10. What are the functions of capital market? Describe the component of capital market.
11. Explain the process involved in announcement of **Rights issue**.
12. What do you mean by **NIM**? Explain the functions of NIM?
13. Explain the mechanics of floating new issues?
14. Explain about the steps involved in public issue when a company approaches the capital market.
15. Define stock exchange. What are the functions of stock exchange?
16. What are the major financial instruments available in the market? Distinguish its features.
17. Explain the new financial instruments which are available at present in the capital market?
18. What is merchant banking? Explain the role of merchant banker in public issues?
19. What are the main objects of merchant banking? Explain obligations and responsibilities under the Act?
20. What are the guidelines issued by SEBI with regard to merchant banker?
21. What do you mean by penalty system? Explain the process in default of a merchant banker.
22. Explain the role of merchant banker in project preparation, appraisal and counselling.
23. Explains the pre-issue and post-issue activities involved by merchant banker in connection with public issues.
24. Define Merger, Acquisition and Takeover and explain the role of Merchant Banker in these aspects.

## REFERENCES

1. Pramod Kumar Agrawal, *Merchant Banking in India, Financial Services*, Delta Publishing House, Delhi 1997, p. 45.
2. *Ibid.*
3. A. Sudhakar, *Merchant Banking—Capital Markets, Financial Services*, Delta Publishing House, Delhi, 1997, p. 65.
4. P.K. Agrawal, *Merchant Banking in India, Financial Services*, Delta Publishing House, Delhi, 1997, p. 45.
5. *Ibid.*
6. *Economic Times*, Dt. 17.11.2003, p. 7.
7. SEBI (PM) Rules, 1993 Published in the Gazette of India Extraordinary Part II, Section 3, Subsection (i) dated 7.1.1993.
8. Van Horne, *Financial Management*, Prentice-Hall of India, 1997, p. 633.
9. *Ibid.*, p. 632.
10. Van Horne, *Fundamentals of Financial Management*, 1997, Prentice-Hall of India, p. 645.
11. *Ibid.*, p. 641.
12. S.N. Maheswari, *Principles and Practice of Financial Management*, S. Chand & Sons, p. E99.
13. Van Horne, *Fundamentals of Financial Management*, Prentice-Hall of India, 1997, p. 647.
14. *Ibid.*

# UNIT II

- Mutual Funds in India
- Venture Capital
- Leasing
- Credit Rating

# 1

# MUTUAL FUNDS IN INDIA

**Introduction**

The investment preferences of households have changed dramatically. In India, the household sector accounts for over **80 per cent** of the **GDP** which plays a significant change in their investment preferences. The investors investment preference may shown an impact on the economy. In the emerging economic environment of competitive markets. The investment pattern has been changed all over the financial landscape as a result of financial liberalisation. The household sector is the main provider of savings in the economy. Hence, the direction into which such savings are channeled determines the direction of growth of the financial sector. The financial development occurred because of the technical invention and through the mode of popular joint stock company. **The Joint Stock** form made the large scale industry possible by collecting large amounts of capital. Subsequent financial innovations have carried the process further the risk reduction and liquidity. The capital is generated out of savings leading to investment which is a part of the financial system. The organised financial comprises of **money market, capital market, new issue market, stock market** etc., led by RBI, DFHI, banks, financial institutions, mutual funds, merchant banks and all other intermediaries regulated by the **SEBI and the RBI**. There are specialised investment institutions which help those savers who do not understand the functioning of the capital market and remain away from the capital market because of the complicated procedure involved in analysing and interpreting the investment opportunities. These institutions which acts as investment, conduits, pool the savings of many individual investors and combine them into a fairly large and well diversified portfolio investments. All these features are available in mutual fund. Mutual funds are an investment vehicle for the investors to enjoy the expert management skills of professional and maximise the return with an accepted risk. There are the trusts for the public savers to pool their savings. In the entire globe, the trend has been for the individual investor shifting from the direct investment in equities to the mutual fund route.

## Definition

Mutual fund can be defined as "is a form of collective investment that is useful in spreading risks and optimising returns".[1] A mutual fund offers safety, it provides the services to the investors and offers a wide variety of securities within the reach of the most modern investors. Mutual funds are fast developing into magic wands for the retail investor. Mutual funds has been defined "Mutual fund is a non-depository, non-banking financial intermediary which acts as an important vehicle for bringing wealth holders and deficit units together indirectly."[2] —Pierce, James L.

According to **Weston J. Fred and Brigham**: "Mutual fund is a corporation which accepts money from the investors and user the same way to buy stocks, long-term bonds, short-term debt instruments issues by the issuers."[3]

The SEBI has defined mutual funds as Section 2(m) "Mutual funds means a found established in the form of a trust by a sponsor to raise money by the trustees through the sale of units to the public under one or more schemes for investing in securities in accordance with these regulations."[4]

## Concept

A mutual fund is an investment company or a trust that pools the resources of thousands of unit holders and invests on behalf of them in security markets. The mutual funds have been functioning as an agent to mobilise the resources from various investors the **Unit Trusts, Investment Trusts, Mutual Funds,** banks, investment companies, real estate, investment trusts, trust companies, personal trust funds etc., all there names contain some common characteristics. The Investment Trust is an investment holding company and very popular in **U.K.** This investment trust will be incorporated under the Companies Act. It has the same type of capital structure like the Industrial Company. The **Unit Trust** is established and is obliged to buy back units wherever an investor wants to sell them. But investment trust cannot buy back its shares and the investor has to sell his shares on the stock market. Investment trust can raise long-term debt and can retain a part of its income. The Unit Trust cannot do either of there things. The unit trust always maintains a direct relation between the value of the unit and the value of the fund. **Mutual savings** banks are popular in **USA.** They offer professional fund management entrusted to them by pension plans of business and institutions. Mutual funds are very popular in **USA, Canada** and **India.** Mutual fund is a trust at law. A mutual fund performs the basic function of buying and selling securities on behalf of its unit holders. Mutual fund provides opportunity to the investors to secure a better rate of return on their savings by utilising the benefit of professional management of portfolios. Mutual funds helps the small investors to obtain **high return-low risk** combinations from their scientifically managed portfolios. Mutual funds are convenient and efficient investment vehicles. They can take a portfolio of securities including the blue-chip companies. The mutual fund cult has spread much faster and over a wider area than the equity cult within a very short period. **The Society for Capital Market Research and Development** conducted a study regarding the investor's preference towards the mutual funds, the study finally concluded that there are **2/3rd** of middle class households in India. The study further reveals that the shift towards mutual funds has resulted in the declining popularity of certain other financial assets like LIC policies, bank fixed deposits, National Savings Certificates and Company Deposits. The Unit Trust is basically a pure intermediary which involves the capital appreciation. The small investors cannot directly invest in the instruments such as **certificates of Deposit, Commercial Paper and Treasury Bills** because they require heavy amount of investment. Mutual funds provide continuous supervision, analysis, investment consultancy, judicious investment decision, expert, experienced, professional management at low costs. The investors have to pay expenses like administrative fee, management expenses and transaction costs forgetting these services.

**Advantages**

The advantages of the mutual fund relative to the stock market are as follows:

1. **Low transaction costs.**
2. **Benefits of high talent and expertise.**

3. **Diversification.**
4. **Tax deductions.**
5. **Low risk and better returns.**
6. **Investor's protection.**

*1. Low Transaction Costs*

The Mutual Fund is a specialised institution which acts as an investment intermediary and channelises the savings of a large number of people. The mutual funds are able to get the economies of large scale because pooling of the large amount at their disposal for investment in the market. This reduces the costs in the form of brokerage fee, commission etc. Thus a small investor gets the benefits of economies.

*2. Benefits of High Talent and Expertise*

The investors in India have no knowledge about the stock market operations. They are unable to know the position of market situation. They do not know about the economy, per capita income, demand, consumption, companies operations, efficiency, their earning capability, profit booking etc. The stock market is a highly volatile and even sometimes the experts may fell in confusion. The entire stock market depends upon many factors. The common investor has no observation about all these movements. The stock market is a **heaven** for those with high expertise, in-depth knowledge, scientific analysis, thorough understanding about the industry, company and pulse of the customer, dynamism, courage, mental stability, financial muscle etc. The Indian investors are highly influenced by the **broker's decision**. They do not take any investment decisions regarding a particular scrip. They simply handover the cheque to the broker on their recommendations. They do not know **when to buy, when to sell, what price, at what price the** scrip should be sold etc. The buying price of a particular scrip in the stock market is the most important factor in determining the profits. The sale price/disposal of a financial asset in the market is also a very important element in designing and constructing a portfolio. The portfolio management is a highly specialised skilful activity. It requires a continuous monitoring and evolution. A small investor cannot be an expert in the portfolio management. If the investor invests in mutual funds, he gets all the benefits of the above said factors. All these activities are performed by the mutual funds. They will appoint a high talented, specially trained experts in the portfolio management, equity analysts, fund managers etc. To achieve the targeted return assured by the fund to the investors. The funds can be professionally employed through the mutual fund ensuring good returns. The fund managers have extensive research facilities at their disposal. They are able to analyse the performance and prospectus of various companies and take good decisions in making the investments fruit full.

### *3. Diversification*

In mutual funds by a large number of investors small savings can be pooled. The investor can also buy shares of one or two companies. Therefore, the mutual funds can be used to buy shares of many different companies. Diversification reduces the risk of a portfolio. Diversification requires an additional amount of investment. In diversification, sometimes more risk may be evolved. Thus the portfolios construction, expansion and diversification is very easy in the mutual funds.

### *4. Tax Deductions*

The Income Tax Act of 1961 provides some tax deductions and exemptions to the mutual funds. The Mutual Funds can be designed to suit the tax payers needs. A large number of mutual funds have come up with the schemes ensuring tax benefits to the subscribers. Generally the tax payers contribute in these funds. According to these schemes, the investors are required to keep the money in the fund for a certain period called **"lock up"** which at present is **3 years**. These funds distribute the profits among the unit holders. The units will be repurchased by the fund at **current NAV**. The pooled amount is used to acquire shares and debt instruments. The **NAV** of the Units varies with values of the financial assets held by the mutual fund.

### *5. Low Risk and Better Returns*

A mutual fund will be operated by the Efficient Fund Managers. The Fund Managers have basic and extra ordinary skills in their areas. They are well versed with the market movement. They know how to move in a highly volatile market. They are able to reduce the risk factor and increase high return to the unit fund. A small investor on the other hand, may not be in a position to minimise such risks. Therefore, the mutual funds can reduce risk and maximise return to the holders.

### *6. Investor's Protection*

Mutual funds in India are regulated by the **SEBI**. The SEBI regulations of 1996 provide better protection to the investors. The mutual funds activities are also monitored by the **SEBI** (Mutual Funds) regulations. The SEBI regulations import a great degree of flexibility and facilitate competition.

## MUTUAL FUNDS IN INDIA

The first Mutual Fund in India was started in 1964. The Unit Trust of India was set up under a special U.T.I. Act in 1963. All Mutual Funds have to be registered with the **SEBI**. The UTI is involved in mobilising small savings and channelising them into productive avenues. The Government of India permitted the Commercial Banks to launch mutual funds in India by Amending the Banking Regulation Act in **1987**. A number of Commercial Banks have started mutual funds to mop up savings in the society. The **SBI** has launched a mutual fund called **The SBI Mutual Fund** in 1987. The first scheme launched was known as **"Magnum Regular Income Scheme"** and another scheme was **"Magnum Monthly Income Scheme"**. It had also introduced **"Magnum Tax Savings Scheme"** with a tax benefit under Section **80 cc** and **"Magnum Regular Income"** with **12 per cent** minimum assured rate of return per annum. The **Canara Bank** formed the Canbank Mutual Fund with the objective of housing investment expertise for the benefit of investors. It had also started two schemes **Canstock** and **Canshare** in 1987. The object of these schemes was a long-term capital appreciation by adopting strategies. The objective was to secure a regular income and growth. The **Indian Bank** had also established a mutual fund called the **Indian Bank Mutual Fund** in 1990. It floated schemes such as **"Swarna Pushpa, Ind Ratna, Ind 88A; Ind Jyothi, Swarna Jyothi"**. Ind 88A was a tax saving growth scheme. The Punjab National Bank set up a mutual fund called The PNB Mutual Fund in 1990. It had floated a PNB Regular Income plus scheme. It had buy back facility after one year. The Bank of India introduced rising monthly income scheme schedule with an objective of doubling the amount after 5 years period. The LIC Mutual Fund was set up in 1989 by the LIC. It had introduced open schemes such as **"Dhanaraksha 1989, Dhanavriddhi, Dhanasahayog and Dhanavidya, Dhanashree, Dhan 80 CCB, Dhan Tax Saver, Dhanasamridhi etc.** The GIC Mutual Fund was set up in 1990. It had launched schemes like **GIC SAFE, GIC Rise**. The Government of India allowed the private sector corporates to join the mutual fund sector on 14.2.1992. Afterwards a number of private sector companies had approached the **SEBI** for permission to set up private mutual fund. The **Alliance Capital** had set up the Alliance Equity **(D)(G)**. The Birla Mutual Fund had introduced **Birla Advantage, Birla MNC (D)(G). The ING** Mutual Fund had set up **IG portfolio (D)(G)**, ING Income Portfolio. **The Templeton** Mutual Fund had introduced **Templeton India Income**, Templeton **MIP**. The Tata Mutual Fund had set up **Tata Income (D/G)**. The Sun Mutual Fund had set up **Sun F and C money.** Kotak Mahindra Mutual Fund had set up **K-30, K-Tech, K Gilt, K Liquid**. Chola Mutual Fund had introduced **Cholagilt Saving, Cholagilt** Investments. The Pioneer Mutual Fund had set up **Pioneer ITI Blue-chip (D)(G), Pioneer ITI Prima Plus (D)**, Pioneer **(IT Index)**. The DSP Mutual Fund had set up **DSPML balanced (D)(G).** The JM Mutual Fund had introduced JM India Bond **(D)(G).** JM Income Bond **(D)(G)**, Reliance Mutual Fund introduced **"Reliance Income (DH)(DY)**, Sundaram Mutual Fund has set up **Sundaram Bond Savers (D)(G)** Schemes, Zurich Mutual Fund introduced **Zurich India** Prudence D, Zurich India Prudence-G scheme Prudential, ICICI Mutual Fund has set up **Prudential ICICI MP, Prudential ICICI MP(G), Prudential Liquid Plan**. The IDBI Mutual Fund introduced **IDBI Principal, IDBI Income Scheme,** Grindlays Bank has set up Grindlays SSI, Grindlays SSI DQ Schemes. HDFC introduced HDFC Income (D) (G), HDFC (Liquid) schemes etc. All of these mutual funds has entered the market with the liberalisation of rules and regulations by the Government. In November 1995, the Government has permitted private sector mutual funds to set up **Money Market Mutual Fund. The SEBI** mutual fund regulations of 1996 provides registration, constitution, management and schemes of mutual funds in India. Money market mutual fund emerged in the **U.S.** in 1972 and is now coming up in many countries. MMF are established for the purpose to purchase large pools of short-term financial instruments. In abroad the average maturity period of investments is about **40 days**. The investors will use the **MMMF** with the prior approval of the RBI and SEBI. Since 1.4.1996 the MMMF is available to only corporates and mutual funds. The maturity period of MMMF has also been reduced. Bank of Madurai, Amro Bank, UTI, IDBIMF, were given clearance to set up **MMMFs**. The first MMMF established by the **Kothari Pioneer** in 1997 did not succeed. The UTI started its MMMF on 23.4.1997 and collected about **Rs. 30 crores**. The scheme is offered to resident individuals, HUFs, trusts, societies and corporates. The MMMF is involved in buying and selling of money market instruments only. They will construct the portfolio with treasury bills. Government securities, call money, commercial paper, commercial bills, certificates of deposits etc.

The period **1996–98** was the worst in the history of the mutual funds. But several AMCs used the opportunity to restructure their portfolios and were ready for the 1999 boom in equities. In the year 1999–2000, the value of assets under the management swelled to Rs. 107946 crores[5] then the equity melt down happened. At present there are **34** mutual fund houses managing 614 schemes and Rs. **94,571 crores** in asset. All of them will not survive, but performance and transparency will prove in the long run.

| *Year* | *Corpurs fund (AMC) (Rs. in crores)* |
|---|---|
| 1964–69 | 65 |
| 1969–74 | 172 |
| 1974–79 | 402 |
| 1979–84 | 1261 |
| 1986–87 | 4563 |
| 1987–88 | 6739 |
| 1989–90 | 13456 |
| 1990–91 | 19111 |
| 1991–92 | 23060 |
| 1992–93 | 37480 |
| 1993–94 | 46988 |
| 1994–95 | 61301 |
| 1995–96 | 75050 |
| 1996–97 | 80539 |
| 1997–98 | 68984 |
| 1998–99 | 68472 |
| 1999–2000 | 107946 |
| 2000–2001 | 90587 |
| 2001– | 94571 |

Private sector funds recorded higher fresh sales as compared from **May 2000–July 2001**. Redemptions were also higher than in

June. It resulted in a net inflow of **Rs. 2430 crores**. Private sector funds utilised this period to increase their product offering. **Tarus Mutual Fund** launched a debt and gilt fund. Bank sponsored funds a net inflow of **Rs. 61 crores**. Institutions backed funds also saw a sharp full in net inflows. Mutual funds can be classified as **"by category" or based on functioning of schemes**. The relevant data for the period May 2000 to July 2001[6] for mutual funds (category) was presented in below.

**Mutual Funds by Category**

(a) UTI mutual fund.
(b) Private sector mutual funds. **(excluding UTI, banks Sponsored and institutions).**
(c) Bank sponsored mutual funds. **(BOB, BOI, Canbank, PNB, SBI).**
(d) Institutions backed mutual funds.

*(Rs. in crores)*

| *Particulars* | *May 2000* | *June 2000* | *July 2000* | *May 2001* | *Jun 2001* | *July 2001* |
|---|---|---|---|---|---|---|
| **(a) UTI Mutual Fund** | | | | | | |
| Sales | 1224 | 1410 | 774 | 376 | 1858 | 237 |
| Redemption | 1100 | 557 | 134 | 2302 | 2265 | 87 |
| Net sales | 124 | 853 | 640 | –1926 | –407 | –630 |
| **(b) Private Sector Mutual Funds (excluding UTI, banks sponsored, institutions backed)** | | | | | | |
| Sales | 5015 | 3931 | 4208 | 6815 | 9886 | 1125 |
| Redemption | 4034 | 3528 | 3580 | 4030 | 6787 | 880 |
| Net sales | 981 | 403 | 628 | 2785 | 3089 | 2430 |
| **(c) Banks Sponsored Mutual Funds** | | | | | | |
| Sales | 95 | 101 | 373 | 389 | 835 | 332 |
| Redemption | 161 | 92 | 90 | 136 | 187 | 271 |
| Net Sales | –66 | 9 | 283 | 253 | 648 | 61 |
| **(d) Institutions backed mutual funds** | | | | | | |
| (a) Sales | 95 | 105 | 66 | 357 | 561 | 531 |
| (b) Redemption | 216 | 91 | 117 | 245 | 225 | 397 |
| (c) Net sales | –121 | 14 | –51 | 112 | 336 | 134 |
| **(e) All mutual funds (including UTI)** | | | | | | |
| (a) Sales | 6429 | 5547 | 5421 | 7937 | 13140 | 1235 |
| (b) Redemption | 5511 | 4268 | 3921 | 6713 | 9464 | 1037 |
| (c) Net sales | 918 | 1279 | 1500 | 1224 | 3676 | 198 |

## Mutual Funds by Schemes

The mutual funds can also be classified according to the schemes—

(a) Growth schemes.
(b) Income funds.
(c) Balanced funds.
(d) Liquid and money market funds.
(e) Gilt funds.
(f) Equity Linked savings schemes.

(*Rs. in crores*)

| *Particulars* | *May 2000* | *June 2000* | *July 2000* | *May 2001* | *June 2001* | *July 2001* |
|---|---|---|---|---|---|---|
| **(a) Growth Schemes** | | | | | | |
| (i) Sales | 1018 | 741 | 1325 | 87 | 112 | 59 |
| (ii) Redemption | 482 | 481 | 960 | 190 | 80 | 135 |
| (iii) Net Sales | 536 | 260 | 365 | **–103** | 32 | **–76** |
| **(b) Income Funds** | | | | | | |
| (i) Sales | 2043 | 2068 | 1423 | 2909 | 6297 | 3759 |
| (ii) Redemption | 1963 | 1400 | 1003 | 1074 | 496 | 368 |
| (iii) Net Sales | 80 | 688 | 420 | 1835 | 4801 | 78 |
| **(c) Balanced Funds** | | | | | | |
| (i) Sales | 698 | 517 | 499 | 64 | 43 | 9 |
| (ii) Redemption | 285 | 290 | 98 | 1725 | 2105 | 115 |
| (iii) Net Sales | 413 | 227 | 401 | **–1661** | **–2062** | –10 |
| **(d) Liquid and Money Market Funds** | | | | | | |
| (i) Sales | 2147 | 1847 | 1850 | 4348 | 5991 | 8074 |
| (ii) Redemption | 2247 | 1573 | 1387 | 3378 | 5550 | 6038 |
| (iii) Net Sales | **–100** | 274 | 463 | 970 | 491 | 2036 |
| **(e) Gilt funds** | | | | | | |
| (i) Sales | 481 | 363 | 318 | 526 | 695 | 489 |
| (ii) Redemption | 522 | 513 | 466 | 152 | 258 | 390 |
| (iii) Net Sales | **–41** | **–150** | **–148** | 374 | 437 | 99 |
| **(f) Equity Linked Savings Schemes** | | | | | | |
| (i) Sales | 42 | 11 | 6 | 3 | 2 | 3 |
| (ii) Redemption | 12 | 11 | 7 | 194 | 25 | 11 |
| (iii) Net Sales | 30 | 0 | **–1** | **–191** | **–23** | **–8** |

## Funds Flow by Category

All mutual funds taken together recorded a net inflow of Rs. **1989 crores,** while fresh sales fell to **Rs. 12359 crores** redemption increased to **Rs. 10,370 crores.**

The Unit Trust of India saw another month of net outflow. The redemption also fell subsequently to **Rs. 873 crores**. There was a net outgo of **Rs. 636 crores. The private sector mutual funds** recorded higher fresh sales as compared to June. Redemptions were also higher than in June and this resulted in a net inflow of Rs. **2430 crores.** Private sector funds utilised this period to increase their product offerings. **Tarus Mutual Fund** launched a debt and gilt fund. Banks sponsored funds saw a net inflow of **Rs. 61 crores**. Institution backed funds also saw a sharp fall in net inflows. The amount in this case was **Rs. 134 crores.**

## Funds Flow by Type

The mutual funds can be classified as **Growth schemes income funds, balanced funds, liquid funds, gilt funds and equity linked savings fund**. All of these schemes are to be discussed in preceding pages. Debt funds saw fresh sales fall by **40 per cent**. Redemptions on the other hand were higher by **46 per cent**. The net result was that net sales fell to double digit levels. The fresh sales were dismally low, reaching single digit levels. In US–64 had fully closed the exit route in July. There were no redemptions from this fund. Liquid and money market funds were the winners during the period **May 2000–July 2001**. The fresh sales increased by **Rs. 2000 crores** over June. Redemptions increased by a little over **Rs. 500 crores** on the whole, this type of fund received a net inflow of **Rs. 2036 crores**. This is a record for the analysis period the strong inflows into liquid and money market funds could also be an indicator of investor's perception that the rally in bond markets is coming to an end. Gilt funds saw fresh sales of **Rs. 489 crores**. The Redemptions stood at **Rs. 390 crores** and the net result was an inflow of **Rs. 99 crores**. Most funds were moving into medium tenure paper and gilt funds can also expect returns to slow down, tax saving funds continued to remain due. Inflows were minimal and there was a net flow of **Rs. 8 crores**.

## Investment Trust

The Investment Trust is a financial institution. It collects a small amount of investible funds from a large number of investors. The trust pools the amount of **savings and invests them in stock market** by constructing a suitable portfolio. A small investor may not have large funds to purchase the securities in many companies. It is fully authorised to deploy the funds as it likes. It is very usual in the stock market, the prices are highly volatile, then there is a danger of loss due to fluctuations. Diversification is the process of risk reduction. The portfolio risk can be reduced by diversification. The investment trust collects the funds from the public by selling the shares of trusts. The trust deploys the funds in the market as it desires. The selection of securities are decided by the Trustees. The trust distributes the income among its members in the form of dividend. The trust will make investments from the consolidated fund created from the subscriptions of various members of the trust. The first investment trust was established by the Royal family of **Belgium**. Scottish American investment trust was established in 1873. In USA the investment trust was established during **1925–1929**. The investment trusts were established due to the substantial expansion of finance area and speculative spirit in that period.

## Industrial Investment Trust in India

The first Industrial Investment Trust was established in **1933** by M/s Premchand Roychand in **Mumbai.** After the establishment of this fund the number of other trusts were formed, such as Investment and Finance Company, Kolkata, General Investment and Trust Company, Kolkata, Tata Investment Trust, Mumbai. Most of the Investment Trusts are established by the industrial groups. These trusts try to make managerial control of the companies whose securities they are going to purchase. The trusts are organised as private companies. The investment trusts are used as a tool to control more and more unity by owning and controlling the shares. The investment trusts are categorised into two types: (a) **Management Investment Trust and (b) Fixed Investment Trusts**. The management investment trusts have full freedom over the funds which they collect the **fixed investment trust** is confined to a fixed list of securities. The management of the fund is not empowered to change the portfolio except in unforeseen situation. The fixed investment trust is better than the trust. Fixed Investment Trust is also known as **"Unit Trust".** The objective of the fund is to protect the investors from managerial manipulations. These trusts suffer from a number of drawbacks. There is no opportunity for diversification of investments. All of these funds are kept in few companies scrips only. The expenses for running the trust is very high. At present there is no existence of fixed investment trusts. These trusts are almost obsolete in these days. The Trusts in India can play an important role in the economy. The trusts should be regulated properly for better management.

**MF Organisation**

The mutual funds in India are regulated by **SEBI**. The SEBI has the authority to register both public and private sector's mutual fund. The Mutual Funds set up by **LIC and GIC** are regulated by the Investment Division, Ministry of Finance. All Intermediaries and players in the capital market are brought under the **SEBI** authorisation and regulation. If the mutual funds are started by the Commercial Banks, they should get the RBI permission also. The SEBI has taken over the responsibility of regulating, inspecting and controlling the activities of all the mutual funds except **MMF**. The mutual funds in India have five key parties involved are:

(a) The Sponsors.
(b) The Board of Trustees.
(c) The Asset Management Company.
(d) The Custodian.
(e) The Chit holders.

**The Sponsors** are the important party in establishing a mutual fund. Every mutual fund is formed by a Sponsor. According to the **SEBI** guidelines, Sponsors can be defined as "Sponsor means any-body corporate who acting alone or in combination with another body corporate, establishes, a mutual fund after completing formalities there-of". The Sponsors could be a registered company or a scheduled bank or all India or state level financial institution. The Sponsors must have a good track record, a positive networth and consistent record of profitability and a good financial standing during the last 5 years. **The Board of Trustees** is another party which plays an import role in the formation and management of the mutual fund. According to the guidelines issued by SEBI. It has defined as **"Trustee** is a person who holds the property of mutual fund in trust for the benefit of the Unit holders". The trustee eligibility is determined on the basis of eligibility and suitability will be examined from the composition of the board of directors. The SEBI will examine and approve the

**"Memorandum of Association"** of the trustee company. SEBI has the authority to examine and approve the draft of the trust deed. **Asset Management Company** means a company formed and registered under the Companies Act, 1956 and was approved by the Board Under Regulation **20**. The approval of the **AMC** was based on good track record, professional experience, net worth etc. **The Custodian** means a person carrying on the activity of safe keeping of the securities or participating in any clearing system on behalf of the clients to effect deliveries of the securities. The Custodian is an independent organisation delinked with the sponsors, the trustees and AMC. The SEBI would approve the custodian when granting the authorisation for setting up mutual fund as a part of the composite authorisation. The custodian is responsible for the coordination with the brokers, the actual transfer and storage of stocks and handling the property of the trust. The custodian is answerable to the **AMC**. The AMC conducts the research and based on it, manages the fund or portfolio the **AMC** is responsible for floating, managing, redeeming the schemes etc. It receives the fee for the services rendered by it. The guidelines of SEBI should be implemented by the trust board. The AMC has to report on a quarterly basis its activities, investments and operations through AMC. It should report to the trustees and to the SEBI separately in respect to their operations and results. The MF should prepare an annual report and submit to the investors of the fund and to the SEBI. The board of trustees is governed by the **Deed** and the policy in respect of each scheme should be laid down forgetting the approval from SEBI. The management of MF is a top decision making function rests with the board of trustees as per the latest guidelines of the SEBI. The brain of the mutual fund is the trustees and it is governed by a trust deed. The experts and specialists will be on the board of trustees. The AMC will look after the routine functions of fund. All MFs should be managed by the experts, high talented skill fund managers and professionals. The experts in this area are **Finance Professionals**. The AMC will manage the funds by making investment decisions. The fund to be invested in major categories which are regular income investments, growth oriented and money market instruments. The MF should concentrate before taking decisions about the fundamental analysis of the economy, industry and company. The fund can invest towards research and appoint experts, investment analysts, portfolio managers and a host of other specialists.

## Organisation Structure of MF

The Mutual Funds in India are regulated by **SEBI**. The SEBI has the authority to register both public and private sectors MF. The MF set up should be done according to the norms of the SEBI. The SEBI has provided **"Four-tier"** system for managing the affairs of the fund. The MFs are designed to suit the needs and preferences of the investors. The choice of the fund will be determined by the investor himself. The investor should frame his investment objectives regarding whether he expects a regular income or capital appreciation or high earnings or low risk etc. Then the objective will help to choose the best fund among different alternatives. The MFs will adopt different strategies to meet the investor's objectives. In India the MFs can be classified into **Five categories**. The classification of funds can be based on various factors:

**(1) based on ownership status,**
**(2) based on schemes of operation,**
**(3) based on portfolio objectives,**
**(4) based on location,**
**(5) others.**

*(1) Ownership Status*

The MFs in India can be established by either public sector or private sector. The public sector mutual funds has been functioning since 1963–64. The **UTI** has been functioning since 1964. In **1987** the second public sector MF was launched by **SBI**. SBI MF was the first among all the Commercial Banks. The Government has given the permission to PSBs for entering the MF sector to curb the monopoly of the UTI, CanBank, BOI, PNB, GIC, LIC mutual funds have joined operations in the business at a short span of time. Private sector corporates have been permitted by the government on February 14, 1992. Since then a number of private companies have approached SEBI for the approval of mutual fund. The SEBI has provided the guidelines for registrations, constitution and management of the mutual funds. They can be classified the basis of their operations. The MFs can be divided into **3 categories,** i.e., open ended, close ended and open-cum-close ended schemes.

*(2) Scheme of Operation*

1. *Open Ended Schemes*: A mutual fund which offers units for sale without specifying any duration for redemption. An investor can subscribe it at anytime the scheme will be opened throughout the year and investor can redeem his holding at anytime. The enter and exit of the scheme is very easy. The MF repurchases the units at periodically announced rates. The repurchase prices are based upon the **Net Asset Value.** The NAV of the scheme will depend upon the stock market prices. The open ended funds provide high liquidity to the investors. The sale price of units are also announced by the fund from time to time for subscription. For example, **US–64, ULIP** of UTI **Dhanavridhi, Dhanaraksha**; Magnum Balance Fund, Magnum Insta Cash Fund of the SBI.
2. *Close Ended Scheme*: A mutual fund which offers units for sale to the public only at the time of initial issue. The scheme is also offered to the investors at a specified period of time. After closing the time, the investor cannot subscribe to the scheme. A close ended scheme of MF, the period of maturity will be announced in advance. The investor can buy or sell the units of the scheme in secondary market. The price in the secondary market is determined on the basis of demand and supply. The close ended scheme can be easily managed by the fund managers. The fund manager can evolve long-term investment strategies depending upon the life of the scheme. **Mastergain-92, Grand Master of UTI, Dhanasamridhi, Dhanasree of LIC MF**, Can Double, Canstar, Cangrowth of Canara Bank, Ind Jyothi, Swarna Jyothi of Indian Bank are some of the examples of close ended schemes.
3. *Open-cum-Close Ended Scheme*: The scheme is offered by the MF is kept open for a specific interval and it runs the scheme as a close end scheme. The scheme is a combination of both open and close ended funds. This kind of schemes are permitted by SEBI in recent years only. In offer document the scheme rules and regulations will be announced. The units of the scheme may be listed in stock exchange. These units may be traded in the stock exchange regularly.

*(3) Portfolio Objective*

MFs can be classified on the basis of portfolio. The schemes are classified as follows:

(a) Balanced funds.
(b) Equity funds.
(c) Bond funds.
(d) Growth funds.
(e) Tax benefit funds.
(f) Specialised funds.
(g) MMMF.
(h) Leveraged fund.

**Balanced Fund means** the amount collected from this scheme is deployed in the market by purchasing equity and fixed income bearing securities. The combination of both the financial assets will be fixed MF. Some MFs spent some amount on the equity preference and debentures. Therefore, the situation may ensure certain amount of interest and dividend. Some MFs maintain a ratio between equity and preference share in **50:50**. The balanced fund ensures both the capital appreciation and regular return in the form of dividend and interest. The investors have advantage both in return and capital appreciation. It is also known as **Income and growth funds**. Examples for balanced fund schemes are: Cantriple of Commercial Bank—Canara Bank, Dhanaraksha 1989 of LIC, ULIP 1971, Unit Scheme 95(D), HDFC Balanced Fund, Tata Balanced Fund, Prudential ICICI Balanced Fund, Alliance 1995 etc.

**Equity Fund** Scheme units will be offered to the investors by the MFs. This scheme proceeds will deploy for purchase of shares. According to this scheme objectives, the funds will be spent for the acquisition of the blue-chip company shares. The fund undertakes risks associated with the investment in equity of the reputed companies. The scheme is also further classified as Income fund and growth funds. Examples for equity fund scheme are: **UGC 10000, UTI Pharma and health care, UTI Service sector**, UTI software, K-Tech Alliance Millinium, Magnam IT, Prudential ICICIFMCG etc.

**Bond funds** proceeds will be spent for acquiring bonds. The bonds ensure fixed and regular income. It ensures regular income to the investors. The bonds are available in the market at lower prices in some situations. Therefore, the net income on these bonds will go higher. Some companies offer non-convertible bonds including shares. Any investor who subscribes for the share will have to take up bonds also. **Example: UTI bond, UTI Mahila Unit Scheme, UTI NRI, Tata Income, Alliance Income fund 5U EAD, IDBI Principal, K-bond deposit, K-bond wholesale, Sundaram bond saver, Templeton Income Fund,** IDBI Principal Deposit, Chola triple fund, Alliance Income Fund, Prudential ICICI, Pioneer ITI Income builder, LIC bond-G, Sun FEC Money value bond.

**Growth funds** objective is to provide capital appreciation for the value of investments. The scheme concentrates on value appreciation of securities. The risk involved in this scheme is very high. The scheme will not give preference for regularity of income. Growth fund is also called as long haul investments. The scheme is a long-term based fund.

**Perhaps Tax Schemes** are designed to meet the tax payers needs. The investor who contributes the scheme is entitled to get the tax concession in Income Tax. The lock in period is **3 years**. The scheme distributes the profits among the chit holders. A large number of MFs have come up with many schemes. These schemes provide benefits like income, capital appreciation and tax concessions. The proceeds of these shares would be deployed to acquire equity and debentures. Usually all the tax payers will contribute for these funds. **For example: Magnum tax gain, Pioneer ITI tax shield.**

**Specialised fund/sector** fund invests in a particular type of securities. The scheme objective is to make investments in a particular area or industry. If any investor wants to invest in a particular security he will prefer a fund which deals in such securities. Example: **Birla MNC, UTI pharma, K-Tech, Magnum IT, UTI Software**, Pioneer ITI.

**Money Market Mutual funds** is a scheme which has been set up with the objective of investing in money market instruments. The fund involves in buying of instruments from the money market like Treasury bills, call money, commercial paper, commercial bill, certificate of deposits, Government securities. The maturity period will be less than 1 year for all these instruments. The MMMF constitutes the only portfolio of **MMMF** Example, UTIMMMF, IDBI principal, Money market fund.

The aim of **Leveraged portfolio** is to maximise the capital appreciation to the investors. In this type of scheme, the financial assets will be purchased by borrowing the fund at a cost. The cost of interest and the gain from holding shares is the profit of leveraged fund. Leverage funds involves in speculative activities to earn more and more profit.

*(4) Based on Location*

Mutual funds may be categorised on the basis of location where they mobilise funds as **Domestic fund and offshore funds**. Domestic funds mobilise savings from public within the country. Offshore mutual funds are the mobilise funds from abroad for investment in India.

Other types of mutual funds such as **Loan funds and Non-loan funds**. These funds are not very popular in the country.

## Objectives of a Mutual Fund

The objectives of the mutual fund are presented below:

(a) To provide a better opportunity to low income group investors.
(b) To provide a better expertise, talent, skilful, scientific approach towards stock market activities.
(c) To manage small investors portfolios that provides regular income growth safety liquidity and diversification.

## Importance of Mutual Fund

The mutual tunds mobilises a large amount of savings from the small investor's savings. The fund attracts resources mainly from middle class families. Their savings potential is very high in India. The pooling of the large amount of resources, operating and the ability to commit the large sums of money for long periods. The mutual funds will enjoy ample resources at their disposal by mobilising from various investors. The mutual funds gain a lot of significance from the investors. It has been proved in the case of **Master gain–92** scheme of the Unit Trust. The scheme has mobilised **Rs. 4500 crores** from the market and created history in the market. But the Unit Trust failed to manage that scheme. In India, the investors do not have any basic knowledge about the portfolio management. Therefore, the investors are investing in mutual funds. They are important due to the following reasons:

(a) The mutual funds have been functioning like financial intermediaries in mobilising the savings of the public.

(b) The mutual fund invest in a variety of securities where there is a demand.

(c) Mutual Funds appoint experts, to get the benefits of speculation activities.

(d) Mutual Funds leads to a general prosperity to the investors.

(e) The mutual funds will handle the investors fund with utmost care and try to fulfil the needs of unit holders.

(f) The fund managers will apply all the stock market techniques to enhance the fund of the NAV.

(g) The mutual funds will attract foreign investments by offering **offshore funds.**

(h) The per capita income of rural and urban middle class people are increasing and their savings are channelised towards mutual fund sector. The fund diverts the resources towards industrial under under taking units by acquiring the financial assets of various companies.

(i) The mutual funds have tremendous scope for growth in the country.

(j) The liberalisation and industrial policies gave a scope for the growth of the country. The Government should prepare an agenda about the utilising of the vast resources available with the mutual funds. There are certain areas to be developed such as **water resources, roads, agricultural, etc.** The Government of India can divert the resources towards construction of dams, water sheds, and creation of irrigational facilities, development of agriculture sector, development of cooperative service sector, benefits will passes to the farmers. The mutual funds may also enter into power sector to improve the production of power by providing large amounts of savings. In future the mutual funds may be like **UTI (Agri), UTI (Power), UTI (Roads), UTI (Housing)** etc.

## Regulatory Framework

The Mutual Funds in India are governed by the UTI Act of 1963, Indian Trust Act of 1882, Companies Act of 1956, Securities Act of

1956, and the other tax laws. The overall monitoring and supervising are done by the **Ministry of Finance**, the RBI and the SEBI. The RBI had issued guidelines for the bank sponsored mutual funds in 1987. Afterwards it also received the guidelines from the Ministry of Finance in 1991. The SEBI also issued guidelines in 1991 and a comprehensive set of regulations in 1993. After the successful growth of the mutual fund industry, it became necessary that all mutual funds in India should follow uniform norms for the valuation of investments and accounting practices. This leads to better comparison for the valuation of fund performance. The SEBI issued new mutual fund regulations in December 1996 based on the recommendations of the mutual fund **2000 report**. All mutual funds in India including the UTI is regulated by the SEBI. The **offshore** funds are governed by the Ministry of Finance, the Government of India, and the RBI. **MMMFs** are governed by the RBI. The SEBI regulations aim at facilitating competition, transparency, investor's protection etc.

## Registration of Mutual Fund

According to the SEBI guidelines the following process is involved for the registration of a mutual fund.

(1) Every mutual fund should be registered with the SEBI under regulation 9.

(2) An application for registration should be made in **Form A** by the fund sponsor and shall be addressed to the SEBI.

(3) Notwithstanding anything contained in sub-regulation **(1)** any application made by a sponsor prior coming into force of these regulations containing such particulars are mentioned in the form shall be treated as an application made in pursuance of the sub-regulation **(1)** and should be dealt with accordingly provided that the fee payable in respect of the application made under sub-regulation shall be the same as is referred to in the sub-regulation of regulation **4** every application for registration under the regulation **3** shall be accompanied with an application fee as specified in **Schedule II** by means of a cheque or bank draft in favour of the SEBI payable at **Mumbai**.

***Regulation 5***

The SEBI regulation indicates that subject to the provisions that under sub-regulation **(3)** of regulation 3, any application which is not complete in all aspects and does not confirm to the particulars specified in the form, shall be rejected provided that, before rejecting any such application, the applicant shall be given an opportunity to remove within the time specified, such objections as may be indicated by the board.

***Regulation 6(1)***

The regulation 6 deals with the furnishing information clarification and personal representation. The SEBI may require the sponsor to furnish such further information or clarification as may be considered necessary for the grant of registration. The sponsor should appear before the SEBI for personal representation.

***Regulation 7***

This regulation indicates the consideration of application. The board on the basis of information furnished in the application and after obtaining such further information as may be required should decide on the application for registration not more than 3 months from the date of receipt.

***Regulation 8***

This regulation deals with the conditions for the registration of a mutual fund. For the purpose of granting the registration the board should take into account all the matters which are relevant to efficient and orderly conduct of the affairs of a mutual fund and in particular the following:

(a) The sponsor must possess a sound track record and experience in the relevant field of financial services for a minimum period of **5 years**. He should possess professional competence, financial soundness and general reputation of fairness and integrity in his business transactions **"sound track record"** means networth, dividend paying capacity and the profitability of the sponsor.

(b) Mutual Fund is in the form of a trust and the trust deed has been approved by the board.

(c) An Asset Management Company who holds an approval of the board has been appointed to manage the affairs of the mutual fund and operations the schemes of such funds.

(d) The sponsor contributes atleast **40 per cent** to the net worth of the **AMC**.

(e) The sponsor or any of its director or the **principal officer** is to be employed by the fund. The management looks after the affairs of its business at any time when it is convicted for any offence involving moral **turpitude** or guilty of any economic offence.

***Regulation 9***

It deals with the grant of registration. The board on being satisfied that the application is complete in all respects and all particulars sought have been furnished and that the mutual fund is eligible for registration may register with fund subject to:

(a) Receipt of registration fee indicated in **Schedule II** of the Act in a manner specified by the Board.

(b) The terms and conditions specified in regulation **12**.

Where a mutual fund is found to be eligible for grant of registration, the board shall grant a certificate in **Form B**.

***Regulation 10***

(a) According to the regulation every mutual fund registered under these regulations, should pay annual fee for every financial year, from the year following the year of registration as specified in **Schedule II.**

(b) The annual fee should be remitted to the board in the manner specified in regulation **(1)** of regulation 4 before the beginning of each financial year.

***Regulation 11***

(1) The regulation deals with the failure of the payment of fee by the mutual fund. If any fund fails to remit the annual fee as

provided in sub-regulation **(2)** of regulation **10**. The board may prohibit the mutual fund from launching any new schemes till the fee has been remitted.

(2) Without prejudice to these regulations, the board may, on being satisfied with the reasons for the delay and subject to such conditions as it may deem fit, permit the sponsor to pay the annual fee at anytime within 2 months from the commencement of the financial year to which such fee relates.

### *Regulation 12*

According to the regulation every fund which is granted registration is subject to fulfil the following terms and conditions:

(a) Complying with the provisions of these regulations.

(b) Informing forth with the board, as soon as it comes to the knowledge of the sponsor or the trustees that any information or particulars previously submitted to the board were either misleading or false in any material respect.

(c) Informing forth with the board of any material change in the information or particulars previously furnished, which have a bearing on the registration granted by it.

(d) The sponsor, the **AMC** trustees and the custodian should comply with the provisions of the regulations.

(e) Allowing examination of the directors, officers and other employees in the course of inspection and extending full co-operation on its behalf.

(f) Agreeing to produce books of accounts, documents and such other information as sought for by the board in the course of inspection.

### *Regulation 13*

It deals with the situation procedure where registration is not granted by the SEBI. The following process involved while denying registration:

(i) Where an application does not satisfy the requirements mentioned in regulation **8**. The board shall reject the application.

(ii) The information about the rejection of application will be communicated to the applicant in writing, stating therein the grounds on which the application has been rejected.

(iii) The applicant, who is aggrieved by the decision of the board under sub-regulation (**2**) may within a period of **30** days from the date of receipt of such intimation can apply to the board for reconsideration of its decision.

(iv) The board shall as soon as possible, in the light of the submissions made in the application and whenever necessary, after giving an opportunity for personal hearing, convey its decision in writing to the applicant.

***Regulation 14***

According to this regulation, it deals with the constitution and management of the mutual fund. The mutual fund shall be constituted in the form of a trust in accordance with the provisions of the Indian Trust Act, 1882 (of 1882).

***Regulation 15***

The regulation informs about the appointment procedure of the trust the process for the appointment of the trust is as follows:

(1) A company shall be appointed as a trustee to manage the mutual fund provided that the board may regarding the special circumstances can permit the appointment of a board of trustees, as trustees of a mutual fund.

(2) The appointment of the trustees should be subjected *inter alia* to the following conditions, namely—

(a) the trustees are persons who have experience in financial services and are not found guilty of any economy offence;

(b) the names of the trustees should be forwarded to the board;

(c) any change in the appointment of the trustees should be subjected to the approval of the board;

(d) no trustee should retire unless another person is appointed in the place of retiring trustee;

(e) no person should be a trustee or a director of a trustee company in more than one mutual fund;

(f) atleast 50 per cent of the trustees should be independent members and no such trustee should be an affiliate or subsidiary of the sponsor;

(g) an AMC, any of its directors, officers or employees should not act as a trustee of any mutual fund.

***Regulation 16***

(1) The regulation deals with the process of registration of a deed under the Registration Act. The investment of the trust shall be in the form of a deed duly registered under the provisions of the Indian Registration Act of **1908** executed by the sponsor in favour of the trustees named in such instruments and shall contain such clauses as mentioned in **Schedule III** and such clauses which are necessary for safeguarding the interests of the unit holder.

(2) No trust deed shall contain a clause which has the effect of—

(a) Limiting or extinguishing the obligations and liabilities of the trust in relation to any mutual fund or the unit holders; or

(b) Indemnifying of the trustees or the Asset Management Company for the loss of damage caused to the unit holders by their acts of negligence or acts of commissions or omissions.

(c) The trust deed should be made available for the inspection by any member from the public at the registered office or the principal place of business of the mutual fund and if so desired, a copy of the same should be made available to any person on payment of a nominal fee as decided by the mutual fund.

***Regulation 17***

(1) The section deals with the obligations of the trustees as per the law. The trustees shall have a right to obtain from the **AMC** such information as relevant to the management of the

affairs concerning the operations of the trust and may also call for periodical reports from the **AMC**.

(2) Where the trustees have reason to believe that the conduct of the business of the mutual fund is not in conformity with these regulations. They should forthwith take such remedial steps as necessary to rectify the situation and keep the board informed of the same with full particulars.

(3) The trustees should take the steps to execute all the documents, which are necessary to secure the acquisitions disposals. It also assures the transactions that are entered into by the AMC are properly made in accordance with these regulations.

(4) The trustees should be responsible for ensuring that the AMC complies with these regulations.

(5) The trustee should enter into an agreement with the AMC which contains the clauses as specified in the **Schedule IV** and such other clauses which are necessary for the purpose of investment of the funds of the mutual fund then such agreement will be approved by the board.

(6) The trustees should be accountable for and be the custodian of the property of the respective schemes and should hold the same in trust for the benefit of the unit holders in accordance with these regulations and the instruments of the trust.

(7) The trustees should take steps to ensure that the transactions concerning mutual funds are in accordance with the provisions of the trust deed and **Schedule III** of these regulation.

(8) The trustees should be responsible for the calculation of any income due to be paid to the fund and also of any income received in the mutual fund for the holders of the units of any scheme in accordance with these regulations and the trust deed.

(9) The trustees should receive a quarterly report from the **AMC** and submit a **6 monthly** report to the board on the activities of the fund.

(10) The trustees should call for the meeting of the unit holders

(a) whenever required to do so by the board in the interest of,

(b) on a requisition of **3/4**th of the unit holders of any scheme or of all the schemes together, or

(c) when the majority of the trustees decide to wind up or prematurely redeem the units or modify any scheme.

### *Regulation 18*

The regulation deals with the process of setting up of the **AMC**. According to the rules and regulations the following steps required for the approval of the **AMC**:

(i) The application for the approval of the **AMC** shall be made in **form A**.
(ii) The memorandum and articles of association of the AMC shall be submitted to the board along with the application for approval under the sub-regulation **(i)**.
(iii) The provisions of regulations **5, 6 and 7** should apply to the applications made under sub-regulation **(1)** of this regulation as they apply to the application for registration of a mutual fund.

### *Regulation 19*

(1) The regulation explains the process of getting of an appointment of the AMC. The act indicates that the sponsor, the trustee, should appoint an **AMC** who is approved by the board to manage the affairs of the mutual fund and operate the schemes of such fund.
(2) The appointment of an AMC can be terminated by majority of the trustees or by **75 per cent** of the unit holders of the scheme.
(3) Any change in the appointment of the AMC should be subjected to prioral approval of the board.

### *Regulation 20*

The regulation deals with the approval of the AMC. For the grant of approval from the AMC. The board may take into account all the matters, which are relevant to efficient and orderly conduct of the affairs of the AMC and in particular the following namely:

(a) The existing AMC has a sound track record, general reputation and fairness in transaction;
(b) The directors of **AMC** are persons of high fame and stand

having at least 5 years of professional experience in the relevant fields, such as **portfolio management, investment analysis, financial administration**;

(c) The board of directors of the AMC has atleast 50 **per cent** directors, who are not affiliate or associated in any manner with, the sponsor or any of its subsidiaries or the trustees;

(d) The chairman of the **AMC** should not be the director of a trustee company or trustee of the board of trustees;

(e) The AMC shall have a minimum net worth of **Rupees Five crores**.

### *Regulation 21*

The regulation explains about the terms and conditions of approval of the **AMC**. The grant of approval of the AMC under regulation 20 shall be subject to the following terms and conditions, namely—

(a) the AMC has professionals with adequate experience in the management of mutual funds;

(b) any director of the AMC shall not hold the position of a director in another **AMC** or of a trustee in any mutual fund;

(c) the AMC shall forthwith inform the board of any material change in the information or particulars previously furnished, which have a bearing on the approval granted by it;

(d) no change in the management of the **AMC** shall be made without prior approval of the board;

(e) the AMC undertakes to comply with these regulations.

### *Regulation 22*

This section deals about the situation, if the approval is not granted to an AMC:

(1) When an application made under regulation 18 for grant of approval does not satisfy the requirements laid down in regulation 21 the board may reject the application.

(2) The decision to reject the application shall be communicated to the applicant in writing stating the grounds on which the application has been rejected.

(3) The AMC which is aggrieved by the decision of the board under sub-regulation (1) may within a period of **30 days** from the date of receipt of such intimation, apply to the board for reconsideration of its decision.

(4) The board shall as soon as possible in the light of the submission made in the application under sub-regulation (3) and whenever necessary after giving an opportunity for personal hearing, communicate its decision in writing to the applicant.

***Regulation 23***

The regulation inform about the restrictions on business activities of the AMC. No asset management company shall:

(a) act as trustee of any mutual fund,
(b) undertake any other business activities except activities like financial services consultancy, exchange of research on commercial basis as long as any such activities of one not in conflict with the activity of the mutual fund,
(c) act as an AMC for any other mutual fund to hold the position of a trustee in a trust or act as a director in any other AMC,
(d) permit any director of the AMC.

***Regulation 24***

The regulation defines the role and obligations of an AMC. The following process tells us about the rule position regarding the obligations of the AMC:

(i) The AMC shall take all reasonable steps and exercise all due negligence and ensure that the investment of funds pertaining to any scheme is not contrary to the provisions of these regulations and the trust deed.
(ii) The AMC shall be responsible for the acts of commission and omissions by its employees or the person whose services have been obtained by the Company.
(iii) The AMC shall submit to the trustee, quarterly reports on March 31, June 30, September 30 and December 31 on its activities and the compliance with these regulations.

(iv) The AMC shall be expected to meet all its expenses and make provisions for:
  (a) office space, personnel including **security analysts** and **portfolio managers,**
  (b) regulatory compliance and reporting services,
  (c) preparation and distribution of the funds prospectus, annual and periodic reports and other investor's communications,
  (d) advertising and other sales material,
  (e) accounting services and preparation of tax returns, and
  (f) insurance coverage and other services.

(v) The trustees of the mutual fund may terminate the assignment of the AMC at any time after receiving a reasonable notice in writing from the **AMC**.

(vi) Notwithstanding anything contained in any contract or agreement, the **AMC** or its directors or the officers shall not be absolved of any civil liability to the mutual fund for their acts of commissions and omissions, while holding such position or office.

***Regulation 25***

The mutual fund shall have a custodian. He is not associated with AMC in anyway.

***Regulation 26***

The regulation explains about the process of **approval** of custodian,

(i) The custodian shall make in application in **form A** for registration.

(ii) The provisions of 5, 6 and 7 shall, so far as may be apply to the application made under sub-regulation (1) of this regulation.

(iii) For grant of approval of the custodian, the board may take into account all matters which are relevant to efficient and orderly conduct of the affairs of the custodian and in particular the following, namely—

(a) the existing custodian has a sound track record, general regulation and fairness in transaction,

(b) the applicant himself or the employees or the persons who have experience in providing custodian services,

(c) the applicant has the infrastructure, office space and personnel to provide custodian services,

(d) the applicant or the director or the partners are not found guilty of any economic offence,

(e) the applicant is not the sponsor or trustee, of any mutual fund.

(iv) The grant of approval to the custodian shall be subjected to the following terms and conditions, namely—

(a) the custodian or its directors, partners will not in anyway be directly or indirectly affiliated or associated with any AMC,

(b) the custodian will not act as sponsor or the trustee of any fund,

(c) the custodian will not act as a custodian of more than one mutual fund without the approval of the **SEBI**.

The rules and regulations framed by the SEBI. Every mutual fund in India has to follow the rules and the regulations from **27 to 39** which indicates about the schemes of the mutual funds.

***Regulation 27***

It deals with the procedure for the announcement of schemes.

***Regulation 28***

It reveals the contents of publicity material.

***Regulation 29***

It contains the rules regarding misleading statement.

***Regulation 30***

It indicates about the steps involved enlisting of the schemes with the concerned stock exchange.

***Regulation 31***

This clause explains about the minimum amount to be raised from the market through various schemes. Close ended **Rs. 20 crores** and open ended **Rs. 50 crores.**

***Regulation 32***

This section tells us that the schemes should be kept open for the public subscription for a period of **45 days.**

***Regulation 33***

It indicates about the process of refund to an investor when the mutual fund scheme fails.

***Regulation 34***

It reveals that the allotted applicant should receive the unit certificates from the fund within **10 weeks** in case of close ended schemes and **6 weeks** in case of an open ended scheme.

***Regulation 35***

This provision deals with the transfer process of unit certificates.

***Regulation 36***

It indicates the winding up process of a mutual fund.

***Regulation 37***

It tells the effect of winding up of the schemes.

***Regulation 38***

It explains the procedure and manner of winding up of schemes.

***Regulation 39***

This provision deals with the declaration of winding up of scheme.

The regulations from **40 to 46** indicates about the investment objectives and valuation policies of the mutual fund. The rules from

**47 to 65** tells about the general obligations of the mutual funds on various aspects. **Regulations 65 to 75** informs about the procedure for an action in case of default regarding various conditions.

**RBI Guidelines**

The Commercial Banks are considered to follow the guidelines which are issued by the RBI on certain aspects as indicated below:

- Every mutual fund should be constituted as a trust under the Indian Trust Act and the sponsoring bank should appoint a board of trustees to manage it. The board of trustees should have at least two outside trustees.
- The trustees in addition to ability and integrity should have the proven capacity to deal the investment decisions and investors protection.
- The overall direction, control, superintendence and management of the affairs and business should vest in the board of trustees.
- The routine functions of the schemes should be looked after by a full pledged executive trustee.
- The executive trustee should not discharge any other responsibility in the concerned bank.
- An healthy relationship should be maintained between the sponsor and the board of trustees.
- Care should be taken so that there will be no clash of interest between the trustee board and the concerned bank.
- The sponsor bank should contribute the corpus fund and specified by the RBI. No additional contribution should be made by the sponsor bank to the corpus without the prior approval of the RBI.
- The sponsor bank should contribute in addition to the corpus fund and maintain in each of the funds schemes by the way of its stake, an amount equivalent to 1 per cent of the amount outstanding.
- The banks should obtain the RBI's prior approval before announcing any scheme of a mutual fund.
- The investment objectives and policies of the mutual fund should be laid down in the trust deed and every scheme

launched by the fund must be in accordance with such broad objectives and policies.

- The MF should make a clear statement while inviting the public about the investment objectives of the fund and its policies.
- The subscription amounts collected by the mutual funds are primarily intended to be chanelised into the capital market instruments.
- The MFs should not undertake direct or indirect lending portfolio[1] funds management, underwriting, bill discounting, money operations etc., which are essentially banking/merchant banking functions etc.
- There is no objection to the mutual funds in investing the amounts initially collected for a scheme in the money market instruments, rediscounting of bills or bank deposits for a period of not exceeding **6** months.
- The mutual funds may also invest their temporary surplus fund in similar instruments upto not more than **25 per cent** of their total investible funds. Such short term/temporary investments can however be made only if they are permissible under the charter of the fund.
- The mutual funds should take delivery of scrips purchased and in the case of scrips sold, give delivery thereof to the purchaser. The scrips purchased should be transferred in the funds name.
- A mutual fund should not make short sale/purchase of securities or carry over the transactions from one settlement period to the next settlement period.
- The mutual funds should not make investments in any other mutual funds of similar collective investment schemes. The funds should not also invest in the shares of investment companies/corporations.
- The mutual funds should not hold under any one scheme, more than **5 per cent** of issued share capital or debenture stock of any company.
- In case the mutual fund operates more than one scheme, the holdings in respect of all its schemes put together should not exceed **15 per cent** of the paid up capital or debenture stock of a company.

- The total amount invested by a fund from any of its schemes in the shares, debentures, of any specific industry should not exceed **15 per cent** of a schemes fund. This provision will not, howevr, apply to a scheme which has been floated for investments in one or more specified industries and a declaration has been made to that effect.
- The maximum spread between the purchase and selling prices of units/shares of any scheme should not be more than **5 per cent**.
- The total cost of managing any scheme under a fund should be kept within **5 per cent** of the total income of the scheme.
- Income distribution by the way of dividend or capitalisation of gains should not be made on the basis of revaluation of the stock holdings or unrealised capital appreciation.
- The fund should create depreciation on investments held and provision for bad or doubtful debts. The auditors should satisfy before declaring any dividend.
- Further, the fund should create a dividend equalisation fund for each scheme by appropriating a part of its surplus income.
- A mutual fund should maintain separate accounts of each scheme launched by it, segregating the assets under each scheme. No switching of assets between the schemes should take place, except with the prior approval of the board of trustees and at the prevailing market rates.
- The board of trustees of mutual funds should prepare an annual statement of accounts in respect of each of the schemes which should contain, statements of assets and liabilities and income and expenditure accounts, duly audited by the qualified auditors. Further an abridged version of the annual account together with the reports of auditors and the board of trustees, should be published for the information of subscribers to the concerned scheme.
- The board of trustees of mutual funds should disclose the NAV of each of the schemes and the method of valuation for the benefit of the concerned subscribers.
- The sponsor bank should furnish to the RBI in duplicate, the following reports on a regular basis:
  - — a half yearly report indicating the performance of the mutual fund as a whole as well as each scheme,

— audited annual statement of accounts, together with the reports of auditors and the report of the board of trustees,

— scheme-wise details of investment portfolio of the funds, value of such investments, changes in the portfolio since the previous annual report and industry-wise exposure.

### *Company Law Guidelines*

Mutual funds generally invest in shares, debentures and other securities of the blue-chip companies and in the money market instruments the guidelines issued by the Government indicates that a mutual fund in a private sector can be sponsored by one or more limited companies having a sound track record. The company or companies which wants to establish a mutual fund should establish the fund as a trust under the Indian Trust Act of 1882. The sponsoring company should incorporate an **AMC**. The AMC should have a net worth prescribed by the Government. The sponsoring company should have at least a 40 per cent stake in the paid up capital of the **AMC**. In order to meet this requirement of **40 per cent** stake, the sponsoring company or companies have to subscribe to the shares of the AMC by complying with the provisions of **Section 372** of the Companies Act (Rule 11). According to the Rule 11(c) the sponsoring company can invest only upto **25 per cent** of the subscribed equity capital. Since the sponsoring company has to invest to the extent of atleast **40 per cent** in the paid up capital of the AMC, the sponsoring company has to get the approval of its shareholders in a general meeting and the Central Government as required by the sub-section **(4)** of Section 372 of the Act for investing in the shares of the **AMC**. As stated above, the mutual fund is required to be established as a trust. Indian Trust Act, Section **(3)** defines the term trust as "an obligation annexed to the ownership of property and arising out of a confidence reposed in and accepted by the owner or declared and accepted by him for the benefit of another, or of another and the owner". Section **41(2)** of the Act provides that a person who has agreed in writing to become a member and whose names entered in the register of members shall be a member of the company. A person means a natural person or a corporation. A trust is not a legal entity. It is only a legal arrangement, it is not a person. According to Section **153** of the Act, no notice of trust shall be entered on the register of members. To overcome, Sections **41** and **153** of the Act, in practice mutual funds get the shares registered with either in the name of the

**Sponsoring Company** or in the name of the **Asset Management Company** or in the name of the **Custodian Company**. According to the Government rules and regulations, every mutual fund should avail the services of the custodian. According to the Government regulations every mutual fund should get the shares purchased and transferred to the fund's name and scheme also.

If the shares are not registered in the name of the mutual fund, the mutual fund should comply with Section **187-C** of the Act by giving the declaration in Form II as prescribed by the Companies Rules of 1975 as contemplated in sub-section (2) of Section 187C of the Act, within **30 days** from the date of registration of transfer of shares should be done by Concerned Company. Consequently, the company in whose name the mutual funds shares are registered has to file Form No. 1 as prescribed by the Companies Rules, 1975, with the company concerned, within **30 days** from the date of registration of transfer of shares as required by sub-section (1) of Section 187C of the Act. When Forms I & II prescribed under Section 187C are filed with the company, the Company is required to file Form No. III prescribed under the Companies Rules, 1975, with the Registrar of Companies within 30 days from the date of receipt of forms I and II from the shareholding company and the mutual fund by paying the appropriate filing fees as prescribed in Schedule X of the Act. Section 187C of the Act does not apply to the shares purchased or acquired by the mutual fund since the shares are registered in the companys name and to the account of mutual fund.

**Section 153–B** of the Act provides that where any shares or debentures exceeding a certain value are held in trust by any person, such person has to make a declaration to the public trustee appointed by the Central Government under Section 153-A of the Act, within 60 days in Form No. I annexed to Trustees Rules, 1964 and send a copy of the declaration to the company concerned within **21 days** after the declaration is sent to the public trustee. In case of Stockholding Corporation of India, such declaration in Form I shall be made in respect of the shares or debentures held by it as such on or before **31st March**, Company-wise, by the **15th** of May every year. If there is any change in the shareholding or debenture holding given in the declaration in Form I, the person who has given the declaration has to send a report in Form II appended to the Trustees Rules, 1964, to the public trustee notifying such change within **30 days** from the date of such change.

According to Companies Act Section 187–B indicates that the public trustee gets all the powers and rights exercisable by mutual fund. The mutual funds and the sponsoring Companies are required to comply with some of the cumbersome provisions of the Companies Act, 1956.

## Risk Factors of a Mutual Fund

Risk is the essence of the valuation of a financial instrument. The value of a financial asset depends upon many factors. Risk means, a chance the expected gain, profit or return may not materialise. The actual outcome of the investment may be less than the expected outcome. If the certainty of outcomes expected variance is zero it is called as risk free. Risk can be defined as "the variability of returns from those that are expected"[7]. The actual return on the investment may differ substantially from the expected return. The risk must be considered in determining the value and making the investment choices. Risk and Return are the foundations for **maximising** the shareholders wealth. The Return can be defined as "Income received on an investment plus any change in market price, usually expressed as a percentage of the beginning market price of the investment"[8]. The return comes from two sources **income plus any price appreciation**. For common stock the one-period return can be computed with the following formula:

$$R = \frac{D_t + (P_t - P_t - 1)}{P_t - 1}$$

$D_t$ = cash dividend at the end of time period *t*
$P_t$ = stocks price at time period *t*
R = actual return
t = a particular time period in the past/future
$p_{t-1}$ = stock price at time period t–1

The return which we expect is different from the return which we receive. For highly risky securities, the actual rate of return can be viewed as a random variable subject to a **"probability distribution"**. It can be defined as "A set of possible values that a random variable can assume and their associated probabilities of occurrence."[9] The probability distribution is based on two factors of the distribution: (a) the expected return, (b) the standard deviation. The expected return is a weighted average of the possible returns, with the weights being the probabilities of occurrence. The expected return can be defined as "the weighted average of possible returns, with the weights being the probabilities of occurrence". The expected return can be calculated by the following formula:

$$\bar{R} = \sum_{i=1}^{n} (R_i)(P_i)$$

$\bar{R}$ = expected return
$R_i$ = return for the *i*th possibility
$P_i$ = the probability of a return occurring
n = the total number of possibilities

The another factor which influences the probable distribution is the **standard deviation**. The expected return is based around the dispersion or variability of a financial asset. The conventional measure of dispersion is the standard deviation. Standard deviation can be defined as "A statistical measure of the variability of a distribution around its mean. It is the square root of the variance".[11] The standard deviation of returns depends upon the variability of returns. The standard deviation σ can be expressed mathematically as:

$$\sigma = \sqrt{\sum_{i-1}^{n} (R_i - \bar{R})^2 (P_i)}$$

σ = standard deviation
$R_i$ = return on investment
$\bar{R}$ = the expected return on investment
$P_i$ = Probability occurrence of the financial asset

The standard deviation sometimes confuses and sometimes makes to fall in dilemma when compared with the risk of a financial asset. To overcome the limitations of the standard deviation it can be better to find out its coefficient of variation. The co-efficient of variation can found by dividing the standard deviation with the expected return. The co-efficient of variation can be defined as "the ratio of the deviation of a distribution to the mean of that distribution. It is a measure of relative risk".[12] The coefficient of variation can be calculated by the following formula:

$$CV = \frac{\sigma}{\bar{R}}$$

σ = standard deviation
$\bar{R}$ = expected return

Thus coefficient of variation is a measure of the risk per unit of expected return. The larger the CV, the larger the relative risk of the financial asset. The average investor is averse to risk. The risky investments should offer higher expected returns than less risky investments in order to make the people and hold it. Therefore, the risk averse can be defined as "term applied to an investor who demands a higher expected return the higher the risk".[13] The low risk investments sometimes produce higher returns. Investors usually make their investments in a single financial asset or they deploy their wealth in a combination of two or more instruments. Therefore, this combination of investments are called as **"portfolio"**. Portfolio can be defined as "A combination of two or more securities or assets".[14] Mutual funds performance depends upon the management of portfolio. The NAV is the barometer of performance of any type of mutual fund. The reflection of better management of portfolio is as indication of the high NAV of the Units. The expected return of a portfolio is a weighted average of the expected returns of the securities comprising that portfolio. The weights are equal to the proportion of total funds invested in each security. The formula for the expected return of a portfolio can be as follows:

$$R_p = \sum_{j=L}^{m} W_j R_J$$

$R_p$ = the expected return on portfolio
$W_j$ = the proportion of the investments in security *j*.
$R_j$ = the expected return for security *j*.
m = the total number of different securities in the portfolio.

The fund managers of the mutual fund will have to concentrate on many factors like **portfolio standard deviation, covariance, correlation coefficient** etc. The portfolio management also concentrates on the **diversification**. The concepts of diversification is to spread the risk across a number of assets or investments. The meaningful diversification reduces risk. The portfolio risk comprises two components.

Total risk = Systematic risk + Unsystematic risk

The systematic risk means the overall movements of the general market or economy. It is caused by a number of factors. This type of risk is inescapable. The systematic risk is also called as market risk or non-diversifiable risk. The systematic risk can be defined as "the variability of return on stocks or portfolios associated with changes in return on the market as a whole".[15] The diversification cannot reduce this risk. Another risk element is **unsystematic risk**. The unsystematic risk is also called as **"non-market risk"** or **"diversifiable risk"**. The non-systematic risk can be reduced by the diversification. The security's total return is not related to the overall market variability. The unsystematic risk can be defined as "the variability of return on stocks or portfolios not explained by general market movements. It is avoidable through diversification."[16] The unsystematic risk is related to a particular company or industry. Unsystematic risk is independent of economic, political and other factors that affect all the assets in a systematic manner. All the risk associated with the market portfolio is the systematic risk. In this context, the capital market and portfolio theories have developed a critical important concept **"Beta"**. Beta is a measure of relative risk of a security. Beta is a coefficient measuring a security's relative volatility. It indicates the extent of the risk for a given financial asset which is non-diversifiable. It is the co-variance of a security return with that of the market for a security class. Beta can be defined as "An index of systematic risk. It measures the sensitivity of a stock's returns to changes in returns on the market portfolio. The beta of a portfolio is simply a weighted average of the individual stock betas in the portfolio."[17] The security with a higher (than 1) beta is more volatile than the market, and the net asset with a lower (than 1) beta would rise or fall slowly than the market. **For example**, $\beta = 1$ is for everyone percentage change in the market return, on an average, the security return also will change by one per cent.

To understand the financial market in a better way it is necessary to know the value of a financial asset. The value of a financial assets are highly influenced by the return and risk. The fund managers should keep in mind about these components in their portfolios. These two elements can be ignored under any circumstances. The fund managers skill reflects in the risk reduction of a portfolio and enhance the returns to efficient portfolio. The risks may be classified in a number of ways. The following are said to be the major types of risks, which a mutual fund should not be ignored while designing the innovative schemes to meet the needs of the unit holders. They are default risk, liquidity risk, financial risk, maturity risk, inflation risk, currency risk, country risk, business risk, interest rate risk.

Unforeseen risk proves that every long-term stock investors too dump a fund at the worst time. A funds past performance tends to be an unreliable guide except for the worst funds. Volatility in the market is a routine consistent. The fund managers have much more control over the risks than returns. The investor may expect ups and downs in the market and can use the risk indicators to choose a relatively well placed fund. Speculators can bear higher risks for higher returns. The technique reveals the risks that are likely to be most rewarding.

Risk indicators involve mathematics. **Beta** is the most common measure of the risk. A **beta of 1**, matches market risk, less than 1, a fund is calmer than the market. **Alpha** is a performance measure adjusted for the risk. A fund that responds more to the markets advances than the declines has a **positive Alpha**.

Growth funds concentrates on the companies which have rapidly increasing earnings and riskier than the value funds, which hunt for those stocks at low multiple of earnings or book value. To reduce the overall risk a balanced portfolio of funds should be placed across the spectrum with perhaps a slight tilt towards small stocks and value for the long-term invest.

## Performance Valuation of Mutual Funds

The SEBI has come out with a standard format of the balance sheet for mutual funds in India. The mutual fund industry does not have a standard accounting policy and comparison may be done after the adjustments. The mutual fund performance is based on the **Net Asset Value**. The NAV of the unit is an important concept and it is the basis for the unit pricing. In the case of open ended and closed end scheme, the NAV can be calculated as follows:

$$\text{NAV} = \frac{\text{Total market value of the assets in the portfilio of the fund} - \text{liabilities}}{\text{Number of funds units outstanding}}$$

In the case of open ended schemes the NAV calculated on daily basis and the sale and purchases are to be made on each day. The following formula can be applied to calculate the sale and repurchase prices of units.

$$\text{Sale price} = \frac{\text{(MVA} - \text{Liabilities excluding CL,ISC, reserve and unit capital)} + \text{Brokerage, Commission, taxes and other example)}}{\text{Number of units outstanding}}$$

$$\text{Repurchase price} = \frac{\text{(MVA – Liabilities excluding CL,ISC, reserve and unit capital) – Brokenage, Commission, taxes and other example)}}{\text{Number of units issued or outstanding}}$$

The expected rate of return on units can be calculated as:

$$ERR = \frac{(NAV_1 - NAV_{t-1}) + \text{Dividends} + \text{Capital gains}}{NAV_{t-1}}$$

ERR = Expected rate of return on units
MVA = Market Value of Assets
CL = Current Liabilities
ISC = Initial Share Capital
$t$ = Current Year
$t$–1 = Previous Year

The NAV is determined by the stock market prices. The stock market prices are influenced by the supply the demand and the other factors. The units are discounted to the extent value of the net asset value, and the average discount have been about **25 per cent** and in certain cases. The discounts are as high as **30 to 50 per cent**. The following factors may give rise to discounts:

(i) The close ended fund units are very limited trading in value and volume.
(ii) The close ended scheme units floating is very small.
(iii) High administrative expenses and management fee causes low dividend which in turn low the price.
(iv) The unit prices are very low because the broker offers low prices which they have to hold them for a more time.
(v) On overall the market for these units is limited while comparing with the corporate shares.

The NAV includes dividends, interest accruals and reduction of liabilities, expenses besides market value of investments. The causes for the **Non-satisfactory** performance of the mutual funds are as follows:

(a) poor investment planning,
(b) too much diversification of portfolio,

(c) blue-chip scrips do not yield more than average return,
(d) high turnover of portfolio leads to huge payment of brokerage, and
(e) wrong prediction about income, profitability, interpretation of government policies etc.

**Efficiency of Mutual Fund**

A good mutual fund always works for the satisfaction of the unit holders. The evaluation of a mutual fund can be done by taking the following factors into consideration:

***Liquidity***

A good mutual fund should create liquidity to its unit holders in the form of listing on a stock exchange.

***Stability***

A mutual fund should be stable and offer a wide range of schemes for a long-term period.

***Growth***

The fund must concentrate on increasing the NAV's consistent growth in dividend and capital appreciation.

***Returns***

A fund should assure better returns to its unit holders and try to achieve the goal.

***Credibility***

Previous track record of issuer. An investor before investing should decide and verify the track record.

***Management Approach***

The management of a fund depends upon many factors, i.e., diversification, risk bearing, return maximisation.

***Method of Valuation of the Investments***

Every Mutual Fund in India should value investments according to the following valuation norms:

**(a) Traded securities.**
**(b) Non-traded securities.**
**(c) Rights shares.**

While valuing the **traded securities**, the following factors should be taken into consideration:

(i) The securities should be valued at the last quoted closing price on the bourse.
(ii) If the scrips are traded on more than one stock exchange, generally the AMC is left to select the appropriate stock exchange. The reasons for selection should be recorded in writing. Usually all the scrips can be valued at the prices quoted on the stock exchange where a majority in value of the securities are principally traded.
(iii) In a particular valuation day, if a security has not been traded on the selected stock exchange, the value at which it is traded on another stock exchange may be taken.
(iv) In same situations, when a scrip is not traded on any stock exchange on a specific valuation day, the earliest previous day quotation may be used for consideration. But such date should not be more than 60 days prior to the valuation date.

**The Non-traded securities** will be valued in the following manner:

(a) A scrip may be treated as a non-traded scrip, if it is not traded on any stock exchange for a period of **60** days prior to the valuation date.
(b) The **Asset Management Company** has the authority to value the non-traded securities in the following procedure:

(i) The Board of Directors of the AMC should prescribe the norms for valuation of non-traded securities.

(ii) The decision of the Board of Directors of the AMC must be documented in the minutes and the supporting data in respect of each security so valued must be preserved.

(iii) The methods used to find out the value of non-traded security should be periodically review by the trustees of the mutual fund.

(iv) The Auditors of the MFs should be reported as **"fair and reasonable"** in their report on the annual accounts of the mutual fund.

(v) The Equity Instruments should be valued on the basis of capitalisation of earnings or NAV method.

(vi) The Debt Instruments should be valued on a yield to maturity basis.

(vii) The value of investments like **call money, short-term deposits, rediscounted bills** should be valued at **cost plus** Accrual.

(viii) The value of other money market instruments should be valued at the yield for which they are currently traded.

(ix) The Government Securities should be valued at yield to maturity based on the current market rate.

(x) For the valuation of the non-traded instruments would be valued as follows:

**Cost of the Non-traded instrument + Interest accrued at the beginning of the day** + [Redemption value–The cost (spread over to the remaining maturity period of the Instrument)]

(xi) For the valuation of non-convertible debenture, it will be treated as Debt instrument and Valued accordingly.

(xii) In case of convertible debentures, the convertible component should be valued as an equity instrument.

(xiii) If the financial instruments have been bought on **repo basis**, the instrument must be valued as:

**The Resale Price – Interest upto the date of resale.**

(xiv) If the Financial Instrument has been sold on repo basis:

**Repurchase price – Interest (upto the date of repurchase price) – The value of the Instrument.**

If the repurchase price exceeds the investment value the depreciation should be provided. If the repurchase price is lower than the value of the Instrument, adjustment must be taken into consideration.

(xv) In case of valuation of equity, the warrants to subscribe for shares attached to instruments can be valued at the value of the share *minus* the cost of **warrant**.

The value of **Rights shares** should be calculated as:

The price of the rights share may either **"Cum-Right Price"** or an **"Ex-Right Price"**. The cum-right price gives the buyer, besides the ownership of shares already held, the right to apply for new shares offered by the company, while the **ex-right price** gives the buyer only the ownership of the existing shares held by the seller and not the right to apply for additional shares offered by the Company. Ex-right price is quoted either after the rights shares have already been allotted by the Company or the time to apply for right shares has already expired. The value of the right can be calculated by the following formula:

$$R = \frac{M - S}{N + 1}$$

R = Value of one right
M = Cum-right market price of a share
S = Subscription price for a new share
N = No. of shares (old) required to purchase one new share.

The valuation of a share ex-right can be obtained by the following formula:

$$P = \frac{MN + S}{N + 1}$$

P = Theoretical market value of a share ex-right
M = Cum-right market price
N = Number of old shares entitling to purchase one new share
S = Subscription price for a new share.

Alternatively the value of a right can also be calculated by the following formula:

$$R = \frac{P - S}{N}$$

R = Value of one right
P = Ex-right market price of a share
N = Number of old shares entitling to new one share
S = Subscription price for one new share.

Alternatively until they are traded, the value of the rights share can also be calculated by applying the following formula:

$$V = \frac{N}{M} \times (P_{ex} - P_o)$$

V = Value of rights share
N = No. of rights offered
M = No. of original shares held
$P_{ex}$ = Ex-right price
$P_o$ = Rights offer price.

While calculating the NAV of the MFs, all expenses and incomes accrued upto the valuation date should be taken into consideration. The management expenses, and other expenses should be accrued on daily basis shall be adjusted. Any changes in portfolio of the mutual fund are to be recorded in the books upto a period of **Seven days** following the date of the transaction. The NAV calculation should not be effected by more than **2 per cent.**

The price of the units must be determined with reference to the last determined NAV unless—

(a) The sale price is determined with or without a fixed premium added to the future NAV which declared in advance.
(b) While determining the prices of the units, it must be ensured that the repurchase price is not lower than **93 per cent** and the sale price is not higher than **107 per cent** of the **NAV.**

## *General Obligations*

Every mutual fund in India should work according to the general obligations which were imposed by the Act. Generally, the Mutual Funds should fulfil the following obligations:

1. **Maintenance of proper books of Accounts.**
2. **Accounting policies and standards.**

3. **Financial year.**
4. **Initial expenses treatment/ issue expenses.**
5. **Issue of warrants.**
6. **Annual report.**
7. **Auditor's Report.**
8. **Disclosure norms.**
9. **Procedure for action in case of default.**

1. *Maintenance of Proper Books of Accounts*

The important obligation of a mutual fund is to maintain the proper books of accounts according to the sub-regulation (2) of the SEBI Regulations, 1993. The mutual funds should keep the books or accounts to explain its transactions and to disclose it any point of time the financial position of the fund in particular give a true and fair view of the state of the affairs of the fund. The Mutual Fund shall inform to the SEBI the place where the books, records and documents are maintained and available.

2. *Accounting Policies and Standards*

The Mutual Fund shall follow the accounting policies and standards to provide appropriate details in the following manner:

(a) The Mutual Funds should present all investments in the balance sheet at market value.
(b) The Mutual Fund while determining the holding cost of investment and the gain or loss on sale of investments, the average cost procedure should be followed.
(c) The income of a scheme is generally earned by a Mutual Fund is in the form of dividend. Dividend income should be recognised by the Fund on the date, the share is quoted on an **ex-dividend basis**.
(d) If the shares are not quoted on the stock exchange the dividend income should be recognised on the date of **declaration** by the concerned company.
(e) In case of debt instruments income must be calculated on a daily basis for the concerned period of the time.
(f) The financial statement of the mutual fund should reflect the

transactions for the purchase or sale of investments for a particular trade date but not as of the **settlement date**.

(g) While evaluating the income of a scheme, **Bonus** shares are also to be taken into consideration. The original shares are valued on **ex-bonus** basis.

(h) In case of rights entitlements, it should be recognised only when the original shares on which the rights entitlement accrues are traded on stock exchange on an **ex-right basis**.

(i) If the accrued income has not been received for a beyond due date, the provision should be made in **Revenue account** of the scheme.

(j) In case of **open ended scheme** units are sold if any positive amount is arised, it should be credited to reserves. And if negative amount found, it should be debited to reserves. The face value will be credited to Capital Account.

(k) If units are repurchased of a open ended scheme, if any **positive** amount is arised should be debited to reserve and if negative should be **credited to reserves**, the face value being debited to the capital account.

(l) Every mutual fund should maintain **an equalisation account** for open ended scheme, on sale of the units, an appropriate part of the proceeds should be credited to it. When the units repurchased by the MF an appropriate amount should be debited to equalisation account. The net balance of this account should be adjusted in **revenue account**.

(m) Every mutual fund should maintain capital account for each close ended scheme. In this scheme, if the mutual fund repurchase its units, the par value of the unit should be debited to capital account. If any positive amount is available, it should be credited to **reserves** and if any **negative**, it should be **debited to** reserves.

(n) A proportionate initial expenses should also be transferred to the reserves.

(o) The investment in different financial instruments should include **stamp charges, brokerage charges** etc.

(p) In case of debt instruments, if any discount is found in purchasing moment, it should be reduced from the cost of the investment.

(q) If any underwriting commission received by the Mutual Fund, it should be treated as **revenue** only when there is no devolvement on the scheme. If there is devolvement. The underwriting commission should be adjusted according to the proportion.

3. *Financial Year*

The Accounting Year for all the schemes shall end on the same date which shall be **March 31**. In case of a new scheme which is commenced the accounting year, the disclosure and reporting requirement would apply for the period beginning from the date of its commenced and ending on the last date of the relevant accounting year of the mutual fund.

4. *Treatment of Issue Expenses*

Every Mutual Fund should identify all expenses clearly and must be appropriate for each scheme. The Asset Management Company **(AMC)** is important organ in mutual fund, it will undertake the functions of buying and selling securities of the each scheme. The AMC renders the investment and advisory sources on turn over basis of the schemes. It will charge the **Fee** to mutual fund which is fully disclosed in the offer document subject to the following:

(A) If the net assets do not exceeds **Rs. 100 crores,** the commission or fee is **one** and a **quarter** of 1 per cent of the weekly average net assets in each accounting year per each scheme.

(B) If the net assets exceeds **Rs. 100 crores, 1 per cent** of the excess amount over **Rs. 100 crores** will be charged.

(C) In addition to the above fee the **AMC** may charge the MF with the following expenses:

(a) Initial issue cost of sponsoring the fund and its schemes.

(b) Recurring expenses such as **brokerage, marketing and selling expenses, Registrar's services for** transfer of shares, agents commission, all of these initial expenses in respect of anyone scheme shall not exceed **6 per cent** of the fund raised under that scheme. In addition to the above expenses, the following expenses may also be charged to the mutual fund:

(i) fee and expenses of trustees,
(ii) audit fees,
(iii) custodian fee,
(iv) cost of funds from location to location,
(v) winding up costs for terminating a mutual fund/ scheme,
(vi) cost of statutory advertisements,
(vii) cost regarding to investor communication,
(viii) any such other costs may be approved by the **SEBI**.

*The Treatment of Initial Expenses*: The initial expenses must be accounted in the books of account of each scheme specified as below:

(i) The issue of scheme can be classified into **two** categories: (a) **load**, (b) **no load basis** or sometimes it may issue as mixed basis. The type of issue should be clearly explained to the investors in the offer document. In the case of a close ended scheme floated on a **load basis** the initial issue expenses should be amortised on a **weekly** basis over the period of the scheme.
(ii) In case of open ended schemes, floated on the load basis. The initial expenses may be amortised over a period not exceeding **5** years. The expenses incurred during the life of an open ended scheme cannot be amortised.
(iii) In case of load basis open end and close end schemes, the unamortised portion of the expenses are to be included in the calculation of **Net Asset Value.** But such portion should not be included for calculation of the advisory service to the AMC.
(iv) If the schemes floated on a **no load basis**, the AMC can levy an additional management fee not exceeding **1 per cent** of the NAV. The AMC is entitled to levy a contingent charges as follows:

(a) It may be entitled to buy a contingent deferred sales charge for redemption during the **first four years** after purchase should not exceed **4 per cent** of the redemption proceeds in the first year.
(b) It is **3 per cent** in the second year.
(c) It is **2 per cent** in the third year.
(d) It is **1 per cent** in the fourth year.

(v) The distribution charges, in case of load schemes should be borne by the scheme of the mutual fund.

(vi) The distribution charges in case of **no load schemes** should be borne by the **Asset Management Company.**

All the initial expenses together should not exceed to **6 per cent.** If any amount exceeds 6 per cent it should be borne by the **AMC.** The total expenses of the scheme excluding **issue/redemption expenses** but including the investment management and advisory fee are subject to the following limits:

(a) on the first **Rs. 100 crores** of the average weekly net assets **2.5 per cent.**

(b) on the next **Rs. 300 crores** of the average weekly net assets **2.25 per cent.**

(c) on the next **Rs. 300 crores** of the average weekly net assets **2 per cent.**

(d) on the balance of the assets **1.75 per cent.**

Any expenditure exceeding limits should be borne by the **AMC/ Trustee/Sponsor.** The SEBI cannot be approved the expenses beyond the certain level of percentage.

5. *Issue of Warrants*

The issue of warrants or dividends to the unit holders must be despatched within **42 days** of the declaration of the dividend. Repurchase proceeds must be paid to unit holder within **10 days** from the date of repurchase/redemption.

6. *Annual Report*

Every Mutual Fund should prepare annual report on scheme-wise basis or an abridged summary. It shall be published through an advertisement within **6 months** from the date of closure of the relevant financial year. The Annual Report or abridged summary shall contain details as specified in **Schedules VII and VIII** of the Act. The Annual Report of the every mutual fund shall be made available for inspection at the Head Office of the Mutual Fund. If any member so required, a copy thereof shall be made available on payment of nominal fee as specified by the Mutual Fund.

7. *Auditor's Report*

The books of accounts of the every mutual fund should be audited by an Auditor. The Auditor shall be different from the auditor of the **AMC**. According to the SEBI regulation **65**, the Auditor may be defined as "Auditor means a person who is qualified to audit the accounts of a Company under Section **224** of the Companies Act, 1956"[18]. An Auditor of the Mutual Fund should be appointed by the Trustees. The Auditor shall submit his report to the trustees. The Audit Report shall form a part of the annual report of the Mutual Fund. The Auditor's should comprise of a certificate to the effect of that;

(a) he has obtained all information and explanations which to the best of his knowledge and belief, were necessary for the purpose of his audit,
(b) the statement of accounts has been prepared in accordance with accounting policies and standards as specified by the **SEBI**,
(c) the balance sheet and the revenue account give a fair and true view of the scheme, state of affairs and surplus or deficit in the fund for the accounting period to which the balance sheet or as the case may be the Revenue Account relates.

8. *Disclosure Norms*

The scheme-wise annual report of a mutual fund or its abridged summary thereof should be published through an **"advertisement"**. And an abridged scheme-wise annual report shall be mailed to all the unit holders within **6 months** from the date of closure of the relevant accounting year. The report shall contain all the information as specified by the SEBI. The report should reflect a true and fair view of the operations of the mutual fund. But the abridged information shall not contain full portfolio disclosure but must contain details regarding fund activities. According to the SEBI norms. If any mutual fund publish full accounts in newspapers, the full portfolio disclosure is **not** required. Every mutual fund should submit all the information to the SEBI within

6 months from the date of closure of each financial year. The mutual fund, **AMC, Trustees,** custodian, sponsor of the mutual fund should make such disclosure or submits such documents as they may be called upon to do so by **SEBI**. The MF should furnish the periodical reports to the SEBI as follows:

(a) Copies of the duly audited annual statements of accounts including the balance sheet and PEL A/C for the mutual fund and in respect of each scheme once a year.
(b) A copy of six monthly unaudited accounts.
(c) A quarterly statement of movements in net assets for each of the schemes of the fund.
(d) A quarterly portfolio statement including changes from the previous periods for each scheme.

The sale of units should be done by the Trustees or the **AMC** after providing sufficient information made available for the investors to take a informed decision. The trustees of the mutual fund are bound to make disclosures to the unit holders. It is the response of the trustees to keep the investors informed about all the available information. SEBI is the most powerful organisation in the financial sector of the nation. It has the full authority in the primary market, secondary market, money market and mutual fund industry. All the Mutual Funds in India shall act as per the guidelines norms issued by the SEBI from time to time in force. **SEBI** is the watchdog of the stock market and mutual fund sector. The SEBI is empowered to suspend registration of a mutual fund. If a mutual fund fails in the following situations:

(a) fails to furnish any information,
(b) fails to furnish wrong information relating to its activities,
(c) fails to submit periodical returns,
(d) fails to comply with directions,
(e) fails to resolve investor complaint,
(f) in guilty of misconduct/unprofessional ethics,
(g) fails to pay any fee,
(h) fails to maintain net worth of the Asset Management Company.

The SEBI has authority to cancel the registration of a mutual fund or impose a penalty on the following grounds:

(a) If the Mutual Fund, Asset Management Company, Trustees of the Mutual Fund involved in **price rigging or manipulation or concerning activities** affecting the securities market and the investories interest.

(b) The Mutual Fund or AMC or Trustees or Custodian is guilty of fraud or is convicted of a criminal offence.

(c) The Mutual Fund has been guilty or repeated defaults which result in suspension of the registration.

(d) The financial position of the mutual fund deteriorates to such an extent that the board is of the opinion that its continuance is not in the interest of investors and other mutual funds.

Therefore, the SEBI has the full authority in either cancellation of a registration of a mutual fund or suspension of registration of the licence of the fund/**AMC/Trustee**. The suspension cancellation of a certificate of the mutual fund should be preceded by an enquiry by enquiry officers. The SEBI has the authority to appoint an inquiry officer under regulation **69 of** the Act for holding an inquiry. The enquiry officer shall issue a notice of the MF/AMC/Trustee/Custodian as the case may be at the registered office or the principal place of business of the concerned. The MF/AMC/Trustee/Custodian may within **30 days** from the date of receipt of such notice furnish to the enquiry officer a reply together with copies of documentary or other evidence relied on by him or sought by the board from him.

The enquiry officer shall give to the concerned person a reasonable opportunity of being heard to enable him to make submissions in support of his reply under the sub-regulation **(3)**. The alleged person or any other person on behalf of him should be presented before an equity officer. But no advocate is permitted on behalf of the person. But in some time, the SEBI will gives permission to attend the advocate on behalf of the **MF/AMC/Trustee**. The enquiry officer shall after taking into account all relevant facts and submissions made by the party submit a report to the board and recommended the penalty to be awarded as also the grounds on the basis of which the penalty proposed in the notice is justified. On the basis of the report, the **SEBI** would issue a show cause notice which the mutual fund must reply within **14 days**. After hearing the reply it would approve the action for default. Every order passed under sub-regulation **(3)** shall be self-contained and give reasons for the conclusions stated therein including justification of the penalty imposed by that order. The board shall send a copy of the order under sub-regulation **(3)** to the MF and Central Government. On and from the date of the suspension, the MF shall **cease** to carry on any activity related to MF during the period of suspension. **On and from** the date of cancellation the MF shall cease to carryon any activity related to that MF. **The order of suspension** or cancellation of registration passed under sub-regulation **(3)** of regulation 71, shall be published in atleast two daily newspaper by the board. **Any person** aggrieved by an order of the board may prefer an appeal to the Central Government.

*Winding up of Scheme*: In mutual fund, there are basically two kinds of schemes available to the investors. They are categorised as (i) **open ended scheme,** (ii) **close ended scheme**. An open ended scheme shall be wound up, if the total number of units outstanding after repurchases at any point of time falls below **50 per cent** of the originally issued number of units. A close ended schemes of a mutual fund may be wound up.

(a) On the expiry of the period of time if any, fixed for the duration of the scheme by that scheme; or
(b) On the happening of any event which in the opinion of the trustees, requires the scheme to be wound up; or
(c) If **70 per cent** of the unit holders of a scheme pass a resolution that the scheme be wound up; or
(d) If the board so directs in the interest of the unit holders.

If a scheme is to be wound up in pursuance to sub-regulation of the Act, the trustees shall give notice of the circumstances leading to the winding up of the scheme on and from the date of advertisement of the winding up the trustees or the AMC as the case may be shall:

(a) cease to carry on any business activities;
(b) cease to create and cancel units in the scheme;
(c) cease to issue and redeem units in the scheme.

9. *Procedure and Manner of Winding Up*

The Mutual Fund of the Trustee shall call a meeting of the unit holders to consider and pass necessary resolutions by simple majority of the unit holders present and voting at the meeting for authorising the trustees or any other person to take steps for winding up of the scheme.

(a) The **Trustee** or the person authorised under the Act shall dispose of the assets of the scheme concerned in the best interest of the unit holders of that scheme. The Trustee or the person authorised under the Act shall dispose of the assets of the scheme concerned in the best interest of unit holders of that scheme.

(b) The proceeds of sale made in pursuance of clause (a) above shall in the first instance be utilised towards discharge of such liabilities as are properly due under the scheme and after making appropriate provisions for meeting the expenses connected with such winding up the balance shall be paid to the unit holders in proportion to their respective interest in the assets of the scheme as on the date when the decision for winding up was taken.

On the completion of the winding up the trustees shall forward to the SEBI and after the receipt of the report, if the board is satisfied that all measures for winding up of the scheme have been completed, the scheme shall **cease** to exist.

## Disclosing Through the WEB Mutual Funds Style

### *Recent Developments*

Over the course of the past year, the returns of many equity mutual funds remained in negative territory. This has been largely due to the direction taken by the markets. The fund managers could not give returns due to market situation. The Mutual Funds now viewed as investments which empower investors to participate in the growth of financial market. Fund investments are transparent as investors are regularly informed about their portfolio. The latest development in the market is, mutual funds are also providing information on websites. The websites of different funds focus on the information required the investors. Daily disclosures of the **NAV**, regular monthly updates and information on dividends and changes in the load structure are the things which all the investors should be aware before investing.

### *www.alliance capital india.com—Case Study 1*

The site provides the first hand information about the Net Asset Value of the fund. The previous days NAV of all the schemes is provided in an easily accessible manner on the site and is updated regularly. The site contains the information such as news about dividend declaration, fund's holdings in its different schemes etc. The quarterly reports also contains the same information. The information about the portfolio usually contains only the top **Ten** holdings of the particular scheme. The website provide the financial data about the funds returns over different time periods as well as the benchmark of the sector.

The site provides **offer document** for all the funds schemes. These can be downloaded in a format. These can also be requested through **e-mail** as well as post. A facility for receiving the **NAV** of the fund's schemes as well as news updates through **e-mail** is also provided on the site.

The site also provides information about the funds as well as its key personnel along with the directors and the trustees. Details about the qualification and the experience of the key personnel are also provided. **Telephone Numbers** and addresses of the funds offices indifferent cities as well as those of its transfer agents are provided. The fund's site has a **learning** centre which has a section of frequently asked questions and an archieve of useful articles from the investment manager. Here also some of the information is outdated. A **Glossary** and a simple savings calculator are also present on the site.

### *www.pioneeriti.com—Case Study 2*

The PIONEER ITI can be reached through above address. The fund is upto the mark by presenting the latest information on **NAVs** of its different schemes. A facility for the daily receipt of NAV through e-mail is also provided.

The portfolio of the funds and different schemes are presented under the heading of the monthly performance reports. Pioneer ITI is among the few funds which provides full disclosure of their portfolios for each month of the year. The information about returns will be provided and is also to be updated on a **weekly basis**.

The fund's site provides a number of tools for the financial planning. These include a savings, networth and inflation calculator.

The savings and net worth calculator require detailed inputs and one's financial position. These concerned parameters provides a realistic time frame for developing a saving plan. The inflation calculator is a simple tool to demonstrate the effect of inflation on the current prices.

Forms required for making the investments, redemptions or switches are provided in a downloaded format. These also includes the slips for the information about the change of address; change of account number and other routine communication between an investor and the fund.

The **Fund's CEO** communicates with the investors on a monthly basis through the site. This is usually as same as the communication as that provided in the monthly fact sheet. This is based on the issues faced by the investor and provides inputs for targets oriented investing. As the proliforation of ranking surveys are being carried out the funds are eager to impress the investors about their performance. This information is also provided by the fund and usually shows the results of the latest ranking exercises. The fund also provide the data of different volatility measures of its different schemes. The significance of these also communicated. The fund provides the detailed information about itself and its sponsors. Information about the fund's key personnel and trustees is also not present. The site's section on the **FAQ** provides a series of questions which take investors through the entire process of investing and the possible questions which arises in an investor's mind. These also indicate general questions on mutual funds and the concept of fund investing. Reports about the funds in different sanctions of the press are included in site. The site provides the addresses and telephone numbers of its offices in different cities.

### (1) Basics of Fund Management[19]

The key objective behind every investment is **to get better returns** out of the same, with a moderate degree of risk associated with it. But, in order to reap the benefits from an investment, be it equity, bonds, MFs. FDs.The investor should be better informed and should be in a position to take a call based on certain analysis, and not just be a layman putting the hard-earned money on rumors and information floating around in the market place.

In case of the assets of a mutual fund, which is the poor of assets from the individual investors, the most significant risk is the poor fund performance. While analysing the performance of a fund, Crisil in its research tries to address only portfolio (market) risk and not the credit, counter party, operation and legal risks. In case of pension funds and insurance companies, sufficient research has taken place on asset liability management. In the banking sector, already these exist sophisticated models to measure and manage the risk. In case of a fund's operations, fund adviser's demands are increasing to understood how performance has been achieved for the risks assumed.

For a majority of funds, performance is assessed as against the prescribed benchmarks for the same. A number of methods to assess portfolio risk do exist and many of the funds adopt standard deviations as a measure of risk, along with a few others. For the simple fact that no single model can predict risk accurately. The basic ideas of evaluation of a mutual fund can be implemented more accurately by taking into account the whole organisation. Also, once the Risk Management process is put in place in a fund house, it would prove better for key people: Chief Investment Officers (CIO), fund managers, research analysts, dealers to take conscious decisions based on the set of defined parameters.

In the context of a fund's performance, diversification is in inverse proportion with the risk, with in certain limits. The market-linked risk from economy-related factors like fiscal policy, industrial policy, money supply, inflation etc..... cannot be eliminated. Thus, the risk that can be, explained by the market conditions is called. **Systematic risk** and the unexplained residual risk (which could be company or industry or instrument-specific) is called unsystematic **risk**.

**(2) Top of the POPS: These are a few of their Favourite Sectors[20]**

***—Caste Study 3***

The scores have changed, so has the popularity. The pharmaceutical sector-riding high on expanding global demand for generic drugs—has emerged as the most popular sector among mutual funds for the quarter ended September 2001. However, even after having lost its sheen during three months, Infosys Technologies still tops the funds' popularity Index chart.

In spite of the ET-Crisil Fund Popularity Index chart, for the September quarter, indicating a 44.8 per cent fall in propensity to invest in Infosys Technologies by Mutual Funds, it still ruled as the most popular stock held by funds.

The propensity to invest by finds in pharmaceutical stocks rosé sharply by 37–76 per cent. However, the propensity to invest fell to 55–62 per cent in case of information technology stocks, for the quarter ended September 2001.

During the same period, most funds pared their holdings in Infosys Technology by 23 per cent. The total percentage to Net Asset Value (NAV) of the Scrip in funds slipped 42 per cent to 4.97 per cent even as the price of the scrip fell 26 per cent to 2.4 per cent.

For the some period, stock preferences of private sector mutual funds (excluding UTI) indicator four of the top 20 stocks in their portfolio are pharma ceutical stocks, two information technology stocks and not a single one from the media and telicom sector.

On the other hand, the remaining 14 of these top 20 stocks belonging to core sector like capital goods, engineering, cement, steel, petroleum products and petrochemicals.

Diversification is clearly the new mantras in the mutual funds industry, as is evident from the ET-crisil analysis of the changing preferences of fund managers. The study excludes all overseas registered Foreign Institutional Investor (FII) without portfolio details as well as domestic mutual funds monolith—Unit Trust of India—due to non-availability of its portfolio for the period ended September 2001.

Analysis of the top equity holding are based on two factors—the number of schemes comprising a particular stock and the simple average of the percentage holdings of each scheme in the particular stock (without considering the absolute value of the holdings). It is therefore an amalgamation of how commonly owned. The scrip is and the extent to which the funds are willing to allocate their portfolios (irrespective of the size of that portfolio) to that scrip. We call this the popularity Index.

The sample size includes 98 equity and balanced schemes which account for over 70 per cent of the total assets of the private sector domestic mutual funds in these two categories (please see accompanying Tables).

**The Value-Weighted Holdings**

| *Scrips* | *Sept 29, '01* | *June 30, '01* | *Ckg (%)* |
|---|---|---|---|
| Ranbaxy labs | 2.96 | 0.96 | 208.84 |
| ACC | 2.63 | 1.32 | 99.54 |
| Dr. Reddy's Labs | 4.93 | 2.84 | 73.68 |
| Hero Honda Motors | 3.61 | 2.13 | 69.55 |
| Cipla | 5.79 | 4.23 | 36.76 |
| HLL | 3.57 | 2.64 | 34.97 |
| Reliance Ind. | 4.74 | 3.85 | 23.12 |
| ITC | 3.6 | 3.01 | 19.74 |
| Grasim Industries | 3.19 | 2.82 | 13.02 |
| Satyam Computers | 2.65 | 2.47 | 7.41 |
| MTNL | 1.05 | 0.98 | 7.06 |
| Avantis Pharma | 2.07 | 2.03 | 1.86 |
| VSNL | 2.16 | 2.12 | 1.68 |
| HPCL | 1.81 | 1.82 | –0.13 |
| BHEL | 2.57 | 2.66 | –3.68 |
| BPCL | 2.57 | 2.66 | –3.68 |
| SBI | 1.81 | 1.99 | –5.23 |
| Hindalco Industries | 1.81 | 2.05 | –11.88 |
| L & T | 3.66 | 4.27 | –13.33 |
| Infosys technologies | 4.92 | 8.49 | –42.04 |

So, which stocks are in and which ones are out of favour with fund managers? The popularity Index of September 2001 has as many as eight new entrants. These includes three pharmaceuticals stocks, two telecommunications stocks and one each from automobiles, Cement and Steel Industry. The eight new entrants comprise of Grasim Industries (in the 9th position), Dr. Reddy's (10th position), Avantis Pharma (11th position), VSNL (16th position), Hero Honda (18th position) and Hindalco Industries and MTNL taking the last two positions respectively.

Information technology stocks such as Digital global software. HCL Technologies, Wipro and Hughes Software, all of which were among the most sought after stocks by funds for the quarter ended June 2001, have dropped out of the top 20 stocks held by funds during the following quarter. Pharmaceuticals ranked 11th June quarter moved out of the top 20 holdings of funds in the September.

Let's take a closer look at the most popular stocks. At the top, Infosys remains the most preferred stock yet, however, the extent of its popularity has been eroding since December 2000. That evident from the intensity of preference or propensity to invest which is measured by the percentage change in the combined score of how commonly owned, the stocks is and the simple average portfolio allocations to it between two periods.

**The Value, Volume, Price Games**

| Scrips | Value (Rs M) Sept '01 | June '01 | Chgl % | Volume (000's) Sept '01 | June '01 | Chg (%) | Price (R) Sept '01 | June '01 | Chg (%) |
|---|---|---|---|---|---|---|---|---|---|
| Infosys Tech | 746.74 | 1543.46 | –51.62 | 311.14 | 406.18 | –23.40 | 2400 | 3799.95 | –36.81 |
| Cipla | 833.86 | 901.40 | –1.95 | 792.70 | 789.32 | 0.43 | 1115.00 | 1142.00 | –2.3 |
| HLL | 547.77 | 537.19 | 1.97 | 2646.23 | 2632.66 | 0.53 | 207.00 | 204.05 | 1.45 |
| L & T | 554.56 | 801.27 | –30.79 | 3532.23 | 3647.11 | –3.15 | 157.00 | 219.70 | –28.5 |
| Reliance Indust | 719.45 | 921.36 | –21.91 | 2705.72 | 2481.11 | 9.05 | 265.90 | 317.35 | –28.5 |
| ITC Ltd. | 550.59 | 558.94 | –1.49 | 949.78 | 741.3 | 28.12 | 579.70 | 754.00 | –23.1 |
| ACC | 398.98 | 308.37 | 29.38 | 3221.45 | 2259.95 | 42.55 | 123.85 | 136.45 | –9.2 |
| BSNL | 474.10 | 685.84 | –30.87 | 3984.03 | 3853.02 | 3.40 | 119.00 | 178.00 | –33.15 |
| HPCL | 275.59 | 297.74 | –7.44 | 2256.20 | 1878.48 | 20.11 | 122.15 | 158.50 | –22.9 |
| Satyam Computer | 400.23 | 590.51 | –32.22 | 3151.41 | 3485.91 | –9.60 | 127.00 | 169.40 | –25.03 |
| VSNL | 328.60 | 322.79 | 1.80 | 1557.73 | 1010.46 | 54.16 | 210.95 | 319.45 | –33.9 |
| SBI | 277.38 | 399.34 | –30.54 | 1681.10 | 1827.67 | –8.02 | 165.00 | 218.50 | –24.4 |
| Hero Honda Motors | 548.75 | 411.42 | 33.38 | 2935.30 | 2837.38 | 3.45 | 186.95 | 145.00 | 28.9 |
| Hindalco Indust | 276.15 | 406.65 | –31.92 | 542.17 | 472.78 | 14.68 | 509.35 | 853.00 | –40.6 |
| MTNL | 160.47 | 196.15 | –18.19 | 1263.57 | 1556.16 | –18.80 | 127.00 | 126.05 | 0.75 |

*Sources*: *The Economic Times*, Dt : 9.11.2002.

The propensity to invest in Infosys technologies dropped by nearly 44.87 per cent for the quarter ended September 2001. In fact the intensity of preference for just three stocks of the top ten in the popularity index dipped dramatically for the September quarter. Satyam Computers slipped 60.18 per cent between June-September, while HCL Technologies fell 63.77 per cent.

Realiance Industries dipped 26.95 per cent and Bharat Heavy Electricals fell by 14.87 per cent. A look at the value-volume figures will corroborate this trend. In the case of Infosys, the Private Sector mutual funds shed 23 per cent of their volume holding in the stock.

**The Popularity Index**

| *Base: Sept. = 100* Company | *Sept. 2001* | | *June 2001* | | *Index Chg. (%)* |
|---|---|---|---|---|---|
| | *Index* | *Rank* | *Index* | *Rank* | |
| Infosys Technologies | 55.13 | 1 | 100 | 1 | –44.87 |
| Cipla | 49.98 | 2 | 43.53 | 4 | 14.8 |
| Hindustan Lever | 40.45 | 3 | 32.11 | 7 | 26.29 |
| Larsen & Loubro | 38.5 | 4 | 34.65 | 5 | 11.13 |
| Reliance Industries | 37.90 | 5 | 52.01 | 2 | –26.95 |
| ITC | 37.92 | 6 | 16.05 | 14 | 105.34 |
| Bharat Heavy Electricals | 31.37 | 8 | 36.85 | 9 | –14.87 |
| Grasim Industries | 29.3 | 9 | 27.05 | NA | 8.35 |
| Dr. Reddy Laboratories | 27.62 | 10 | 10.38 | NA | 166.12 |
| Ranbaxy Laboratories | 26.82 | 11 | 5.11 | NA | 424.89 |
| Aventis Pharma | 24.03 | 12 | 17.52 | NA | 37.2 |
| Bharat Petroleum Corpo. | 17 | 13 | 16.93 | 17 | 0.38 |
| Hindustan Petroleum Corpo. | 16.08 | 14 | 13.86 | 18 | 15.95 |
| Satyam Computer Services | 14.2 | 15 | 35.66 | 3 | –60.18 |
| Videsh Sanchar Nigam | 13.18 | 16 | 7.18 | NA | 83.56 |
| State Bank of India | 13.13 | 17 | 10.47 | 19 | 25.39 |
| Hero Honda Motors | 12.4 | 18 | 9.49 | NA | 30.68 |
| Hindalco Industries | 9.09 | 19 | 8.53 | NA | 6.56 |
| Mahanagar Telephone Nigam | 8.99 | 20 | 5.9 | NA | 52.2 |

*Source*: *The Economic Times*. Dt. 9.11.2000, p. 7.

This, coupled with nearly 36 per cent erosion in the price of stock between June-September 2001 has resulted in a 51.62 per cent decline in the actual value of the fund's Infosys holding, which came down to Rs. 746 mn as of September 30, 2001.

On the other hand, Cipla, the second most popular stock witnessed a 14.8 per cent increase in the propensity to invest by funds in September 2001 over June 2001. Funds shed 0.43 per cent of the volume of their Cipla holdings even as price dipped 2 per cent in the same period.

So the pure value of the funds holdings in cipla, came down by nearly 1.9 per cent to Rs. 883.86 m. Other pharmaceutical stocks like Dr. Reddy's Laboratories and Ranbaxy Laboratories entered the popularity index chart in September 2001. The sharpest jump in popularity is seen in new entrant Ranbaxy Laboratory. It is the only stock in top 20 list, in which funds value holding jumped a whopping 229 per cent to Rs. 453.4 m. The same can be attributed to a 147 per cent increase in the volume holdings of the scrip in funds. The share price of the stock rose 33 per cent to Rs. 645 in September 2001.

**Mutual Funds Sponsoring Agency**

The SEBI was authorised by the Government to register and regulate the mutual funds both in the public and private sectors. All intermediaries and players in the capital market are brought under the SEBI authorisation and regulation. The mutual funds set up by financial institutions like LIC and GIC are regulated by the Ministry of Finance. The SEBI has taken over the responsibility of regulating, inspecting and controlling the activities of mutual funds. The authorisation is a package of approval.

(1) The sponsor of the mutual fund is to be a public company, or scheduled bank or all India or State level financial institution.
(2) Sponsor means any body corporate, who acting alone or in combination with another body corporate establishes a Mutual Fund, after initiating and completing formalities thereof.
(3) Every mutual fund shall be constituted in the form of a trust in accordance with the provisions of the Indian Trusts Act, 1882.
(4) A company shall be appointed as a trustee to manage the mutual fund. The appointment of the trustee shall be subject to the following conditions:

    (a) the trustees must have experience in financial services and are not found guilty of any economic offence,
    (b) the names of the trustees shall be forwarded to the board,
    (c) any change in the appointment of the trustees shall be subject to the approval of the board,
    (d) no trustee shall retire unless another person is appointed in the place of the retiring trustee,

(e) no person shall be a trustee or a director of a trustee company in more than one mutual fund,

(f) at least 50 per cent of the trustees shall be independent members and no such trustee shall be an affiliate or subsidiary of the sponsor, and

(g) An Asset Management Company, any of its directors, officers or employees shall not act as a trustee of any mutual fund.

**Registration of the Trust Deed**

A Mutual Fund can be constituted in the form of a trust. The instrument of trust shall be in the form of a deed duly registered under the provisions of the Indian Registration Act, 1908 executed by the sponsor in favour of the trustees named in such instrument and shall contain such clauses as are prescribed in schedule and such clauses which are necessary for safeguarding the interest of the unit holders. No trust deed shall contain a clause which has the effect of:

(a) Limiting or extinguishing the obligations and liabilities of the trust in relation to any mutual fund or the unit holders; or

(b) Indemnifying of the trustees or the Asset Management for loss or damage caused to the unit holders by their acts of negligence or acts or commissions or omissions.

The trust deed shall be available for inspection to any member of public at the registered office or the principal place of business of the MF and if so desired, a copy of the same shall be made available to any person on payment of a nominal fee as may be decided by the MF.

**Rights and Obligations of Trustees**

The trustees and the Asset Management Company should with the prior approval of the SEBI must enter into investment management agreement. The agreement contains the various clauses for the purpose of making investment. The Investment Management agreement contains the following information:

(a) The AMC would be responsible for floating schemes for the mutual fund in various schemes in accordance with the provisions of the trust deed and SEBI regulations.

(b) The AMC would undertake the management of mutual funds only.

(c) The AMC can also be involved such other activities as financial service consultancy, exchange of research and analysis on commercial basis, without the approval of the SEBI.

(d) The AMC should invest only in accordance with the provisions of trust deed and the SEBI regulations.

(e) The AMC should not take any activity with the contravention of the SEBI regulations.

(f) The AMC should not acquire any of the assets out of the scheme fund.

(g) The AMC should not disclose any information without the trustees prior approval in writing.

(h) The AMC can disclose the basis of calculating the repurchase price and NAV of the various schemes of the mutual funds as specified by the trustees or SEBI.

(i) The trustees should have the right to obtain the information from the AMC.

(j) The AMC should comply the provisions in accordance with the trust deed and SEBI regulations.

(k) The trustees have the power to call any information from the AMC.

(l) The trustees would have the power to dismiss the AMC with the approval of SEBI and its regulations.

(m) The trustees should ensure before the launching of any scheme that the Asset Management Company has the best infrastructure facilities such as office space, best talented competent staff, and appointment of all key personnel including fund managers, registrars and brokers.

The Asset Management should submit the quarterly report about the functioning of the various schemes of the mutual fund to the trustees. The trustees should ensure that the AMC has not given any undue or unfair advantage to any deal with the interest of the unit holders. The trustees should ensure that the mutual fund schemes have been managing independently. The investors benefits should not be overlapped. If the trustees believe that the conduct of business of mutual fund is not in accordance with the SEBI regulations, it should take such remedial steps and in form immediately to the SEBI. The trustees would be accountable for and be custodians of all the properties of the fund. The trustees should take steps to ensure that the activities of the fund in accordance with the provisions of the trust deed. The trustees should obtain the consent of unit holders in the following circumstances:

(a) According to SEBI norms, it is required to do so, or
(b) The majority of the trustees decide to wind up or prematurely redeem the units, or
(c) The 3/4th of the unit holders to do, so
(d) If any change in the fundamental attributes of any scheme or the trust.

The trustees should call for the information by the key personal of the asset management company to submit to the SEBI as per the Act. The trustees should review all transactions on quarterly basis carried out between the mutual fund, AMC and its associates. The trustees should also review the networth of the AMC on quarterly basis. If in case of any shortfall, it should make up for the shortfall as stipulated by the SEBI. The trustee should review all service contracts periodically and satisfy themselves that such contracts are executed in the interest of the unit holders.

**Trustees Code of Conduct**

The trustees of the fund should abide by the code of conduct as presented below:

(a) The schemes should be organised in the interest of all classes of unit holders.
(b) The trustees should provide all information to all unit holders in simple language about the investment policies, objectives, financial position and general affairs of the scheme.
(c) The trustees should avoid excess concentrations of business with broking firms.

(d) They must avoid conflict of interest in managing the affairs of the schemes.

(e) They must ensure scheme-wise segregation of bank accounts and securities accounts.

(f) The trustees should carry out the business and invest in accordance with the investment objectives of the schemes.

(g) The trustees must not use any unethical means in the affairs of the schemes.

(h) The trustees should maintain high standard of integrity and fairness in the transactions of the business affairs.

(i) The trustees should render at all time with high standard of service, ensure proper care and exercise independent professional judgement.

(j) The trustees should submit to the SEBI on a half yearly basis with the required documents. A brief report on the activities of the mutual funds. A certificate indicating that the affairs are carried out properly in accordance with the rules and regulations of the Act.

(k) The trustees should exercise general and specific due diligence as follows:

    (1) The trustees should review the desirability of the AMC.
    (2) The trustees should ensure that the trust property is properly protected.
    (3) The trustees must ensure that all service providers are registered with the SEBI.

(l) The trustees should pay specific attention to the following situations:

    (1) any service contract with the associates of the AMC.
    (2) selection and nomination of individuals to fill vacancies of independent directors.
    (3) check all the service contracts with all the key persons.

**Asset Management Company**

The sponsors of mutual funds would appoint the Asset Management Company with the approval of the SEBI. The AMC can be terminated by a majority of trustee or by **75 per cent** of the unitholders of the scheme. The application for the grant of the AMC shall be made in

**"A Form"**. The memorandum of association and articles of association of the AMC shall be submitted to the SEBI alongwith the application. For grant of approval of the AMC by SEBI, the applicant has to fulfil the following conditions.

(a) The AMC should have a sound track record and fairness in transaction.
(b) The AMC should have the directors with adequate professional experience in financial services aspects.
(c) The Directors of the AMC should not have been found guilty or convicted of any economic offence.
(d) The Directors of the AMC shall not hold the position of a director in another AMC or a trustee in any mutual fund.
(e) The AMC should inform any change to the SEBI.
(f) No change in the Management of the AMC shall be made without approval of the SEBI.
(g) The Chairman of the AMC should not be a trustee of any other mutual fund.
(h) The AMC should have a net worth of Rs. 10 crores.
(i) The net worth of the AMC will be calculated as follows: Paid up capital + Free reserves – Misl. exp. unwritten deferred revenue expenditure/intangible assets.

**Grant of Approval of the AMC**

For grant of approval of the AMC, the SEBI may take into account all matters which are relevant to efficient and orderly conduct of the affairs of the AMC and in particular the following as:

(a) The existing AMC should have a sound track record and general reputation.
(b) The Board of Directors of the AMC are persons of high repute and standing having at least 5 years of professional experience in the relevant field.

**Restrictions on Business Activities**

The Asset Management Company cannot act as a trustee of any mutual fund. It cannot undertake any other business activities. The AMC should engage itself in the activities of financial services like portfolio management services, advisory services to offshore funds, pension funds, provident funds, venture capital funds, financial consultancy, management of insurance funds and exchange of research on commercial basis. If the SEBI accepts any work can be undertaken by the AMC. The AMC must disclose full information to the unit holders.

**Obligations**

The AMC must take all precautions in accordance with the provisions of the regulations and the trust deed. It should take care of all the investment decisions. It should be responsible for the acts of behaviour by its employees. The AMC should submit to the trustee about the activities of the fund as quarterly basis. The AMC is required to file with the trustees and SEBI as follows:

(a) A detailed bio-data of all its directors.
(b) The other particulars should be submitted within 15 days of their appointment.
(c) Any change in board of directors.
(d) A quarterly report to the trustees.
(e) A statement of securities holding in the AMC by the Director.
(f) A brief note on investment made by the Directors in other mutual fund organisations.

A mutual fund should not buy/sell securities through any broker who is associated with the sponsors. The mutual fund is not allowed to purchase **5 per cent** or more of the aggregate purchases in all of its scheme for a block of any three months. If the purchases/sales exceeds 5 per cent limit a justification report should be submitted to the trustees on quarterly basis. The AMC should not utilise the services of the sponsor or any of its associates for the purpose of business transactions. The mutual fund should disclose at the time of declaring half yearly results: (a) underwriting obligations of the schemes with reference to issue of shares of associate companies, (b) if any devolvement, (c) worked as a lead manages to the issue of shares of the associated companies, (d) any participation in private placement.

The AMC should not appoint any person as key personnel who has been found guilty of share transfer agents. The AMC should assign the processing work to the least charged company. It has to abide by the same code of conduct as specified in the case of **trustees**.

## Custodian

The mutual fund should appoint a custodian to look after the custodial services for the schemes. The MF should inform the SEBI within 15 days of the appointment of the custodian. The MF should enter into a custodian agreement regarding the service contract, terms and appointment conditions. The appointment will be confirmed with the approval of trustees.

## REFERENCES


1. Growth and emerging of mutual funds, A. Sudhakar, K. Gangappa, "*Finarcial Services*", Deep and Deep Publications, p. 173, 1997.
2. N. Gopalaswamy, *Inside Capital Market*, Deccan Publications, Chennai, p. III-164.
3. *Ibid.*
4. *Ibid.*
5. *Business Today*, 10th anniversary issue, Jan. 20, 2002, p. 69.
6. Kumar, Amit, *The Economic Times*, 27.8.2001, p. 5.
7. Van Horne, *Fundamentals of Financial Management*, p. 91, 1997.
8. *Ibid.*
9. *Ibid.*
10. *Ibid.*
11. *Ibid.*
12. *Ibid.*, p. 95.
13. *Ibid.*, p. 95, 1997, PHI
14. *Ibid.*, p. 95.
15. *Ibid.* p. 100, 1997, PHI
16. *Ibid.*, 100.
17. *Ibid.*, 102.
18. N. Gopalaswamy, *Inside Capital Market*, Deccan Publications, p. III-164.
19. *Economic Times* at 9 Nov. 2001, p. 7.
20. *Economic Times*, 9 Nov. 2001, Crisil Fund Tracker, p. 7.

# 2

# VENTURE CAPITAL

## Introduction

Venture capital is a type of financial intermediary emerged in **USA**. It is a financial intermediary very popular during **1970** in **America**. Early 1980 in Britain, in the mid-1980s in **Japan** and Canada. It has become popular in **1987** in India. It is a long-term investment which involves in high **risk** industrial projects with reward possibilities. It is involved in financing the new business and professional activities carrying higher expectation to come up with the success. It is a source of long-term finance for innovative projects. It plays a vital role in providing the long-term capital to a wide variety of enterprises.

Venture capital provides finance or risk capital to little known **unregistered, high risky, technology oriented, knowledge** based activities or industries which have long development cycles, small private business etc. It also renders the management and marketing expertism to the units. It is an organised financing with relatively new enterprises to achieve substantial benefits. The venture capital is the part of the primary market. It is an important source of funds for technology based industries. It helps the commercial enterprises where conventional financing agencies cannot reach. The business concern requires a sizeable equity contribution to the project cost where scientists and **technocrats** cannot always provide. The venture capital provides the equity to help the projects to get out of research laboratory and into the market. Financial resources will be provided not as a **loan** but as an investment in the venture. It is regarged as "pre-public" financing venture capital companies generally support the management as a **minority** partner. The venture capital financial assistance is made available in **3 kinds. They are equity, conditional loans and Income notes**. The VC firm contributes in the form of equity which does not exceed 49 per cent of the total equity. Another type of assistance is available in the form of conditional loan ranging between **2 per cent and 15 per cent** of the required. It is repayable in the form of **Royalty** between 2 and 15 per cent after the venture is able to generate sales and no interest is paid on such loans. The **Income notes** has combining features of conventional and conditional loans. The entrepreneur has to pay both the interest and royalty on sales at low rates. The rate of royalty is based on the profitability of the business. All these types of assistance are tailored to meet the investment needs of entrepreneurs at different phases. Development start up, launching the financing, for meeting the growth of expansion are the **3 phases**. The development start is the riskiest and requires utmost attention.

## Features of VC

Venture capital fund has the following features:

(a) Venture capitalists assume risk.
(b) It is a long-term financial instrument with capital appreciation.
(c) Venture capitalists provide—technical, commercial, managerial, financial and entrepreneurial services.
(d) It involves investment in small industries with high risk and assures a better return in future.

Venture capital companies has to appoint marketing specialists in product launching to capture the market. The V.C. board should consist of private business executives academic scientists, engineers patent attorney, bankers and brokers.

## Financial Support

The various kinds of financial requirement involves the following:

(a) See capital to bring a research idea to the development stage.
(b) Financial requirement to set up initial infrastructure on manufacturing, distribution, sourcing and marketing without any cash in flows from sales.
(c) This stage of financing is to **add** to their range of products or switch over from unsuccessful product range.

(d) This is the final stage of capital requirement for expansion or diversification.

Whether to finance these projects, in order to finance, it is based on the information available, research and selection etc., venture capital research team will evaluate the investment proposals based on the factors like **ROI**, track record of entrepreneurs, market considerations, exit routes. The success of the venture capital depends upon the business environment, statutory regulations, taxation levels, future revenue costs, capacity utilisation, and sales levels. Investors of venture capital have no liquidity for a period of time. Venture capital proposals are attractive in **high technology** area. The VC funds require professionals. The preferred form of organisation for the VC is the limited company. VC firms are not permitted to money market operation, portfolio investments, broking, fundamental management and financial services.

**Instrument**

The methods of financing are practiced by the VC companies:

**(A) Shares.**
**(B) Debt.**

***(A) Shares***

The following types of shares are available for investment in the venture capital firms:

1. Equity shares.
2. Preference share.
3. Convertible preference share.

The equity shares are usually issued by the Companies. They are a good growth of the unit. There is an anticipation that there would be a significant growth in the value of equity over a period of time. In the form of equity the contribution does not exceed **49 per cent** of the total equity, ranging between **2 and 15 per cent** of the investment. The other instruments are in general nature. The types of assistance are tailored to meet the investment needs of entrepreneurs at different stages.

**Technological Revolution**

The present technological revolution has witnessed the re-emergence of small and medium firms. These firms play an important role in the development of technology. The introduction of **Computer Aided Design/Computer Aided Management CAD/CAM** flexible manufacturing system, Bio-technology. These developments have increased the global competitiveness of small and medium hightech firms. There is a tremendous scope of development in agriculture. The role of small and medium technology firms can easily spread into the entire country in agriculture sector. The venture capital firms can also concentrate on farm-management, development of seed capital with quality, low duration period of cultivation, development of water resources, land development, soil technology, agro based industries like food processing etc.

The introduction of appropriate changes in the company law and banking law are considered advisable to enable their successful participation in the current technological revolution. Certain positive policies should be formulated for sustainable development.

The investments of VCFs differs from organisation to organisation. The VCFs are usually characterised by substantial control over management decisions and protection against downside risk. Some VCFs have a seat on the company's board of directors. VC is a high risk-high return business. Because these projects are untested and are undertaken by new persons without experience. The expected returns from VC investment are very high. The funds are usually expected to be tied up for **Three to Ten years**. Usually VCFs in addition to using their own funds, are banking upon the sources to get funds in the form of equity through All India Financial Institutions, **FIIs, private sector**, nationalised banks, private sector, public sector and NRIs.

Venture capital firms can recover their investments if the organisation has a commercial run. There are various alternatives are available for the venture capitalists are presented below:

(a) Initial public offering.
(b) Buy back of the shares.
(c) Sale of the firm to another company.
(d) Sale to new investors.

Initial public offering is the opportunity for a venture capitalist to offer their holdings for public sale and liquidate the investment. **Buy back of shares** mans the promotors of the investee company buy the shares held by the venture capital companies as investment. It provides liquidity to VCFs by encashing their holdings. Sometimes the venture capitalists can recover their investments by selling the holdings of their investments to outsider who is interested in purchasing the whole enterprise. **Sale to investor** is the final alternative to the venture capitalist. Venture capitalist can sell its equity holding to a new venture capital company who is interested in buying the ownership position of the venture capitalist.

**Guidelines Issued by the Government/SEBI**

The Union Finance Ministry has issued guidelines for the establishment and functioning of the venture capital activities:

(1) Any company can undertake VC finance activities by agreeing to abide by these guidelines.
(2) Interested companies can put an application and details of the proposals to the SEBI with a suitable explanatory note.
(3) Application for the issue of share capital by the companies should be made to the SEBI under capital issues act.
(4) In case of all India public sector financial institutions the SBI and other Scheduled Banks, if they want to establish a venture capital firm, they should get the approval from the RBI.
(5) VCFs are managed by the professionals with an adequate experience in industry, finance, accounts etc.
(6) If the VCFs are established by the subsidiaries of banks/ institutions or in house schemes. They should maintain their independence and an arm length relationship. However, they would be free to draw the professional expertise and infrastructure of the parent organisation with the interests of their shareholders and clients and minimising costs.
(7) The Full time chairman/**president/Chief Executive/ Executive Directors/Wholetime director** should not hold any position in any other company.
(8) VC assistance should go basically to high risk involved and high technology based concerns.

(9) The financial assistance mainly be equity support through loan support to supplement this may also be done.

(10) VC assistance should cover those enterprises which fulfil the following parameters:

(a) The total investment of the concerns should not exceed Rs. 10 crores.

(b) The concern should be in the new technology development concept and it must be like a pilot project.

(c) The project should be in a position from pilot to commercial stage which is an innovative technology.

(d) The project promoters/entrepreneurs should be relatively new or professionally or technically qualified with sufficient financial resources.

(e) Investment in the firms engaged in trading, broking, investment or financial services agency or liaison work should not be permitted.

(f) Investments in assisted units for their expansion or strengthening or investments for the revival of sick units would be permitted.

(g) The assisted company should be in the form of a limited company and it must employ professionally qualified persons to maintain its accounts.

(h) The VCF should invest at least 60 per cent of its funds into VCF activities.

(i) The VC investment during the first **12 months** permissible investment is a level of **30** per cent should be reached for VC financing activity by the end of the second year, **60** per cent by the end of third year-**75** per cent by the end of the **Fifth Year** of its operations. The **balance** may be invested in any new issue or existing company of equity, debentures, bonds, CCPS, or other securities approved for the these purposes by the SEBI.

(j) Investment on leasing sector should not exceed **15** per cent of the total founds deployed including the first year.

(k) The VC firms can raise funds through public issues or private placements.

(l) Foreign equity upto **25 per cent** would be permitted in the venture capital firms.

(m) The NRI investment would be permitted upto **74 per cent** in venture capital concerns (on Non-Repatriation basis).

(n) The NRI investment would be permitted **25/40** per cent on a Repatriable basis.

(o) For NRI investment, an application should be submitted to the **Ministry of Finance** with a copy to the chairman, SEBI.

(p) The maximum debt equity ratio will be permitted by **1:1.5**.

(q) The VCFs can be listed according to the prescribed norms.

(r) The VC issue may be underwritten at the discretion of the promoters.

(s) The pricing of shares at the time of disinvestment by a public issue of general offer for sale by the VFCs may be done by them.

(t) The pricing of shares will be based on the factors like **book value profit earning** capacity. All these factors should be disclosed to the public.

(u) The tax exemption treatment would be available to the approved capital firms only.

(v) The venture capital firms which want to enjoy these tax benefits should obtain a letter of eligibility from **IDBI/ ICICI** or any nominated agency of the government.

## Tax Concessions

According to the Income Tax Act, 1961 **Section 10 (23D)** deals with tax concessions to the VCFs. The VCFs are exempted from the payment of capital gains tax and Income Tax. For preferential tax treatment under the capital gains. The VCF should follow the guidelines issued by the Central Government. The VCF should operate like the mutual funds. According to the guidelines, mutual funds are not allowed to invest more than **5 per cent** in the equity of a single company and **15 per cent** in a particular industry. If the investments are made in sick units and export oriented units then the exemptions will be provided. Various liberalisation measures have been taking deep roots in the economy. The Government is in favour of effective steps to boost the VC outfits. In the present environment, many path breaking technologies in the fields of micro electronics, biotechnology

**computers** have raised small units with the support of venture capital. The dynamism, the trust of innovations and entrepreneur cannot be ignored. The globally reputed firms like **Microsoft, Gentech, Apple, DEC, Micro, Intel, Lotus** and **Federal** express backed venture capital support they emerged industry standard in their fields. After implementation of liberalisation and globalisation policies, more steps are required by the Government, financial institutions, private sector and other agencies for the development of VCFs. The long-term capital gains are subjected to a tax of **20 per cent**. These are some distinctions between public sector VCFs and private sector venture capital firms. Tax concessions are discretionary in case of public sector. The long-term prospects of the industry remains **high**, hightech projects should be encouraged by various methods.

Entrepreneurship introduces a critical element of dynamism into an economic system. It is not a coincidence that the worlds leading economy, The **United States** is believed to be the most entrepreneurial society in the world. In USA 4 Indian American venture capitalists creating wonders in the industry. According to **Forbes**[1], the following ranks were found:

| *S. No.* | *Name of the Person* | *Rank in Terms of efficiency* | *Prefitability* | *Market value* |
|---|---|---|---|---|
| 1. | Vinod Khosla | 7 | 94 | 2 |
| 2. | Hauque | 72 | 51 | 26 |
| 3. | Yogan Dala | 68 | 48 | 58 |
| 4. | Atiq Raja | 94 | 14 | 100 |

## Venture Capital in India

In India the venture capital industry is located in **four centres**. They are Mumbai, Delhi, Kolkata and Bangalore. The venture capital in India can be classified into four categories:

(a) Companies set up by Financial Institutions.
(b) Companies set up in the Private Sector.
(c) Companies set up by Commercial Banks.
(d) Companies set up by State level Financial Institutions.

In India, if any person wants to establish venture capital, he has to get approval from the Ministry of Finance. Now the SEBI has the power to grant licences for venture capital firms. The venture capital firms in India are run by professionals. The venture capital firms have been established in India in the form of a limited company. The firm should invest atleast 60 per cent of its funds in venture proposals. The remaining amount may be invested in the form of new issue of equity, debentures, bonds and CCPs. The venture capital firms can invest upto **15 per cent** of the total employed in the leasing sector. The venture capital firms in India are not permitted to enter into the money market operations, broking, portfolio investments and fund management and financial services. Funds may be raised through public issue/private placement.

Today, India has over **50 VC**[2] funds and equity funds operating in the country. The estimated investment of risk capital in 2001 is Rs. **7200 crores** against just over Rs. **4800 crores** in 2000. To get world class entrepreneurs from India, the role of risk capital needs are to be emphasised. The IT and non both fields must be nurtured. India's top venture capital funds[3] and their business turnover is presented below:

| | *(Rs. in crores)* *(2001–2002)* |
|---|---|
| (a) Warburg Pincus | 3360 |
| (b) ICICI Venture Funds Management Company | 1200 |
| (c) Chrysalis | 672 |
| (d) Indocean Chase | 648 |
| (e) Citibank Private equity | 480 |
| (f) Hongkong and Shangai Banking Corporation | 336 |
| (g) Bank of America | 312 |
| (h) Walden International | 264 |
| (i) Baring Private Equity Partners | 240 |
| (j) GE Capital Services | 240 |
| (k) Global Technology | 192 |
| (l) Infinity Technology Investments | 168[4] |

Venture Capital Investments trends as estimated by venture capital Association sector-wise and year-wise particulars are presented below:

| *Year* | *Figures in $ million* |
|---|---|
| 1997 | 20$ |
| 1998 | 80$ |
| 1999 | 250$ |
| 2000 | 500$ |
| 2001 | 1200$ |
| 2002 | 1100$ |
| 2003 | 1500$ |

The opportunity areas for venture capital are **software services, software products, internet based services, infotech, bio-tech, wireless,** agri-products and processed foods. The following are some of the institutions which offer venture capital finance:

1. IDBI Venture Capital Fund.
2. Technology Development and Information Company of India Ltd. (TDICI).
3. Risk Capital and Technology Finance Corporation Ltd. (RCTC).
4. Canbank Venture Capital Fund.
5. 20th Century Venture Capital Fund.
6. Indus Venture Capital Fund.
7. APIDC Venture Capital Ltd.
8. India Investment Fund.
9. Credit Capital Venture Fund.
10. Gujarath Venture Finance Ltd.

The venture capital plays a vital role in providing long-term capital to a wide variety of enterprises.

## REFERENCES


1. The *Economic Times*, Dt. 3-2-2002, p. 1.
2. The promise of risk capital, Sudhir Sethi, *Business India*, p. 133, Jan. 20, 2002.
3. Jump start, India's Top Venture Capital Funds, *Business Today*, Anniversary Issue, 2002, p. 128.
4. Welcome the new entrepreneur, Seema Sukla, *Business Today*, Anniversary Issue, 2002, p. 13.

# 3

# LEASING

## Introduction

The important function of Finance is to provide the funds required by the firm for capital investment. The capital investment includes investment in **Fixed Assets**. The fixed assets such as land, building, plant, machinery and other properties which are necessary for long-term use in the business activities. For all the requirements, the company has to meet the funds either through internal financing or through external borrowings. The heavy amount of expenditure in the capital assets is a **sunk** investment. The capital investment is involved in some consequential gains and losses and such assets are to be disposed of at a later stage. To overcome these consequences an alternative is to own and use the capital assets to get them on **lease**. The leased assets will be utilised as per the terms and conditions of the leasing agreement. Leasing has emerged as a source of long-term financing of the corporate sector. A lease represents a contractual agreement between two parties.

## Definition

Lease can be defined as "A contract under which one party, the lessor (owner) of an asset, agrees to grant the use of that asset to another the lessee in exchange for periodic rental payments."[1]

A contract of lease may be defined as "a contract whereby the owner of an asset **(Lessor)** grants to another party **(Lessee)** the exclusive right to use the asset usually for an agreed period of time in return for the payment of rent".[2]

A lease is an arrangement under which a lessee acquires the right to use the asset, without ownership title of it, in return for a series of periodic lease rentals to the lessor (owner). The lease has been defined by Equipment leasing association of UK as "A lease as a contract between the lessor and lessee for the hire of a specified asset selected for a manufacturer or vendor of such assets by the lessee."[3]

The International Accounting Standard defines lease as "an agreement whereby the lessor conveys to the lessee in return for rent the right to use an asset for an agreed period of time."[4]

Lease is a written agreement allowing the economic use of the assets for a stipulated period of time. The lease agreement takes between both the parties, the lessor and the lessee. The lessor is the **owner** of the asset and the uses is known as **"lessee"**. The owner of the asset **(lessor)** permits the lessee **(user)** to utilise the asset for a specified amount of payment then it is called **"lease rental"**. Leasing represents as an alternative sources to ownership. It can be viewed as a specialised means of financing. A lease can be treated as the functional equivalent of debt. Lease is a form of **hire** for which rent is paid. The provisions for payment of taxes, **insurance, maintenance expenses, provision for renewal of the lease** are usually provided by the **lessor**. But in some countries like **USA and UK** where leasing is most popular, leases which meet certain criteria are capitalised in the books of the **'lessee'** on the contrary in India. The depreciation and other tax shields connected with the leased assets are claimed by the **lessor**. The total amount of rental collected from the leased asset is treated as **income in** the books of the **lessor** and as expense in the books of the **lessee**. Any type of fixed assets can be leased. **For example,** construction equipments, **plant and machinery, aircraft, ships, computers, office machines, motor transport vehicles, passenger cars, agricultural equipment, heavy industrial equipments, etc.**

## Objectives of Leasing

Lease financing may enhance the growth of industries and services. The main objects of leasing are presented below:

(a) To carry on the business of buying, selling, leasing, letting on easy payment system.
(b) To promote industrial finance in the form of advance, deposit or lend money, securities and properties to or with any company, body corporate, firm, person or association falling under the same management.

(c) to manage to funds of investors by investing in various avenues.
(d) to carry on and undertake the business of portfolio investment in **equity shares, preference shares, stocks and debentures.**
(e) to provide a package of investment/merchant banking services by acting as managers to public issues by underwriting securities.

**Steps Involved in Leasing**

A contract of lease provides a person an opportunity to use an asset which belongs to another person **(lessor)**. The following steps involved in a leasing transaction may be summarised as follows:

(1) At the first instance, the lessee has to take a decision regarding the required asset. Then he has to select the manufacturer or the supplier. Before selecting the type of machine, he takes, or he considers various factors like **design specifications, the price, warrantees, terms of delivery, installation and servicing.**
(2) In the second stage the lessee enters into a lease agreement with the lessor. The lease agreement contains some obligations between the lessor and lessee:
    (a) during the lease period, the lease is irrevocable,
    (b) the quantum amount of periodical rental during the lease period,
    (c) details of any option to renew the release or to purchase the asset at the end of the basic lease period. If there is no indication about the option to the lessee, the lessor takes possession of the asset and is entitled to any residual value,
    (d) the details regarding the responsibility for the payment of cost maintenance and repairs, taxes, insurance and other expenses,
    (e) the payment of expenses in lease transactions depends upon the types of lease agreement.
(3) After fulfilling the formalities like signing of lease agreements, the lessor approaches the manufacturer or supplier to supply the asset.

(4) On receipt of the order from the lessor, the lessor makes payment to the supplier after the asset has been delivered, tested and accepted by the lessee.

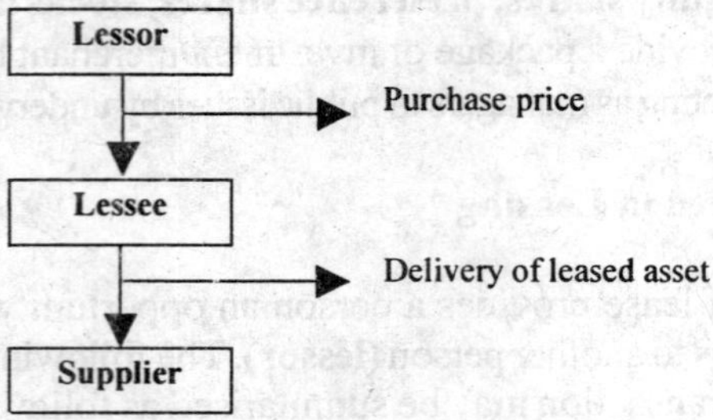


The above chart explains the relationship between supplier, lessor and lessee.

The following factors give more meaningful explanation for thorough understanding about the **lease finance**:

(a) **Fair Market Value:** The Fair market value can be defined as "The price at which property can be sold in an arm's length transaction".[5]

(b) **Residual Value:** The Residual value may be defined as "the value of a leased asset at the end of the lease period."[6]

(c) **Net Lease:** The net lease have been defined as "A lease where the lessee maintains and insures the leased asset."[7]

(d) **Operating Lease:** The operating lease is relatively short term phenomenon. It is often cancellable at the option of the lessee with proper notice. It does not give lessee all the benefits and risks that are associated with the asset. The lessor is responsible for the maintenance of asset, insurance and all other relevant expenditure. **Operating leasing** has been defined as **"A short-term lease that is often concellable"**[8] The operating lease is shorter than the assets economic life. The lessor does not recover its investment during the first lease period. It includes the leasing of **copying machines, computers hardware, word processors, and automobiles.**

(e) **Financial Lease:** Financial lease can be defined as "A long-term lease that is not cancellable".[9] It is long-term in nature and a sources of financing. It is also known as **"capital clause"**

It may be leveraged or non-leveraged. It is non-concellable and requires maintenance, property taxes and insurance which is to be provided by the lessee. Financial lease is availed in connection with leasing of land, buildings, **industrial plants, warehouses, retail stores, heavy industrial machinery, aircraft etc.** In this lease, all the risks incidental to the ownership of the asset and the benefits which arise, will be transferred to the lessee except the legal title the lease should bear cost of insurance, repairs and maintenance of the end lease. The financial lease is also known as **"close and lease"**. The rental payments are fixed. It also ensures a return of the total investment at a **predetermined** rate of return. Financial lease is one which satisfies one or more of the following conditions:

(a) the owner of the asset transfer title to the user at the end of the lease period,
(b) the lease facilitates an option to buy the asset at a bargain price,
(c) the lease period shall be equal or greater than 75 per cent of the estimated economic life of the asset, and
(d) at the commencement of the lease, the present value of the minimum lease payments equals or exceeds 90 per cent of the fair value of the property.

## Factors Influencing Leasing

Now-a-day, lease financing is very popular. It can boost the productivity of industry. It is more helpful in implementation of expansion, modernisation and diversification. A number of factors account for the **lessees** preferring arrangements. These are:

(a) the user is willing to pay more to reduce his debt.
(b) It provides 100 per cent deductability of cost.
(c) It facilitates long-term finance without dilution of ownership.
(d) It allows piecemeal procurement of assets according to the needs and convenience of the user.
(e) The lessor is the owner of the equipment and is entitled to depreciate on lease rates under the Income Tax Act, 1961 and enjoys tax exemptions.

(f) It facilitates after tax cost of leasing could be less than the after tax cost of equity financing.
(g) The lease is self-liquidating position.
(h) There is no interruption in the utilisation of machines and equipments except in case of **default** by the lessee.
(i) The user/**lessee** need not make heavy investment in the asset on lease and it utilises, this margin for **working capital of the firm**.

## Types of Lease Financing

The following are the **Financial lease** arrangements:

**(a) Sale and lease back.**
**(b) Direct leasing.**
**(c) Leveraged leasing.**

### *(a) Sale and Lease Back*

Under this method a business concern sells an asset to another party, and this party leases it back to the firm. The equipment/asset is sold at its market value. This method is very popular with the firms which are facing short-term liquidity crunch. The firm receives the sale price in cash and gets the right to use the asset during the basic lease period. The firm makes regular rental payments to the owner/lessor. The title of the asset lies with the lessor. He is also naturally entitled to any residual value of the asset might have at the end of the lease period. This method is beneficial both for the user and owner. The owner gets the benefit in terms of tax credit due to depreciation. The sale and lease back can be defined as "the sale of an asset with the agreement to immediately lease it back for an extended period of time."[10]

### *(b) Direct Leasing*

According to this method the vendor sells the asset to the lessor who in turn leases it to the lessee. The lessee/**user** can use the asset along with a contractual obligation to make lease payments to the lesser. The major types of lessors are manufacturers, **finance companies banks, independent leasing companies**, special purpose leasing companies and firms. In this type of leasing, a company acquires to use of an asset which is unable to own previously. A wide variety of direct which is leasing arrangements meet various needs of firms.

### *(c) Leveraged Leasing*

Leveraged leasing is popular in financing big assets such as **aircraft, oil rigs, and railway equipment**. These assets require large capital outlays. Such a type of lease arrangement involves **three parties**—the lessee, the lessor and the lender. The lessee contracts make periodic payments over the basic lease period and in return, is entitled to the use of the asset over that period of times. **The lessor** procures the asset according to the terms of the lease arrangement and finances. The acquisition in part by an equity investment the remaining is provided by a lender. Generally the loan is secured by a mortgage as the asset and the lessor is himself a borrower. **The lessor** is entitled to deduct all depreciation charges associated with the asset. Leveraged leasing can be defined as "A lease arrangement in which the lessor provides an equity portion **(generally 20 to 40%)** of the leased assets cost and third party lenders provide the balance of the financing.

## Advantages of Leasing

Investing in capital assets generally needs substantial cash outlay. It is not possible always to incure the heavy expenditure of amount in cash, therefore, the leasing is the best alternative sources of financing. Leasing facilitates as a source of long-term funds that can be used for acquisition of capital assets. The advantages leasing can be presented as follows:

1. **Leasing** facilitates a firm without heavy amount of investment to utilise the asset. The firm is only to make periodical rental payments. Leasing saves considerable funds for alternative uses.
2. Leasing provides assets in **cheaper and faster** sources. Leasing organisations are providing finance faster than the bankers. The rental payments are fixed according to the expected profits.
3. **Leasing** enables the lessee to utilise the funds in a proper and better way in place of **low yielding** fixed assets. Lease finance does not effect the **debt equity ratio** of the lesser. Therefore, the lessee can utilise his funds more effectively.

4. The lessee role is limited to utilise the assets for a fixed period of time and he does not bare the risk of **obsolescence of** the asset.
5. **Leasing** arrangement is more beneficial to small firms because they are unable to raise the funds on account of paucity of financial resources. It is best source of financing for technocrats who are unable to arrange funds for promoters contribution of margin money as required by financial Institutions.
6. **Leasing** facilitates lower rental charges to the lessee, because of the tax advantages.
7. According to the lease arrangement, the lessee gets a right to use the asset without title. The asset acquired as lease basis does not become a part of the property of the lessee. The rental payments are revenue in nature. The lessee can avail the chance of **several government** incentives. The lessee can escape from the MRTP Act on a large asset based situation.

## Disadvantages of Leasing

Acquisition of assets through lease finance results in some disadvantages which are presented below:

(a) In lease financing the lessee never gets the ownership of the asset. He gets only a right to use. There is no chance for the sale of the asset.
(b) In the lease agreement, if the lessee is in default position in rental payments. The lessor will take over the asset and the lessee has no right to prevent him from doing so.
(c) In the lease financing system the lessee has no right and no power in possession of the asset.

## Choosing a Lessor

Due to rapid industrialisation, leasing is gaining tremendous popularity in India. Leasing facilitates a long-term relationship between **lessor and the lessee**. Each party should understand others difficulties. Leasing agreement is to work effectively as a source of modern business finance. The following factors influence in selecting a lessor:

(a) **Market rate.**
(b) **Accurate information.**
(c) **Quality of service.**
(d) **Professional spirit.**
(e) **Systematic documentation.**

### *(a) Market Rate*

The prospective lessee enquires about the prices of required asset within the specific technical design. The lessee must ensure that the comparisons are made on the basis of rentals. He should verify all the model prices which are available in the market as competitive basis. The lessee should remember the rental value, scrap value, life period of the asset would have an impact as the profitability of the firm.

### *(b) Accurate Information*

The lessee and lessor, both the parties need accurate information to avoid all future problems. The lessee should provide the lessor all the available information relating to nature of his business and its operations. It will help the lessor in understanding. The actual requirement of the lessee. The lessor is also likely to have the details about the lessy's company financial position, technical capabilities etc. The lessor should also provide full information regarding the lease financing like **lease period, amount and number of rental payments, the liability** for repairs and insurance of the asset etc.

### *(c) Quality of Service*

In lease financing the maintenance of leased assets lies with the lessor. The maintenance of the leased asset depends upon the competency of the educated and trained staff in technical aspects etc., of the lessor. This is the most important element in the selection of the lessor.

### *(d) Professional Spirit*

Lease finance requires a highly talented professional skill. The lessee is not in a position in familiar with all consequences of the less financing. The lessor should act as a guide. The lessor should be familiar with all aspects of the lease financing. The lessor should be able to brief about

(a) the legal aspects involved in leasing transactions,
(b) rental payment, tax implications, etc.,
(c) advice the lessee regarding all the aspects of transactions.

### *(e) Systematic Documentation*

In financing aspects, the documents are most important elements and maintenance of proper documentation is very necessary. Generally the lease financing is a long-term based activity and the documents should be kept for a long period of time. The lease documents cover all aspects of the lease transactions in a legally satisfactory manner. The terms and conditions should be clearly defined to avoid overlapping.

## Lease Evaluation

Lease financing is beneficial to both the parties, i.e., lessor and lessee. Each party can evaluate the transactions from its dimension. The relation between lessor and lessee will continue for a long period of time. The evaluation of lease deals will be done by two parties, namely:

**(A) Evaluation by lessor.**
**(B) Evaluation by lessee.**

## (A) Evaluation by Lessor

A lease is a financial proposal. Generally leasing is an alternative to debt financing. In lease transactions the cash flows are in the form of rentals received from the lessee. **The Internal rate of return** is generally the accepted technique by the lessor for evaluating a lease transaction. The IRR is the rate which discounts the cash flows to **zero**. The IRR is computed on the basis of these cash flows. Therefore, a comparison will be made with weighted after tax average cost of capital of the lessor. If the **IRR** is more than the weighted after tax average cost of capital, the investment should be made. The lessor makes an assessment the risk involved in the leasing transaction while appraising the lease, the lessor is concerned with **six as characters,**

**capacity, credit, conditions, competition and collateral.** After appraising of lease. If the lessor finds the use transaction is more **risky**, he may demand higher rental, higher security deposit, additional collateral security, shorter lease term, personal guarantees etc.

The following illustration will help in understanding how to evaluate a lease transaction from the view of the lessor:

**Illustration–1**

From the following information evaluate the lease proposal in point of the lessor.

XYZ Ltd. is a leasing company involved in equipment leasing, the details regarding the lease transactions are:

(a) The cost of equipment to the lessor is **Rs. 2,00,000**, it is financed **80 per cent** through debt and the remaining by equity. The cost of the debt amounts to **16 per cent** and equity **14 per cent** before tax.
(b) The company is in **55 per cent** tax bracket. The equipment is used for three shifts. The rate of depreciation is normally **15 per cent** and **7.5 per cent** for each additional shift. The depreciation is charged according to the diminishing balance method.
(c) The scrap value of the equipment is **Rs. 32,000.**
(d) The direct cost of the lessor is **Rs. 1,000** in the Ist year.
(e) The estimated cost for maintenance and general administration is **Rs. 3,000** per annum.
(f) The lessee has been charged to pay the following:
   (i) the annual rent Rs. 72,000 for 5 years. The rental should be made at the end of each year.
   (ii) the security deposit is of Rs. **6,000**. It is refundable at the end of the lease term.
   (iii) A sum of Rs. **2,700** as non-returnable management fee is payable at the time of commencement of the lease.

From the above information, suggest whether it is beneficial for the lessor to lease the equipment using **IRR** technique.

***Solution***

The evaluation of lease can be done as follows:

(1) It requires finding of cost of capital for lessor.
(2) Computation of annual tax liability.
(3) Calculation of annual net cash in flows.
(4) Cashout flows at zero year.
(5) Computation of Internal Rate of Return.

*(1) Calculation of Cost of Capital for Lessor*

| *Sources* | *Amount* | *After Tax Cost* | *Total Cost* |
|---|---|---|---|
| 1. Equity | 40,000 | 14.0% | 5600 |
| 2. Debt | 1,60,000 | 7.2%* | 11,520 |
| | | | 17,120 |

16 × 45/100 = 7.2%

$$\text{Tax adjusted average cost of capital} = \frac{17120}{2,00,000} \times 100$$

$$= 8.56\%$$

*(2) Computation of Annual Tax Liability*

The computation of annual tax liability of the lessor can be shown by considering of all the expenses.

| *Particulars* | *Years* | | | | |
|---|---|---|---|---|---|
| | 1 | 2 | 3 | 4 | 5 |
| 1. Land Revenue | 72,000 | 72,000 | 72,000 | 72,000 | 72,000 |
| **(–) Expenses** | | | | | |
| (a) Direct cost | 1000 | — | — | — | — |
| (b) Maintenance and admin. cost | 3000 | 3000 | 3000 | 3000 | 3000 |
| (c) Depreciation | 60,000 | 42,000 | 29,400 | 20,580 | 14,406 |
| **Income before tax** | 8000 | 27000 | 39600 | 48420 | 54594 |
| (–) Income tax | 4400 | 14850 | 21780 | 26631 | 30026 |
| Income after tax | **3600** | **12150** | **17820** | **21789** | **24568** |

### (3) Compuiation of Annual Net Costs Inflow

| | Particulars | Years | | | | |
|---|---|---|---|---|---|---|
| | | 1 | 2 | 3 | 4 | 5 |
| 1. | Lease Revenue | 72000 | 72000 | 72000 | 72000 | 72000 |
| | *(+) Scrap value* | — | — | — | — | — |
| (a) | Direct cost | 1000 | — | — | — | — |
| (b) | Administration cost | 3000 | 3000 | 3000 | 3000 | 3000 |
| (c) | Refund of deposit | — | — | — | — | — |
| (d) | Income tax paid | 4400 | 14850 | 21780 | 26630 | 30026 |
| | Annual Net cash inflo | **63600** | **54150** | **47220** | **42370** | **64974** |

### (4) Cash Outflows at Zero Year

| | Rs. | Rs. |
|---|---|---|
| Cost of equipment | | |
| (–) Management fee | 2700 | 2,00,000 |
| (–) Security deposit | 6000 | 8700 |
| Net Cash Inflow | | 191300 |

A number of alternative financing sources like **retained earnings, hire purchase, bank loans, factoring, equity issues, bank over drafts** etc.

The valuation and the choice will depend upon many considerations. The evaluation is based on quantitative financial measurement. There are some differences between buying and leasing. In buying of an asset the **initial cost** should be incurred by the buyer. But in case of leasing there is no need of it. The investment allowances and depreciation charges for the purpose of tax are available in case of buying an asset. But these benefits are not available to the lessee when he make a decision regarding leasing. The scrap value is enjoyed by the buyer in buying process whereas it is not possible in lease finance. Management fee and lease rentals are not payable in case of buying and it is necessary in case of leasing.

The comparison of benefits which are available under buying and leasing can be made according to NPV or IRR method. **The NPV** is one of the methods in evaluation process and the following steps are required.

(a) A close observation of the PV of cash flows under buying process.
(b) An analysis of the present value of cash flows under the process of lease financing.

(c) The decision between buying and leasing will only be made by comparing the net present value.

(d) The alternative which shows higher NPV will be preferred.

**Illustration–2**

A proclainer, which has a service life of 10 years, can be purchased for Rs. 3,60,000. The same machine is available on hire basis at the rate of Rs. 90,000 per annum payable at the beginning of each year. Operating costs are borne by the Lessee. A Technocrat requiring the use of the proclainer. He expects to utilise it for 2 years and after that he sells it at 80 per cent of the purchase price. The Lessee can finance its purchase by his own resources to the extent of Rs. 160,000 and the remaining by borrowing at 18 per cent p.a. The interest on the loan will be paid at the end of each year and the loan can be repaid out of the sale proceeds of proclainer.

For tax aspect purpose the depreciation is available as deduction at 25 per cent on diminishing balance method. If any excess realisation is available, it is subject to tax. The tax rate is 50 per cent, the tax be paid at the close of each year.

The Technocrat expects a minimum internal rate of 10 per cent net of taxes on his own resources. Prepare your analysis and advise him clearly about the basis of your recommendation.

***Solution***

Before the lessee, two alternatives are available, i.e. **(a) Buying, (b) Leasing**. While evaluating the two alternatives, the gross revenues are the same. The operating costs are also the same. Therefore, the cash inflows and outflows are different in two methods.

**(a) Purchase of a proclainer.**

**(b) Hire/Leasing of a proclainer.**

*(a) Purchase of a Proclainer*

The evaluation of this proposal requires a close observation about the cash inflows and cash outflows the cash outflows analysis is presented below:

***(i) Outflow***

| *Outflow* | *Amount Rs.* | *e 10% PV factor* | *Discounted Value* |
|---|---|---|---|
| (a) Cash outflow on purchase | 1,60,000 | 1.000 | 160000 |
| (b) Interest on borrowings for Ist year **(after tax effect)** | 18,000 | 0.909 | 16362 |
| (c) Interest on borrowings for second year | 18,000 | 0.826 | 14868 |
| (d) Income tax payable on profit on sale of the proclainers* | 42,750 | 0.826 | 35111 |
| **Cash outflows** | 2,38,750 | | 2,26,541 |

*** The payments of interest will attract a income tax exemption, therefore, the value of interest will be taken as 50 per cent of interest cost.**

*Working Notes*

(1) Amount of Interest =

$$\text{Amount of borrowed} \times \frac{\text{Rate of Interest}}{100}$$

| | |
|---|---|
| The total cost of the asset = | 3,60,000 |
| (–) **Funds from own resources =** | **1,60,000** |
| borrowed at 18% = | 2,00,000 |

$\therefore$ Interest $= 2{,}00{,}000 \times \dfrac{18}{100} = 36{,}000$

$\therefore$ After tax effect $= 36{,}000 \times \dfrac{50}{100} = 18{,}000.$

(2) The written down value of the asset after two years of use is **Rs. 2,02,500.00**

**The depreciation will be as follows:**

| | |
|---|---|
| The cost of the asset is | Rs. 3,60,000 |
| (–) Ist year depreciation | **90,000** |
| **(e 25%)** | 2,70,000 |
| (–) IInd year depreciation (25%) | **67,500** |
| WDV after two years | 2,02,500 |

The profit after sale of the asset after two years.

| | |
|---|---|
| The book value of the asset is = | Rs. 2,02,500 |
| The sale price of the asset (80% on purchase price) | 2,88,000 |
| (–) WDV of the asset | 2,02,500 |
| **Profit** | **85,500** |

The income tax payable on the profit = 85,500 × $\frac{50}{100}$ = 42,750.

***(ii) Cash Inflow***

| *P/S* | *Amount Rs.* | *PV factor 10%* | *Discounted value* |
|---|---|---|---|
| 1. Cash received on sale of the proclainer after repaying the borrowings **(see note 1)** | 88,000 | 0.826 | 72,688 |
| 2. Savings in tax due to depreciation (Ist year) | 45,000 | 0.909 | 40,905 |
| 3. Second year | 33,750 | 0.826 | 27,878 |
| *( see note 2)* | 1,66,750 | | 1,41,471 |

*Therefore, the purchase of the proclainer will result a net dcf of*

Rs. 85,070 $\frac{22,654}{14,147}$

*Working Notes*

*Note*: (1) (a) Cash realised on the sale of asset is Rs. **2,88,000** but Rs. 2,00,000 loans has to be paid back. Therefore, the net cash inflow is Rs. **88,000**

(b) Tax effect of depreciation is Rs. 90,000

∴ the income tax rate is (50%) 90,000 × $\frac{50}{100}$ = 45,000.

Savings due to tax exemption as depreciation.

(2) The second year depreciation is Rs. 67,500

∴ The savings in depreciation after tax adjustment

67,500 × $\frac{50}{100}$ = 33,750

∴ Savings is Rs. 33,750.

## (b) Hire Purchase of the Proclainer

The evaluation of the leasing requires a close observation of outflow and inflow.

### *Outflow*

| *P/S* | *Amount Rs.* | *PV factor 10%* | *Discounted value* |
|---|---|---|---|
| Hire purchases for Ist year | 90,000 | 1.000 | 90,000 |
| Hire charges for IInd year | 90,000 | 0.909 | 81,810 |
| | 1,80,000 | | 1,71,810 |

### *Cash Inflow*

| *P/S* | *Amount* | *PV factor 10%* | *Discounted value* |
|---|---|---|---|
| 1. The tax savings in the first year on hire basis | 45,000 | 0.909 | 40,905 |
| 2. Tax savings on hire charges for the second year | 45,000 | 0.826 | 37,170 |
| | 90,000 | | 78,075 |

The net cash outflow in case of the proclainer hired, it will be **Rs. 93,735.00** (Rs. 1,71,810–78,075).

The analysis of the above information indicates that the net discounted outflows in case of the proclainer is purchased are lower than the net discounted outflows in case of it is taken on Hire basis. Therefore, the technocrat is advised to purchase the proclainer.

If the amount realisable on the sale of the proclainer at the end of two years Rs. 2,88,000 is uncertain and 80 per cent of the original cost appears to be high, the conclusion may will be in favour of **Hiring of** the asset. However, the rate of return is 10 per cent.

## Internal Rate of Return Method

This is the other method of evaluation of lease proposal which will be made by the lessee. The internal rate of return is that rate at which the sum of discounted cash inflows equals the sum of discounted cash outflows. It is the rate which discounts the cash flows to **zero**. The Internal rate of return is the maximum rate of interest which an organisation can afford to pay on the capital invested in a project. A project would qualify to be accepted if the **IRR** exceeds the cut off rate. While evaluating two alternatives, a project which gives a higher internal rate of return would be preferred.

Three steps are involved in the process of evaluating the lease proposals.

(a) At the first instance we should compute buying alternative under the IRR method.

(b) At the second stage leasing alternative may be evaluated under the IRR method.

(c) In the final stage, a comparison between leasing and buying of alternative should be done and the alternative which have a higher IRR will be selected.

The following illustration helps us to understand the IRR method thoroughly.

**Illustration–3**

ABC Ltd. is interested to get the services of a **Gowthami Machines** to expand its activities. The Company studies whether it is preferable to lease or buy the machine. The cost of the machine is **Rs. 90,000.** The machine would have a life of **8 years** and at the end of the period its scrap value is **Rs. 9000**. In the event of purchase, the Company would claim in the first year a capital allowance of **100 per cent**. The taxable profits would exceed this allowance in the first year. If the machine is not purchased, it may be leased for 8 years at the annual rental of Rs. 19000 payable annually in advance.

The cost of capital is **15 per cent P.A.** after the corporate tax. The Company's tax rate is **50 per cent** that the Gowthami Machines would be purchased or leased with effect from the commencing of a financial year. The income tax would be payable one year after the end of the financial year.

From the above information you are required to analyse the situation whether the asset may buy or **lease.**

***Solution***

The calculations of buying or leasing alternative methods of the internal rate of return are presented forthcoming:

**ABC Ltd. Analysis of Purchasing Instead of Leasing**

| Year | *Cash Inflows* Leasing cost saved | Tax saved | Sale | Total | Cash outflows | *Net cash flows* Actual | DF at 15% | PV at 15% | DF at 20% | PV at 20% |
|---|---|---|---|---|---|---|---|---|---|---|
| 0 | 19,000 | | | 19000 | 90,000 purchase | –70,000 | 1.00 | –70,000 | 1.00 | –70,000 |
| 1. | 19,000 | 45,000 | — | 64,000 | 9500 | +54,500 | 0.87 | 47,415 | 0.83 | 45,235 |
| 2. | 19,000 | | — | 19,000 | 9500 | +9500 | 0.76 | 7220 | 0.69 | 6555 |
| 3. | 19,000 | | — | 19,000 | 9500 | +9500 | 0.57 | 5415 | 0.60 | 5700 |
| 4. | 19,000 | | — | 19,000 | 9500 | +9500 | 0.57 | 5415 | 0.48 | 4560 |
| 5. | 19,000 | | — | 19,000 | 9500 | +9500 | 0.50 | 4750 | 0.40 | 3800 |
| 6. | 19,000 | | — | 19,000 | 9500 | +9500 | 0.43 | 4085 | 0.36 | 3420 |
| 7. | 19,000 | | — | 19,000 | 9500 | +9500 | 0.38 | 3610 | 0.28 | 2660 |
| 8. | | | 9000 | 9000 | 9500 | –500 | 0.33 | –165 | 0.23 | –115 |
| 9. | | | — | — | 4500 | –4500 | 0.28 | –1260 | 0.19 | –855 |
| | | | | | | | | +77910 | | +71930 |
| | | | | | | | | –71425 | | –70970 |
| | | | | | | NPV | | +6485 | | +960 |

$$\text{IRR} = 15\% + \frac{6485}{6485 + 960}$$

$$= 15\% + \frac{6485}{7445}$$

$$= 15\% + 0.87 = \mathbf{15.87\%}$$

From the above analysis, the cash flows are not only one of the important factors but also there are some other important considerations; should have their impact while taking a buying or leasing decision. These factors include the impact of lease on lessee's tax position **unforeseen contingencies** etc. The lessee would like to be ensure that he will have an uninterrupted use of the leased asset.

## Accounting for Leases

The accounting for lease is in much controversy in abroad. The controversies are related to the disclosure of the lease transactions. In the initial stage, lease transactions were not required to disclose the financial statements. Gradually, the disclosures require the lease transactions in the form of footnotes to the financial statements. **The International Accounting Standard 17**[11] has defined certain important terms as follows:

**(a) Lease.**
**(b) Financial lease.**
**(c) Operating lease.**
**(d) Face value.**
**(e) Inception of the lease.**

The **Lease** has been defined as **"An agreement whereby the lessor can convey to the lessee in return, for rent the right to use an asset for an agreed period of time".**

The **Financial lease** has been defined "A lease which transfers substantially all the risks and rewards, incidental to ownership of an asset, the title may or may not eventually be transferred."

The **Operating lease** was defined as "A lease other than the Finance lease".

The **Face value** has been defined as "the amount for which an asset can be exchanged between acknowledgeable willing buyer and acknowledgeable willing seller in an arm's length transaction.

The **Inception of the lease** has been defined as "the earlier of the date of lease agreement or of a commitment by the parties to the principal provisions of the lease."

The accounting process in the leasing firms can be categorised into two kinds.

1. Accounting for leasing in the Financial statements of the lessor.
2. Accounting for leasing in the Financial statements of the lessee.

**Computation of Internal Rate of Return**

| *Year* | *Cash outflow* | *Cash inflow* | *DF at 15%* | *PV* | *DF at 12%* | *PV* |
|---|---|---|---|---|---|---|
| 0 | 191300 | — | — | — | — | — |
| 1 | | 63600 | 0.8695 | 55300 | 0.8928 | 56782 |
| 2 | | 54150 | 0.7561 | 40942 | 0.7971 | 43163 |
| 3 | | 47220 | 0.6575 | 31047 | 0.7117 | 33606 |
| 4 | | 47370 | 0.5727 | 24265 | 0.6355 | 26926 |
| 5 | | 64974 | 0.4971 | 32298 | 0.5674 | 36866 |
| | | | | 183852 | | 197343 |
| | The Net present value | | | **–7448** | | **+6043** |

$$IRR = 12\% + \frac{6043 \times 3}{6043 + 7448}$$

$$= 12\% + \frac{6043 \times 3}{13491}$$

$$= 12\% + 1.34 = \mathbf{13.43\%}$$

The weighted average cost of capital is **8.56 per cent** and the Internal rate of return from the asset is **13.43 per cent**. Therefore, it is beneficial to the lessor to lease out the equipment.

**(B) Evaluation by Lessee**

**Before going to take an asset on lease finance, the lessee will also evaluate the lease transaction. The lessee will consider the benefits which are available in buying of the asset or taking on leasing basis. He will select the alternative which is most beneficial to him. The prospective lessee would take into account the factors such as accounting treatment, purchase and renewal options, maintenance, taxes and insurance, length of lease, local taxes, competition. The lessee should also consider and compare.**

***I. Accounting for Leasing in the Financial Statements of the Lessor***

The Accounting treatment of leases has undergone radical changes over the past decades. One time leases were not disclosed in the financial statements at all. The lessor will disclose his financial statements as follows:

**(a) Finance lease.**
**(b) Operating lease.**

*(a) Finance Lease*

If any asset acquired under a finance lease, it should be recorded in the Balance Sheet not as an asset, plant, equipment or property. But it will be shown as a **"Receivable"** at an amount equal to the net investment in the lease. According to the rules and regulations of the finance lease, the recognition of the finance income will be based on pattern which reflects a constant periodic rate of return on the net investment in respect of **Finance lease**. The vendors or manufacturers or dealer lessors may include the selling profit or loss in the Income by the business concern for outright sales. If low rates of interest are quoted, selling profit should be restricted. In the financial lease, the initial direct costs should be charged income at the commencement of the lease.

*(b) Operating Lease*

If any asset is acquired under the operating lease, should be recorded as an asset, property, plant and equipment in the lessor's balance sheet. The rental income may be recognised on a straight line method for a leased period. The lessor should maintain the accounting process for depreciation which is based on the firm's policy. The depreciation would be charged according to the conditions set out in the **International Accounting Standards.**

***II. Accounting for Leasing in the Financial Statements of the Lessee***

The accounting treatment of leasing in the financial statements of lessee presented below:

- **(a) Finance lease.**
- **(b) Operating lease.**

*(a) Finance Lease*

In the financial statements of the lessee, the acquired asset will be shown on both sides of the balance sheet. At the commencement of the lease, the acquired asset value should be shown on the asset side at the present value of the minimum lease payment. If it is possible to determine amount may be arrived through the interest rate implicit in the lease as the discount factor, if not, the lessee's incremental interest rate shall be used for this occasion. Another important element is that, if the fair value of the acquired asset is lower than the present value of the minimum lease payments, the acquired asset shall be presented at the fair value. The lease obligations of the acquired asset should be shown on the **liability** side of the balance sheet. It is reasonable to show the present value of payments due within one year as a **Current liability**. If the present value of payments due exceeds one year, it will be treated as **non-current liability**.

According to the finance lease conditions, the rentals should be apportioned between **finance charges** and the reduction in outstanding liability. The depreciation on the acquired asset should be charged according to the guidelines of the **International Accounting Standards**[4] **"Depreciation Accounting".**

*(b) Operating Lease*

The rental charges paid by the lessee should be charged in a systematic way as the revenue expenditure for the accounting period.

**Leasing in India**

Leasing is the important sources of the finance. It is the best sources of financing capital equipment. It has proved itself as an effective system for financing assets in **Europe, Japan and U.S.A.** The leasing is popular in India. Land leasing is the traditional system which exists in our country since old times. It has been emerged in India from 1970. The first leasing organisation was **"First Leasing Company of India Ltd."**, established in Chennai. The Company has started its business in **1973** and it has grown over years. A number of other leasing companies have come into existence. They are **Mazda Leasing, 20th Century Leasing Company, Ross Morarka Leasing Company, Pioneer Leasing Company, Express Leasing Company, HB Portfolio and Leasing Company** etc. A large number of public sector undertakings like **ONGC, SAIL, HMT, HAL, BHEL, Air India, ISRO and Coal India** considering the leasing as a means of financing for their ongoing projects. Commercial Banks also entered in this sector through their subsidiaries. Railways are also acquiring the leased assets from the **IFRC**. The MTNL has been raising its own resources through bond issues for capital expenditure and for acquisition of leased assets. The Banking Law Amendment Act of 1983 has authorised banks to open the leasing subsidiaries. The **ICICI** has fully involved in leasing activities in large volume. The Commercial Banks can engage in leasing in four kinds. They are:

(a) By the way of separate subsidiary leasing company.
(b) As a departmental activity.

(c) By participating in the equity of leasing companies.
(d) By entrusting the management to a reputed finance company.

The rapid growth of equipment leasing has led to its expansion into areas like **aircraft, autos, ships, computers, communication equipment, earthmoving equipment, industrial plant and machinery, medical equipment, office equipment, hotels** etc. The present structure of leasing companies can be categorised into five kinds:

(a) Hire purchase and investment companies.
(b) Subsidiaries of manufacturing companies.
(c) Independent leasing companies.
(d) All India Financial Institutions.
(e) Group Leasing Companies.

The RBI has also permitted the SBI and others to enter into this area. The Commercial Banks have an edge over other lessors. The Commercial Banks enjoy a low cost fund averaging **7.5 per cent to 9 per cent** as compared to leasing companies. The leasing companies have an average of **14 per cent** to **16.5 per cent** based on their capital structure. The Margins available to the leasing companies are in between **4 per cent and 10 per cent** depending upon the credit risk. The profit margins in case of banking subsidiaries are getting more. The lease rentals of quotations of the banks can be finer than finance companies.

**Shah Committee**

With the growth of the leasing sector, it is considered necessary to have prudential norms for the **Non-banking finance companies.** The Narasimham Committee was appointed in **1991** to study the growing role of leasing and hire purchase institutions in the financial intermediation process. The Committee involved in designing of new norms in addition to the existing conditions. The Committee recommended that there should be some prudential norms and guidance for conducting the business system offsite supervision on periodic return should be instituted by a **unified supervisory authority.** Dr. A.C. Shah Committee was therefore appointed on May 5, 1992 for carrying out an indepth study on the role of **NBFCS** and suggested regulatory and control measures. The Committee had submitted its report in **September 1992.** The major recommendations of the Committee were:

(a) Category-wise classification of the financial companies should be abolished and uniform regulations should be applied to all the financial companies.

(b) Regulatory attention by the Reserve Bank should be confined to companies with net owned fund of **Rs. 50 lakhs** and above.

(c) Entry norms, i.e., minimum net owned fund of Rs. 50 lakhs and a cooling period before accepting the deposits, should be prescribed for the new financial companies.

(d) The regulations should be directed to the asset side such as limit on credit concentration, prohibiting investments in undesirable activities etc.

(e) Capital adequacy standards should be laid down based on the risk assessment of assets and the credit conversion factors for off balance sheet items.

(f) The exempted category of deposits should be removed and all the deposits should be treated alike. A clear distinction should be made between deposits and borrowings from banks/ institutions and inter corporate deposits should constitute a part of deposits.

(g) **Net owned fund** of a financial company should be redefined to exclude investments in other NBFCs and subsidiaries as also loans and advances to subsidiaries to the extent of the aggregate of such investments, loans and advances exceed **10 per cent** of the amount of the paid up capital and free reserves of the company as reduced by the amount of a accumulated balances of losses, deferred revenue expenditure and other intangible assets.

(h) Aggregate amount of funds under portfolio management scheme should be related to the net owned fund of the company.

(i) NBFCs should be allowed to accept the deposits for a period ranging between **12 months and 84** months. Further so long as the interest rates on the bank deposits are regulated, interest rates on deposits accepted by NBFCs should be **2 to 3** percentage points more than those offered by the Commercial Banks.

(j) Prudential norms for income recognition, transparency of accounts and provisions for bad and doubtful debts, should be prescribed.

(k) Auditors should be assigned with more responsibilities in regard to compliance of regulations.

(l) The group had also made a few other recommendations, such as formation of a self-regulating organisation, compulsory credit rating after **5 years** initiating public awareness programmes for educating the depositors.

## Amendments

By accepting the recommendations of the Shah Committee in principle, the RBI said that a few recommendations have to be modified to fit into the overall framework of the financial sector reforms. If it is added that few others may require legislative changes. The RBI said that to avoid the difficulties in the transition, a phased programme of implementation has to be worked out. Therefore, the RBI announced several amendments to the NBFCs. The amendments cover deposits period, types of deposits, investment and registration of these companies, they aim at better regulation of the NBFCs. The amendments announced by the RBI are:

(i) The minimum period of deposits for all the financial companies has been brought down to over 12 months instead of 24 months. The maximum maturity period has been brought down from 120 months to 84 months for the residuary non-banking companies. The existing maximum period for other categories of financial companies, however, remains unchanged upto **60 months.** It is as a part of gradual move to bring into alignment the maturity range of deposits of different types of companies.

(ii) Intercorporate deposits and borrowings and funds received from the directors/shareholders of the private companies will be treated as regulated deposits and will not longer be in the exempted category. Funds raised through debentures and bonds secured by the immovable properties have also been removed from the exempted category. Sufficient time is being given to the companies to bring down any excess deposits if presently held, to the required level.

(iii) Hire purchase finance and equipment leasing companies maintain liquid assets at **10 per cent** on the revised definition of deposits, which include intercorporate deposits/ borrowings effects from **April 12, 1993** instead of 15 per cent of deposits, excluding intercorporate deposits/ borrowings. At least one half of these liquid assets, i.e. **5 per cent** of the deposits will have to be maintained in the form of Central and State Government securities or government guaranteed bonds. Loan and investment companies in respect of which no liquid asset requirement were stipulated till now, will effectively from July 12, 1993, be required to maintain liquid assets, to the extent of **5 per cent** of their deposits. At least half of these liquid assets i.e., **1/2 per cent** of their deposits will have to be in the form of Central or State Government securities. In case of the residuary non-banking companies which are required to invest at least **70 per cent** of their deposit liabilities in approved securities a minimum investment in government securities is being prescribed. These companies will be required to invest at least **10 per cent** of their aggregate liabilities to depositors in government securities or government guaranteed bonds.

(iv) All financial companies, including residuary non-banking companies, with net owned funds of **Rs. 50 lakhs** and over are required to register with the RBI. They should furnish the necessary details in the prescribed proforma. The registration would, in due course, be vital for the companies expanding their operations.

**Prudential Norms**

The RBI announced on June 13, 1994 regarding prudential norms for income recognition, accounting standards, provision for bad and doubtful debts, capital adequacy and concentration of credit etc. The RBI issued a circular letter No. **DFC (COC) 828 174/92–93, dated 4.12.1993** regarding guidelines for the **NBFCs** and the residuary non-banking companies in pursuance of the recommendations of the working group on Financial Companies. The norms which are introduced by the RBI presented below:

(1) The RBI will introduce capital adequacy norms based on risk weights for different types of assets and off balance sheet items. The **Financial Companies** are also advised regarding prudential norms for income recognition, **transparency** of accounts, provision for bad and doubtful debt and concentrate on credit. The RBI decided to introduce these norms. As per the guidelines, the companies are required to submit a half yearly return in the prescribed form.

(2) RBI has directed the finance companies which are not classified as an equipment leasing or a hire purchase finance company to accept deposits to the extent of **25 per cent and 15 per cent** of its net owned funds from the public and shareholders respectively. Now the registered companies are allowed with a higher limit equal to their net owned funds. Such companies are required to maintain liquid assets to the extent of **10 per cent** of its deposit liabilities. The deposit liabilities consists of deposits from **public and shareholder**, intercorporate deposits/borrowing, money raised through issue of bonds. At least one-half of the assets should be in the form of government securities or government guaranteed bonds. If any finance company fails to get the minimum credit rating it will not be allowed to accept the fresh deposits or renew the maturing deposits.

(3) According to the guidelines issued by the RBI regarding the accept of deposits until RBI is satisfied on a scrutiny of the half yearly returns with a satisfied credit rating. After satisfying the scrutiny, the RBI will issue a specific advice regarding the non-applicability of limits on deposit acceptance.

(4) All the NBFCs and residuary non-banking companies which have been registered with the RBI required to get themselves rated for the fixed deposits by anyone of the three credit rating agencies **i.e. CRISIL, CARE, ICRA.** The Companies should get fresh rating atleast once in a year. A copy of the ratings should be sent to the RBI alongwith half yearly returns. The Finance companies should get the minimum credit rating as follows:

(a) CRISIL — FA
(b) ICRA — MA
(c) CARE — CARE BBB (FD)

(5) The guidelines issued by RBI contains *the income recognition and accounting standards* of the finance companies. The policy on income recognition is based on the record of recovery. The income

from the **Non-performing Assets** may not be recognised on the basis of accruals. If an asset becomes non-performing when it ceases to yield any income, the income from the **NPAs**[12] shall be recognised. Interest on the NPA should not be booked as income in such interest outstanding for more than **6 months**. An amount which is treated as due, remains unpaid for **30 days** beyond the due date. The basis treating a credit facility as NPA as follows:

(a) In case of team loan.
(b) In case of lease rental.

If interest amount remains unpaid for six months, a term loan is to be treated as NPA. If the instalment is overdued for more than **six months** the entire outstanding loan inclusively unpaid interest if any should also be treated as **NPA**.

If lease rental/**hire purchase** instalments are past due for six months, the entire dues from the lesser should be treated as **NPA**.

A bill is to be treated as NPA if it remains overdue and unpaid for **six months** overdue interest is not taken into income account. All other credit facilities in the nature of short-term loans/advances should be treated as NPA.

(6) The guidelines issued by the RBI regarding accounting for investments is presented as follows:

(a) All the investment in securities can be classified into current investment and long-term investments.
(b) A current investment means an investment which is converted into cash. Any investment which is intended to hold for more than one year from the date on which such investment is made. It should be valued at lower cost and market value for each investment individually.
(c) A long-term investment is an investment other than a current investment. It should be valued at cost.
(d) The unquoted shares are to be valued at cost or break up value of the shares as per the audited balance sheet of the company whichever is less.
(e) The units of mutual funds should be valued at lower cost or latest NAV.
(f) Commercial papers and treasury bills should be valued at carrying cost.

(g) The unquoted debentures are to be treated as long-term loans for the purpose of income recognition and asset classification.

(7) According to the RBI guidelines, the **NBFCs** credit be classified into **four** broad categories:

**(a) Standard assets.**
**(b) Substandard assets.**
**(c) Doubtful assets.**
**(d) Loss assets.**

**Standard Assets** do not have any default in repayment of principal or payment of interest. It does not disclose any problem. It does not carry more than normal risk attached to the business. **Substandard Assets** has been classified as **NPA** for a period not exceeding **two years**. An asset where the terms of loan agreement about interest and principal have been re-negotiated or rescheduled after the commencement of operations are also called as substandard assets. The asset should remain in such category for atleast two years of satisfactory performance under the re-negotiated or rescheduled terms. The substandard asset may be upgraded if there is satisfactory compliance of the above situation. **Doubtful Asset**, which an asset has remained **NPA** for a period exceeding two years. The term loans, of the instalments have ramained overdue for a period exceeding two years will be treated as doubtful. The **Loss Asset** means where the loss had been identified by the **NBFC** or internal auditors or the RBI inspection but the amount has not been written off, wholly or partly. The provisions regarding loans and advances of the NBFCs have been decided according to the guidelines. The provisions against substandard assets, doubtful assets and loss assets are presented below. **For substandard assets** a general provision of **10 per cent** of total outstandings should be made. **For loss assets** the provision should made the entire asset value be, write off. If the assets remain in the books 100 per cent of the outstanding should be provided. **In case of doubtful assets** the provision should be made to the extent of 100% where the advance is not covered. The realisable value is to be estimated on a realistic basis. The provision for doubtful asset depends upon the following basis:

| *Period for which the asset*<br>*provision* | *Percentage of*<br>*is treated as doubtful* |
|---|---|
| (a) Upto *one year* | **20%** |
| (b) One to three years | **30%** |
| (c) More than three years | **50%** |

(8) According to the guidelines the capital adequate norms are to be fulfilled by all the NBFCs. The capital is divided into two tiers—**Tier I and Tire II. Tier** I capital is the core capital. It provides permanent in nature and it is ready to face the unexpected losses. **Tier-II** capital is not permanent in nature. It is not readily available. Tier I capital contains paid up equity capital, free reserves, balance in share premium account and capital reserves but not reserves credited by the Revaluation of Assets. **Tier II** capital consists of **preference shares**, Revaluation reserves, general provisions and loss reserves, hybrid debt capital and subordinated debt. The registered NBFCs should achieve a minimum capital adequacy norm of **6 per cent** of the risk weighted assets, the capital adequacy norms for off balance sheet items by 8 per cent. The total of Tier II elements will be limited a maximum of 100 per cent of total of Tier I elements for the purpose of compliance with the norms. The guidelines further reveals that the risk weighted assets which contains degree of credit risk involved in balance sheet items. The aggregate will be taken into account for reckoning the minimum capital ratio. The weights allotted to each of the items of assets and off balance sheet items are furnished forthcoming data.

(9) According to the guidelines issued by the RBI, that every registered NBFC should furnish **half yearly return** in duplicate indication about the details, capital fund and risk asset ratio, calculation of risk weighted assets and off balance sheet exposures and other certain data. The return should be submitted within the period of two months and certified by the Auditor.

| *Weighted Assets (Balance Sheet Items)* | *Percentage Weight* |
|---|---|
| (a) Cash and Bank balances (Including FDRs, CDs) | 0 |
| (b) Investments in Government and approved in securities as Banking Regulation Act, shares/debentures/bonds/ units of mutual funds/CPS | 0 |

(Contd.)

(Contd.)

| | |
|---|---|
| (c) *Current Assets* | |
| (i) Stock on Hire | 100 |
| (ii) Intercorporate deposits | 100 |
| (iii) Loans and advances fully secured | 0 |
| (iv) Loans to staff members | 0 |
| (v) Other secured loans | 100 |
| (vi) Bills purchased/discounted | 100 |
| (vii) Others (to be specified) | 100 |
| (d) *Fixed Assets* (net of depreciation) | |
| (i) Assets leased out | 100 |
| (ii) Premises | 100 |
| (iii) Furniture and Fixtures | 100 |
| (e) *Other Assets* | |
| (i) Income tax deducted at sources | 0 |
| (ii) Advance tax paid | 0 |
| (iii) Interest due on government securities | 0 |
| (iv) Others (to be specified) | 100 |

**Off Balance Sheet Items**

| *Nature of Items* | *Credit Conversion Factor* |
|---|---|
| (a) Financial and other guarantees | 100 |
| (b) Shares/debentures underwriting obligations | 50 |
| (c) Partly paid up shares/debentures | 100 |
| (d) Bills discounted/Rediscounted | 100 |
| (e) Lease contracts | 100 |
| (f) Other current liabilities | 50 |

## Legal and Tax Aspects of Leasing

A leasing business provide tax implications under the Act. The tax aspect of leasing pertains to both **Income Tax and Sales Tax.**

### *Income Tax*

Leasing offers tax benefits both to the lessor and the lessee. Leasing is the way for tax avoidance, reduction/deferment of tax liability and sharing tax savings. It provides a technique for transferring the benefits of tax incentives from the lessor to the lessee of the asset. The tax implications have the dimension of the two parties which are presented below:

**(a) Benefits/tax aspects to the lessor.**

**(b) Tax considerations to the lessee.**

## (a) Tax Aspects or Lessor

The Lessor (owner) has the right to claim deduction of depreciation from his taxable income. The rate of depreciation will be applicable as per the Income Tax Act. The tax aspects of the lessor depends upon the following factors:

**(a) Lease rentals.**
**(b) Allowable expenses.**

The computation of taxable income of an assessee under the Income Tax Act, 1961 involves computation under various heads of income. The income from all sources will be aggregated and reduction will be allowed as per the Act. The different sources of income will be computea and the provisions will be applied. The provisions apply to leasing companies. There are no specific provision to leasing business. The assessment of the leasing companies will be done under the head of **"profits and gains of business and profession"**. For other companies the income from lease is taxed as **"Income from other sources"**.

The **allowable expenses** are termed as deductibility of expenses. While computing the income of lessor from leasing, some expenses are allowed as a deduction to determine the taxable income. The following expenses will be deductible from the income of the lessor:

(a) Depreciation.
(b) Rent, rates, taxes, repairs and insurance of the leased asset, if the expenses are borne by the lessor.
(c) Bad debts.
(d) Interest on borrowed capital.
(e) Travel expenses as per approved conditions.
(f) All expenses incurred in the trade/business.
(g) Ammortization of certain preliminaries.

The expenses such as preparation of project report, feasibility report, market survey, legal charges for drafting of memorandum of association and articles of association, registration expenses, public issue expenses other than debt and loans, subject to maximum of **2.5 per cent** of the cost of the project, allowable in 10 equal instalments.

The depreciation and interest is the most important factors while computing the income of the lessor. The depreciation claim by the lessor involves tax shield on the leased asset. The depreciation plays an important role on the taxable income of the lessor. The salient features of depreciation element in the tax assessment is presented below:

(1) The Companies Act prescribed provisions for depreciation to the accounting purpose.

(2) The Income Tax Act prescribed provisions for depreciation element to income tax purpose.

(3) Leasing Companies in India are regulated by the Companies Act.

(4) The Act prescribes the rates of depreciation for various types of depreciable assets on WDV basis as well as straight line basis.

(5) The Act permits companies to charge depreciation on any other basis.

(6) Leasing Companies follow the provisions of the Income Tax Act with the basic objective of tax deductibility.

(7) The provision also facilitate an incentive to investment in specified assets leased out for leasing business.

(8) Section 32 of the Income Tax Act contains the provision regarding deductibility of depreciation as expenses. The section envisages three important conditions for allowing depreciation. They are:

   (a) The asset must be owned by the Assessee.
   (b) The asset must be used for the purpose of business.
   (c) The asset is in the form of buildings, furniture, machinery, plant, ships, vehicles, books scientific apparatus and surgical equipment.

(9) The lessor is eligible to claim depreciation tax shields. But the lessor is not eligible for any other investment related tax shield.

(10) The amount of annual depreciation on an asset is determined by:

(a) the actual cost of the asset,

(b) classification in the relevant block of assets.

(11) The depreciation is computed at the block-wise rates on the basis of WDV method only.

(12) The computation of the amount of depreciation, a significant implication of the categorising assets into blocks.

**(b) Tax Considerations for Lessee**

The income tax consideration for the lessee are:

(a) Allowability of lease rentals.

(b) Deductibility of expenses.

(c) Tax planning.

***(a) Lease Rentals***

The Income Tax Act permits the lease rentals as a normal business expenditure for lessee. The lease rental payment will be treated as revenue expenditure. It is not a personal expenditure. It relates exclusively to business purpose of the lessee.

***(b) Deductibility of Expenses***

The Lessee is required to bear the routine expenses associated with the leased asset. These incidental expenses such as repairs and maintenance, insurance are allowed as a deduction by the I.T. Act from taxable income of the assessee.

***(c) Tax Planning***

Tax Planning is the most important factor both for the Lessee and Lessor. The tax planning saves tax to both the parties. The claiming of depreciation by the lessor is the main device of saving taxes. The lessees can use deduction of lease rentals in two ways: (a) flexible structuring of lease rentals and (b) transfer of unabsorbed capital allowance to the lessor.

## Sales Tax Aspects

The Government levy sales tax on sale of goods in India. The levy of sales tax consists of the Central Sales Tax Act, 1957 (CST) and State Sales Tax of various states. The CST is levied by the Government of India. The collection of Sales Tax as inter-state sale of goods only. The sale of goods within the state is administered by Respective Sales Tax Authorities. A lease has the three important elements in view of the Sales Tax.

(1) Purchase of an asset by a Lessor.
(2) Lease Rentals.
(3) Sale of the Asset.

The **purchase of an asset by a lessor** for the purpose of leasing to a lessee involves the inter-state sale. The business affair attracts the provisions of the CST. According to the CST the normal rate of sales tax **10 per cent** or the appropriate rate will be levied to inter-state purchase/sale of goods in the respective state, whichever is higher, will be imposed. If the goods sold by a registered dealer to another registered dealer are levied a concessional rate of **4 per cent** of the sale price subject to conditions. The asset supplier is not entitled to the concessional rate of sales tax.

**Lease rentals** are the most important element in levying the sales tax. There was no tax as lease rentals prior to 1982. In 1982, the tax is also levied on this aspect. Accordingly tax on transfer of the right to use any goods for any purpose for cash, deferred payment or other valuable consideration was included in the tax as purchase/sale of goods. Therefore, the leasing was brought within the scope of sales tax. Lease rentals attract sales tax under the sales tax authorities in all the states except Maharashtra. The salient features of the lease rentals and its sales tax process are presented below:

(1) The sales tax is payable on the annual taxable turnover of the lessor.
(2) The rates of tax vary from state to state.
(3) The rates of tax vary between a minimum and maximum.
(4) Surcharge on sales tax, additional surcharge, additional sales tax on excess turnover are levied on the lease rentals.

(5) High turnover leasing companies may have to obtain multiple registrations.

(6) Sales tax on lease is related to the actual use of the asset.

**Sales of the asset** is the another important aspect in the Sales Tax Act. Generally, the second sale have tax exemptions within the state. But lease transactions does not attract the exemptions. The lease transactions suffer a multi-point levy irrespective of the goods covered by the transactions.

## REFERENCES


1. James C. Vanhorne, *Fundamentals of Financial Management*, PHI, 1997, p. 585.
2. S.N. Maheswari, Principles and Practice, *Financial Management*, p. E-53.
3. V. Gopalaswami, *Capital Market*, Deccan Publications, Madras, 1996 p. 217
4. *Ibid.*
5. James C. Vanhorne, *Fundamentals of Financial Management*, PHI, p. 585, 1997.
6. *Ibid.*
7. *Ibid.*
8. *Ibid.*
9. *Ibid.*
10. Van Horne, *Fundamentals of Financial Management*, PHI 1997.
11. S.N. Maheswari, *Financial Management, Principles and Practice*, p. E-68, 1996.
12. NPA is an asset in respect of which interest has remained unpaid and has become past due.

# 4

# CREDIT RATING

## Introduction

The debt market in India has been increasing. The number of companies that have been borrowing directly from the capital market also create a healthy situation. The industrial environment has become more and more competitive demanding the funds for the supply of funds. The investors have been increasingly towards the capital market and they find a borrowers assurance in timely payment of interest and principal. At the present situation, the investors need an independent and credible agency which judges impartially and gives a better direction in this regard. The quality of debt obligations depends upon many factors. The Companies needs are different. The investors expectations are different. The financial institution's environment is different for making the investment decisions . For a thorough understanding of the concept of credit rating, it is necessary to know the definitions given by some authorities in this field. It is a process of evaluating risk associated with the credit instrument.

## Definition

Credit Rating can be defined as "Credit Rating is designed exclusively for the purpose of grading bonds according to their investment quality."[1]

According to **Moody's Investor Service,** "Ratings are designed exclusively for the purpose of grading according to their investment qualities."[2]

**Standard Poor** defined the Credit Rating, "AS&P's Corporate or Municipal debt ranging is a current assessment of the credit worthiness of an obligator with respect to specific obligation".[3]

The **CRISIL** has defined the Credit Rating as "The crisil rating symbols indicate in a summarised manner CRISIL's current opinion as to the relative safety of timely payment of interest and principal on a debenture preference share, fixed deposit or short-term instruments."[4]

Credit rating is not a recommendation to the investor's/ buyers of a financial product. It is not a method of evaluation of the company. It is not a one time evaluation of risk. It has to be done by specialised, expert, reputed accredited institutions. The rating process is meant for debt instruments. It is not graded the whole organisation. It is only confined to the financial affairs of the concern. It reflects the issuer's financial strength, the soundness of operations, efficiency of top level management and overall performance of the organisation. Generally the rating firms undertake the task of rating financial instruments on a request the organisation issuing that instrument. It is an act of assigning values to financial instruments by estimating the solvency. The rating reflects the financial **status** of the company in the market. Credit Rating is just like getting of the **ISI** mark to a commodity. It is an observation made by the outside concern regarding the financial capabilities of a firm. Equity shares cannot be rated like **bonds, debentures** or any debt instrument.

The first credit rating services emerged in **USA in 1909**. It was first introduced by **John Moody**. His ratings become very popular with investors. In U.S.A. the SEP ratings become very popular in 1920. They began to rate the companies and governing bodies issuing bonds to the public. The first credit rating was done by the **CRISIL** in 1988 in India. The ratings have been the indicators of the current opinion of the relative capability of timely servicing the debts and obligations. Different instruments of the same company may carry different credit rating. The credit rating is highly beneficial to both investors and the borrowing companies.

The benefit to various parties concerned with the rating are listed below:

**(a) to investors;**
**(b) to borrowers;**
**(c) to government;**
**(d) to credit rating companies.**

### *(a) To Investors*

The following are the advantages to the investors due to the credit rating services:

(i) The investors will get the best quality of information at low cost.

(ii) The investors can take the calculated risk in their investments.

(iii) The credit rating services encourage the common man to invest his savings towards capital market for getting higher returns.

(iv) CR will provide safeguard against bankruptcy and other malpractices by the corporate sector.

(v) CR will guide the investors by rating the instruments of various companies for the investment making decision.

***(b) To Borrowers***

(i) Companies with good rating can enter the capital market confidently.

(ii) For sincere and honest corporate buyers they can raise large resources of funds from the market at cheaper rates.

(iii) It can be used as a marketing tool.

(iv) The good rating can attract the foreign collaborators.

(v) It is the barometre of financial discipline among the corporate borrowers.

(vi) There is no scope for propaganda among companies during the rise of resources from the market.

***(c) To Government***

(i) Fair and good ratings motivate the investors towards investment therefore the idle fund will be channelised for the productive uses.

(ii) Mega issues can enhance employment opportunities which will be attracted by the credit rating.

(iii) It provides investors protection without any burden on the part of the government.

(iv) It facilitates the formulation of public policy guidelines on institutional investments.

***(d) To Credit Rating Companies***

(i) Honest and impartial credit rating agencies would definitely survive in the market.

(ii) The existence and development of credit rating companies largely depends upon their performance.
(iii) The credibility is the life of the rating companies.
(iv) There will be tremendous scope for other allied financial services.

**Types of Credit Rating**

Credit ratings are of various types, depending upon the needs of the rates. The following are the common types of credit rating:

(a) Debentures /bond rating.
(b) Commercial paper rating.
(c) Equity ratings.

**Debentures /Bond rating** is the major business of the credit rating agencies. Rating the debentures/bonds or debt securities issued by a Company or Semi-Government is called bond rating. **Commercial paper** means a short-term, unsecured promissory notes. These papers are generally issued by the Large Companies. These commercial papers are very popular in **U.S.A.** It is mandatory on the part of a company to obtain the rating approved by the rating agency to issue commercial paper. In USA there is much demand for rating of these papers. The rating of equity capital is called **equity rating**. For corporates **Debt is Jam, equity is ginger**[5]. According to the *Economic Times* reports, the corporate sector raised debt and equity just **Rs. 1101 crores** and **Rs. 6 crores** respectively in the first half of the fiscal year **2001– 002.** The debt private placement market managed more than **Rs. 22,500 crores.** Significantly, a total of **Rs. 12,272 crores** was raised by the **AAA** rated paper. On the other hand, **Rs. 2025 crores** of paper was not the rated paper. Corporate debt issues become very popular in the last 3 years.[6] To put things imperspective **Rs.1,60,000 crores** corporate debt was issued in public issues/structured of private placements in last 3 years. In the first six months of this financial years **Rs. 45,00,000 crores** worth corporate debt is raised in the global markets. This provides the big picture of funds availability and potential to grow. Corporate debt issues are preferred to bank borrowings because of flexible structuring with multiple options, floating or indexed interest coupons, better pricing, debenture trustee supervision, credit rating.

**Credit** enhancement facilitates decision making by issuers and investors. It provides a better fit on expectations, corporate debt issues also help in reaching the retail investors who get a better yield.

**Limitations of Credit Ratings**

The credit ratings are important to the investment activity in the capital market. But the ratings have the following limitations:

(a) Ratings of the financial debt instruments are only the indicator of risk.
(b) Ratings are only a time bound gradings of quality of a financial product.
(c) Ratings carry some weight because opinions are made by the experts in the field and poor grade instruments will get flop in the market.
(d) If the rating agencies are not retaining the best talented expert professionals, then the ratings will become undependable.
(e) Rating agencies do not give the ratings of equity.

Credit rating provides a relative ranking of the credit quality of the debt instruments. The credit rating does not evaluate about the reasonableness of issue price, possibility of capital gains, liquidity in the secondary market, risk of prepayment by issues or interest or exchange risks. Credit rating is an opinion expressed by an independent professional organisation. It helps the issuers of debt instruments to price their issue correctly and to reach out the potential investors. The credit rating is compulsory for the following cases:

(a) All Non-Banking Finance Companies that have not owned funds of more than **Rs. 50 lakhs** are required to register with the **RBI** and get themselves compulsorily credit rated every year.
(b) In case of Finance Companies which have not owned funds of less than **Rs. 2 crores** should get their first credit rating done.
(c) Credit rating is compulsory for issuing of FCDs which have a conversion period of more than 18 months.
(d) Credit rating is compulsory in case of non-convertible debentures whose maturity period exceeds **18 months**.

(e) All commercial paper issues will have to be credit rated and the rating should be a minimum of P2/A2/PR2 as the case may be. The rating should not more than two months between the date of rating and the date of issue.

## Scope of Credit Rating

The scope of credit rating in India is restricted to debt instruments. The financial instruments such as **Debentures, bonds, fixed deposits, commercial papers** are rated. But in developed countries like the USA and the UK equity shares are also rated. In present environment the CR has become an obligation. There is a strong need of CR in the market. Because the lack of information in the market about the issuer and the instrument led to the need for CR. The corporate sector entirely depends upon public for project finance has resulted in the issuance of a number of debt instruments. The capital market is dominated by share brokers and the other intermediaries. Sometimes they canvas for themself interest and motivate the investors in favour of a particular financial instrument. Therefore to overcome this problem, it is necessary for the safety of the investors to rate the debt instruments in the market. If the CR does not exist in the market, the investors may fell in dilemma and there will be chance to cheat the innocent investors. After the introduction of free pricing of securities by the Companies. The CR has become a weapon in the hands of investors to analyse the financial instruments floated by the issuing company.

## Objectives of the Credit Rating

The basic objective of the credit rating is to provide the best and low cost information to the investors to take investment decision in a particular instrument. The following are the objectives of the credit rating system:

(a) It imposes a financial discipline on the borrowers.
(b) It helps the financial intermediary in discharging the functions relating to debt issues.
(c) It guides the investor regarding his commitment towards a particular debt instrument for his better returns.
(d) It facilitates the formulation of public guidelines on the institutional investment.

(e) It may provide adequate funds for the high rated companies at a low rate of interest.
(f) It lends greater credibility to financial and other representations.
(g) It encourages transparency of information and better accounting standard.

## Credit Rating Process

The credit rating process involves the following procedure:

1. The issuing company approaches the rating agencies.
2. On the basis of client needs, rating agency appoints a team of experts to appraise the financial position of the company.
3. The experts team makes report to the agency after evaluating the clients financial position.
4. Credit rating agency submits its observation about the quality of debt instrument through symbols.

## Credit Rating Agencies in India

Credit rating is a specific evaluation about the credit quality of the issuer of securities and is done for a particular financial instrument. It has assumed great importance for **individual investors, brokers, and financial advisers** with the expansion of the capital market. The credit rating agencies not only rate the instruments of private corporate sector but also rate the public sector units debt instruments. The proposed bond issued by the PSUs should be evaluated by **SEBI** and credit rating agencies. The permission has been granted with a view of making the PSU bonds more attractive in the market. Credit rating agency does not create a fiduciary relationship between the credit rating agency and the rating users. Generally the credit rating agencies undertakes the assignment of rating an instrument on a proposal made by the issuing company. Therefore, if once the instrument rated, it becomes its obligation towards investors to periodically announce. The status of grading of the instrument whether the issuer wants it or not. Unsolicited credit rating exists in abroad. Credit rating is based on the information provided by the issuing company. Credit rating agencies take into consideration of the various factors such as **risk composition, market situation, operating efficiency, track record, accounting quality,**

**planning and control systems financial flexibility, profitability, liquidity and asset quality of the issuer** company. The credit rating agency completes task and assign the grades. The ratings are continuously monitored by the agency and the grades are changed, suspended or withdrawn by it at any time according to the new information. Credit rating is not only to guide the investors, fund managers, brokers, financial analysts, but it is also be used to misguide them, which depends upon sincerity and honesty of the agency.

In India, the following agencies are fully involving in the credit rating activities:

1. **Credit Rating and Information Services of India (CRISIL).**
2. **Investment Information and Credit Rating Agency of India Limited (ICRA).**
3. **Credit Analysis and Research Limited (CARE).**
4. **Onida Individual Credit Rating Agency of India Limited (ONICRA)**

## 1. CREDIT RATING AND INFORMATION SERVICES OF INDIA (CRISIL)

The CRISIL was established in January 1988. It was floated by **ICICI, UTI, LIC, GIC, Asian Development Bank and SBI.** The other share holders include Housing Development Finance Corporation, General Insurance Corporation, Bank of India, Bank of Baroda, Allahabad Bank, Indian Overseas Bank, Canara Bank, UCO Bank, Standard Chartered Bank, Vyshya Bank, Bank of Madura, Bank of Tokyo, Grindlays Bank, Hongkong and Shangai Banking Corporation, Deutsche Bank and Citi Bank.

Its objective is to undertake the assignments of credit rating is based on the proposal made by the issuer companies for their financial products. They are **Debentures, fixed deposit programmes, commercial paper programmes,** short-terms borrowing instruments and preference shares. The CRISIL rating is necessary for the authorities and banks. The CRISIL provides not only the credit rating but also renders services to the corporate sector covering the topics like structure of the industry, degree of competition and business situations.

The CRISIL entered a strategic alliance with the standard and poor's in 1995. Its services includes information services, infrastructure services and consultancy. Its information services offer corporate research reports. It also prepares **CRISIL 500 Index** which will be very useful to the corporate sector. Its consultancy using render assistance to power, telecom and infrastructure financing. It rates the rupee denominated debt instruments. The CRISIL informs its current opinion about the relative safety of timely payment of interest and principal on the rated financial instruments. It assigns rating after taking into consideration all the factors of the borrowing company. It takes into consideration all the things about the issuer company. It review's principal business fundamentals like competitive position, strategies, policies, plans, strength, weaknesses goals and philosophy of the management, and past performance. It also undertakes the assignment of **finance companies**. Finance companies review includes about the regulatory and competitive environment, capital adequacy, **financial asset quality, liquid position, profitability and financial position, interest burden and tax aspects.** The CRISIL's instrument grade rating symbols are categorised into **"Highest Safety", "High Safety"** and **"Adequate Safety".**

### CRISIL's Rating Process

The CRISIL takes the assignment from the issuer company for a fixed rate of charges for rendering the services. It appoints highly skilled talented experts, equity analysts market specialists, the evaluation of a particular financial instrument is carried out by professionally qualified persons. The evaluation includes data collection, financial analysis and discussions with key personnel in the company. The Company should render all the latest information to the CRISIL on the desired aspects at the time of requesting for a rating. On receipt of the issuing company's request for rating the CRISIL assigns the work to a team of experts which will be responsible for carrying out the rating assignment. The team obtains all the information and interacts with the company officials. The findings of the team is presented to an **internal committee** of the CRISIL thereafter the findings will be transited to the Rating Committee. The **Rating Committee** comprises some directors (outside persons) to take a decision on the rating. The rating assigned by the rating committee will be informed to the issuing company. In this Juncture, if the Company wants to submit any information, it can do so. The rating process involves a careful analysis and strict confidentiality of the client information. The directors of the issuing company do not get involved in the rating process. Once the confirmation of rating is made by the CRISIL, it is obligated to monitor the rating over the life of the debt instrument.

The CRISIL also undertakes the ratings of mutual funds. The Company offers a package to the corporate customers. Credit rating has a much broader connotation than the financial analysis. CRISIL has recently announced its first rating of **real estate projects**. The ratings indicate the relative ability of the developer to specify and build to agreed quality levels and to transfer clear title within stipulated time schedules.

**The Investment Research Division offers** various services to the investors and borrowers. All of these services are based on the analysis of the published information on the corporate sector. It also provides the **CRISIL CARD** which is a corporate data based on 500 companies with individual cards on each company. It also runs **CRISIL BANKCARD** which is a data base on 30 public and private sector banks. **CRISIL ECOSCAN** is a database providing the data on major sectors of the Indian economy. It also publishes **CRISIL VIEW**, which publishes its opinion on the credit quality of a company and provides indepth analysis of published information. This bulletin is meant for institutional investors and brokers. The CRISIL has also established **Advisory Services division** to provide more services to the needs of corporate sector and investor community. The division offers the following services:

(a) Funds mobilisation for public sector undertakings.
(b) Evaluation of privitisation/disinvestment to PSUs.
(c) Upgrading of credit evaluation for banks and other lending institutions and also monitoring system.

The CRISIL has carried out credit evaluation for a few State Governments and State Electricity Boards for the use of private investors planning infrastructure projects. State Governments and Municipal Bodies seek to raise funds from the debt market, these issuers are expected to use ratings in the future.

## CRISIL's Rating Process

The credit ratings are based on the latest information which are provided by the issuer company to the rating agency. In evaluation of credit worthiness of a issuer company's financial product, it will analyse all the factors regarding **business analysis and financial analysis** for a manufacturing concern. It also undertakes the credit rating to the assessment of financial companies. The CRISIL generally rates the following concerns:

**(A) Evaluation of Manufacturing Companies.**
**(B) Evaluation of Financial Companies.**

### *(A) Evaluation of Manufacturing Companies*

The credit rating process involves a detailed exercise regarding the financial data of the Company. The evaluation also includes visits to factories and offices of the company for holding discussions with the company officials, **bankers, creditors, auditors** for clarity of information. The evaluation process requires a desk work, outdoor work and other allied works. The key factors usually considered in evaluation of a manufacturing concern are:

**(a) Business Analysis.**
**(b) Financial Analysis.**

#### *(a) Business Analysis*

It is the most important factor in evaluation of a manufacturing concern. Under this analysis, it will examine about the risks involves in the operation of the smooth functioning of the company. The **Risk** is the essence of the valuation of a firm. The value of a financial asset depends upon their return and risk. The risk is measurable. The Risk can be defined as **"The variability of returns from those that are expected".**[7] The total risk of a firm comprises two components which are presented below:

***Total Risk: Systematic Risk + Unsystematic Risk***

The systematic risk means, it effects the overall market of the nation, such as the changes in economy, tax reforms introduced by the Government, or a change in the world environment. The systematic risk is inescapable. The systematic risk is also caused by a wide range of factors like **recession, war, and structural changes in the economy.** The systematic risk is also known as **"Market risk or non-diversifiable risk".** The systematic risk can be defined as "The variability of return on stocks or portfolios associated with changes in return on the market as a whole".[8] Another risk component is unsystematic risk, which is unique to a particular company or industry. The unsystematic risk is independent of **economic, political and other factors.** Unsystematic risk accounts between **60 to 75 per cent** of the total risk involved in a company. Unsystematic risk can be defined as "variability of return on stocks or portfolios not explained by general market movements. It is avoidable through diversification".[9] The unsystematic risk can be reduced or even eliminated through diversification. The unsystematic risk is also known as **"Non-market risk"** or **"Diversifiable risk"**. Industry risk means the level of competition from others in the market. It also includes market factors such as demand and supply position of a particular product, the government policies regarding industry position. **Marketing risk** means the association of competitive advantages, or disadvantages, market share, selling and distribution channels. The review also includes quality of customer service rendered by the client. The customer service is highly influential factor in enhancing the sales volume of a commercial enterprise. The review also focuses on operating efficiency of the firm. The volume of profitability will depend upon the utilisation of capacity installed. The mass production of the commodities will boost up the gross marginal profit. The CRISIL team will study about locational advantages, raw material availability and prices, labour relationship, and product cost structure. The industrial peace is the other important element in evaluation of a firm. The better industrial relationship between management and labour definitely enhances the production level of a manufacturing concern which reflects in profitability of a company. The team also studies the **cost reduction control** system which is followed by the issuer company. Thus undertake the close study about the legal position of the company. The position includes the terms and conditions of prospectus, the trustees and their duties and responsibilities and the system of timely payment. It also observes the protection against forgery and frauds. The experts will also evaluate the management and promoters position. It examines the relation of the track record of managers, top level executives and promoters. They also study about their qualifications and experience regarding business capabilities. The team also observes the planning and control system adopted and implemented by the Company. They study about the business capacity to adjust with the flexibility of latest environment. The CRISIL team examines the **Fundamental analysis**. Under this analysis the CRISIL will examine. The liquidity, profitability and solvency position of the rating company.

### *(b) Financial Analysis*

Under this head, the CRISIL examines the earning capability, accounting quality, financial status and cashflows. The factors which reflects the financial analysis presented below:

**(1) Earning capability.**
**(2) Accounting standards.**
**(3) Financial Status.**
**(4) Analysis of cash in flows.**
**(5) Management evaluation.**

*(1) Earning Capability*

The team examines the earning capacity of the issuer company. They will also assess about the future earnings and earning protection. Earning protection is the most important element in the growth of a company. Retaining the present earnings are the most problematic aspect in the business environment. The business is uncertain and no one knows what happens tomorrow. Though the present earning is low but the future capabilities may turn the status of the company. The earning capability is based on the general economy of the state. It is based on the quantum level of production.

*(2) Accounting Standards*

The profits of the corporate sector are declared by the Accounting Department. The Accounting Department fully involve in book-keeping and maintenance of records. After completion of the routine process of the accounting, the company submits its reports to the share holders in **AGM.** The overstatement/understatement of profits depends upon the maintenance of the accuracy of accounts. The team verifies the auditor's qualification and experience. They also examine the method of income recognition. The team also scruitinises the method of inventory valuation and depreciation policies and thorough check will be done on all the items of the balance sheet on both sides.

*(3) Financial Status*

The team analyses the financial plans of the Company and their implementations. The procurement of funds and disbursing of the fund is the most important task of the finance department. The team also examines the efficiency of the finance being in all aspects. They also verifies the **EPS, profitability ratios, proportion of interest and net profit.**

*(4) Analysis of Cash in Flows*

The CRISIL team investigates the debt equity mix and variability of future cash flows. They assess about the requirement of fixed capital and working capital. The adequacy of cash flows reflect in working capital management, current ratio, inventory to sales etc. The financial flexibility also examined in terms of capital financing plans, flexibility in financing through alternative method etc.

*(5) Management Evaluation*

The experts examine about the relation to track record of promoters, managers and top level executives. The experts examine the abilities, skill talent dynamism, managerial skill, problem solving capacity implementation of the plans, strategies, decision making capacity etc. They evaluate the targets, company philosophy and financial strategies. They also check about the capacity of adjusting with flexibility. Foresight is the most important element to a commercial enterprise. The top level management have a foresight about the company future that enables the company to move in a right direction.

***(B) Evaluation of Financial Companies***

The following aspects are covered by the CRISIL expects while evaluating the **Finance Companies:**

- **(a) Regulatory and structural environment.**
- **(b) Fundamental analysis.**

They closely examine the **Regulatory and Structure** framework of the financial system. The rules and regulations are to be followed by the Finance Companies. SEBI, RBI, MOF, ROC and department of company affairs all these bodies are statutory concerns with reference to finance companies. The RBI issues guidelines to finance companies, the SEBI gives direction to the finance companies in regard to the mobilisation of resources. The trends in regulation/deregulation and their impact on the company will be examined.

**The Fundamental Analysis** will be done by the CRISIL'S group of experts. They will analyse the liquidity position of the company, asset quality, profitability, financial sound etc. The term also checks the interest and tax sensitivity of the Company. The analysis of **liquidity** position includes **capital structure, matching of assets and liabilities.** The top level management policy on liquid assets in relation to financing commitments and refunding of deposits. The capital structure refers to the make up of a firms capitalisation. It represents the mix of different sources of long term-funds in the total capitalisation of the company. The term capital structure is used for the mix capitalisation. The experts should undertake the pattern of capital structure in case of newly established companies. The Company can undertake any of the following four patterns:

(a) Capital structure with equity share only.
(b) Capital structure with both equity and preference shares.
(c) Capital structure with equity shares and debentures.
(d) Capital structure with equity shares, preference shares and debentures.

The choice of an appropriate capital structure depends on a number of factors such as the nature of the Company's business, regularity of earnings, conditions of the market, attitude of the investor. The other factor in **fundamental analysis is** the asset quality. The Asset Quality depends upon the Company's credit risk management. The Committee undertakes a system for monitoring credit affairs of the Company. They also examine the sector's risk involved in a particular position. The exposure to individual borrowers and management of credit will be studied indepth. **The profitability** analysis is the other factor in evaluation of finance companies. The team also examines the historic profits and fund deployment. The quantum of revenues arose on non-fund based services. The team observes the financial position of the Company. The team closely observes the financial leverage of the company. They examine about the exposure to interest rate changes. They observe the hedge against interest rate and tax law change,

**The evaluation** is carried out by the CRISIL team which effects its credit evaluation of the Company. The Companies will present information to the **CRISIL** on the areas which are discussed about at the time of requesting for a rating. The credit rating process generally involves a period of time **for 4 to 6 weeks.** Ratings of company deposits are made compulsory under the new companies bill of 1993. The RBI also made it compulsory for all the **NBFC**s registered with it to get themselves rated before they approach the public. The CRISIL adopted the conventional rating system which is available in the advanced countries. The symbols are assigned by the CRISIL for different financial instruments in different ways. The CRISIL undertakes the ratings of various financial instruments as follows:

**(i) Rating of Debentures.**
**(ii) Rating of Fixed Deposit Schemes.**
**(iii) Rating for short-term Instruments.**

*(i) Rating of Debentures*

The CRISIL does not rate the equity shares or the performance of the Company as a whole. The rating is confined only to **Debentures, fixed deposits, and short-term instruments.** The symbols that are used in credit rating of debentures and meanings are presented below:

| *Symbol* | *Meaning* |
|---|---|
| **(1) AAA**<br>(Triple A)<br>*Highest Safety* | The Debentures which are rated **AAA** are judged as the highest safety debt instrument in timely payment of the interest and principal. This ratings reflect that the issue is fundamentally very strong. |
| **(2) AA**<br>(Double A)<br>***High Safety*** | The debentures which are rated **AA** are judged as high safety of timely payment of interest and principal amount. They deffer slightly from AAA issues. |
| **(3) A**<br>*Adequate Safety* | The debentures which are rated **A** are judged as adequate safety of timely payment of interest and principal amount. But any change in circumstances adversely affects such issues more than the above graded categories. |
| **(4) BBB**<br>Triple B<br>*Moderate Safety* | The Debentures which are rated **BBB** are judged to provide adequate safety of timely payment of **Interest and principal amount** at present. But changes in circumstances are likely to lead to weakened capacity to pay interest and repay the principal than higher rated categories. |
| **(5) BB**<br>Double B<br>*Inadequate Safety* | The debentures which are rated **BB** are judged to carry inadequate safety of timely payment of interest and principal amount. The uncertainties will lead the issues to inadequate capacity to make timely interest and principal payments. |

*(Contd.)*

*(Contd.)*

| | |
|---|---|
| **(6) B** *High Risk* | The Debentures which are rated **"B"** category are treated as greater susceptibility to default. Though currently interest and principal payments are met, any adverse situation would lead to lack of ability or willingness to pay interest or principal amount. |
| **(7) C** *Substantial Risk* | The Debentures which are rated **"C"** category reveals that, the investment made in this instrument to default. Therefore, the investor should think twice before investing in this category of debt instruments. The timely payment of interest and principal is possible only if favourable situations continue. |
| **(8) D** *Default* | The debentures which are rated **"D"** are in defaults. If the company is in arrears of interest or principal payments. It is doubtful on maturity. These debentures are more speculative and the interest may be received only on liquidation or reorganisation. |

### *(ii) Rating of Fixed Deposit Schemes*

The fixed rating made by the CRISIL carries a symbol **"F"**. The ratings are classified as follows:

| | |
|---|---|
| **(1) FAAA** Triple A *Highest Safety* | The fixed deposit which carries **"FAAA"** reveals the degree of safety regarding the prompt payment of interest and principal amount. |
| **(2) FAA** F Double A *High Safety* | This rating reveals that the amount of interest and principal will be paid within a stipulated period of time. |
| **(3) FA** *Adequate Safety* | This rating carries the degree of safety regarding the timely payment of interest and principal amount. The financial position of the company is satisfactory. |
| **(4) FB** *Inadequate Safety* | This rating reveals that the company is not in a position to pay interest and principal amount within a stipulated period of time. |
| **(5) FC** *High Risk* | This rating indicates that the payment of interest and principal amount is doubtful. |
| **(6) FD** *Default* | This rating indicates that the issue is either in default or is expected to be in default and there is no assurance for the payment. |

### *(iii) Ratings of Short-Term Instruments*

The short-term instruments are also rated by the CRISIL. The ratings of the short-term instruments commences from the letter **"P"**. The ratings have been presented in below:

|  |  |
|---|---|
| **(1) P1** *Highest Safety* | The rating reveals that the interest payment will be made according to the time and the principal amount will also be paid in time. The investment in this instrument is very safe. |
| **(2) P2** *High Safety* | This rating indicates that the payment of interest is within the stipulated time and the principal amount will be paid on maturity. |
| **(3) P3** *Adequate Safety* | This rating reveals the degree of safety for timely payment of the interest and principal amount. |
| **(4) P4** *Inadequate Safety* | This rating reveals that the timely payment of interest on the instrument is minimal. |
| **(5) P5** *Default* | This rating indicates that the company is unable to refund the amount on the maturity. |

The overall ratings of the CRISIL to various debt instruments is as follows:

| *Debentures* | | *Fixed deposits* | | *Short-term instrument* | |
|---|---|---|---|---|---|
| AAA | *Highest Safety* | FAAA | Highest Safety | *P1* | **Highest Safety** |
| AA | *High Safety* | FAA | High Safety | *P2* | **High Safety** |
| A | *Adequate Safety* | FA | Adequate Safety | *P3* | **Adequate Safety** |
| BBB | *Moderate Safety* | FB | Inadequate Safety | *P4* | **Inadequate Safety** |
| BB | *Inadequate Safety* | FC | High Risk | *P5* | **Default** |
| B | *High Risk* | FD | Default | | |
| C | *Substantial Risk* | | | | |
| D | *Default* | | | | |

The investors must decide themselves how much of their portfolio would like to invest either in Fixed Deposits or debentures of a Company. After taking the decision he must identify what the risk he is willing to take. The above ratings indicate about the degree of risk level in various instruments. For rating of the Debt instruments the CIRSIL charges the fee as follows:

**Fee Structure for Fixed Deposits**

The fee charged by the CRISIL two kinds—**(A) Initial rating fee,**

**(B) Annual Surveillance fee.** The initial rating fee will be charged by the CRISIL as **0.05 per cent** of the outstanding amount of the fixed deposits subjected to a minimum of **Rs.40,000**. The minimum fee for the initial rating would depend on the nature and size of the operations of the Company. **The Annual Surveillance** fee is **0.03 per cent** of the outstanding amount of the fixed deposits subjected to a minimum of Rs. 25,000 per annum. The charges are subjected to change but will not exceed **0.05 per cent** of the outstanding amount of the fixed deposits. In addition to the above charges any additional expenses incurred (if any) will be charged to the client by the CRISIL.

**Fee Structure for Debentures Programme**

The fee charged by the CRISIL in case of debenture are a follows:

(a) Initial rating fee will be charged as **0.10 per cent** of the amount of debenture issue size and it is subjected to a minimum of **Rs. 40,000**. The minimum fee for initial rating depends upon the nature and the size of the Company.
(b) **The Annual Surveillance** fee will be charged as **0.03 per cent** of the amount of debenture issue size and subjected to a minimum of **Rs. 25000** per annum. The charges are subject to change.
(c) **Any other expenses** incurred by the CRISIL will be charged to the client company.

**Fee Structure for Commercial Paper Programme**

The fee charged by the CRISIL in case of Commercial paper programme is presented below:

(a) **Initial rating fee** will be charged by the CRISIS as **0.10 per cent** of the amount of commercial paper permissible under the RBI guidelines. The minimum fee for the initial rating would depend upon the nature of the business and the size of the operations.
(b) **Surveillance fee** should be charged as **0.03 per cent** of the amount of commercial paper permissible by the RBI. It is subjected to a minimum of **Rs. 25,000 per annum**. The rates are subjected to change. All other expenses will be charged if any incurred by the CRISIL.

CRISIL offers services to the clients and the evaluation of information will be kept under confidential until announcement of rating officially.

## 2. INVESTMENT INFORMATION AND CREDIT RATING AGENCY OF INDIA (ICRA)

The ICRA has promoted by the Industrial Finance Corporation of India. It has come into existence in **August 1991**. It has its headquarters at Delhi. It is an independent company limited by shares with an authorised share capital of Rs.10 crores. The paid up share capital of the agency is **Rs. 5 crores**. The IFCI has contributed **26 per cent** of the share capital and the balance is contributed by **UTI, GIC, PNB Central Bank of India, Bank of Baroda, UCO Bank etc.**

The ICRA is the second rating agency in India. It is established as a competitor to the **CRISIL**. This sanction is subjected to some conditions. The agency should be self-supporting for the first two years. Afterwards it should not require any subvention from the **IFCI**. The rating agency should be managerially independent. The share holders of the agency are as follows:

**IFCI, UTI, SBI, PNB, LIC, GIC, EXIM, Allahabad Bank, Canara Bank, Central Bank of India, Citi Bank, Indian Bank, Indian Overseas Bank, Oriental Bank of Commerce, UCO Bank, UBI, United Bank of India, Vyshya Bank Ltd., Housing Development Finance Corporation Ltd., Infrastructure Leasing and Finance Services Ltd., and 20th Century Finance Corporation Ltd.** It is managed by a board of director. The Board Comprises of seasoned professionals with finance and economic background. The Board includes the nominees from the Government and the RBI.

### Objectives

The main objective is to assess the credit instruments and assign a grade constant to the risk associated with such instrument. The rating is based on an objective analysis of the information provided by the client company. The main objectives of the ICRA is as follows:

(a) To guide the investors in making well informed investing decisions.

(b) To assist the issuer company in raising funds from wider investor.

(c) It acts as a marketing tool.
(d) To create a healthy competitive environment in the capital market.

**Services**

The ICRA provides the services in **credit assessment** and general assessment. The credit assessment involves in taking up of assignments for credit assessment of the companies intending to use the same for obtaining the financial assistance from **Commercial Bank, Financial Investment Institutions.** Factoring companies, and Financial service companies. The assessment reveals the opinion of the ICRA. The **General assessment** involves in providing services. If any banker approaches, it prepares as per the requirements of the general assessment report. The services are also likely to be useful to the NBFC's for the purpose of **merger, amalgamation acquisition, Joint Venture. Collaboration and factoring of debt.** It does not specify any symbol in respect of general assessments. It provides a report on various aspects of the companies.

**The Rating Process in ICRA**

The Rating process will commence, when the issuer company approaches the ICRA for rating the issue. Then the ICRA informs to the issuer company about the required data. Therefore, the desired data will be procured by the client. A group of analysts takes up the work of collection of data and procures information from the looks and records of the concerns. The rating agency also interacts with its executives. For the rating purpose of the issuer, the ICRA will utilise the services of inhouse research and database as well as Industry studies of reputable agencies. It ensures the Confidentiality of all the information collected during the rating process. Once the rating Agency assigns a symbol, the agency should monitor the rating till the redemption/repayment of the debt obligation. The following are the various steps involved in the Rating process of debt instrument.

(a) The rating process is not restricted to any examination of the financial measures.
(b) The analytical framework is divided into several categories.
(c) The analysis indicates the financial discipline of the issuer company.

The ICRA undertakes a close observation of various parameters. They are presented below:

1. **Industry Risk.**
2. **Market Position.**
3. **Operating Efficiency.**
4. **Evaluation of Management.**
5. **Accounting Standards.**
6. **Financial Capacity.**
7. **Cash Flow Adequacy.**

***(1) Industry Risk***

The experts team examines the industry growth. It also observes the evaluation of strengths and weaknesses of the unit. They also gather information about the intensity of Competition to the issuing Company. The volume of the market, the number of players in the market, the market share of each Company, threat from the new entrants, technology used by competitors/new entrants. The risk means a chance of occurring a future loss. The risk can be classified as **Systematic risk and Unsystematic risk.** The systematic risk is associated with the overall movements in the general market or economy. The risk is inescapable and is caused by **recession, war and structural changes in the economy.** The systematic risk is known as **Market risk or Non-diversifiable risk.** The unsystematic risk is not related to be overall market variability. It can be eliminated or reduced. It is known as **Non-market risk or diversifiable risk.** They examine the nature and extent of regulations.

***(2) Market Position***

The assesses the market situation. They examine the abilities which would increase the market share of the Company. They will assure the future estimation of the sales while meeting the market players. The competition from the existing and the new companies will be taken into consideration. They study about the brand strengths and also the position of the issuer company in the market. The team examines the price variability of the different brands which are available in the market. The experts should analyse the distribution and marketing strengths of the issuer company. They also examine the weakness of the marketing/distributional channel. A detailed study will be done by the experts to strengthen the effective channel of distribution.

### *(3) Operating Efficiency*

The group of experts analyse the production schedules of the issuer company. They examine the abilities which are going to reduce the cost. They procure and compare the data regarding the installed capacity and produced units. A high level of production capacity utilisation enhances the level of production and reduces the cost of production per unit. They compare the issuer company data with competitors data. Then they draw a conclusion about the efficiency of the issuing company. The team examines the labour relationship in the issuer company. **Industrial peace** is the most important factor to achieve the production targets. **The access to raw material** also shows substantial cost savings in the form of transportation charges. **The latest sophisticated technology** also saves the time and the cost more effectively.

### *(4) Evaluation of Management*

The experts closely evaluate the track record of the issuer company management. They check the capabilities of the top level management, their qualifications and experience. Their technical, financial and managerial capabilities are closely monitored and evaluated by the team of experts. The experts may check the process of the systems for financial and strategic planning. They will review about the control process and budgeting of the issuer organisation. The team also examines about the credibility of management plans and the extent of commitment towards achieving the **Organisational goals.** They also study about the organisational structure and layers in the management with the operating environment and management strategy. They focus on the skill and quality at different levels of workers and managerial capacities. The team checks the process of delegation of authority and succession about the planning.

### *(5) Accounting Standards*

The team thoroughly checks the accounts which are maintained by the Accounts Department of the Company. Financial statements are the most important factors. They decide the results of the issuer company. The profits that are declared by the Company depends upon the accuracy of the accounts. The quality of the accounts depends upon the Accounting standards.

### *(6) Financial Capabilities*

The team focuses on the financial strengths of the issuer Company. They evaluate the financial position of the company by observing the parameters like **EPS, PE-Ratio, Gross-Profit Ratio, Earnings before depreciation and tax, Profit before tax, Profit after tax, Capital structure, Cost of Capital, management of working capital, the ratio between current assets and fixed assets**, the return on Capital employed, the Financial leverage, liquidity ratio, cash flows, the balance between accounts receivable and payable and the other areas.

### *(7) Cash Flow Analysis*

The information required for evaluating the cash flow analysis is the magnitude and variability of future cash flow relative to credit affairs. The experts also examine the cash flows from its group Companies.

All the above parameters will be closely monitored by the team of experts. The required information will be submitted by the issuer company to the rating agency. Sometimes the rating agency can procure the data from its own sources. However, the following parameters may be gathered through meeting and visits.

**(a) Internal Sources.**
**(b) External Sources.**

The information from the **internal sources** is the most important element in the assessment of a firm. The team visits the plant and discussions are made with factory officials regarding the type of technology they adopted. They examine the records of the departments like **Production, Finance, Accounts, Marketing and Personnel.** The internal sources are procured from **Operating personnel, top management and business unit heads.**

The information which is available from the outside perview of the company is known as **External Sources.** The information can be procured from the bankers of the issuing company. They provide all the financial aspects of the issuing company on request. The **Auditors** of the issuing company provides a valuable information and guides the rating firm. **The competitors** are also one of the important external sources of the information. The Competitor reveals all the facts regarding strengths and weaknesses of the issuing company. **The Industry experts** is another important source of information. Their suggestions and criticism play an important role in evaluation of a firm. They judge the position of the issuing company in the market. The Industry experts know all the aspects of the market players and their comments will influence the image of the company. **The Suppliers** can have the first hand information about the issuing company. The suppliers tell about the capacity utilisation and technical details of the issuing company. **The Dealers/Distributors** of the issuing company can have the first hand information about the market position. They are able to know the pulse of the consumers and their behaviour. The dealers can suggest about the product modification, if necessary. **The Consumers** have the final authority to comment about the product, its quality, price and availability etc. The consumer is the king in the market.

**Rating Scale**

The primary objective of the ICRA is to provide guidance to the investors and creditors in determining the credit risk associated with the debt securities. The ratings reflect an independent, professional and impartial assessment of such credit risk. The ratings are not the recommendations to buy or sell or hold securities. The rating is a symbolic indicator of the current opinion **/comment** about the capability of the issuer company. The rating is an objective analysis of the information and clarification obtained from the concerns. The ICRA rates long-term, medium-term and short-term debt instruments. The rating symbols and their implications are as follows:

(1) Long-Term Instruments Rating Scale.
(2) Medium-Term.
(3) Short-Term.

### *(1) Long-Term Instruments Rating Scale (Debentures, Bonds, Preference Shares)*

| *Symbol* | | *Description* |
|---|---|---|
| **LAAA** | **Highest Safety** | The debentures/ bonds/ PS which are rated **"LAAA"** indicates fundamentally very strong position . There is no risk factor involved in this issue of debt instrument. In any adverse situation also the degree of safety does not affect the timely payment of **principal and interest** as per the terms and conditions of the issue. |
| **LAA** | **High Safety** | The debt instruments which are rated as **"LAA"** reveals the risk position of the issue. In this category, the risk factors are moderate and may vary slightly. The fundamentals are very strong that the perspect of timely payment of **Principal and Interest** will be paid even in an adverse situation. |
| **LA** | **Adequate Safety** | The financial instruments which are rated as **"LA"** reveals that the risk factors are more variable and greater in periods of economic stress. The protective factors are average. If any adverse situation arises, it may effect the timely payment of **Principal and Interest** as per terms of the issue. |
| **LBBB** | **Moderate Safety** | The debt instruments which are rated as **"LBBB"** indicates considerable variability in the risk factors. The protected factors are below average. Any adverse changes in **business/economic** circumstances are likely to affect the payment of **Principal and Interest** as per terms and conditions of the issue. |
| **LBB** | **Inadequate Safety** | This symbol reveals about the payment of principal plus interest on an adequate safety. The timely payment of interest and principal are more likely to affect the present or prospective changes in business or economic circumstances. The protective factors fluctuate in case of changes in the economic conditions. |
| **LB** | **Risk Prone** | The debt instruments which are rated as **"LB"** indicates that the protective factors are narrow. Obligations may not be fulfilled. Any adverse changes in the business or economic conditions results in inability to redeem the debt as per terms and conditions of the issue. |

*(Contd.)*

*(Contd.)*

| | | |
|---|---|---|
| **LC** | **Substantial Risk** | The rating symbol **"LC"** reveals that the investment in this issue involves risk and timely servicing of debts is possible only in case of continuous existence of favourable circumstances. |
| **LD** | **Default** | The rating reveals that it is an extremely speculative instrument. It is already in default in the payment of **interest and principal.** As per terms, it is expected to default. The refund is possible only on **liquidation** or reorganisation. |

## *(2) Medium-Term Rating Scale (Fixed Deposit)*

| *Symbol* | | *Description* |
|---|---|---|
| **MAAA** | **Highest Safety** | The instruments which are rated as **"MAAA"** indicates the highest safety. It is the best one as per terms in the timely payment of **principal and interest.** |
| **MAA** | **High Safety** | Investment in this category of instrument is very safe. The prospect of timely servicing the interest and principal as per terms is high but not as high as in the above category. |
| **MA** | **Adequate Safety** | The rating reveals the timely servicing of the interest and **principal is adequate.** Debt servicing may be affected by the adverse changes in the business or economic conditions. |
| **MB** | **Inadequate Safety** | The timely payment of interest and **principal** are more likely to be affected by the future uncertainties. |
| **MC** | **Risk Prone** | The rating reveals that the susceptibility to default is high. Any adverse changes in the business or economic conditions results in inability to service the debts on time as per terms and conditions of the issues. |

## *(3) Short-Term Instrument Commercial Paper*

| *Symbol* | | *Description* |
|---|---|---|
| $A_1$ | **Highest Safety** | The rating indicates that the prospect of timely payment of **debt/ obligation** is the best. |
| $A_2$ | **High Safety** | The relative safety is lower than $A_1$ **rating.** |

*(Contd.)*

*(Contd.)*

| | | |
|---|---|---|
| $A_3$ | **Adequate Safety** | The prospect of timely payment of interest instalment is adequate. The fundamental strength may affect any adverse change in the business or economic conditions. |
| $A_4$ | **Risk Prone** | The rating indicates that the degree of safety is low. Any adverse change in business or economic conditions results in default. |
| $A_5$ | **Default** | The rating indicates the default position or the position which is expected to default. |

## Schedule of Fee

| | |
|---|---|
| **(i) Initial Rating Fee:** | (a) Fixed Deposits—**0.05 per cent** of the outstanding amount of the fixed deposit.<br>(b) Debentures—**0.10 per cent** of the issue size.<br>(c) Commercial paper—**0.10 per cent** of the issue size. |
| **(ii) Annual Surveillance Fee:** | **0.03 per cent** of the outstanding amount. |
| **(iii) Credit Assessment Fee:** | **0.05 per cent** of all outstanding debts as on the last balance sheet. It is subjected to a minimum of **Rs. 25,000** and maximum of **Rs. 5 lakhs.** |
| **(iv) General Assessment Fee:** | A flat fee of **Rs. 50,000** for each company is to be assessed. It is subjected to a maximum of **Rs. 10.00 lakhs**. This, however, does not apply to general assessment of overall portfolio fees for which would be decided according to the nature and volume of work involved. |

*Notes*:

(1) All fees are non-refundable.

(2) The minimum and maximum fee rating should be **Rs. 50,000** and **Rs. 20.00 lakhs** respectively.

(3) The minimum and maximum surveillance fee should be **Rs. 30,000** and **Rs. 10.00 lakhs** respectively.

(4) In case of convertible debentures, no rating fee should be payable for a part of the debenture if they are convertible within a period of **12 months.**

(5) All other pocket expenses are to be charged to the issuing company on actual basis.

(6) The fee for other rating instruments/services would be decided on the basis of financial instruments.

(7) A separate fee should be charged for involving in the preparation of project appraisal.

The ICRA rating are helpful to the borrowing companies to access capital market and money market for raising a larger volume of resources from a large investor's base. If the ratings are done by the ICRA, the less known companies are also able to access the capital market and money market.

## 3. CREDIT ANALYSIS AND RESEARCH LTD (CARE)

### Introduction

The CARE is the third credit rating agency in India. These ratings are accepted by the SEBI, the RBI and the Government of India. It is promoted by the IDBI and the other institutions. The regulatory authorities have made rating a necessary grading for entering into the market. It is incorporated as a Public Limited Company under the Indian Companies Act. It has commenced its operations in October 1993. The CARE is run by the Board of Directors comprising of eminent persons with a varied experience in financial services and allied areas. The Company is an autonomous body and enjoys full freedom in its operations and the ratings are also accepted by the market. It maintains its integrity, independence and credibility. It offers a wide range of products and services in the field of credit information and equity research. It has had the benefit of close relations with reputed credit rating agencies in the world.

The **Shareholders** of the CARE includes **IDBI, Canara Bank, UTI, Credit Capital Venture Fund of India Limited, Sundaram Finance Limited, The Federal Bank Ltd.,** The Vyshya Bank Ltd., First Leasing Company of India Ltd., ITC Classic Finance Ltd., Kalimathi Investment Company Ltd., The Investment Corporation of India Ltd., Varuna Investments Ltd., 20th Century Finance Corporation Ltd.

The CARE fully involves in rating all types of Debt Instruments such as:

(1) Fixed Deposits.
(2) Certificate of Deposits (C.D's).
(3) Commercial Paper.
(4) Debentures.
(5) Structured Obligations.

It also undertakes general credit analysis rating of the Corporate Sector for the use of lenders, bankers and other institutions. The ratings and symbols are presented below for a detailed discussion:

| *Symbol* | *Explanation* |
|---|---|
| **(A) Long-Term and Medium Term Instruments** | |
| **CARE AAA CARE AAA FD/CD/SO** | The Debt Instruments which carries **"CARE AAA"** ratings are considered to be the best quality, carrying no investment risk. This category of Debt Instruments are protected by the stable cash flows with good margin. This is a strong payment signal even in an adverse situation. |
| **CARE AA CARE AA FD/CD/SO** | The Debt Instruments carrying this grading are judged to be of **high quality** by all standards. These are also categorised as high investment grades. They are rated lower than securities. Any change in the assumption may have a greater impact. The risk involved in this category of securities are quite different from **"CARE AAA"** instruments. |
| **CARE A CARE A ED/CD/SO** | The Debt Instruments which are classified as **"CARE A"** ratings are considered as Upper medium grade instruments. It has many favourable investment attributes. Adequate safety is available for **principal and interest amount** of the Debt Instrument. Adverse situation of the business / economic conditions may not show an impact on this issue. |
| **CARE BBB CARE BBB FD/CD/SO** | The instruments which are classified as ratings are considered as investment grade. It indicates the adequate safety for the payment of **interest and principal** amount at the time of rating. Any adverse situation in business or economic conditions may more likely to weaven the debt servicing capability compared to the high rated instruments. |
| **CARE BB CARE BB FD/CD/SO** | This category of Debt Instruments are considered to be **speculative** within adequate protection for **interest and principal** payments. |
| **CARE B CARE B FD/CD/SO** | The Debt Instruments are classified as susceptible to **default**. The adverse situation in business or economic conditions lead to default. |
| **CARE C CARE C FD/CD/SO** | These Debt Instruments carry high investment **risk**. They may lead to default in the payment of **interest and principal.** |

*(Contd.)*

*(Contd.)*

| *Symbol* | *Explanation* |
|---|---|
| **CARE D CARE D FD/CD/SO** | These categories of investments are in the least safety position. They are either in **default** or likely to be in default. |

**(B) Short-Term Instruments**

The Debt Instruments rated by the **CARE** for Short-Term Instruments are presented below:

| | |
|---|---|
| **PR-1** | The Short-Term Instruments which are rated as **"PR-1"** reveals that the issuing company has **superior** capacity for the repayment of short-term promissory obligations. Issuers of such type of instruments will normally be characterised by the leading market positions in established industries. High rates of returns on funds are possible. |
| **PR-2** | The issue of these categorised instruments have strong capacity for the repayment of **short-term promissory obligations**. The issuers have the characteristics which resemble the PR-1 instruments but to a lesser degree. |
| **PR-3** | The Instruments have an adequate capacity for the repayment of short-term obligations. The variability in earnings profitability results in changes in the level of debt protection. |
| **PR-4** | These category instruments have minimal degree of safety regarding the timely payment of short-term promissory obligations and the safety is likely to be adversely affected by the short-term in less favourable conditions. |
| **PR-5** | This category of instrument is in **default** or it is likely to default on maturity. |

**(C) Credit Analysis Rating**

| | |
|---|---|
| **CARE-1** | This rating reveals the excellent capability in debt management. The management of debt can be done more effectively. Such business concerns will be normally market leaders in the respective sectors. |
| **CARE-2** | This rating indicates a very good debt management capability. These companies are normally regarded as close to those rated CARE-1, but with a lower capability to withstand the changes in assumptions. |

*(Contd.)*

*(Contd.)*

| | |
|---|---|
| **CARE-3** | This rating reveals that the company has good capability for debt management. These companies are regarded as minimum grade. The assumptions that do not materialise may impair debt management capability in future. |
| **CARE-4** | This rating indicates the satisfactory capability for debt management. The capacity to meet the obligations is likely to affect the short-term adversity or in less favourable conditions. |
| **CARE-5** | The rating deals with the poor capability of the debt management. These companies are in default or likely to default in meeting their debt obligations. |
| | The debt management capability covers a wide range of services. The rating are expressed only in limited number of symbols. It assign **+ or –** signs to be shown after the assigned rating to indicate the relative position within the brand covered by the rating symbol. |

*Source*: Information pamphlet issued by the CARE.

## Summary

The investment preferences of households have changed dramatically. In India, the household sector accounts ones **80 per cent** of the GDP which plays a significant change in their investment preferences. The financial development occurred because of the technical invention and through the mode of popular joint stock company. **The joint stock** form made the large scale industry possible by collecting large amounts of capital. The capital is generated out of savings leading to investment which is a part of the financial system. The organised financial system of comprises with **money market, capital market, new issue market and stock market.**

In the entire globe the trend has been for the individual investor shifting from the direct investment in equities to the mutual fund route. The mutual fund offers safety and it provides services to the investors. The Unit Trust is established and is obliged to buyback chits whenever an investor wants to sell them. Mutual savings banks are popular in **USA.** Mutual funds helps the small investors to obtain **high return, low risk** combinations from their scientifically managed portfolios. The small investors cannot directly invest in the instruments such as **Certificate of Deposit, Commercial Paper** and **Treasury Bills**. The

Mutual funds facilitated advantages to the unit holders. In India all mutual funds have to be registered with the SEBI. The Government of India permitted the commercial banks to enter into this segment. The Government has also permitted private sector to set up **Money Market Mutual funds.** Mutual funds can be classified as by category and by scheme-wise. The Investment Trust is a financial institution. It collects a small amount of investible funds from a large number of investors. The Mutual Funds have five key parties—the sponsors, the board of trustees, the AMC, the custodian, the unit holders. The Mutual funds can be classified into five categories. They are based on ownership status, schemes of operation, portfolio objectives and location. The mutual funds should be registered with **SEBI**. The SEBI regulations from **1 to 75** informations about various rules and regulations to be followed by mutual funds. The RBI issued guidelines for commercial to enter into mutual fund sector. The mutual funds should also follow the guidelines which are issued by the Company Law. Risk is the essence of the valuation of a financial instrument. The return which expect is different from the return which we receive. The total risk is consisting of systematic risk and unsystematic risk. The risk can be classified in several ways like **default risk, liquidity risk, maturity risk, inflation risk, purchasing power risk, currency risk, exchange risk, business risk**. Risk indicators involves mathematics. **Beta** is the most common measure of the risk. **Alpha** is a performance measure adjusted for the risk. The Net Assets Value is determined by the stock market prices. The stock markets are influenced by the supply, the demand and the other factors. A good mutual fund always works for the satisfaction of the unit holders. The mutual funds in India should be evaluated on the valuation norms **Traded securities, Non-traded securities and Rights shares.** Every mutual fund in India should work according to the general obligations like maintenance of proper books of accounts, audit, annual report disclosure norms, procedure for action in case of default. The winding up of the mutual fund can be done by the Trustee. The Trustee of the mutual fund shall call a meeting of the unit holders to consider and pass necessary resolution by simple majority of the unit holders present. On the completion of the winding up the trustees shall forward to the SEBI. **Venture capital** is a type of financial intermediary emerged in USA. Venture capital provides finance or risk capital to unregistered, high risky technology oriented units. The VC contributes in the form of equity upto **49 per cent** of the total equity. VC firms has to appoint marketing specialists in product launching to capture the market. The methods of financing are practiced by the VCF shares and Debt. The present technological revolution has witnessed the reemergence of small and medium firms. The introduction of appropriate changes in the company law and banking law are considered advisable to enable their successful participation in the current technological revolution. The Union Finance Ministry has issued guidelines for the establishment and functioning of the venture capital activities. Income Tax Act, 1961 deals with tax concessions to the VCFs. Entrepreneurship introduces a critical element of dynamism into an economic system. In India, the VCFs are located in Mumbai, Delhi, Kolkata and Bangalore. **Leasing** has emerged as a source of long-term financing of the corporate sector. A lease represents contractual agreement between two parties. Lease financing may enhance the growth of industries and services. A contract of lease provides a person an opportunity to use an asset. Now-a-days lease financing is very popular. Leasing facilitates a firm without heavy amount of investment to utilise the asset. Leasing provides assets in cheaper and faster sources. Leasing arrangement is more beneficial to small firms. Acquisition of assets through lease finance results some disadvantages. Due to rapid industrialisation leasing is gaining tremendous popularity in India. The factors influence in selecting a lessor, i.e. **Market rate, accounting information, service, professional spirit, systematic documentation.** Credit Rating helps investors by providing an easily recognisable, simple tools that couples a possible unknown issues. The rating is an opinion on the future ability and legal obligation of the issuer to make timely payments of principal and interest on a specific fixed income security. CRISIL has been promoted by ICICI and UTI as a public limited company with its head quarters at Mumbai. The main objective of CRISIL has been to rate debt obligation of Indian Companies. ICRA has been promoted by the IFCI with head quarters at New Delhi. ICRA was established to provide information and guidance to institutional and individual investors and creditors. **CARE** is promoted by IDBI. It provides credit rating, information services, equity research and to the customers. **Onida Individual Credit Rating Agency** has been promoted by well known **Onida** group. ONICRA is India's first Individual rating system.

**Review Questions**

1. What is a mutual fund? Define the concept of a mutual fund.

2. Explain the framework of regulations of the mutual fund industry in India
3. Examine the role of SEBI in Mutual fund sector.
4. Briefly discuss the future of mutual funds in India.
5. Critically examine the SEBI guidelines pertaining to mutual fund investment.
6. Examine the role of **Asset Management Company** of a mutual fund.
7. Explain the RBI guidelines in case of mutual funds set up by a commercial banks
8. Define "Risk". Explain the various risk factors involved in mutual fund sector
9. What do you mean by **Net Asset Value**? How it is calculated?
10. Explain the different methods of valuation of the investments in a mutual fund
11. What are the general obligations to be fulfilled by a mutual fund in India?
12. Explain the role of Trustees in a mutual fund
13. Explain the recent developments emerged in the mutual fund sector.
14. What do you mean by venture capital?
15. What do you mean by Credit Rating? Explain the Credit Rating agencies operating in India.

## REFERENCES

1. L.M. Bhole, *Financial Institutions and Markets*, p. 264. Tata McGraw, Hill, 1999.
2. *Nabhi Manual of SEBI*, p. 528, Nabhi Publications, 1995.
3. *Ibid.*
4. *Ibid.*
5. Rushi Chopra, *Economic Times*, Dt. 31/10/2001.
6. A.J. Mehta, Debt concerns, *The Economic Times*, Dt. 21/11/2001, p. 9.
7. Van Horne, *Fundamentals of Financial Management*, p. 91, PHI, 1997.
8. *Ibid.*, p. 101.
9. *Ibid.*

# UNIT III

- Underwriting
- Registrars
- Securities and Exchange Board of India (SEBI)
- National Stock Exchange
- Derivatives Trading
- Bombay Stock Exchange (BSE)
- Over the Counter Exchange of India (OTC)
- Brokers
- Depository System

# 1

# UNDERWRITING

## Introduction

In public issues, after the merchant bankers, the next position goes to the Underwriters. They play an important role in the public issues. In the primary market the major activity is related to Underwriting and their marketing. The Underwriters give guarantee for the public subscription and in turn they receive the commission. They agree to subscribe to a guaranteed number of shares when the public do not subscribe them Underwriting can be defined as **"bearing the risk of not being able to sell a security at the established price by virtue of purchasing the security for resale to the public; also known as firm commitment underwriting".**[1]

The person who assures is called as "Underwriter"; and the consideration for the assurance is known as "Underwriting Commission". Underwriting is the nature of an insurance against the adverse situation in the timing of the public issue. The SEBI has defined the Underwriting as "an agreement with or without conditions to subscribe to the securities of a body corporate where the existing shareholders of such body corporate or the public do not subscribe to the securities offered to them".[2] The Underwriter has been defined as "a person who engages in the business of Underwriting of an issue of securities of a body corporate".[3] The Underwriting is mandatory for the public issue. The stock exchange regulations clearly specifies that no stock broker is allowed to underwrite more than 5 per cent of the public issue and the concerned stock exchange should approve the appointment of broker underwriters. Usually the bankers can underwrite upto 10 per cent of the public issue. The Underwriting Commission cannot be paid on the amounts contributed by promoters, employees, directors, business associates. The Underwriting is an important element of the primary market. It is appointed by the issuing company in consultation with the merchant bankers. The name of the Underwriter and his obligations should be disclosed in the prospectus. There are a number of financial institutions, commercial banks, insurance companies as well as a number of private companies which provide underwriting. An Underwriter issue is the safe way of marketing securities and the investors are influenced by the prestige of underwriters. The issuing company may appoint anyone or more of the following parties:

**(A) Financial Institutions.**
**(B) Brokers.**
**(C) Bankers.**
**(D) Investment Companies.**
**(E) Trusts.**

The Underwriters may be appointed on the following basis:

(1) Guidelines of the SEBI.
(2) Financial capacity.
(3) Past experience and track record.
(4) Outstanding Underwriting Commitments.
(5) The Network of investor clientele of the Underwriter.
(6) Good reputation.

The person/firm who has been appointed as an underwriter for an issue should fulfil the following conditions:

(a) he has to underwrite a certain number of shares,
(b) the company should not charge the terms of the issue without the permission of the Underwriter,
(c) he should take up the responsibility of the unsubscribed issues by the public,
(d) he authorises the company to allot such balance of shares.

**Need for the Underwriters**

There is a strong need to underwrite the issue because of the following situations:

(1) If the project is new to the market.
(2) The project is promoted by **Technocrats**/Technicians.

(3) The large issues may not be possible for a broker.
(4) The project may not provide a better return on the investment.
(5) When the project is located in a backward area.

**Objectives of the Underwriting**

The objectives of the Underwriting are presented below:

(1) It guarantees the sale of securities at a given price.
(2) It facilitates the provision of money during the financial crisis of the company.
(3) The Underwriter helps the new company in its reorganisation.

The following are the salient features of an underwriting agreement:

(1) The Underwriter may not be able to sell the issues in some situations. The unsold securities are distributed among the underwriters in the agreed proportion.
(2) The offering price must be maintained for the successful distribution of the securities.
(3) The company makes a delivery of the securities to the manager and receives the payment on the closing date.
(4) At the termination of the underwriting, the manager must make the final accounting for each underwriter. He should also remit the commissions and accounts for the expenditure incurred.

Underwriting is an insurance for the new securities of the public. It is one of the methods of marketing securities. The other methods are **Prospectus method, offer for sale, private placement etc.** The Prospectus method is the most popular method in India. Raising the capital from this method is the most popular method marketing the issue of securities. The distribution expenses may be substantially saved. **Offer for sale** is another method of issue of securities. In this method the sales are sold largely to some brokers/**issue houses**. The issue house/brokers again sell the shares to the public at a fixed price. This method saves the company, the cost and the trouble of selling the shares to the public. In this method, a **Third party** takes over the responsibility. **Private placement** is another source of issue of securities. It has become more popular in India. In this process, the funds are raised in the primary market by selling the security issue to one investor or a **small group** of investors without resorting to underwriting. In this method, the cost of the issue is minimal. It is the most effective way of procuring the long-term funds. There is no need to follow the statutory formalities. The offer is made to select a group of known persons. The issues in the private placement markets are **Companies, Statutory Companies, Government and Financial Institutions**. The subscribers in this market are **Mutual Funds, Financial Institutions, Investment Banks and Individual Investors.**

## Kinds of Underwriting

The following are the various kinds of underwriting agreements:

(A) The Purchase Contract.
(B) Agreement between Underwriters and Representatives.
(C) The Selling Agreement.

### *(A) The Purchase Contract*

According to the Purchase Contract, the sale of shares are made to the underwriters at an accepted level of proportion. There will be an agreement among several underwriters to purchase the securities from the company.

### *(B) Agreement between Underwriters and Representatives*

This is an agreement between the Underwriters and the Representatives or Managers. The agreement include all the aspects of the issue of securities.

(a) to fix the time of offering;
(b) to reserve a proportion of securities for the selected dealers and institutions;
(c) place, date and delivery of securities;
(d) provisions regarding the termination and settlement of the underwriters account;
(e) underwriters' responsibilities.

### *(C) The Selling Agreement*

In this method, the issuer company will make an agreement with the dealers to subscribe the new securities. The agreement includes the offering price, selling concession and provisions for delivery and payment.

### Types of Underwriting

Underwriting in India may be broadly classified into two kinds:

(A) Institutional Underwriters, and
(B) Non-Institutional Underwriters.

### *(A) Institutional Underwriters*

The Institutional Underwriters include specialised financial institutions such as **IDBI, IFCI, ICICI and others**. The following are the Institutional Underwriters:

**(1) Development Banks.**
**(2) Commercial Banks.**
**(3) Insurance Companies.**
**(4) State Finance Corporations.**
**(5) Unit Trust of India.**

The **Development Banks** are also known as **Industrial Banks.** The industrial banks have got the long-term deposits and they are in a position to enter into the long-term investments.

The Industrial Banks help the industries by permitting the loans and **by underwriting** their shares and debentures. When an Industrial Unit approaches for underwriting the shares and for direct financial aid, the industrial banks investigate the prospects of the industry, the soundness of the financial requirements, the feasibility and the utilities of the schemes. If the shares and debentures are not fully **subscribed** or the minimum subscription is not taken up by the public within a specific period, the **Development Banks** come to the rescue and take up the residual amount of shares and debentures. **The Underwriting** facilitates the direct financial aids to the new industrial set up. **Industrial Finance Corporation of India** was established in **1948** with the intention of providing the long-term credits and underwriting of **equity preference** and debentures issues. The IFCI is empowered to supplement its resources through borrowing from the market. The IDBI was established under a special status as a wholly owned subsidiary to the **RBI**. The IDBI provides the financial assistance in the form of direct finance and term loans. It also agrees to buy the securities which are not subscribed by the investing public. It provides a **direct subscription** to the shares and debentures issued by the Companies. **The ICICI** was set up in 1955 as a public limited company with the support of the Government and the World Bank. The objectives of the ICICI are to assist in the creation, expansion and modernisation of the industrial enterprises and to sponsor and undertake the new issue of securities. Underwriting is one of the main objectives of the corporation. **Commercial Banks** perform the routine banking. These banks are also called Public Banks. Lending and Underwriting of the issues are the main objectives of the Commercial Banks. A few Commercial Banks have been rendering their services as syndicators of loans and managers to the issue. The Commercial Banks normally act as passive agents by supplying the forms only on request rather than on their own initiative and earn brokerage. **Insurance Companies** are basically investment institutions but not development institutions. **LIC and GIC** of India are the premier institutions in the country which involve in the insurance sector. These two conventional investment institutions supply funds mainly to provide the liquidity to the investments for developing the corporate sector. The objectives of these organisations are **direct lending to industry, subscription to shares and bonds of special industrial financial institution**, and purchase of securities of the Joint stock companies from the capital market. The government corporations also involve in the underwriting business. **The State Financial Corporations** also involve in the underwriting business for stimulating the capital market. **The Unit Trust of India** is the other conventional investment institution which enjoys superiority as an organisational device because of some activities. The UTI involves in continuous sale of units, Redemption of units at **NAV**, convenience to the small investors of small amount.

### *(B) Non-Institutional Underwriters*

There are two types of non-institutional underwriters in India:

1. Stock brokers.
2. Individuals.

**The Stock brokers** act as intermediaries in the purchase and sale of securities in the primary market and the secondary market. These persons have a network of sub-brokers who spread throughout the length and breadth of the country. They are known as sub-brokers. These people spread message and give publicity about various issues in the offering. They readily supply application forms or even go to the extent of collecting money from the investors. They play a very crucial role in the area of underwriting. The brokers can influence their clients by persuasion. **Individuals/Investment Companies** also involve in the underwriting business. The Investment Companies obtain funds from a large number of investors by selling the shares. The pooled funds are placed before the experts to deploy the purchase of financial assets. The benefits derived from the capital market will surpass that of the shareholders. These are two types of investment companies namely **(a) Fixed Investment Trusts and (b) Management Investment Trusts.**

## Disadvantages of the Underwriting System

The Underwriting is an agreement between the issuer and the financial intermediary. The Underwriting institutions in India are suffering from some weaknesses. The Underwriting system is not developed in India. In India, we do not have any special institutions to carry out underwriting business. The Underwriting activities are dominated by the development banks which are primarily the leading institutions. They are burdened with other responsibilities like **guaranteeing** deferred payments, making direct subscription to the corporate securities and doing entrepreneurial work. In India, the small enterprises are unable to utilise the services of the underwriters. There is a strong need to develop this sector to build confidence among the small organisations. The establishment of large number of small enterprises create more employment opportunities. This also enhances the per capita income. The Indian primary market does not have the organised machinery to facilitate these services. There is no arrangement to pursue the investors towards the small savings.

## Measures to Improve the Underwriting System

(a) In India, a lot of efforts should be made to develop the present structure of underwriting organisations; and also to enlarge the underwriting facilities.

(b) There is a strong need to create the financial syndication in the activities of the underwriters. The consortium creates the confidence among the corporate clients.

(c) The project evaluation is the most important one in the industrial finance process. A detailed investigation should be done by the technical and financial experts about the viability of the project. For this purpose, a permanent body should be established with the eminent personalities who are drawn from all the fields, i.e., marketing, technical, finance etc.

(d) **The project evaluation board** creates the confidence among the small concerns. The body services that are offered by the best expertise will be definitely useful to the small concerns.

(e) To encourage the small concerns, underwriting by the stock brokers should be invited with adequate financial and other incentives.

(f) The services of the project evaluation board could be made available to the stock brokers with a nominal fee.

(g) The underwriting business should be developed by observing the U.S. pattern.

(h) The underwriting syndicate should create a large network of retailers and dealers.

(i) The Underwriting should become an occupation of a profession as in the case of the **Merchant Banking**.

(j) The encouragement to stock brokers, commercial banks, lead to the development of the underwriting profession. A separate body should be constituted the Chartered Accountants; and a special curriculum should be introduced at post-graduate level for this specialised skilful operations.

(k) The Government should think about the scale of underwriting commission and brokerage.

## Registration

An underwriter is a financial intermediary in the primary market. Underwriters are appointed by the issuing companies after consulting the merchant bankers. To act as an underwriter, a certificate of registration must be obtained from the SEBI. The SEBI has the full authority to grant the certificate of registration. No person should act as an underwriter unless he holds a certificate granted by the SEBI.

The stock broker or the merchant banker should hold a valid certificate or registration u/s 12 of the Act.

According to the SEBI guidelines (Underwriters) Regulations 1993, Section 30, the prospecting person should apply for the grant of the certificate to the SEBI in **FORM A**. On receipt of this form, the board may ask the applicant to furnish further information or classification regarding the matters relevant to underwriting. If the board asks to present the applicant before it, he should be available to the SEBI. After scrutinising the Form A, the application will be rejected, if it is incomplete. But before rejecting any such application, the applicant should be given an opportunity by the board to remove such things within the specified time. The board takes into account all the matters that are relevant to underwriting and particularly regarding the below facilities before granting the certificate:

(a) The applicant has the necessary infrastructure.
(b) The applicant should have the experience otherwise he should appoint two experienced members.
(c) The underwriter should satisfy the capital adequacy requirement of the networth of **Rs. 20.00 lakhs.**
(d) The purpose of networth means, the applicant might be a proprietary concern or a firm or an association of persons or anybody of individuals, the value of capital plus free reserves of business.
(e) In the case of a body corporate, the value of the **paid up capital** plus **free reserves** should be disclosed in the looks of account of the applicant.

If the SEBI believes that the applicant is eligible, then it sends an intimation to the applicant that he is eligible for the grant of certificate; and thus it grants the certificate in **Form B** after the payment of the prescribed fee. An underwriter should make an application in **Form A** for the renewal of the certificate before the expiry of **3 months**. If the **registration is not granted** by the board, it will communicate with **30 days** of such refusal. After receiving the information from the SEBI, the applicant should furnish the required information within **30 days**. On receipt of the information, the board reconsiders its decision and communicates its findings in writing to the applicants. Every applicant who is eligible for the grant or renewal of the certificate should pay the fee. If the board satisfies with the cause shown, it permits the underwriter to pay such fee at any time before the expiry of **six months** from the date on which such fee becomes due. If an underwriter fails to pay the fee, the board may suspend the certificate.

### Fee

The Underwriters should pay the fee for the grant or renewal of the registration to the SEBI on the date of granting the certificate. The underwriter should pay **Rs. 2.00 lakhs** for the first and second years respectively; and he should pay **Rs. 1.00 lakh** for the third year to the SEBI. Every year a renewal fee of **Rs. 20,000** should be paid. Since 1999, the SEBI has raised the registration fee to **Rs. 5.00 lakhs**. The renewal fee of **Rs. 2.00 lakhs** should be paid for every 3 years from the date of registration.

### General Obligations and Responsibilities

The SEBI Regulations 1993, Chapter III deals with the general obligations and responsibilities of an underwriter. Every underwriter at all times abide by the code of conduct as specified in the Act. Regulation 13 reveals the characteristics of an underwriter.

***(Code of Conduct)***

(a) Every underwriter has to maintain high standards of integrity, dignity and fairness in all his dealings with his clients and other underwriters in the conduct of business.
(b) An underwriter should ensure that he and his personnel will act in ethical manner in all his dealings with the issuing company.
(c) Every underwriter should at all times render high standards of service, exercise due diligence, ensure proper care and exercise independent professional judgement.
(d) Every underwriter should disclose to the issuer company his possible source or potential areas of conflict of duties and interests while providing the underwriting service.
(e) An underwriter should not indulge in any unfair competition.
(f) No underwriter should make any statement either oral or written which would misrepresent.

(g) No underwriter should divulge to other issues.
(h) No underwriter should wilfully make untrue statement or suppress any material fact in any documents, reports, papers or information furnished to the board.

Every underwriter should enter into an agreement with a body corporate or whose behalf he is acting as an underwriter. The said agreement amongst other things should have the following:

(a) The period for which the agreement should be in force.
(b) The amount of underwriting obligations.
(c) The period within which the underwriter has to subscribe to the issue after being intimated on behalf of such body corporate.
(d) The amount of commission or brokerage payable to the underwriter.
(e) Details of the arrangements, if any, made by the underwriting for fulfilling the underwriting obligations.

## General Responsibilities

According to the SEBI guidelines, the underwriter has the following responsibilities while discharging his duties:

(a) The Underwriter should not derive any direct or indirect benefit from underwriting the issue, other than commission or brokerage payable under an agreement.
(b) The total understanding obligations under all the agreements should not exceed **twenty times** the networth.
(c) The Underwriters have to subscribe the securities under the agreement within 45 days of the receipt of intimation from the issuers.
(d) Every Underwriter should keep and maintain the following books of account and documents, namely:

(1) If the Underwriter belongs to a body corporate—

(i) A copy of the balance sheet, profit and loss account as specified in the Sections **211** and **212** of the Companies Act, 1956;
(ii) A copy of the auditor's report referred in Section **227** of the Companies Act, 1956.

(2) If the Underwriter does not belong to a body corporate.

(i) The records in respect of all the sums of money received and expended by them; and the matters in respect of the receipt and expenditure.

(ii) Their assets and liabilities.

(e) Every underwriter should furnish to the board company's balance sheet, profit and loss account, statement of capital adequacy and such other documents after the close of each financial year before **six months**.

(f) Every underwriter should maintain the following:

1. The details of the agreement.
2. The total amount of securities each body corporate has subscribed in pursuance of an agreement.
3. The statement of capital adequacy requirements.
4. Such other records as may be specified by the board for underwriting.
5. Every underwriter should intimate to the board the place where the books of account, records and documents are kept.

(g) Every underwriter should pressure the books of account, other records and documents for a minimum period of **five years**.

(h) The board may at any time call for any information from an underwriter pertaining to the underwriting business.

(i) If any information is called for, it is the duty of the underwriter to furnish such information.

**Inspection and Disciplinary Proceedings**

The SEBI has the full authority to grant the certificate, renewal of licence, giving directions from time to time. The following process is involved in inspection and disciplinary proceedings:

(a) The SEBI's right to inspect.

(b) Procedure for inspection.

(c) Obligations for underwriters.

(d) Submission of report to the board.

(e) Information of findings to the underwriter.
(f) Appointment of Auditor.

The **SEBI** has the whole right to inspect the books of account, other records and documents of the underwriter for any purpose as specified in the Act. The purposes referred in the Act are as follows:

(a) to ensure that the books of account, other records and documents are being maintained in the required manner;
(b) the provisions of the Act, rules and regulations are being compiled;
(c) to investigate into the complaints received from the investors, other underwriters or any other person on any matter after listening about the activities of the underwriters; and
(d) to investigate suo-moter in the interest of securities business or investor's interest into the affairs of the underwriter.

The SEBI **has the procedure for inspecting** any underwriter in the country according to the regulation **19** of the Act. The SEBI gives a reasonable notice to the underwriter for the purpose of inspection. Sometimes there is no need to give such a notice to the underwriter. With the **investors/public**, the SEBI has the full authority to conduct the inspection without notice. The inspecting authority is bound to discharge its obligations as per the **regulation 21** of the Act.

**After the inspection of the SEBI**, there will be obligations for an underwriter. According to the SEBI regulations, it is the duty of every director, proprietor, partner, officer and employee of the underwriter to assist him in providing the inspecting authority with such books of account and other documents in his custody or control. It is also their duty to furnish him with the statements and information relating to the underwriter within such time as the inspecting authority may require. The underwriter should allow the inspecting authority to have a reasonable access in the premises occupied by such underwriter or by any other person on his behalf. He should allow the inspecting authority to examine the books, records, documents and computer data under his possession. The inspecting authority is entitled to examine the record statements of any principal officer, director, partner, proprietor and employee.

After the completion of the inspection process, the inspecting authority should submit the inspection report to the SEBI. After the submission, the board should communicate the findings to the underwriters and give an opportunity of being heard before taking any action. **On receipt** of the explanation, if any, from the underwriter, the board may call upon the underwriter to take such measures as the board may deem fit. **The appointment of the auditor** is the final step in the process of inspection and disciplinary action/proceeding by the board. The board may appoint a qualified auditor to investigate the books of account or the affairs of the underwriter. He should be appointed according to the Companies Act, Section 226 to fulfil the statutory norms.

### Procedure for Action in Case of Default

The liability for action in case of default will vest with the underwriter, if he fails to get licence from the board. Every Underwriter/**Stock broker/Merchant banker** is entitled to carry on the business of underwriting without obtaining a separate certificate. If the underwriter contravenes any of the provisions of the Act, he will be liable to any of the penalties specified in the Act. The penalties may be either suspension of registration or **cancellation of registration**. The penalty is levied to the underwriter on the following situations:

(a) violates the provisions of the Act, rules or regulations,
(b) does not follow the code of conduct specified in the Act,
(c) fails to furnish any information relating to the business/ furnishes wrong or false information/does not cooperate in any enquiry conducted by the SEBI,
(d) indulges in manipulation or price rigging or cornering activities,
(e) is guilty of misconduct or improper or unbusiness or unprofessional conduct,
(f) fails to maintain the capital adequacy requirement,
(g) fails to pay the fee as specified in the Act,
(h) violates the conditions of registration, and
(i) fails to fulfil his underwriting obligations.

The reasons for the failure will be recorded by the Board. In case of repeated defaults, it imposes a penalty of cancellation of certificate. The SEBI guidelines 28 indicates that no order of penalty of suspension or cancellation should be imposed after holding an enquiry in accordance with the Act. The SEBI should verify all the movements of the underwriter before **suspension or cancellation of registration.** The following manner should be followed by the SEBI before taking an action.

1. The SEBI should appoint an enquiry officer under Regulation 27.
2. The enquiry officer should issue a notice to the underwriter at the register office or principal place of business of the underwriter.
3. The underwriter may within **30 days** from the date of receipt of such notice should furnish to the enquiry officer a reply together with the copies of documentary or other evidence relied on him or sought by the board from the underwriter.
4. The enquiry officer should give a reasonable opportunity to the underwriter to enable him to make submissions in support of his reply made under the Act.
5. Before the enquiry officer, the underwriter may either appear in person or through any person duly authorised by the underwriter. But no advocate should be permitted to represent the underwriter at the enquiry. The advocate will be appointed by the Board as a **presiding officer.** It will be lawful for the underwriter to present his case through an advocate.
6. If it considers necessary, the enquiry officer may ask the Board to appoint a presenting officer to present its case.
7. The enquiry officer after considering all the relevant facts and submissions made by the underwriter, submits a report to the board and recommends the **penalty** to be awarded.
8. The Board issues a **show-cause notice** after receiving the report from the enquiry officer.
9. The underwriter should send a reply to the SEBI within **21 days** of the date of the receipt of the show-cause notice.
10. The board after considering the reply to the show-cause notice passes such order as it deems fit before **30 days** from the date of receipt.
11. From the date of suspension of the registration, the underwriter ceases to act as an underwriter.
12. The order of the Board should be published at least in two daily newspapers by the SEBI.

13. Any person aggrieved by the order of the board under the regulations may appeal to the Central Government under the SEBI Rules 1993.

**Commission of Underwriters**

The Central Government has prescribed the following rates of underwriting commission:

| *P/S* | *On Amounts in Developing on the under Writer* | *On Amounts Subscribed by the Public* |
|---|---|---|
| (a) Equality shares | **2.5%** | **2.5%** |
| (b) Preference shares/convertible and non-convertible debentures | | |
| for amounts upto Rs. 5 lakh | 2.5% | 2.5% |
| for amount in excess of Rs. 5 lakh | 2% | 1% |

The above ceiling limits and companies are free to negotiate for lesser rates with the underwriters. The underwriting commission is not payable for the securities taken up by **promoters, employees, directors and business associates**. Financial Institutions charge concessional rates of underwriting commission for the projects set up in **backward areas**.

The underwriting commission is different from the brokerage. The brokers are paid brokerage for their services to place shares or debentures and not to take them. The amount of commission payable to the underwriters is statutorily regulated. The underwriting also depends upon the market conditions and the attractiveness of the investment to the public. An underwriting contract should not be treated as a mere guarantee. It is also an application for the allotment of the shares or debentures not taken up by the public. The issuing company is entitled to allot the shares of debentures in terms of the underwriting contract. The underwriting commission is paid only in accordance with the **Section 76** of the Companies Act. The statutory regulations and other obligations regarding the underwriting commission are presented below:

(a) The underwriting commission should be paid only with the acceptance of the articles of association of the company.
(b) The underwriting commission should be paid according to the rules and regulations as prescribed by the Government.

(c) In case of shares, the amount or rate of commission which is not offered to the public, should be disclosed in the statement in lieu of prospectus.
(d) The number of underwriters and their proposition should be indicated in the statement.
(e) An underwriting agreement copy should be submitted to the **Registrar of Companies** at the time of delivery of the prospectus. The names of the underwriters must be stated in the prospectus.

**Guidelines Issued for Underwriters by the Government**

The following guidelines are to be followed by the **stock exchanges, merchant bankers** and other agencies that are associated with the management of the public issue.

(a) The regional stock exchange should satisfy with the company's securities which are being underwritten for the public issue.
(b) The underwriter should satisfy that the company has duly complied with the listing regulations.
(c) The governing bodies have the discretion to refuse the permission in respect of underwriting the securities by members.
(d) No underwriter is allowed to the underwriting commitment exceeding **5 per cent** of the public issue.
(e) The stock exchange should be prescribe the procedures for underwriting arrangement.
(f) The stock exchange should ensure that no permission is granted for the underwriters those who default in the past underwriting commitments.

**SEBI Guidelines**

According to the SEBI guidelines the following factors are to be fulfilled:

(a) The minimum requirement of **90 per cent** subscription is mandatory for each issue of capital to the public. This clause is applicable for both public and rights issue.

(b) If the company is not able to receive of the issued amount from the public subscription plus accepted development from the underwriters within from the date of opening of the issue, then the company refunds the amount of subscription.

(c) The underwriting agreement should be filed with the stock exchanges.

(d) The registration number of the underwriter is to be quoted in all correspondence with the SEBI and government authorities and clients.

(e) The SEBI may issue warning letters or penalty advances by which the underwriters would be forewarned in respect of their omissions.

(f) In order to standardise the legal relationship between the issues company and the underwriters, the SEBI has formulated the model underwriting agreement.

(g) The total underwriting obligations under all the agreements should not **exceed twenty times** the network of the underwriter.

**The Model Agreement**

The model agreement suggested by the **SEBI** provides the following information and these should be scrupulously followed to avoid the disputes:

1. The number of shares agreed by the underwriter if the public do not subscribe fully.
2. The rate of underwriting commission is to be paid, and should be paid within **15 days** from the date of finalisation of allotment of shares.
3. In case of development, the process should be disclosed in the agreement.
4. The issuing company should deliver the application forms and abridged prospectus at least **15 days** before the date of finalisation of allotment of shares.
5. The subscription list for the public issue should open before **three months(s)** from the date of the agreement.
6. The subscription list should be kept open by the company for a maximum period of 10 days.

7. The company should file the prospectus with the ROC within 30 days from the date of the underwriting agreement.
8. The company should indicate the number of shares to be taken up by underwriting within **30 days** from the date of closure of the subscription list.
9. The underwriter would be discharged from his obligation to the extent of applications bearing his stamp.
10. The underwriter should procure the shares within 30 days from the date of receipt of communication from the company.

**Devolvement**

According to the SEBI guidelines, if the company does not receive minimum **90 per cent** of the issues including accepted devolvement from the underwriters within **120 days** from the date of opening the issue, then the company refunds the application money. The underwriter should be called upon to honour their devolvement within **120 days** from the date of opening the issue. The underwriters are exempted from the "**Development Rules**" only when the issue is fully subscribed. The company is required to get the subscription accounts audited. The auditor has to certify the net devolvement against each underwriter. The underwriter is not be liable for devolvement if the subscription list has not opened for **ten days (10)** in the case of public issue and **60** days in the case of Rights issue. The underwriter is not responsible if the issue is closed at any time before **10** days in case of public and **60** days in case of Rights issue. In the event of devolvement, all the legal formalities relating to underwriting are to be followed. If the underwriters do not fulfil their commitments during the previous year, they should not normally be allowed to underwrite further issues till they demonstrate their capacity to honour their requirements. The SEBI has proposed that the arrangement could be made for the firm allotment to mutual funds, Indian financial institutions **NRIs** and regular employees of the issues company to the extent of **70 per cent** of the issue most.

The following rules are prescribed for the devolvement of underwriting:

1. All the underwriters will be discharged from their commitments, if the issue is fully subscribed.

2. An underwriter will be discharged from his commitment if the company received valid applications bearing his seal.
3. In case of under-subscription, the surplus applications procured by anyone underwriter would be apportioned to all other underwriter, in the ratio of their gross underwriting obligations the balance left will be devolvement on him.

**Consequences of Underwriting Defaults**

If the underwriter do not accept and subscribe for the shares and debentures that are devolved on him it is assumed that he is in default. Hence, it is a breach of contract. The contract **Section 73** reveals that "When a contract is broken, the party who suffers by such breach is entitled to receive, from the party who has broken the contract, compensation for my loss or damage caused to him thereby, which naturally arose in the usual course of things from such breach or which the parties knew when they made the contract to be likely to result from the breach of it". Therefore, the compensation will not be provide for any indirect loss or damage sustained for reason of the breach.

All issues that are made to the public will not get response. Some issues fail to attract the public. In this situation the underwriter should come into picture and rescue. But some underwriter escape from their commitments. Often these reasons are known to the underwriter even before the issue opens for the subscription. In order to keep a close watch over such underwriter, they should be debarred from underwriting public issues in future. Therefore, all the merchant bankers are required to provide the information to the SEBI regarding the defaulting underwriters.

**Sub-Underwriting**

The underwriter has the option to make the issue with another person called **sub-underwriter** who shares the commitments and revenues. The person who codes is called the principal underwriter. It is like **re-insure** by an insurer. In such a sub-underwriting contract, there will be nó privity contract between the company and the sub-writer. The contract is only between the **principal** underwriter and the sub-underwriter. The company is in no way concerned with the **sub-underwriter**. The names of the sub-underwriter do not appear anywhere and the sub-writing contract need not be filed with the stock exchange of **Registrar of Companies**. Sub-underwriting is resorted in the following situations:

(a) In the underwriter wants to share his risk and ensure subscription.
(b) For smooth sailing of an issue, the involvement of the broker is necessary.
(c) To enable a seasonal underwriter to participate in an issue.

In case of under subscription, the **principal underwriter** is called upon to pay, who in turn may step into the shoes of his sub-writer.

**Evaluation of an Underwriter**

If any part of an issue is underwritten, it should be indicated in the prospectus. The prospectus should contain a statement from the board of directors of the company that the underwriter have sufficient resources to discharge their respective obligations. Therefore, the underwriter plays an important role in the public issues. It is necessary to evaluate the capacity of the underwriters to honour their financial commitment in need. The networth of the underwriters should be verified from the financial statements. Before the company approaches the public issues, the underwriter has to evaluate the company's performance, if he is going to invest in the company. A through understanding of all the aspects regarding the company's track record should be examined by the underwriter:

(a) Company's past record.
(b) Competence of the management.
(c) Objects of the issue.
(d) Project particulars.
(e) Pricing and limiting of the issue.
(f) Marketing arrangements.
(g) Terms of the issue.
(h) Balance sheet liabilities.
(i) Pending legal hurdles.
(j) Clearances and permits.
(k) Market environment.
(l) Distribution pattern of the stationery.

The underwriter should examine the company's reputation in the market. The underwriter should verify the company's product and its customer range. The underwriter should also verify the facts regarding the **sales, profitability, divisible profits, payout record, market share**, dividend, stock market data with reference to **high-low** in the last one year. The underwriter should examine the competency of the management of the issuer company. The evaluation of performance of the top level arrangement regarding **qualification, experience, performance knowledge composition of the board, general reputation** is necessary. The objectives of the issue depends upon the purpose of **expansion, diversification working capital management, financial requirements, cost escalation of the project**. The underwriter should investigate the nature of the project, location of the project. The appraisal of the project by any financial institution, demand supply position of the products, schedule of the implementation of the project and the likely gestation period. He should also observe the pricing and timing of the issue and also the marketing arrangements of the issue. The terms of the issue are the most important aspects in the underwriting process. Generally every prospective buyer would view the price of the product. The underwriter should do a lot of home work regarding **the size of the issue**, the nature of instrument, the conversion terms, justification of price, etc. He should also be cautious about the liabilities of the issuing company's balance sheet. The current states and its impact on the financial position of the company should be considered. The underwriter should enquire about the states to my clearances and permits.

## REFERENCES

1. James C. Van. Horne, *Fundamentals of Financial Management*, p. 527 PHI.
2. Nabhi, *Manual of SEBI*, p. 512.
3. *Ibid.*

# 2

# REGISTRARS

## Introduction

According to the SEBI guidelines the appointment of the **Registrar** is compulsory in all the public issues. The Registrar is an intermediary in the primary market. The Registrar's activity is to collect the application forms from the investors. The Registrar to the issue is also called the issue house. They provide several important services to the issues of securities companies and investors. They coordinate and handle various issue activities such as collection of application forms from banks, allotment of shares, posting of shares, certificates or allotment letters, filing of return of allotment with Registrar of Companies filing listing application with stock exchanges. The functions of the Registrar are presented below:

(a) to prepare a suitable design format to share application,
(b) to assist the issuing company in finalising the application forms,
(c) to coordinate the activities during the issue time,
(d) to conduct the meeting with the brokers on behalf of the client,
(e) to involve in the scrutiny of the application forms,
(f) to assist in the allotment process and to prepare the allotment register,
(g) to prepare refund orders and to maintain the refund register,
(h) to assist in printing the refund orders,
(i) to print the share certificates,
(j) to assist the company in fulfilling the legal formalities with the SEBI.

The registrars involve mainly in the post issue work. According to the SEBI guidelines in terms of Section 12 of the Act, the Registrar should hold a certificate of registration, before they carry on their respective business as an intermediary.

### Responsibilities

The following are the responsibilities of the Registrar to the issue:

(a) They should hold a valid certificate from the SEBI.
(b) Their tasks are time bound activities such as allotment of shares, posting of share certificates, filing of return with **ROC** listing application to the stock exchange etc.
(c) The Registrars coordinate various activities with the lead managers, bankers, stock exchange authorities etc.
(d) The Registrars authorise the stock invest applications directly from the investor, if there are no mandatory collection centres nearest to them.

### Definition

The SEBI has defined the Registrars as, the person appointed by a body corporate or any person or group of persons to carry on the following activities on its or his or their behalf, namely:

(a) collecting the applications from the investors in respect of an issue;
(b) keeping a proper record of application and money received from the investors paid to the seller of the securities; and
(c) assisting the body corporate of person or group of persons in
    (i) determining the basis of allotment of securities in consultation with the stock exchange.
    (ii) finalising the list of persons entitled to the allotment of securities.
    (iii) processing and despatching the allotment letters, refund orders or certificates and other related documents in respect of the issue.

### Registration

The Registrars must register with the SEBI. They can also renew the certificate of registration. The registration is granted by the SEBI on same parameters. The registration involves the following statutory process:

(1) Application for the grant of certificate.
(2) To furnish further information for clarifications.
(3) Application to conform with the requirements.
(4) Consideration of application.
(5) Capital adequacy requirement.
(6) Procedure and registration.
(7) Renewal of certificate.
(8) Procedure if registration is not granted.
(9) Effect of refusal to grant or review certificate.
(10) Payment of fees and the consequences of failure to pay the fees.

### *(1) Application for the Grant of Certificate*

(a) The Registrar should apply to the SEBI for the grant of registration in **Form A.**
(b) The application can be made in two categories.

### *(2) To Furnish Further Information for Clarifications*

On receipt of the Form A, the board may require the applicant to furnish further information for clarifications regarding the activities and matters connected. The applicant or its principal officer if required should appear before the board for personal representation.

### *(3) Application to Conform with the Requirements*

Subject to the provisions, any application which is in complete in all respects and does not conform to the instructions specified in the form, should be rejected. Before rejecting any such application, the applicant should be given an opportunity to remove within the time specified such objections as may be indicated by the Board.

### *(4) Consideration of Application*

The **SEBI** considers all the matters which are relevant to the activities for granting a certificate. Particularly it considers the following, namely whether the applicant:

(a) has necessary infrastructure like adequate office space, equipments and manpower to effectively discharge his activities,
(b) has any past experience in the activities,
(c) or any person directly or indirectly connected with him has not been granted the registration by the Board under the Act,
(d) fulfils the capital adequacy proceedings under the Act,
(e) is subject to any disciplinary proceedings under the Act,
(f) of any of its director, partner or principal offices is or has at any time been convicted for any offence for involving in immoral turpitude or has been found guilty of any economic offence.

***(5) Capital Adequacy Requirement***

The Registrar should meet the capital adequacy requirements according to the Act. It should not be less than the networth of the applicant. The networth of the applicant should be:

(a) Category I — Rs. 6,00,000
(b) Category II — Rs. 3,00,000

The networth means the value of capital contributed + **free** reserves of the business. (In case of a body corporate, the value of the paid up capital and the free reserves as disclosed in the books of accounts of the applicant at the time of making the application).

***(6) Procedure and Registration***

If the SEBI satisfies with the eligibility of the Registrar it will send an intimation to the applicant mentioning the category for which the applicant is eligible. Then the SEBI will grant a certificate in **Form A** subject to payment of prescribed fee.

***(7) Renewal of Certificate***

The Registrar, if he desires, makes an application in **Form A** or renewal for which the applicant has been found eligible for the grant of certificate and grants a certificate before **3 months** of the periods of certificate.

### *(8) The Procedure if Registration is not Granted*

The Registrar should apply to the SEBI for the grant of certificate/ **renewal** of certificate. It should be in the same manner, does not fulfil the requirements in the regulation the SEBI may reject the application after giving a reasonable opportunity of being heard. The refusal of grant or renewal of the certificate will be communicated by the SEBI within **30 days** of such refusal to the applicant. The applicant has the chance to present his abilities to the board within 30 days of the receipt of the intimation. On receipt of the application the SEBI will reconsider its decision and communicate its findings there on as soon as possible in writing to the prospective.

### *(9) Effect of Refusal to Grant/Renew Certificate*

Any Registrar whose application has been refused by the SEBI should on and from the date of receipt of the communication base to carry on any activity.

### *(10) Payment of Fees*

The Registrar whose application is considered by the SEBI should pay such fee in such manner and within the specific period. Sometimes, the board may grant the time for a period of **six months** from the date on which such fee becomes due.

## General Obligations and Responsibilities

The General Obligations and Responsibilities of the Registrars lie in two aspects:

(A) Code of conduct.
(B) Maintenance of records

### *(A) Code of Conduct*

The Registrar to an issue is the most important person in the mobilisation of resources in the public issues. The Registrar fully involves in the **post issue activities**. The Registrar to an issue has to maintain a high integrity and fairness, in all the dealings with his clients. The Registrar should act with more skill, and care. He should be nearest in the business activities. He should not indulge in unfair competition for competing any assignment. Therefore, he should not make any exaggerated statement orally or in written to the clients. The Registrar should always think about the possibility of rendering his best services to the investors. Investors satisfaction depend upon the level of services which are offered by the registrars. They should **divulge** to other clients. They should maintain the confidentiality of the information about the valuable clients. They should provide prompt service with the best efforts.

(a) Enquiries from the investors are adequately dealt.
(b) As per the law they should complete the process of allotment without any delay.
(c) They should also referred the application money without any delay.
(d) They should not generally participate in the creation of **false** market, price rigging, manipulation, providing unpublished price sensitive information to the market, to the members of the stock exchanges and to other practices.
(e) The Registrar to an issue should not involve in inside trading. The directors, partners, managers, their business associates, family members, relatives or friends are prohibited from participating in inside trading.

### *(B) Maintenance of Records*

Every registrar has to maintain proper records and keep records as per the law. The Registrar should maintain records regarding all the applications from the investors in respect of an issue. The Registrar should maintain the records regarding the following aspects:

(a) The applications received from the investors in a public issue.
(b) The rejected applications and the reasons for it.
(c) The basis allotment of shares in consultation with stock exchange.
(d) Terms and conditions for the purchase of securities.
(e) Allotment of securities.
(f) Names list of the allottees.
(g) Refund orders to the non-allottees.
(h) Any other such records directed by the SEBI.

The Registrar should inform to the SEBI the place where the books of accounts, records and documents are maintained. Every registrar to an issue being a body corporate should keep and maintain the following books of accounts and documents in respect of **3 preceding** financial years, namely

(i) in relation to the registrar being a **body corporate:**

(a) A copy of balance sheet, profit and loss are as per the Sections **211 and 712** of the Companies Act, 1956.
(b) A copy of the auditors report referred to in Section **227** of the Companies Act, 1956.
(c) A statement of capital adequacy requirement for each quarter.

(ii) if the registrar to an issue is not being a body corporate:

(a) Particulars of their assets and liabilities.
(b) A statement of capital adequacy requirement for each quarter.

The Registrar should preserve the books of accounts and other records and documents maintained for a minimum period of 3 years. The Registrar submit the required documents to the SEBI whenever it requires. The registrar after the close of each financial year as soon as possible but not later than **6 months** from the close of the said period should furnish the documents to the SEBI. If the board requires, the registrars should submit the copy of the balance sheet, P&C A/c, the statement of capital adequacy requirement and other documents.

**Procedure for Inspection**

The SEBI is the most powerful organisation in controlling the activities of financial intermediaries. The SEBI is authorised to inspect the books of accounts, records and documents. Before commencing the inspection, the board should give a reasonable notice to the registrar. If the board satisfies with the investors interest or public interest no such notice will be given and it may direct the registrar regarding this. It is the duty of every director, partner, officer, proprietor and employee of the Registrar to produce the inspecting authority with such books, accounts and other documents in his custody. They should furnish him with the statements and information relating to the transactions in the securities market within such time as the officer may require.

The Registrar should allow the SEBI inspecting officials to access their premises and also extend reasonable facility for examining any books, records, documents and computer data in their possession. The Registrar should be provided with the required documents asked by the authorities. The inspecting authority is entitled to examine the record statements of everyone. It is the duty of every director, partner and proprietor of the registrar to give to the inspecting authority all the assistance in connection with the inspection. It should submit the inspection report to the board as soon as possible. After receiving the report, the board communicates the findings to the register, so as to provide an opportunity to protect himself before it takes any action. **On receipt** of the explanation from the registrar, the SEBI may call him to take such measures as the board may deem fit. The SEBI appoints a qualified auditor for the company **u/s 226** of the Companies Act, 1956 to investigate into the books of account or the affairs of the registrar. The Appointed Auditor will have the same powers as the inspecting authority. The obligations of the registrar will be applicable to the investigation.

### Procedure for Action in Case of Defaults

A Registrar who fails to comply with any condition is not subjected to the grant of registration. If the registrar fails to comply with the other norms such as **Securities and Contract Regulation Act, 1956, Byelaws of the stock exchanges and the provisions of the SEBI Act, etc.,** a penalty can be imposed after the enquiry. The SEBI has the full authority to cancel or suspend the activities of the Registrar, if he:

(a) violates the provisions of the Act, its rules and regulations,
(b) does not follow the code of conduct,
(c) fails to furnish any information,
(d) furnishes wrong information,
(e) does not submit the periodical returns as required by the Board,
(f) does not cooperate in any enquiry conducted by the Board,
(g) fails to resolve the investors' complaints,
(h) fails to give a satisfactory reply to the SEBI on any matter,
(i) violates the conditions of the registration,
(j) fails to pay the fee as specified in the Act,

(k) fails to maintain the capital adequacy requirement,
(l) is guilty of misconduct, improper business or unprofessional conduct.

The SEBI is a powerful organ in monitoring the activities of the **financial intermediaries**. A penalty of cancellation of certificate may be imposed on the following grounds, if they—

(i) are guilty of fraud or convicted a criminal offence,
(ii) violate any provisions of the insider trading regulations or take over regulations, and
(iii) indulge in deliberate manipulation, price rigging or concerning activities,

In case of their repeated defaults, the certificate of registration can be cancelled. Suspension or cancellation can be imposed after holding an enquiry. The following process is used for conducting the enquiry:

1. At the first instance, the board should appoint an enquiry officer to look into the affairs of a particular registrar.
2. The enquiry officer should issue a notice to the registrar.
3. On receipt of the notice from the SEBI, the registrar should within 30 days from the date of receipt of such notice, furnish a reply together with the copies of documents.
4. The enquiry officer should give a reasonable opportunity of hearing to the registrar.
5. The registrar or his nominee should appear in person before the enquiry officer, but no advocate on his behalf is permitted.
6. If the enquiry officer feels necessary, the board appoints a presenting officer to present its case.
7. After considering all the factors, the enquiry officer should submit a report to the board.
8. On receipt of the report from the **enquiry officer**, if the board observes the same, it issues a **show cause notice**.
9. The Registrar should respond to the show cause notice within **21 days** from the date of receipt of the notice.
10. After receiving the reply for the **show cause notice**, the reconsideration should be taken within **30 days** from the date of receipt of the reply.

11. The orders passed should be self-contained and give reasons for the conclusion.
12. The SEBI should send a copy of the order to the Registrar.
13. The Registrar should cease to carry on any activity on and from the date of suspension or cancellation of certificate.
14. The order of suspension/cancellation should be published in at least **two daily newspapers** by the SEBI.
15. Any person/registrar may appeal to the Central Government in the prescribed manner.

Registrar will also face penal action, if he fails to deliver the share certificates and debentures to a shareholder or a debenture holder within **3 months** from the date of allotment. The Registrar is also liable to punishment, if he fails to refund the access money within **Eight Days (8)** from the date of allotment The Companies Act, 1956, Section 113 reveals that the Registrar will be punished for the non-delivery of the share certificates. The default Registrar will be imprisoned for **two years with fine**.

# 3

# SECURITIES AND EXCHANGE BOARD OF INDIA (SEBI)

## Introduction

The Government of India set up the SEBI on April 12, 1988 for regulation and orderly function of the capital market. It is likely to promote the measures for fair trading in the securities and to protect the rights of the investors. The capital market in India has to develop on the right lines for which a component government agency in USA and UK need.

Initially the SEBI was established as an interim body under the administrative control of the Finance Ministry. Later it was given statutory powers. The SEBI is the most powerful organisation in the capital market. It is the watchdog of the stock market. The tremendous growth in the capital markets led to the establishment of the SEBI. Every company in India is required to register with the SEBI to work under the limitations and rules laid out by the SEBI. Until May 1992, the issue of capital by the Companies was controlled by the Central Government through the office of the Controller of Capital Issues. The CCI regulated the pricing of the issues. These controls have been removed with the repeal of the Capital Issues Control Act on May 1992.

The SEBI has emerged as an important constituent of the Indian financial system. The powers of the Indian financial system have been delegated to the SEBI. Let us start with a brief discussion of these constituents, i.e. **The Companies Act, The Securities Act, 1956, The Capital Issues Act, 1947**. The Companies Act deals with the financial and non-financial aspects of the corporate sector. The aim of the Act is to develop an integrated relationship among the promoters, investors and company managements. The Act seeks to protect the interest of the shareholders and their effective participation in the corporate sector. The Act is administered by the Department of Company Affairs and the Company Law Board. All these wings are working under the control of **Ministry of Law, Justice and Company Affairs**. The provisions of the Companies Act from Sections 55 to 68A are related to the issue of prospectus. If any prospectus is issued against the **contravention** of Section 57 or 58, the company and every responsible person, would be punishable with the fine up to **Rs. five thousand**. The ROC will not register the prospectus unless it is satisfied with the requirements of **Sections 55 to 58**. The shares allotment made by the company should be in accordance with the **Sections 76, 77, 78, 79, 80, 80A, 81, 85, 86, 113** of the Companies Act. **The Securities Contracts Act, 1956** deals with the secondary market operations. Section 3 deals with the recognition of the stock exchanges. Any stock exchange for the purpose of recognition, should apply to the Central Government in a prescribed proforma and it should be accompanied with a copy of the **byelaws** of the stock exchange. The Central Government is empowered u/s 4 to grant the recognition. According to Section 5, the Central Government also has the power to withdraw the recognition. According to the **SCRA** every recognised stock exchange should submit its annual report before 31st January of every year. The Annual Report should contain all the activities of stock exchange, trading securities, change in rules, byelaws, changes in governing bodies, admission or readmission or resignation of members, defaulters, securities delisted etc. The SCRA lays down the rules and regulations about the listing of securities in the stock exchanges. A company as defined public limited under the Companies Act desires of getting its securities listed on a recognised stock exchange should apply to the Central Government along with its application and required documents and information. The powers under the SCRA are transferred to the SEBI. The rating is an opinion on the future ability and legal obligation of the issues to make timely payments of principal and interest on a specific feed income security. CRISIL has been promoted by the ICICI and UTI, as a public limited company with its headquarters at Mumbai. The main objective of the CRISIL has been to rate debt obligation of Indian Companies. The ICRA has been promoted by the IFCI, with headquarters at New Delhi. The ICRA was established to provide information and guidance to the institutional and individual investors and creators. The CARE is promoted by the IDBI. It provide the credit rating, information services, equity research and miscellaneous to the customers. Onida Individual Credit Rating

Agency has been promoted by well known Onida group. The ONICRA is India's first Individual Rating System to control, regulate and monitor all the activities of the secondary market. The SEBI is the most powerful organ in the control, monitoring and in the evaluation of both the primary and secondary markets of the capital market in India. The Capital Issues Control Act, 1947 has been playing an important role in the functioning of the Indian Capital Market since 1947. Its provisions are administered by the **Controller of Capital Issues** in the Ministry of Finance, Department of Economic Affairs. The SCRA mainly regulates the secondary market and the primary market is mostly regulated by the Capital Issues Control Act, 1947. The main objectives of the Capital Issues Control Act are to protect the investor, no malpractice by the corporate sector, better financial position of the corporate sector, better financial position of the corporate sector, no undue congestion of public issues to monitor the foreign investment. The Capital Issues Control Act provisions have now become the powers and functions of the SEBI. The CICA was repeated and the office of the CCI was abolished in **1992**. Certain powers and certain sections of the SCRA and Companies Act were delegated to the SEBI. The regulatory powers of the SEBI increased the securities laws. The SEBI has now become a very important constituent of the financial regulatory frame work in India. The SEBI was established on the same pattern of the **Securities Exchange Commission** in USA.

## Organisation of SEBI

The SEBI restructured its organisation and got rationalised. It has divided its activities into the following **seven** departments, each headed by officials of the rank of Executive Directors. All these departments are further sub-divided into following divisions:

(1) Primary Market Department.
(2) Issue Management and Intermediaries Department.
(3) The Secondary Market Department.
(4) The Secondary Market Department (Administration).
(5) The Institutional Investment Department.
(6) Legal Department.
(7) Investigation Department.

The **Primary Market Department** deals with the policy matters, financial intermediaries, investor grievances etc. The issue management takes care of prospectus and registration, regulation and monitoring of issues related to financial intermediaries.

**The Secondary Market Department** involves in the preparation of policy matter, stock exchange operations, control of secondary market trading activities, development of the new innovative financial products, price manipulation monitoring market surveillance, insider trading etc., all the other things related to it. It also involves in the inspection of the non-member intermediaries and stock sub-brokers.

**The Institutional Investment Department** concentrates on the mutual funds and foreign institutional investment affairs. It looks after the corporate mergers and acquisitions. It fully involves in research and publications and international affairs.

**The Legal Department** undertakes all the legal affairs of the SEBI. It guides the SEBI on legal obligation. It carries out inspection and investigation of activities. The SEBI is the member of the **International Organisation of Securities Commission** (IOSCO). It is an international organisation which consists of other security regulators from over **100 countries**. The SEBI is the active participant in the development committee of IOSCO.

## Objectives of the SEBI

The SEBI is constituted by the Central Government as a supervisory body to regulate and promote the securities market. The objectives of the SEBI are as under:

(a) to promote fair dealings by the issuers of securities,
(b) to provide a better market place for the corporate sector to raise funds at a low cost,
(c) to provide investor protection and safeguard their rights and interest,
(d) to regulate and develop the skills of the financial intermediaries with a view to make them more competitive and professional in spirit,
(e) to regulate the securities market.

## Powers of the SEBI

The SEBI cannot act independently and it is governed by the Central Government. It is obliged to make an annual report to the Union

Government every year. The annual reports should be laid down before the Parliament. The SEBI is entrusted with the following specific powers/functions:

1. Regulating the securities markets.
2. Regulating the affairs in stock exchanges.
3. Power to call for periodical returns from the recognised stock exchanges.
4. Power to call for any information from the stock exchanges.
5. Power to grant the approval to byelaws of recognised exchanges.
6. Registering and regulating the work of the stock brokers.
7. Registering and regulating the work of bankers, registrars.
8. Registering and regulating the work of merchant bankers, underwriters.
9. Registering and regulating the work of the portfolio managers, STAs.
10. Power to prohibit the insider trading.
11. Power to promote the investors education.
12. Power to levy fees.
13. Powers to make or amend the byelaws of recognised stock exchange.
14. Power to prohibit the unfair trade practices.
15. Power to regulate the acquisition of shares and take over of companies.
16. Registering and regulating the work of depositories, custodians, FIIs, credit rating agencies etc.
17. Registering and regulating the work of venture capital funds.
18. Power to call for information, undertaking inspection, conducting inquiries and audits of the stock exchanges, financial intermediaries, mutual funds and self-regulatory organisations.
19. Power to prescribe the maintenance of certain documents by the stock exchange.
20. Compel a public company to list its shares in the stock exchange.
21. Power to give directions to the stock exchanges.
22. Power to suspension of business of a recognised stock exchange.

23. Power to grant the recognition to the stock exchanges.
24. Power to withdraw the recognition of a stock exchange.
25. Regulation and control of the business dealings in spot delivery contracts.
26. Power to prohibit the contracts in certain cases.
27. Licensing the decree in securities in certain areas.
28. Power to declare the applicability of Section 17 of SCRA in any state or area and to grant licences to the dealers in securities.

## SEBI Act, 1992

The SEBI Act provides for the establishment of a board to protect the interests of the investors in securities and to promote the development and to regulate the market. The **Chapter I** deals with the preliminaries and definitions. The **Chapter II** deals with the establishment and incorporation of the board, management of the board, terms and conditions of the services of the Chairman and its members, the removal process of members from the office, the procedure for conducting meetings, the appointment procedure of the officers and the employees of the board. The **Chapter III** contains the process of transfer of assets, liabilities of the existing board. The substantive part of the powers and functions of the board are incorporated in **Chapter IV**. The Registration process of stock brokers, sub-brokers, share transfer agents, bankers to an issue were presented in **Chapter V**. The **Chapter VI** deals with the grants provided by the Government to the board, maintenance of fund, accounting procedure and audit of the board. **Chapter VII** contains all the miscellaneous factors regarding the powers of the Central Government to the issue directions, and to supersede the board, returns and reports delegation of powers, appeals, savings, employees of the board who are treated as public servants, penalties. Exemptions from tax on wealth and income, cognisance of offences by courts, offences by companies, power to exempt, powers to make rules, regulations, etc.

## Constitution of the SEBI

The SEBI, as a regulatory and development board, has wide and varied powers. Its efforts include measures with a body of **six** members consisting the Chairman, two members from the Central Government dealing with **Finance and Law** ministries. Two members who are professional experts in the securities market and one member from the **RBI**. All these members except the RBI nominee are appointed by the Central Government. The Central Government has the full authority regarding the appointment of its members, terms of office, tenure conditions of service, removal of a member from the office etc. The Central Government is the supreme authority to supersede the SEBI in public interests. The general superintendence, the direction and management of the board's affairs rests in the board of members who may exercise all the powers and do all the acts and things which may be exercised or done by the board. The Chairman exercises all the powers that are exercised by the board. The **Chairman and the other members** should be the persons of ability, integrity and have a special knowledge or experience in law, finance, economics, accountancy and administration etc. The term of the office and the service of the Chairman and the members are prescribed by the Central Government. The Central Government has the full authority to terminate the services of **the Chairman/Members** before the expiry of the period. The Government by giving him notice of not less than **three** months in writing or 3 months salary and allowances in lieu thereof, and the Chairman or members as the case may be, should have the right to relinquish his office at anytime before the expiry of the period prescribed. The Central Government has the authority to remove a member from his office if he—

(a) is or at any time adjudicated as insolvent;
(b) is of unsound mind and stands so declared by a competent court;
(c) has been convicted of an offence which involves a moral turpitude; and
(d) has in the opinion of the Central Government, so abused his position as to render his continuation in office detrimental to the public interest.

The SEBI formed **two** advisory committees, namely **the primary market advisory committee** and **secondary market advisory committee**. The Committees are non-statutory in nature and the SEBI is not bound by the advise of the Committee. The SEBI has recently opened its regional offices in **Kolkata, Chennai and Delhi** and the head office in Mumbai. The regional offices help the investors in their complaints and liaise with the issuers, intermediaries and stock exchanges in the region. All the approvals are centralised at the head office.

The SEBI endeavours to provide a regulatory framework which would facilitate an efficient mobilisation and allocation of resources through the securities market. The SEBI has issued the following guidelines for the smooth functioning of the securities market:

1. SEBI Guidelines 1992 (Disclosure and Investor Protection), 1992.
2. SEBI Merchant Bankers, 1992.
3. SEBI Debentures Trustee Rules and Regulations, 1992.
4. SEBI Stock brokers and Sub-brokers Rules and Regulations, 1992.
5. SEBI Insider Training Regulations, 1992.
6. SEBI Guidelines for FII, 1992.
7. SEBI Registrars and Share Transfer Agents Rules and Regulations, 1993.
8. SEBI Underwriters Rules and Regulations, 1993.
9. SEBI Portfolio Managers Rules and Regulations, 1993.
10. SEBI Mutual Fund Regulations, 1993.
11. Guidelines for Foreign Brokers, 1993.
12. Advertising Code Primary Issues, 1993.
13. Guidelines for MMMFs.
14. SEBI Bankers to the Issue Rules and Regulations, 1994.
15. Guidelines for Disclosure and Investors Protection.
16. Guidelines for Preferential Allotment by Listed Companies to FIIs, 1994.
17. Guidelines for Advertisement of Schemes of the Mutual Funds, 1994.
18. SEBI Significant Acquisitions and Take Others Regulations, 1994.

**Registration**

The SEBI has the power to grant the certificate of registration to the stock brokers, sub-brokers, registrars, merchant bankers, underwriters, share transfer agents, lead managers, portfolio managers, investment advisers and such other financial intermediaries. The other intermediaries like depository, custodian, FII, credit rating agency commences the business after obtaining the Registration Certificate from the SEBI. No intermediary will be allowed without registration certificate from the SEBI. The SEBI has the authority to order, suspend, or cancel a certificate of registration in such manner as may be determined by the regulations.

**Financial Support from the GOI**

The Central Government will look after the financial needs of the SEBI. The Government has the authority to provide sufficient funds for the smooth functioning of the board. The Central Government may after the due appropriation made by the Parliament by law on its behalf make the grants to the Board on such sums of money as that Government may think fit for being utilised for the purpose of this Act. A fund should be constituted as the **SEBI general fund** and it should be credited by all grants, fees and charges received by the Board, penalties realised under the Act and any other sources of income as decided by the Government. The SEBI general fund should be utilised for the purpose of payment of salaries, allowances, and other for the remuneration of the members, officers and other employees of the Board. The expenses should be made according to the specifications of the Act. The SEBI should maintain proper accounts and other relevant records. The Board should prepare the annual statement of the accounts in such a form as prescribed by the Government. The Central Government may direct the SEBI in consultation with the Comptroller and Auditor General of India. The accounts of the Board should be audited by the **Comptroller and Auditor General of India** at a specified schedule. The audit expenses should be borne by the SEBI. The **CAG** or his nominee has the right to demand the production of books, accounts, concerned vouchers, and other documents. The audited accounts should be submitted to the Central Government which in turn laid before the house of Parliament.

**Penalties**

The SEBI has the whole authority to levy penalties and impose fines, if a person/intermediary fails to obey the specifications of the Act.

Every financial intermediary/person who is associated with the securities market must honour the rules and regulations issued by the SEBI from time to time. If any person who fails to furnish any document, return or report should be liable to a penalty not exceeding **Rs. 1.50** lakh for each such failure. If any person who fails to file any return or furnish any information books or the other documents within the time specified, he should be liable to a penalty not exceeding **Rs. 5,000** for everyday during which such failure continues or **Rs. 5,00,000** whichever is higher. If any person who registers with the SEBI fails to despatch unit certificates of any scheme in the specified manner is liable to a penalty not exceeding **Five thousand** rupees for each day during such failure continues.

- If any person who registers with the SEBI fails to refund the application money paid by the investors within the period specified in the regulation, he is liable to the penalty not exceeding **Rs. 1,000** for each day during such failure continues.
- If any person who registers with the SEBI fails to invest money collected by him in the manner, he is liable to the penalty not exceeding **Rs. 5,00,000** for each such failure.
- If any person who registers as a stock broker fails to issue contract notes in the prescribed manner, he should be liable to the penalty not exceeding **five times** the amount for which contract notes is to be issued by the broker.
- If any **Asset Management Company** of a registered mutual fund fails to comply with any of the regulations, such AMC is liable to the penalty not exceeding **Rs. 5,00,000** for each such failure.
- If any broker fails to deliver any security or fails to make the payment or the amount due to the investor in the manner, he is liable to the penalty not exceeding **Rs. 5,000** for each day during which such failure continues.
- If any person who registers with the SEBI, charges an excess amount of brokerage as specified in the manner, he is liable to the penalty not exceeding **Rs. 5,000** or five times of the excess brokerage charged whichever is higher.
- If any insider who deals with the securities of a body corporate on any stock exchange on the basis of any unpublished price

sensitive information or communicates any unpublished price sensitive information to any person then he should be liable to penalty not exceeding **Rs. 5,00,000.**

- If any person who is required under this Act fails to disclose the aggregate of share holding in the body corporate before he acquires any share of that body corporate or make a public announcement to acquire the shares at a minimum price he should be liable to the penalty not exceeding **Rs. 5,00,000.**

For the purpose of adjudging u/s of the above failures by the concerned persons/intermediaries, the board should appoint any officer not below the rank of division chief to be an adjudicating officer for holding an inquiry. The inquiry should be done in the prescribed manner. The adjudicating should think about the quantum of penalty after considering the following factors:

(1) The repetitive nature of the default.
(2) The amount of loss caused to an investor as a consequence of default.
(3) The amount of disproportionate gain or unfair advantage.

**Appellate Tribunal**

The SEBI has acquired the statutory status. The study of various regulations of the Act gives the impression. The Central Government has the authority to establish the Appellate Tribunal. The Central Government should by notification, establish one or more Appellate Tribunals known as the **Securities Appellate Tribunals**. The Securities Appellate Tribunal consists of one person only who is to be appointed through notification by the Central Government. The **Presiding Officer** of a Securities Appellate Tribunal should be a judge of a **High Court**, and he should be a member of the Indian Legal Service and held a post in **Grade-I** for at least 3 years. He should work at the presiding officer of a tribunal for at least three years. He should hold the office for a term of **five years**. He should hold the office until he attains the age of **65 years** or for a period of 5 years whichever is earlier. The Securities Appellate Tribunal fixes the salary and all allowances payable to and the other terms and conditions. The presiding officer should not be removed from his office except by an order from the Central Government, on the ground of proved misbehaviour of in capacity after the inquiry made by a judge of the Supreme Court. The Central Government may investigate about the misbehaviour or incapacity of the presiding officer. The staff of the SAT should discharge its functions under general superintendence of the presiding officer. The SAT should have the discharging functions under this Act, the same powers as rested in a **Civil Court** under the Code of Criminal Procedure, 1908 while trying a suit in respect of the following matters:

(a) Summoning and enforcing the attendance of any person.
(b) Requiring the production of documents.
(c) Receiving evidence of affidavits.
(d) Issuing commissions for the examination of witness.
(e) Dismissing an application for default.

**Government Control**

The Central Government has the authority to make rules and regulations to monitor the activities of the SEBI. The power of the Central Government to issue the directions are as follows:

1. Regarding policy matters of the SEBI, the Central Government may give directions in writing to it from time to time. The Board should as far as practicable be given an opportunity to express its views before any direction. The decision of the Central Government is final in any matter.
2. The Central Government may by notification supersede the board for such period not exceeding **six months** as may be specified in the notification.
3. The Central Government is considering the publication of a notification regarding **superseding** the board that—

   (a) all the members shall, as from the date of suppression vacate their offices as such,
   (b) all the powers, functions and duties which may by or under the provisions of this Act, be exercised or discharged by or on behalf of the board shall until the board is

reconstituted be exercised and discharged by such person or persons as the Central Government may direct, and

(c) all property owned and controlled by the board until the board is reconstitutes should vest in the Union Government.

4. On the expiration of the period of **supersession** specified in the notification the Union Government may reconstitute the board by a fresh appointment and in such case any person or persons who vacated their offices under the regulation of the Act, shall not be deemed disqualified for appointment provided that the Central Government may at any time before the expiration of the period of super session, take action under the rules.

## Steps Taken by SEBI to Reform Capital Market

The Capital Market in India has witnessed a speculation as growth during the decade. The trend has been till recently overwhelmingly. The market is being broadened further with the listing of securities. Therefore, the SEBI has taken several initiative steps to promote, develop and regulate the capital market. These reforms include primary and secondary market. The reform as presented below:

1. Abridged prospectus.
2. Proportional allotment allowed in case of oversubscribed issues.
3. Insider trading illegal.
4. All financial intermediaries to be registered with the SEBI.
5. Credit rating made compulsory.
6. Underwriting for issues made mandatory.
7. Deployment of issue proceeds.
8. Fixation of promoter's contribution.
9. Risk factors are to be disclosed in prospectus.
10. Lock in period for promoter's quota shares.
11. Capital adequacy norms prescribed for the stock brokers.
12. Circuit breaker system introduced at stock exchanges.
13. Forward trading and carry over system are banned.
14. Uniform settlement system.
15. Flexibility in issue pricing.

16. Guidelines for the DFI for disclosure and investors protection.
17. Brokers to keep clients money in the separate bank accounts.
18. Audit inspection on the books of stock exchange member.
19. Norms for multiple membership in stock exchanges.
20. Introduction of Jumbo Transfer Deeds.
21. Precautions in transactions between clients and brokers.
22. Guidelines for preferential allotment of shares.
23. PSU bonds that are brought under the preview of the SEBI.
24. Private mutual funds are permitted.
25. Constitution of governing councils for stock exchanges.

**Buy Back of Securities**

The SEBI has allowed the companies to buy back its own securities by the following methods:

(1) Buy back through tender offer.
(2) Buy back through open market.

***(1) Tender Offer***

According to the rules and regulations, a company can buy its securities from the existing shareholders or any others through negotiated deals. A company may also buy its shares through any private arrangement. The SEBI would not permit the insider trading in this aspect. If any company is interested to buy its own securities from any sources, a special resolution is required. The copy of the SR should be filed with the SEBI and the stock exchanges concerned within **seven days** from the date of passing the resolution. The notice for the special resolution should be served along with the company's explanation regarding the buy back of its shares. The explanation document contains the following matters:

(a) The date of approval of the proposal at the board meeting.
(b) The situation for buy back of the shares.
(c) The mode of buy back of the company's securities.
(d) The sufficient provision of money for buy back the securities.
(e) The base point for the fixation of the buy back price.
(f) The number of securities to be purchased by the Company.

(g) The intention of the promoters regarding their scheme.
(h) The details regarding the repayment of loans to FI/Banks.
(i) The details regarding the refunding of fixed deposits, debentures etc.
(j) The auditor's report addressed to the Board of Directors.
(k) The details regarding the repayment of preference shares.
(l) The assurance of the Board of Directors regarding company affairs.
(m) The details regarding the general meeting of shareholders.
(n) The Board of Directors should give assurance that its state of affairs would not become **insolvent** within a period of **one year** from that date.

In the tender method of option to buy back its own securities from the existing security holders on proportionate basis. In addition to the above information they should furnish some additional information regarding the buy back price of the securities. If a Company wants to buy back its shares, it should made a public announcement at least in **one English daily, one Hindi, and one regional language**. The announcement should contain the following information in the media:

1. Full information about the offer.
2. The schedule time for opening and closing of the process.
3. The details about the authority for the offer of the buy back.
4. The full details and complete disclosure of all material factors.
5. The environment for the buy back.
6. The methodology to be adopted for the buy back.
7. The maximum amount to be invested in this method.
8. Information about the company.
9. The auditors report for the last three years.
10. The full details of the capital structure of the company.
11. The full information about the statutory approvals obtained.
12. The lead manager should ensure that the financial data should be latest.
13. The details about the collection and binding centres.
14. The public announcement date should be confirmed by the Board of Directors.
15. Present capital structure and the shareholding pattern.

16. The information regarding any change in the management structure.
17. The other disclosures as may be specified by the SEBI from time to time.
18. The details about the persons who are in control of the company.
19. The full information about **escrow account.**
20. The information regarding the financial ratios as specified by SEBI.
21. The listing details of the company's scrip with stock exchange.
22. The stock market data regarding **high, low and average** marketing price of scrip.
23. The monthly high and low price for the 6 months from the date of announcement.
24. The information regarding the number of securities traded on the above (23) period.
25. The market price immediately after the date of approving the buy back.
26. The volume of securities traded in each month during 6 months preceding the date of the public announcement.
27. The specified date must be earlier than 30 days and not later than 42 days from the date of public announcement.
28. The draft letter of offer should be submitted with the prescribed fee to the SEBI.
29. The SEBI will change the following fee for a proposed buy back of the security **transactions**:

| *Size of the Buy Back Offer* | *Fee (in Rs.)* |
|---|---|
| If the issue size more than Rs. 500 crores | 5,00,000 |
| If the issue size between Rs. 100–500 crores | 2,00,000 |
| If the issue size between Rs. 50–100 crores | 1,00,000 |
| If the issue size between Rs. 10–50 crores | 75,000 |
| If the issue size between Rs. 5–10 crores | 50,000 |
| If the issue size up to Rs. 5 crores | 25,000 |

According to the Companies Act **Section 77A**, the Company should file along with draft letter of offer and declaration of solvency in a prescribed manner.

The buy back of the securities must open to the shareholders for a period of minimum **15 days** and maximum for **Thirty days**. The buy back offer should not be earlier than seven days or later than thirty days after the specified date of the buy back securities. After the process of completion, a communication should be made within **15 days** from the closure of the offer.

## Escrow Account

Before commencing of the buy back process the company should deposit sum an escrow account. It is an account for which the bank acts as an uninterested third party to ensure compliance with the terms of the deed between the two parties only upon the fulfilment of same stated conditions. It becomes operative as soon as the stated event occurs. The banks hold such accounts in which the funds, then accumulated to pay taxes, insurances on mortgage property etc. The escrow account consists of—

(a) cash deposited with a scheduled bank,
(b) the bank guarantee in favour of the merchant banker, and
(c) a deposit of margin with the merchant banker.

The Company should keep the amount in escrow account and make it available to merchant banker. The merchant banker is empowered to operate the escrow account according to the situation. On payment of consideration to all the shareholders who have accepted the offer and after the completion of all the formalities of the buy back, if any amount, securities, and guarantee available in the escrow account should be released to the Company. The SEBI has the full authority if in case of **Non-fulfilment** of obligations under these regulations by the company **forfeit** the escrow account either in full or impart. The amount of forfeited sum can be distributed on *pro-rata* basis amongst the security holders who accepts the offer. If there is any balance available, it would be deployed for the investor's protection.

## Payment of the Consideration

After the closure of the offer, the Company is required to open a special account with a banker and deposit, then in such sum together with the amount lying in the **escrow account** must be utilised for the payment of consideration in cash to those security shareholders whose offer has been accepted or returned.

## Destruction of the Share Certificates

After the payment of consideration to the accepted shareholders, the Company may collect the shares physically and **destroy** the security certificates brought back in the presence of a merchant banker/STA/ Registrar and the statutory auditor within **7 days** from the date of acceptance of the securities. If the buy back securities are in the form of **"Dematerialised"**, they should be extinguished and destroyed according to the Act of the SEBI **(Depositories and Participants)** Regulations, 1996 and according to the byelaws. The Company should submit a certificate to the SEBI signed by a Registrar/Merchant banker and MD with the statutory auditor of the company within **seven days** of extinguishments and destruction of the certificate the Company should maintain a separate account for cancelled and destroyed certificates. The particulars of the destroyed share certificates should be submitted to the concerned stock exchanges within **seven days** of destruction of the certificates.

## Buy Back from the Open Market

A Company can buy its own securities by the method of open market. The shares may be further categorised in the following manner:

**(A) Book building process.**
**(B) Stock Exchange.**
**(C) From odd-lot holders.**

### *(A) Book Building Process*

The buy back of securities through book building process can be made by the Company with a special resolution. The Company should pass a special resolution by specifying the maximum price. The Company should make a public announcement at least **7 days** prior to the commencement of the buy back. The Company has to appoint a merchant banker for this purpose. The Company has to deposit in the **escrow account** before the date of public announcement. After the announcement of the book building process. The Company has to submit a copy to the **SEBI** along with the specified fees within two days. The public announcement should reveal the following matters:

(i) the methodology of book building process,
(ii) the manner of acceptance,
(iii) the formal acceptance, and
(iv) details of bidding centres.

The book building process involves with the latest technology and transparent. For the book building process, the Company should arrange bidding centres with a minimum number **of thirty**. There should be a computer terminal connecting all the bidding centres. The offer should remain open to security holders for a period of **15 days** and not exceeding **thirty days**. The Company should decide the buy back price along with the merchant banker's opinion. The offer price should be paid to all the holders who have accepted the buy back method.

***(B) Stock Exchange***

The shares are also repurchased by the Company through the stock exchanges. For this purpose, a special resolution has to be passed by the Company. The special resolution should specify the maximum offer price. The shares cannot be purchased from the promoters or interested parties. If a Company wants to buy back its shares by the stock exchange process, it should make a public announcement at least **seven days** prior to the commencement of the buy back. The Company has to appoint the merchant banker. A copy of the public announcement should be submitted to the SEBI within two days along with the specified fees. The public announcement should reveal all the information regarding the details of the brokers and stock exchanges etc. The buy back should be made only through—

(a) the stock exchange which has an electronic trading facility,
(b) order matching mechanism.

The merchant banker and the Company should furnish the information to the controlled stock exchange on a daily basis regarding the developments of the process. The furnished information should be published in a national daily newspaper. The Company identity should appear on the electronic screen. The process for destroying the share certificates will be applicable on par with the earlier methods. The Company should complete its legal informalities within **15 days** of payment.

### *(C) From Odd-Lot Buy Back*

The rules and regulations pertaining to the buy back scheme through the odd-lot method are applicable in the same manner.

## General Obligations

The Company can buy back its own securities through either tender offer method or open market system. The method to be adopted by the Company depends upon the decision of the Company. The Company should fulfil the obligations in the following manner:

(a) The Company should furnish true, factual information in a letter of offer or in a public announcement or any other advertisement, circulars, brochure or publicity material.

(b) The announcement should indicate that the information is true and the Board of Directors have to accept the responsibility of the information.

(c) The Company should ensure that during the offer period no bonus issue will be made under these regulations.

(d) The Company should pay consideration only in the form of **cash only**.

(e) The Company should not withdraw the offer if once the announcement is made.

(f) If the Company announces the offer to buy back its own securities through any of the sources the promoters or the person in control should not involve in the securities of the company in the stock exchange during the offer period.

(g) The Companies Act does not allow the buy back offer of the companies if the **amalgamation** method is in pending.

(h) The Company should appoint a compliance officer for redissolving the investor's problems.

(i) The particulars of the destroyed/extinguished security certificates should be furnished by the Company to the concerned stock exchanges within **seven days** of the destructions.

(j) The Company should not buy back its own securities in the following situations:

  (i) locked in securities,
  (ii) non-transferable securities till the pendency of the lock in period.

(k) The Company should issue an advertisement in the national daily within two days of the completion of the process by disclosing the following factors:

  1. The number of securities brought under this office.
  2. The price of the security with which the offer is made by the Company.
  3. The total amount paid in consideration with the securities.
  4. The full details of the security holders who have offered their securities under this process exceeding one per cent of the total securities.
  5. The Company should also reveal about the consequences of the capital structure before and after the buy back of the securities.
  6. The Company should follow all the rules and regulations of the SEBI in addition to the Companies Act and other applicable laws.

**Obligations of the Merchant Banker**

The Merchant Banker plays an important role in the buy back process. The merchant banker is also responsible for fulfilling all the formalities by the offer made company being a client to him. The merchant banker has to ensure that

(a) the offer will be implemented by the Company without any hurdles,
(b) the obligations of the company towards the **escrow A/c,**
(c) payment of consideration in the form of cash,
(d) the announcement of the buy back should be dare according to legal formalities,
(e) the letter of offer should be filed with the SEBI,
(f) the contents of information regarding the public announcement should be fair and true.

(g) the compliance of the Sections 77A, 77B of the Companies Act and another law is necessary,
(h) fulfilment of the obligations of the **escrow A/c** must be maintained by the Company,
(i) a final report should be furnished in a specified manner within **15 days** from the closure of offer,
(j) if the merchant banker fails to comply with the obligations of these regulations immediate action against the financial intermediary should be taken.

**Penalties and Procedure**

The SEBI is the most powerful organisation in India and it controls the activities of all the financial intermediaries like Registrars, Merchant Bankers, Underwriters, etc. The penalties that are imposed by the SEBI are as follows:

(a) Power to order investigation.
(b) Power to issue directions.

The SEBI has the power to order the investigations on **suo motu or** upon the information received by it, to conduct the affairs of any person associated with the process of buy back. The SEBI is empowered to appoint an officer for the following purposes:

(a) to monitor the activities of any person who involved in malpractice;
(b) to investigate into any complaint of any contravened to any of these regulations;
(c) the suspected person should be bound to produce before the SEBI such as books, accounts, documents as he may require;
(d) the suspected person should extend cooperation to the investigating officer for examining the books of accounts and other documents;
(e) the investigating officer has the full powers to summarise and enforce the attendance of the persons;
(f) after completion of the investigation process, the investigating officer should submit a report to the SEBI;
(g) on receipt of the report from the investigation officer, the SEBI

takes an initiative action depending upon the degree of guiltiness by such person.

The SEBI has the power to issue directions with the interest of the securities market and the investors.

(a) It has the power of directing the person concerned not to involve in any further deal in the securities in any manner.
(b) The SEBI has the power to direct the concerned person not to participate in any activities which leads to the violation of the Companies Act.
(c) The SEBI can direct the person concerned to divert or sell the shares which are acquired by violating the rules and regulations of the Companies Act.
(d) It has the power to take action against the registered financial intermediary.
(e) Any person who involved in the insider trading against the provisions should be dealt in accordance with the provisions of the **SEBI Insider Trading Regulations, 1992** and SEBI (Prohibition of Fraudulent and Unfair Trade Practices) Regulations, 1995.

Therefore, the SEBI has been set up to protect the interest of the investors and it is the watchdog of the market. The SEBI is empowered to look after the welfare of the individual investors, institutional investors, financial intermediaries and the corporate sector. The SEBI has now full powers to regulate the primary market and the secondary market operations.

**Takeover and SEBI Regulations**

At present the takeover wave is sweeping the country. It is known that there have been number of takeover bids commenced recently. The takeover becomes a quite common phenomenon. The takeover can be defined as "The acquisition of another company that may take the form of a friendly or unfriendly merger". The shareholders of the target company realise an appreciable increments in wealth relative to the market value of their holdings prior to takeover activity. The appreciation in wealth is possible only due to the premium paid by the acquiring company. Once the announcement has been made to the takeover of a particular company. The target company's stock tends to rise in the market usually in takeover process, the acquiring companies simply pay **too much**. Therefore, the acquiring company's worth will be decreasing. All acquisitions may not be fruitful but some are worthy because of some elements enhances the value of the worth. The combination of these two companies is treated either as a **purchase or** as a pooling of interest.

The benefits of taking over a company is the availability of readymade manufacturing facilities, well established brand, market share and potential no need of licences and well planned distribution network. The takeover is a device for the companies which try to enter into the new business areas or expansion in the same line of activity. The various Acts such as **FEMA, MRTP, IDRA 1961** have further added the needed impetus. The takeover can also be known as **"unwanted undertakings"** or buying up their competitors. The BIFR becomes a facilitator of **MeA deals**. After the introduction of the SEBI regulations the legal hurdles dismantled. The Government is also in non-interference attitude in the takeover process. The availability of the cheap fund in the global and domestic markets made their contributions to strengthen the takeover method.

The takeover is a method of amalgamation of companies. In amalgamation, one company makes an offer to purchase the shares of the members of another company.[1]

Takeover is different from the merges in approach. The takeover is a unilateral step and the offer company decides the maximum price in consideration with the existing rules and regulations. The takeover takes less time while the merger requires a time consuming method. The takeover decisions are influenced by various considerations. The goodwill of the company, large scale production, increase in earnings capacity by acquiring the same line sector company, a high calibre to meet the ROD expenditure, all these factors lead to take over by a company. On the hand acquisition is the purchase by one company of a controlling interest in the share capital of another existing company. The acquisition may arise in the following situations:

(a) agreement with the majority shareholders in the company,
(b) buying of shares in open market,
(c) buying of new shares by private treaty,
(d) an offer to the existing shareholders,
(e) the payment of consideration in the form of **cash, debentures and issue of shares**.

Amalgamation has been defined by **Halsway** as "a blending of two or more existing undertakings into one undertaking the shareholders of each blending company becoming substantially the shareholders in the company which is to carry on the blended undertaking".

## Amalgamation and Merger Process

Amalgamation means the creation of a new organisation by combining two or more units. In the process of amalgamation, two or more companies may liquidate themselves under the law and sell their assets and transfer liabilities to a new company which issues its own stock in exchange for the **new worth** of property received from the amalgamating companies. No one company can exist after the completion of amalgamations. The merger is also known as **Absorption.** The absorbing company retains its identity and expands the size through a merger. **Reconstruction** means purchase of one undertaking by the other, transfer of shares from one undertaking to the other and an order of Central Government in regulation of the **Sections 394, 395, 396** of the Companies Act, 1956. According to Sections 391 of the Companies Act, 1956, a compromise should be done with the creditors to carry out the scheme of reconstruction or amalgamation.

The court may order for a compromise or arrangement or by a subsequent order make provision to facilitate the reconstruction or amalgamation. The Section **391** empowers that 3/4th of the value of the creditors of members affected. The following steps are involved in the scheme of **amalgamation**:

(a) the acquirer prepares a scheme of amalgamation,
(b) defining the transferor and transferee,
(c) authorised, issued and subscribed capital or transfer or and transferee company,
(d) basis of scheme—evaluation report, transfer of assets and liabilities, specified date, consolidation of capital,
(e) change of name, object and accounting year,
(f) protection of employment,
(g) dividend position and prospects, and
(h) conditions of the scheme.

The Mergers, Acquisitions and takeovers are regulated by the SEBI. The SEBI Regulations, 1994 deals with the substantial

Acquisition of shares and takeovers. The Act contains five chapters indicating the rule position regarding the takeover methodology, **Chapter I** reveals the preliminary aspects such as definitions and concepts of various terms. The **Chapter II** deals with the disclosure of share holdings as per regulations 5 to 8. The **Chapter III** indicates the applicability of the regulation for takeover process. The **Chapter IV** contains the bail out takeover process. The last chapter discloses the information regarding the investigation process as per the regulations 33 to 40.

## Exemptions

According to the regulations from **9 to 25** takeover provisions are not applicable to the acquisitions of shares in the following cases **(exempted cases)**:

(a) Application of shares are made in pursuance of a prospectus issued shares (public shares issue).
(b) Underwriting arrangement.
(c) Shares acquired under **Sections 391 and 394** of the Companies Act.
(d) The shares acquired under **Sections 18** of the Sick Industrial Companies Act, 1985.
(e) Acquisition of shares in the general course of business by a registered stock broker.
(f) The shares of unlisted companies.
(g) The SEBI is empowered to grant exemption.

## Minimum Offer Price

The minimum offer price is regulated by the SEBI provisions under **Regulation 19.** It deals with the declaration of the minimum price by the acquirer. The acquirer should made the public announcement at least in one English newspaper and one in regional newspaper. An acquirer who holds shares carrying 10 per cent or less voting rights should not acquire further shares from the open market which when taken together with his existing holdings would carry more than 10 per cent of the voting rights unless he makes a public announcement. When shares are more than 10 per cent of the voting right are held, to acquire further shares, the acquirer has to make a public announcement. The purchasing offer should be made through a registered merchant banker. The takeover announcement copy should be furnished to the SEBI at least **24 hours** before its issuance. The Regulation **17 of** the SEBI Act reveals that the acquirer should submit the draft of a letter to the board of the approval within **14 days** of the public announcement. A certificate is to be submitted by the merchant banker. The acquirer should pay a fee of **Rs. 25,000** to the Board. The letter of offer should be sent to all the shareholders of the company for the purpose of acquisition under the regulations. The minimum offer price may be payable in cash or by exchange of shares or combination of both. According to the regulation **9**, the minimum offer price is the negotiated price or quoted price on the stock exchange whichever is **higher** under the regulations 10 of the Act. The minimum offer price, the highest price in the open market or quoted price on the stock exchange whichever is **higher**. The regulations **21, 23 and 25** deals with the minimum number of shares to be acquired, competitive acquisition and withdrawal of offer respectively. The regulation **20** indicates the general obligations which are to be fulfilled by the acquirer. The obligations which are to be fulfilled are presented below:

(a) The acquirer company should be able to implement the offer.
(b) The acquirer should submit a letter of offer to the Board of Directors of the Company whose shares are being acquired.
(c) The acquirer should indicate the period for which the offer should be kept open.
(d) The acquirer should declared accepting the responsibility for the information presented by him.
(e) The acquirer should also give an assurance for not making any further public announcement for the acquisition of shares in the **succeeding 6 months.**

## Bailout Takeover

Bailout takeover means the promoter who is taking over a financially weak company in pursuance of the rehabilitation scheme approved by a public financial institution or scheduled bank. The provisions pertaining to bailout takeovers would not apply to **sick industrial companies**. The sick industrial companies are governed by the Sick Industrial Companies **(Special Provisions)** Act. The financial weak company may not be a sick company. According to the regulation **26** of the Act financially weak company means, a company which has accumulated loss at the end of the previous financial year and which has resulted in the erosion of more than **50 per cent** but less than **100 per cent** of its networth. The networth of the company is the sum total of the **paid up capital and free reserves.** This regulation excludes sick industrial unit. For the better understanding of the context, we must know the difference between sick company and financially weak company. The sick company has been defined by the **Sick Industrial Companies (Special Provisions) Act, 1985** "an industrial company (being a company registered for not less than **five years**) which has at the end of any financial year accumulated losses equal to or exceeding its entire networth".

Substantial acquisition means a total acquisition of not less than **20 per cent** or more of the shares. The Regulation **30** reveals that the substantial acquisition held by the public should not be less than **20 per cent** of the paid up share capital of such company. The lead financial institution appraises the company in financial viability, assess fund requirements for revival and draw up of the **rehabilitation** scheme. The rehabilitation scheme should also specifically provide the details of any change in the management. The rehabilitation scheme may provide for the acquisition of shares or exchange of shares in the financially weak company in the "outright purchase of shares or exchange of shares or a combination of both". According to the Rehabilitation programme, the lead institution should invite offers for the acquisition of shares from at least **three parties.** The lead institution would have to select one party among the three, based on the managerial competence; technical capability of the person/party adequacy of financial resources etc. The lead institution should also provide necessary information to any interested person regarding the present management capabilities, technologies range of products, shareholder pattern, financial holding, five years balance sheets and any other information desired by that person. The lead institution evaluates the bids received with reference to the purchase price or exchange of shares track record, financial muscle, goodwill of the management of the person acquiring shares. After making the evaluation, the financially weak company accepts one of the bids the selection of bid decision should be informed to the lead institution which in turn invites the acquirer of the determination of offer price. The promoter of the weak company, financial institutions and also the shareholders together determine the offer price by a mutual negotiation between the person acquiring shares and the lead institution.

The acquirer should make a public announcement of his intention for the acquisition of shares. The public announcement should contain relevant details about offer process. Therefore, the acquisition process should be completed as the procedure laid down in the Act.

The SEBI has the full authority to investigate the affairs of the acquired company as per the SEBI Act. The **Chapter V** of the SEBI Act deals with the investigation process about the affairs of the acquired company.

## SEBI and Insider Trading

Insider trading is an unfair and unhealthy practice. The SEBI prohibited the insider dealing or trading. It may be defined as "sale or purchase of securities by persons who possess price sensitive information about the company".[2] It damages the integrity of the market. Insider trading may be the brain child of the brokers and top level management of the corporate sector. The favourable and unfavourable trends of the particular company leads to the insider trading. The favourable trends for a particular company is **takeover, diversification and takeover**. The unfavourable trends are occasions of the poor performance and loss of earnings. The unpublished price sensitive information occupies an important role in the insider trading. For example, financial results, interim and final dividends, right issues, bonus issue, amalgamation, mergers, takeovers. The company executives, journalists, banks, financial institutions, top level management have access towards this information. Insider trading is considered as committing the offence. The SEBI has the full authority to investigate the malpractice on the basis of complaints from the investors or intermediaries or **suo-motu**. The SEBI can carry on the inspection of books of account, other records and documents of a suspected person. It has the power to issue directions to the suspected person not to involve in the securities in any specific manner. According to the Section **24** of the SEBI Act, it has the power to initiate criminal prosecution against the responsible person. The Securities Act also imposes the penalty up to **Rs. 5.00 lakhs** for indulging the insider trading. The insider trading can be curbed with only effective enforcement of the Act. The effectiveness can be established through the strict actions like **fine, withdrawal of licence etc.**, and treating such activities like criminal cases. But the criminal case requires a high standard of evidence. Therefore, the insider trading could be watched and controlled by who holds more than **5 per cent** of stock.

**Prohibition of Fraudulent and Unfair Trade Practices**

The insider trading is extremely difficult to **pin down**. It includes the market manipulation. Market manipulation means no person should buy or sell the securities in a fraudulent manner or no person should indulge in any unfair trade practices should take part or enter either directly or indirectly in the transactions of securities, which are likely to have the effect of artificially raising or depressing or stabilising the prices of securities. No person should involve in or creating a falls or **misleading** appearance of trading on the securities market or results in the rejection of prices of securities based on transactions. No person should involve in increase, depress or cause fluctuations in the market price of the securities, the prohibiting unfair trade practices are presented below:

(a) No person should engage in any Act which appears as a fraud in connection with the purchase or sale of any securities.
(b) No person should delay the transfer of securities.
(c) No person should indulge in the falsification of his books of accounts and records for the purpose of market manipulation.

The SEBI has the right to investigate the affairs of the suspected person. The board can inspect the books of accounts, records and documents of any person buying or selling the securities. The SEBI has the authority to investigate into the complaints received from the investors or intermediaries or any other person or any matter. The board has also the power to investigate the **suo-motu**. The SEBI sends a notice before going to an investigation under regulation **6** to the concerned persons. Sometimes according to the situation, the SEBI is empowered to investigate the affairs of a person without complaint and notice with the interest of public. The concerned person should obey the rules and regulations imposed by the Act. The person should submit all the required documents to the inspecting officer submits a report to the board after the verification of the records and facts. On receipt of the report from the inspecting officer, the board takes measures as it may deem fit including issuing directions with the interest of securities market. The SEBI is empowered to give the directions in the following situations:

(a) The SEBI can direct the person not to deal in securities in any particular manner.

(b) It can direct the person to call up any of its officers, employees or representatives to refrain from dealing in securities.
(c) It can prohibit the person from disposing of any of the securities acquired in violation of the regulations.
(d) It can take the disciplinary action against the person/intermediary holding a certificate of registration u/s 12 of the SEBI Act.

**Procedure of Action in Case of Default**

The SEBI is empowered to take the action in case of default by any person/intermediary. The procedure for action in case of default is presented below:

(a) If any person/intermediary violates the provisions then he is liable to suspension or cancellation of registration or imposition of civil penalty.
(b) The penalty should be imposed after the completion of detailed investigation.
(c) For the purpose of holding an enquiry u/s 13, the Board may appoint an enquiry officer.
(d) The enquiry officer should issue a notice to the person at the registered office or the principal place of the business of the person.
(e) The person should furnish a reply to the enquiry officer within **30 days** from the date of receipt of such notice.
(f) The person should appear in person or through any authorised person before the enquiry officer.
(g) During the period of enquiry, the officer should have the power to some any person relevant to the subject matter of the enquiry.
(h) If any person neglects or refuses the enquiry, the officer may proceed with the enquiry in the absence of such person.
(i) The enquiry officer will give a chance to appoint a presenting officer on behalf of the board.
(j) The enquiry officer should recommend the penalty to be awarded.
(k) On receipt of the report from the enquiry officer, the board can issue a show cause notice to the person.

(l) The concerned person should submit a reply to the board on receipt of the notice within **21 days.**

(m) On receipt of the reply from the concerned person, the board should take the action as early as possible but not later than **thirty days** from the receipt of the reply. The order copy should be sent to the concerned person.

The board has the power to take criminal proceedings before the court of competent jurisdiction. **The Metropolitan Magistrate** or Judicial Magistrate of the first class is empowered to punish the concerned person under these regulations of the Act. According to the Section **24**, if any person gives a false explanation in an enquiry, he should be imposed **penalty**. If any person is aggrieved by an order of the board, he may appeal to the Central Government.

## SEBI Guidelines for Stock brokers/Sub-brokers

The entry into the stock market is not open to the public. The buying and selling of shares and securities is done through the members of the stock exchanges. The financial assets such as **equity, preference shares, bonds, debentures** issued by the Companies and books, securities issued by the Government are traded on capital markets. The buyer and seller of the financial asset do not meet directly in an organised stock market. The transactions takes place through the brokers. The brokers work as agents only. They charge a commission on each transaction they execute. The stock brokers play an active role and support the stock the stock exchanges by performing the following useful economic services.

(a) Ready market ability and price stability for the securities.
(b) Contributes the growth of savings.
(c) Contributes the growth of industrial sector development.

The brokers meet in the stock exchange at specified hours for executing the transactions of their clients. All the transactions of the stock exchange will be entered in the slips and they confirm. The transactions will be settled through bids and offer. The broker is responsible for the delivery of the share certificates to the buyers. The sale or purchase of shares procedure is presented below:

(a). Orders are placed with the broker for buying and selling of shares at best rates.

(b) The order price may inclusive of a broker's commission at market price, i.e., excluding broker commission. The broker commission has to be added.

(c) The transactions will be settled through the system of clearing transactions.

(d) The clearing house acts as the coordinator of all the activities between the members of the stock exchange.

(e) The competition among the bidders for buying and selling of the securities may stabilise the securities prices in the market.

(f) The settlement period is generally a week and the transactions made during the settlement period are settled either by payment or by delivery on the specified days of the clearing programme.

(g) After the closing hours of the market, every member should submit his **sauda sheets** to the computer centre about the purchase and sale of shares during that day. All the activities of all the brokers will be checked by the computer itself. All the adjustments are made in the computer during the settlement period. A statement of all the saudas thus adjusted is printed out. A **balance sheet** for the member in total receivable or payable is also printed out. The sum of the total shares to be delivered should be equal to the sum of the total shares received for each security. Every member is provided with a statement showing the details of deliveries to be effected by him to others and to him by others. A total transaction will be prepared after adjusting all the transactions. The details of the unmatched transactions will be printed out.

(h) In case of specified shares, the settlement transactions are settled through **three options**. The broker has to terminate his contract of sale or purchase by a cross contract or squaring up to complete the contract by delivery or payment or to carry over the contract to the next settlement.

(i) The settlement system offers greater liquidity to the authorities in the secondary market.

## Registration of the Stock Broker

The interested person should make an application for the grant of certificate in **Form-A** through the stock exchange. It may forward the application form to the SEBI within **30 days** from the date of receipt. After receiving the application from the concerned stock exchange, the SEBI will scrutinise the application. It may ask for any further information or clarification regarding the dealings in the securities for the grant of a certificate. The applicant or its principal officer, if necessary should appear before the board for personal representation. The SEBI on being satisfied that a person is eligible as a stock broker, it grants a certificate in **Form-D** to the stock broker and sends an intimation to that effect to the stock exchange. The person who holds the stock broker certificate should at all times abide by the **Code of Conduct** as per the Act. Sometimes, the SEBI may reject the application of an interested person for registration. Then the person should follow the following process for the grant of certificate.

The SEBI may reject the application on the following grounds:

1. (a) If the broker has no eligibility.
   (b) If he does not have necessary infrastructure facilities.
   (c) If he does not have any past experience in dealing the securities in the market.
2. The refusal of the grant of registration certificate should be communicated by the SEBI within **30 days** of such refusal to the applicant and concerned stock exchange.
3. On receipt of the information from the SEBI, the applicant should apply again within a period of **30 days** from the date of receipt of such intimation for reconsideration of its decision.
4. Finally the SEBI may communicate its decision in writing to the applicant and to the concerned stock exchange.
5. A stock broker whose application for the grant of a certificate has been refused by the board should deal the securities as a stock broker.

Every applicant who is eligible for the grant of a certificate should pay the fee as specified in the act from time to time. Sometimes, the board may give time for the payment of fee before the expiry of **six months** from the date on which such fee becomes due. If a stock broker fails to pay the fee as prescribed, the board may suspend the registration certificate.

**Registration of the Sub-Broker**

The stock sub-broker should apply to the SEBI in **Form-B** for the grant of a certificate. The application for registration should contain a recommendation letter from the stock broker in **Form-C** along with the recommendation from his banker. The application should be submitted to the concerned stock exchange. The concerned stock exchange on receipt of the application should verify the information contained and it should also certify that the applicant is eligible for the registration as per the act. The eligibility criteria for the registration as a sub-broker is as follows:

(a) for individuals,
(b) for partnership firms/body corporate.

In case of registration for individuals the following norms should be fulfilled by the applicant:

(1) The applicant should be **21** years of age.
(2) The applicant should not convict in any offence which involves **fraud or dishonesty**.
(3) The applicant should have the minimum educational qualification, i.e. **10+2 or its equivalent examination** recognised by the Government.

In case of registration for **firm/corporates**, the above regulations should be fulfilled. If the board satisfies with the eligibility of the stock sub-broker, then it should grant a certificate in **Form-E** to the sub-broker; and also an intimation to the concerned stock exchange. The sub-broker should pay the fee as specified in the Act and abide by the code of conduct. The sub-broker should enter into an agreement with the **Stock broker** for specifying the scope of his authority and responsibility.

**Code and Conduct of the Stock broker**

Stock broking is a high specialised skilful work. It needs talent, knowledge, sincerity, a thorough understanding about the economy, a clear idea about the government policies, etc. He must fully acquaint with the latest developments in the national programmes. He should be decent. He must be a dynamic personality and have his own style and have his own style of functioning. The broker must be in a good position to maintain relations with all the parties as below:

**(A) General relations.**
**(B) Investors relations.**
**(C) Relationship with other colleagues.**

### *(A) Relations with General Public*

The stock broker should maintain high standards of integrity, promptness and transparency in his business affairs. A stock broker should act with due skill, care and diligence while conducting his business affairs. A stock broker should not involve in manipulative, fraudulent, deceptive or spread rumours with a view of making personal gains. The stock broker should not create any false market or indulge in any Act detrimental to the investors. A stock broker should not involve himself in the **excessive** speculative business in the market. A stock broker should abide by all the provisions of the Act and the rules, regulations issued by the Government, the SEBI and the stock exchange from time to time.

### *(B) Relations with the Investors*

The stock broker should maintain better relations with the investors. The **customer** is the king in the market. The broker should possess sincere nature towards the investors. He should deal with his clients more faithfully in executing the orders for buying and selling the securities at the best available market price. He should not refuse to deal with a small investor merely on the ground of the volume of business involved. The stock broker should promptly inform his client about the **execution or non-execution** of an order. He should make a prompt payment in respect of the securities sold and arranged for the prompt delivery of securities purchased by the investors. The broker should issue a contract note to his client without any delay in prescribed form by the stock exchange. The stock broker should maintain a high confidentiality in the transactions involved with a number of parties. He should not disclose any information to any other person. The broker should not encourage his clients for the sale or purchase of the securities with the object of generating brokerage or commission. The stock broker should not furnish false or misleading quotations or misleading advice or information to the clients with a view to earn commission or brokerage. The stock broker should not deal or transact for a defaulted client with other brokers. A stock broker should not make a recommendation to any client or investor. The stock broker should be adequately trained, skilful, talented staff and make arrangements to render fair, prompt and competence services to his clients.

***(C) Relations with Other Brokers***

The stock broking is a highly talented skilful job. It requires a careful handling of the assignments. The stock broker should maintain a healthy relation with the other brokers. The broker should be in a cooperative manner with the other contracting parties while comparing the unmatched transactions. He must be careful in the delivery of shares and cooperate in finding of **bad delivery**. The stock market must cooperate with other broker in protecting the interests of his clients for their rights to **bonus rights and dividends** related to securities. A stock broker should maintain the transactions with other stock brokers and should cooperate for smooth settlement of transactions. The stock broker should advertise only with the permission from the concerned stock exchange. The stock broker should submit a correct and accurate required returns to the SEBI and the concerned stock exchange.

**General Obligations and Responsibilities**

The following obligations have to be fulfilled by every registered broker in India. The stock broker should keep normally the following books of accounts, records and documents. All these books should be maintained by all the brokers:

(a) Sauda book (Register of transactions).
(b) Clients ledger.
(c) General ledger.
(d) Journal.
(e) Cash book.
(f) Bank pass book.
(g) Documents register.
(h) Members contract books.
(i) Margin deposit book.

(j) The Register of accounts of the sub-brokers.
(k) The duplicates of the contract notes issued to the clients.
(l) An agreement with the sub-broker.

The stock brokers who registers with the SEBI should intimate to the officials about the place of keeping the books. Every stock broker should submit the accounting information after closing the books of accounts to the SEBI not later than **six months** from the closure of the financial year. Every registered broker should preserve the books of accounts and other records for the minimum period of **five years**.

## The Procedure for Inspection

The SEBI has the full authority over the financial intermediary. It controls, regulates, monitors, evaluates and directs the market. It can inspect any stock brokers premises who registers with the SEBI. The Board may appoint one or more persons as the inspecting authority to inspect the books of accounts, records, documents of the stock broker for any purpose. Basically the SEBI undertakes the inspection for the following purposes:

(a) to check the maintenance of the books of accounts as per the Act,
(b) to observe, whether the registered broker has fulfilled all the legal formalities or not,
(c) to investigate into the complaints received from the investors and other stock brokers,
(d) to investigate the **suo-motu** with the interest of securities business or investor's interest into the affairs of the stock broker,
(e) the board should give a reasonable notice to the broker before undertaking the inspection,
(f) if the Board feels, it is necessary to inspect the registered stock broker, it can commence the inspection without sending any notice to the broker in the interest of investors,
(g) the stock broker should be bound to discharge his obligations,
(h) during the tenure of the inspection, it is the duty of every director, partner, officer and employee of the broker to produce

the records, book of accounts and other documents as the inspecting officer may require,

(i) the inspecting authority should submit the inspection report to the Board after the completion of the inspection,

(j) on receipt of the inspection report the Board should communicate the findings to the stock broker. Before taking the action the Board may give him an opportunity of being heard his version,

(k) the Board may appoint a qualified auditor to investigate into the books of accounts or affairs of the broker,

(l) the appointed auditor should have the same powers of the inspecting authority.

## Procedure for in Case of Default

The SEBI has the power to take the action in case of default by a registered stock broker in India. If a stock broker fails to comply with any conditions subject to which the registration has been granted then he is liable for taking action. A broker who contravenes with any of the provisions of the Act, rules or regulations there is liable to take the action against such broker. The broker should strictly follow the rules and regulations of the Stock Exchange and Securities Contract Act. If he fails to comply with the norms, he should be liable to pay the **penalties** as specified in the Act. The penalties in case of default may be either suspension of registration or cancellation. The suspension of registration of a broker may be imposed on the following grounds, if:—

(a) the broker violates the provisions of the acts, rules and regulations,

(b) the stock does not follow the code of conduct,

(c) the broker fails to pay the fees,

(d) the broker violates the conditions of the registration,

(e) the broker fails to resolve the complaints of the registration,

(f) the broker indulges in the manipulation of share prices,

(g) the broker is improper or unbusiness or unprofessional conduct,

(h) the membership of the broker is suspended by the stock exchange,

(i) fails to respond to the board communication,
(j) the broker involves in price rigging or concerned activities in the market,
(k) the financial position deteriorates the broker,
(l) the broker fails to furnish any information to the board,
(m) the broker furnishes wrong or false information,
(n) the broker does not submit the periodical return,
(o) the broker does not cooperate during the enquiry period.

The stock brokers registration can be cancelled by the SEBI, if

(a) the broker violates the takeover regulations or any provisions of the insider trading regulations,
(b) the cancellation of the membership by the stock exchange,
(c) the broker convicts a criminal offence,
(d) the broker is guilty of fraud.

Any broker who is aggrieved by an order of the Board may appeal to the Central Government under the provisions of the Act.

**SEBI and Investors' Protection**

The investors are the most important persons in the capital market. They come under the preview of **Consumer Act**. Generally in India, they face the problems like, **Non-receipt of refund, allotment order, delay and non-receipt of interest, dividend, non-receipt of brokerage and underwriting commission**. These problems arise due to the negligence of the **Corporate bodies and financial intermediaries**. The problems will be solved by the regulatory authorities like the SEBI and the stock exchanges. The basic redressal of grievances are done by the stock exchanges and corporate sectors. All the stock exchanges in India have investor services cell to resolve the grievances. But there will be inordinate delays in resolving such grievances. There the SEBI initiated various measures to maintain discipline in the financial intermediaries and stock exchanges by issuing guidelines. The guidelines include the aspects like insider trading, inspection of stock exchanges and their records, scrutiny of prospectus for adequate disclosures, credit rating for financial instruments like debentures, deposits. The stock brokers are also required to disclose the statutory requirements. They should bring transparency in the clients transactions. The SEBI has issued guidelines to the companies and stock exchanges with regard to the following aspects:

(1) Inspection of books of brokers.
(2) Transparency in prices and volume of trade in stock exchanges.
(3) Enforcing the margin norms strictly.
(4) Amendments to the byelaws of the stock exchanges with regard to capital adequacy.
(5) Indicating the brokerage and security price separately in contract note.
(6) Reviewing the redressing the investor grievances promptly.
(7) Amendment to the relevant byelaws for the issue of contract note by the broker to the client mandatory.

The **Joint Parliamentary Committee** had expressed its opinion for providing the protection to the small investors. The Committee recommended an effective system to handle the complaints and taking of the follow-up action within specified time frame. The SEBI has been vested with the adequate powers through the ordinance to protect and safeguard the interests of the investors. The following elements covers the investors protection and grievances:

**(A) Investor Protection**—SEBI plus investors associations.
**(B) Provisions of the Companies Act.**
**(C) Provisions of the SCR Act.**
**(D) Listing guidelines on the Investors protection.**
**(E) Investor or guidance series.**
**(F) Computerised process of redressal of investors grievances.**
**(G) Company Law Amendment.**
**(H) Companies Act Anomalies.**

### (A) Investor Protection

The SEBI has the full authority to monitor the stock market activities. It has decided to intensify the efforts to redress the complaints of the investors in collaboration with the recognised investor associations. The recognised investors association is empowered to facilitate the filing of class action **suits** in the consumer courts against the concerned companies. In India, the sharing of information is first done with the **Consumer Education Research Centre (CERC)**, Ahmedabad. Section 12 of the Consumer Protection Act, 1986 enables the Consumer associations to file the suits in district forums. The suit by the investor Associations in the district is based on the information as investors complaints. It implies saving in the legal cost apart from benefiting a large number of complaints through a single suit. The SEBI publishes the names of the top **twenty** defaulting companies every fortnight. **It puts** pressures on the companies. The SEBI has the power to issue the **show cause notices** and award penalty points under the SEBI guidelines. The SEBI has the power to issue the **No Objection Certificate** to the companies for releasing their **one per cent** deposit with the stock exchange. It emerged as a major check point for complaints. The SEBI has the power to recommend the suitable legal action against the defaulters to the Department of Company Affairs and for suspension of trading of their shares to various stock exchanges from time to time.

**(B) Provisions of the Companies Act**

The Government of India has been flooded with a number of complaints from time to time. The complaints have been made by the shareholders, investors, debenture holders regarding the delay in the transfer of shares, delay in the issue of allotment letters and share/debenture certificates or refund of share/debenture application money to non-allottees to the applicants of public issue.

The following provisions of the Companies Act V imposes various penalties depending upon the severity of the defaults:

1. The **Section 113** of the Act indicates that every company should within **three months** after the allotment of shares/ debentures has any default in compliance of the provision of law it is punishable.
2. If any company fails to register the share after transferring such share within two months, then it is liable to punishment accordingly.
3. The Companies Act, 1956 has issued the listing guidelines in this regard:

(a) According to the listing guidelines the companies must issue the allotment letters or shares certificates to the allottee immediately after the allotment of shares is made but it should not be later than **two months** from the closure of the subscription list.

(b) The Company should issue letters of regret, along with refund orders to the non-allottees.

(c) The listed company must issue the share certificate within **one month** of the date of lodgement of transfer of shares.

(d) If a company refuses to register any transfer of shares to the transferee within **two months**, the Section 111 of the Act permits to file an appeal before the **Company Law Board**.

(e) After closing the public issue process, Section 73 of the Companies Act imposes conditions for the despatch of allotment letters/certificates as to shares and debentures within the stipulated period of time.

(f) Companies entering the capital market are required to pay to unsuccessful applicants and liable to pay the interest for delayed period from the date of closure of the subscription list.

(g) Section 621 of the Companies Act, 1956 authorised a shareholder to file the prosecution against the company and its officers the companies concerned are advised to ensure that they should strictly follow the provisions of the Companies Act otherwise they would punished.

## (C) Provisions of the Securities Contract Regulations Act, 1956

The **Section 22A** of the Securities Contract (Regulations) Act, 1956 deals with the registration and transfer of shares. A Company fails to register the transfer of shares as one (or) more of the following situations:

(a) If the transfer of the security is in contraventions with any law.

(b) If the transfer of the security is prohibited by any order of any court/tribunal.

(c) If the financial instrument of the transfer is not in proper method.

(d) However, the Company should make a reference to the **Company Law Board** on the above grounds within **60 days** of the lodgement of the instrument of transfer.

**(D) Listing Guidelines on the Investors Protection**

The listing guidelines on the investors protection has been issued by the **Department of Economic Affairs**. The shareholders can take up the matters with the Concerned Register of Companies in regard with non-compliance of the guidelines. A reference may also be made to the concerned stock exchange.

**(E) Investor's Guidance Series**

The investor's guidance series is issued by the SEBI in the interest of public to educate the investors on the basic features of various investments. They are required to make precautions before choosing an investment or dealing with the intermediary. The Indian investors simply depend upon the advices but not on their own assessment. They simply handover the cheques to the brokers. They do not know how to select a scrip. They do not know the product which is manufactured by the selected companies. Even they do not know same basic stock market parameters like **EPS, PE ratio, Debt equity ratio, leverage**, and about the company's market share, company's expansion or diversification, products lifecycle etc. Therefore, they motivate the investors to develop the capital market the SEBI will create an awareness about the investor's right and remedies. The investors should take their investment decisions in the light of their individual circumstances. The SEBI has issued the following series of guidance to enlighten the investors:

1. **Investor's Guidance** (Debentures).
2. **Investor's Guidance** (Transfer of Securities).
3. **Investor's Guidance** (Stock Investment Scheme).

***1. Investor's Guidance (Debentures)***

In India some companies are not able to do service to the debenture holder. The Companies are unable to pay the redemption amount because of financial difficulties. Some other companies delay the interest on debenture or may not redeem the debentures on schedule. The debentures are issued by the Companies, secured against the assets. The assets are mortgaged on the names of the trustees which are mostly **Financial Institutions**. A trust deed is executed between the company and the trustee. The trust deed contains all the conditions and involvements of the two parties. According to the guidelines issued by the Ministry of Finance, the trustees are more powerful in protecting the interests of the debenture holders. The trustees observes the affairs and the activities with regard to debentures aspect the trustees should verify whether a debenture redemption reserve is created or not. The trustees have the responsibility in monitoring the activities regarding the creation of security for the debentures and debentures redemption reserves. The India Trust Act indicates that a trustee may do all acts which are reasonable and proper while protecting a beneficiary. The following steps are involved in case of complaints:

(a) The Section 113 of the Companies Act deals with the issue of debenture certificate to the debenture holder within the specified period. Every company must within **three months** after the allotment of debentures should deliver the certificate.
(b) Company should transfers the registration within **two months** after applying for transfer of registration.
(c) The Companies Act specifies the above schedule for the delivery of certificates and transfer process. The extension of time will be granted by the Company Law Board. Any default in compliance with the provision is **punishable** with fine u/s 113(2) of the Act.
(d) An aggrieved debenture holder may apply to the **CLB** to direct the company to deliver the debenture certificate.
(e) The investor can also file a complaint before the **Magistrate Court** or forward his complaint to the stock exchange decision of the Department of Economic Affairs.
(f) The Companies Act, Section 118 permits the debenture holder to obtain the copies and inspect the trust deeds and other documents.
(g) According to Section 56 of the **Indian Trust Act**, he has the right to ask the trustee for the enforcement of the security created in case of default, in the payment of interest and principal.

(h) The investor has the right to bring the matter to the notice of the SEBI, stock exchange and also financial institutions for the redressal of the grievance.

(i) The debenture holder can compel the trustees to perform any particular act or duty.

(j) The debenture holder can also approach the civil court for the recovery of the due amounts, when the company is unable to pay its debts he can fine a winding up petition under Section 433 of the Companies Act to a **High Court**.

(k) The debenture holder has the right to approach the Consumer Disputes Redressal Forum (District Forum), a State Commission, National Commission for Claims at various levels stipulated by the Act.

### *2. Investor's Guidance (Transfer of Securities)*

This is another set of series issued by the SEBI with public interest to enlight the investors on the basic features of Investor's rights and remedies. The major problems faced by the Investors is delay in the transfer of securities. The following are the steps involved in the settlement of the investors problems:

**(i) Transfer of Securities.**
**(ii) Registration of Transfer.**

**Transfer of Securities** are the obligation to the corporate sector. They are to be delivered through registered post or personally. The Companies Act, **Section 113(1)** reveals that every company has to compulsorily within **2 months** from the date of application made for registration of securities to the buyers party. The Company Law Board has the power to extend the time for not more than **9 months** within the stipulated period to deliver the certificates. A Company is required to send the share certificates duly endorsed within **one month** of the lodgement of the transfer deed.

**Registration of Transfer** can be refused by a company, by sending the notice to the buyers and seller and giving the reasons for such refusal. The **Section 111** of the Companies Act provides that a Company can refuse the transfer of registration on some grounds. Besides the **Securities Contract (Regulation) Act** provides the following grounds for the refusal of registration of transfers of securities. They are:

(a) that the financial instrument of transfer is not proper,
(b) that the transfer of financial asset is in contravention with any law,
(c) that the transfer of security is harmful to the existing investors,
(d) that the transfer of financial instrument is prohibited by any Court of Tribunal.

If the Company has no interest to transfer the shares it should intimate to the investor with a reference to the **CLB**. On the other hand of the Company has the interest to transfer the securities to such registration it should intimate to the buyer and seller in a prescribed form. A reference has to be made within two months to the CLB and reference copies to the concerned parties. The Company should inform to the applicant whether his applicant is refused or transferred before 2 months from the date on which the instrument of transfer is lodged.

### *3. Investor's Protection and Guidance (Stock Investment Scheme)*

The Stock Investment Scheme has been recognised by the **RBI**, the Department of Company Affairs and the Government of India. It has been treated as one of the tools by which the application money for subscription to shares and debentures may be paid. The RBI has issued instructions to all the Scheduled Commercial Banks to make the stock invest scheme a friendly investor. The stock invest may be described as a postal order. It can be used for the payment of money instead of cash. In the appraisal of the stock invest scheme, three persons involve in the process:

**(a) Issuing banks.**
**(b) Investors.**
**(c) Registrars.**

#### *(a) Issuing Banks*

At present all the Scheduled Commercial Banks are issuing the stock invest instrument to the investors, while issuing this instrument, the Issuing Bank has to observe carefully:

(i) before issuing the instrument it should be properly dated and issued under the signature of the authorised signatory,

(ii) every issuing instrument should contain the particulars as to the name and code number of the branch,

(iii) it should be marked as non-negotiable transfer crossed and payable to the bankers,

(iv) it should contain the name and full address of the purchases on its reverse,

(v) the issuing bank should have branches or make necessary arrangements to facilitate the payment against the stock invest,

(vi) the Registrars to the issue are required to return the stock invest duly cancelled to the unsuccessful applicants.

*(b) Investors*

The following steps are needed to participate in the primary market through the stock invest instrument:

(i) The investor can approach any Scheduled Commercial Bank for the issue of stock invest in desired denominations for the payment of money while applying for shares in the primary market.

(ii) The investor should not withdraw the money from the account until the payment has been made on this instrument.

(iii) The investor should take care about the use of stock invest. Because it should be used within **ten days** from the date of issue.

(iv) The investor should indicate all the particulars about the stock invest instrument in the specified place of the application forms.

(v) The investor should use only one stock invest along with each application for subscription to an issue.

(vi) The investor should not make available the stock invest to the third party. It should be utilised by the account holder only.

(vii) After the allotment it will be sent to the issuing bank through the controlling branch.

(viii) The inquiries relating to the stock invest should be addressed to the Registrar only.

(ix) After closing the public issue, the controlling branches of the collecting banks will forward to the Registrar with a clear segregation of the information.

### *(c) Registrars*

The following steps are involved to complete the process of a public issue:

(i) The Registrars should receive the applications for subscriptions accompanied by the stock invest from the controlling branches.

(ii) On receipt from the controlling branches, the Registrar should give the house number on the back side of the stock invest. The stock invest should be detached from the application and kept in the safe custody.

(iii) The Registrar should process the applications. He should work out on the purpose of allotment and despatch of the certificates to the allottees.

(iv) The Registrar should report to the non-allottees and cancel their stock invest and return to the applicants.

(v) The Registrar should deposit the stock invest, duly filled in the bank-wise and branch-wise and thus further process should be completed.

(vi) The Registrar should reject the multiple applications received with a single stock invest.

(vii) The Registrar should maintain a proper record of applications which are received with the stock invest.

## (F) Computerised Process of Redressal of Investors Grievances

The problems of the investors lie with companies and financial intermediaries. In view of the large number of complaints, the Department of Company Affairs has set up a machinery for handling these complaints. It has decided to take strict action against the defaulter companies. The procedure for handling the complaints is by introducing a fully computerised system of processing. The information should be furnished by the Companies regarding the action taken on each complaint within a stipulated period of time. The senior officials have been carefully observing the progress of action taken on investors complaints. The Department of Company Affairs has succeeded in settling the investors grievances. The **Senior Officers** will hold the meetings of the companies against whom a large number of complaints are registered. Therefore, the Companies may concentrate in solving the problems of the investors by the pressure from senior officials. If the Company and Registrar show negligency towards the investor's complaints. They can directly report to the SEBI for appropriate action against such Registrars. The computer system in the investor is protection cell will solve the problem by designing the status system of complaints.

## (G) Company Law Amendment

The Company Law Amendments are made by keeping in view to benefit to the investors:

(a) The Companies Act has permitted the companies to hold shareholders meeting on **Sundays** to attract more gathering.
(b) The shareholders, the debenture holders and fixed deposit holders can now enjoy the nomination facility.
(c) Credit Rating made mandatory.
(d) Auditing standards would be enhanced to the extent of international standards.
(e) The Defaulted Companies are prohibited from raising further loans from the market.
(f) The Directors of the Companies are made more accountability.
(g) The debenture holders can enforce the CLB for the payment of their principal and interest.
(h) The unpaid dividends are transferred to the investors protection fund.
(i) Enforcement of free transferability of shares and debentures.

The advantages of the Companies Act Amendment are presented below:

(a) There is no need to disclose the information regarding drawing large remuneration drawing employees along with the Director's report.
(b) The Companies can now file all the returns and records through floppy discs to the Department of Company Affairs.
(c) The share premium amounts will be included in the free reserves.

(d) The Companies have freedom to convert the loans/debentures into equity without the approval of the Government.

(e) The Companies can now issue non-voting shares subject to certain limitations and regulations.

(f) The Companies will be happy because they can buy back their shares and can retain the control of the company.

(g) The Companies have freedom to maintain the records in loose leaf forms.

(h) The Companies need not submit the full list of shareholders particulars along with annual returns.

(i) If the Shareholders accept the amendments of the objective clause, there is no need to get the approval from the CLB.

(j) The Companies can now get the quick approvals for Mergers and Acquisitions from the Government.

(k) The Directors of the Company can now have the tax free payments from the Company and their relatives can accommodated in the board.

(l) The limit for managerial remuneration of directors is increased.

(m) The concept of deemed public company is removed from the Act.

(n) Inter-corporate funding are increased to a certain level of the specified amount.

## (H) Companies Act Anomalies

According to the Companies Act, 1956, **Sections 73 and 113,** the allotment process of the share capital is offered to the public. Every company should approach the public for the issue of share capital, to get its shares listed within **10 weeks** from the date of closure of the subscription list. The Company should despatch the share certificates within three months from the date of allotment. Therefore, the time gap between the legal formalities logically pushes the share price up. After the despatch of share certificates the investors may increase the supply position in the market. Then automatically the supply of shares in the market becomes more and more, it leads to the decline of prices in the market. The situation will be encashed by the well experienced market men to book profits by covering their position. These people will never loose money in such deals. Therefore, the legal experts feel that, the company should not be allowed to trade even after listing until the company management certifies that the despatch of certificates is completed. Therefore, the situation leads to control the share price accordingly.

The concept of **Non-voting shares** facilitate is available in Western countries and there is a strong demand from industry in our country. The non-voting shares are introduced for the first time in India with certain safeguards and proceedings for minimum extra dividend. Some other changes under consideration by the Government will lead to the development of the corporate sector. The changes include such as **provision from disqualification** for certain categories of managerial personnel, provision of uniforms tenure, provision of the number of companies in which a person can be appointed as **MD** (or) **Manager**, provision for the payment of increased commission to the non-working directors. Freedom given to considerable flexibility and operational in the area of appointment and remuneration to their directors and managers.

The SEBI is the powerful organisation to implement the rules and regulations of the corporate sector from time to time. The SEBI has made it mandatory for the companies to provide full and complete balance sheet to the shareholders for enabling them to an analytical investment decision.

## Summary

In public issues, after the merchant bankers, the next position goes to the underwriters. The person who assures is called as Underwriter and the consideration for this assurance is known as "Underwriting Commission". It is one of the marketing securities. Underwriters in India may be broadly classified into two kinds—Institutional Underwriters and Non-Institutional Underwriters. The Registrar is another intermediary in the primary market. His activity is to collect the application forms from the investors. SEBI is established for regulation and orderly function of the capital market. It is likely to promote the measures for fair trading in the securities and to protect the rights of the investors. It is empowered to control, regulate and monitor all the activities of the secondary market. It has divided its activities into the seven departments each headed by officials of the rank of executive directors. It was established on the same pattern of the Securities Exchange Commission in USA.

**Questions**

1. What is a Underwriter? Explain his position in the public issue.
2. What are the general obligations and responsibilities of the Underwriter?
3. Write an essay on Registrar status in public issues.
4. What is SEBI? State the functions and powers of the SEBI.
5. Describe the nature of government influence on securities market.

**REFERENCES**

1. Van Horne, *Fundamentals of Financial Management*, p. 641.
2. N. Gopalaswamy, *Insider Capital Market*, p. Va 125. Deccan Publications.

# 4

# NATIONAL STOCK EXCHANGE

## Introduction

The Indian stock markets have come a long way since the early **18th century** when securities trade was initiated under a sprawling banyan tree in front of town hall in **Mumbai.**[1] The Companies Act that was passed in 1850 signalled these of the era of the joint stock companies in India. The creation of NSE by the leading financial institutions in 1992 led to move the screen based trading for equities debt and hybrid instruments. The process of globalisation began with the opening up of the Indian capital markets to the FIIs in 1992. This led to foreign custodians and brokerages setting up base in India. They brought their best global practices in the Indian markets. Equity research gained prominence. The globalisation of markets made the Indian financial markets more vulnerable to the external events as a result of which any movement in the global markets have a corresponding ripple affect in India.

**The NSE** was sponsored by the IDBI and co-sponsored by the CIC, GIC, SBI capital markets, Stockholding Corporation, Infrastructure Leasing and Finance Corporation. It emerged as a part of the capital market reform process due to the failure of the conventional stock exchange. It was established to provide transparent and efficient securities market. It was set up in **Mumbai** in November 1992 with a paid up capital of **Rs. 25 crores**. It was recognised by the Government. It started its operations in June 1994 in **Debt** market and in equity trading in November 1994. There was no trading floor in the exchange. Trading was done on the computers with the help of the PC terminals in the broker offices. It has a fully automated, electronic, screen based trading system. It was an order driven and not based on quota driven market. It allows two kinds of traded securities such as listed and permitted. It prevents the price rigging and insider trading.

The Pherwani Committee recommended to establish the NSE with a view to provide single market.

**Objectives**

The objectives of the NSE are:

(a) to cover wide area geographical location;
(b) to provide an equal access and fair, efficient and transparent;
(c) to provide the shorter settlement cycles;
(d) to provide the book entry settlement system;
(e) to provide the Indian investors with international standard service;
(f) to check the insider trading and price rigging;
(g) to protect the interest of the investors;
(h) to protect the brokers frame default;
(i) to provide the listing facilities to PSUs;
(j) to spread the investment and cult to the savers in the rural and semi-urban areas;
(k) to encourage the debt market;
(l) to professionalise the members to more competent;
(m) to create more employment opportunities for the finance professional in the orbit of the capital market;
(n) to protect the members from the default risks.

Indian premier stock exchange today, NSE is evident that it has revolutionised trading in India. Through its network of **3075 VSAT**[2] exchanges across **379** cities, millions of Indians who previously could not, are able to trade in the stocks. The number of companies listed in the NSE and average daily turnover are presented below:

(*Rs. in crores*)

| *Year* | *No. of Companies Listed* | *Average Daily Turnover* |
|---|---|---|
| 1994–95 | 678 | 17 |
| 1995–96 | 1269 | 276 |
| 1996–97 | 1484 | 1176 |
| 1997–98 | 1357 | 1520 |
| 1998–99 | 1254 | 1651 |
| 1999–2000 | 1152 | 3303 |
| 2000–2001 | 1029 | 5337 |

In October 1995, the NSE became the largest exchange in India in terms of stocks transacted volumes in 2000–01, its total turnover was **Rs.17,70,457** crores.

## Constitution

The NSE offers the screen based trading with national network transparency and it ensures cost effectiveness. The investment counters are spread wide in the country under the NSE electronic network. The NSE has two separate segments:

**(a) The Wholesale Debt Market Segment.**
**(b) The Capital Market Segment.**

**(a) The Wholesale Debt Market Segment (WDMS)** deals with banks, financial institutions, other institutional participants and in **PSU** bonds, treasury bills, government securities, call money, commercial papers, certificates of deposits etc. In these segments all are big, they are big deals, mega players, mega investors etc.
**(b) The Capital Market Segment (CMS)** deals with equities, convertible debentures. This segment includes the securities which are traded on other stock exchanges. The CMS operates from 3.11.1994. It introduced trading in **repos** from 23.6.1995. The RBI has identified the NSE as the only conduit for the inter-bank security deals. The NSE is free from all speculative activities. It has also become a speculator's paradise basically in the speculative market. A separate membership is required for each segment.

The NSE has created competition to the BSE. It has dominated the BSE within a short time period and exceeded the business of the **150 years** old BSE. NSE is set up as a cash and delivery market. But it has become a circular market. In this circular market the transactions are mostly squared. The example for circular market is **X selling to** Y, **Y selling to** Z and **Z selling to** X.

## WDM

The **WDM** segment consists of two parties. They are trading members and participants. The trading members are recognised as the members of NSE. Generally the financial institutions, body corporates, commercial banks are eligible to become the trading members. They are selected on the basis of same selection criteria. The trading member should possess at least two years experience regarding the financial services. They must possess a networth of **Rs. 2 crores**. The NSE charges **Rs. 30 lakhs** as fee from the trading members. The trading member should not withdraw his membership up to **Five years**. The trading member must engaged in securities business but not is fund based activity. The trading members can trade on their own purpose or on behalf of their clients. The participants are another party in this segment. The participants involve in buying and selling of the securities. They are responsible for the settlement of trade. The participants can be treated as the buyers of the securities for their own requirements. Their transactions are executed through trading members. The participants can monitor all the market movements. The participants have to access the NSE trading system.

**Trading System in WDM**

Trading has become a sophisticated way at present. The conventional system of trading has less changing with the development of information technology. Trading is fully computerised. The Indian stock market has transformed the trading ways into **Online trading system**. The system has increased the trading velocities and reduce the time horizon. The NSE provides a facility for the screen based trading with order matching facility. The scattered trading members are connected from their respective offices to the main system at the NSE centralised premises through a high speed efficient satellite telecommunication network. The trading process is an automated order matching system. It does not reveal the identity of the parties to an executed order or a seller. It is an advantage to the members because no identity would be found. It operates on a **Pricetime priority**. In screen based trading system orders are automatically matched by the computers. If an order does not find a suitable match it remains in the system and will be displayed on the screen till a fresh order matches. The trading system facilitates a flexibility to the parties according to their ordering method. The process provides an excellent environment for placing an order. Several conditions like, **volume related**, price related and time related can easily be placed on the system. The rapid technology development of the information system provides the **online** market information through various facilities. In the screen based system, the entire information regarding a particular scrips or about all scrips will be available in the market. The detailed information regarding the total order in a security, the quantity traded, the high, the low and the last traded prices are available through screen at anytime. The debt market is easily accessible to three types of users. They are trader uses, privileged user and inquiry users. The trading members should keep in touch with the users. But the **participant parties** are allowed privileged user and inquiry by users only. The trader user is an important component in the online trading system. The traders user gives access for entering the orders on the trading system **the privileged** user has the right to set up a counter party. The inquiry user cannot enter orders or trade or set up exposure limits. The inquiry user can have the market information and the right to set up the market watch screen. The volume of trade in the debt market segment can be executed in the negotiated (or) continuous market. In the continuous market, the orders are automatically matched by the computer system. If the order does not find a suitable element, it will be entered in the order books. The entry in the order book is known as **passive order**. It may tallied lated with any forthcoming order and result into a trade. The forthcoming orders which match with the existing order is known as the **active order**. The debt market trading system facilitates trading in debt and other instruments either as outright purchase and sale as **Repo** or as non-repo traders. Repurchase agreements can be defined as "Agreements to buy securities (usually treasury bills) and to resell them at a specified higher price at a later date".[3] The Government security dealers offer repos to the corporations. The trading member has to indicate the trade type repo/non-repo and the desired settlement term. The NSE permits the settlement terms from T+0 to T+5. The Repo term ranges from 3 to 14 days. The online trading system works on the basis of **price time** priority. There are two types of orders which may be placed by the trading members as **Repo trade and Non-repo trades**. In case of repo trades, it facilitates the lowest buy rate in case of the buy order and in case of the sell order, it arranges higher sell rate. The transactions are based as passive order rate. If the busy order in case of non-repo trades is the highest buy price and the best sell order is with the lowest price then the orders are matched automatically by the system based on the passive order price. All the orders should be placed according to the specifications of the NSE. The entered transactions are identified on the subject matter of the trade and they are divided into **six parts**. This classification is known as **security depositor**. All the orders are matched on the basis of the descriptors. The transactions are categorised on **security type, security, issue, settlement, trade type and repo term**. The order transactions will be tallied on the basis of security descriptor, price, volume, order type and conditions. The value of the order is indicated in "Rupees Lakh" in the trading system. In the trading system every participant can set up counter party exposure limits. All the traders executed by the trading members for their participants will not affect the trading members counter party exposure.

**Settlement System in Debt Market**

The debt market transactions are settled in Mumbai. The settlement in the debt market segment lies with the participants and the exchange monitors. The trades are settled as per the procedure laid down:

(a) The transactions are settled individually.
(b) Trades are settled directly between the participants.
(c) There is no settlement through the clearing house mechanism.
(d) The settlement takes place on rolling basis.
(e) Each order will be settled on the basis of specified settlement date.
(f) The NSE presently allows the settlement periods ranging from T+0 to a maximum of (T+5).
(g) On the scheduled settlement date, the NSE provides the information to the concerned members regarding the trades to the settled on that day.
(h) All the Government securities are settled by the participants through their **Subsidiary General Ledger** account with the RBI (or) through exchange of physical certificates.
(i) The information regarding the required settlement are reported by the members to the NSE.
(j) The other instruments are settled through the delivery of physical securities.
(k) On receipt of the information from the participants, the NSE closely monitors the information.
(l) If the cancellation of trade participants are required to get its prior approval.
(m) If any disputes arises during the process, one can approach the arbitrator for resolving the dispute.
(n) The arbitration mechanism has been established by the NSE.

Capital Market Segment covers the trading in equity and retail debt. In this segment, there is a strong need to upgrade the professional standards of intermediaries. The intermediaries are still to develop their skills and to become more competitive. The admission standards to this segment are very vigorous. The rules and regulations are framed by the NSE. There is much stress on factors such as **capital adequacy, track record, education and experience**. Admission into this segment involves two stages. The interested person is required to go through a written examination followed by an interview. The trading members in this segment are corporates, registered firms, individuals and institutional members. The applicant should engage in fee based services only. The individual members and registered firms must have minimum networth requirements of **Rs. 75.00 lakhs**. The corporate bodies should have **Rs. 1 crore**. The minimum prescribed educational qualification is graduation and two years experience in financial services/as broker/authorised assistant. The experience in any financial aspects are welcome.

### Trading Systems in CMS

The screen based system is fully automated and workers on the basis of an **order driven market**. The trading system provides flexibility to the members in their placement orders. Orders received for the first time are stamped and immediately processed for a potential match. If the suitable order is not found it will be stored in different books. The orders are stored in best price and within price time sequence. The order matching rules of the NSE system reveals that the best buy order matches with the best sell order. Sometimes an order may match partially with another order resulting in multiple trades. The orders will match as the buy order is with the highest price and the sell order is with the lowest price. Members may enter orders in the system, the order will be displayed till another party puts in a counter order. On the other hand, the members may be reactive and put in orders that match with the existing orders on the system. The orders which are lying unmatched in the system are passive orders. The orders that match with the existing orders are called **active orders**. The active orders are always matched at the passive order price. Therefore, the earlier orders will get priority over the orders that come in later. The trading members can enter into the various types of orders depending upon their requirements. There are three conditions—

(a) time related conditions,
(b) price related conditions, and
(c) volume related conditions.

### *(a) Time Related Conditions*

These transactions are executed on the basis of time conditions. In this type of orders, the orders will stay in force only for a few days. The time conditions further may be classified as: (a) day order, (b) a good till cancelled, (c) a good till days, (d) an immediate (or) cancel. **The day order** is valid for the day which the order is placed. In case the order is not matched during the day, it gets cancelled automatically. A good till cancelled order means, the order will remain in the trading system until it is cancelled by the members. A good till days means the order allows the trading members to specify the days, it will be kept in the system up to that day afterwards it is flushed out from the system. An immediate order (or) cancel means, it allows a trading member to sell (or) buy a particular security when the order is released into the market. If it fails the order will be removed from the systems.

### *(b) Price Related Conditions*

This is the most important condition in the capital market segment. The price conditions is known as "on stop" this order allows the member to place an order and gets activated only when the market price of the security exceeds a threshold price until then this situation the order does not **focus** in the market. In the case of sell order, it gets triggered if the last price will be less than the sell order price.

### *(c) Volume Related Conditions*

The NSE may set a minimum disclosed value from time to time. In this condition the trading members may disclose only a part of the order value in the market. For example, an order of 5000 with a disclosed value condition of 500. It means that 500 is released into the market. After the order is traded, another 500 will be automatically released and so as the full order executed. The quantum of disclosed value will be fixed by the NSE.

## Settlement System in the Capital Market Segment

The NSE operates a well defined schedule for the welfare of the investors. Trading in this segment has been growing rapidly. An important growth in the segment is the short settlement cycles. The following features involve in the settlement process of the NSE:

1. The settlement cycles will be announced well in advance by the NSE.
2. The transactions will be settled through the clearing house only.
3. There will be no settlement among the brokers.
4. The NSE maintains the gap between inflow and out of the fund is for only one day.
5. The NSE takes the responsibility of bad deliveries, rectifying short delivies.
6. NSE assures legal guarantee to the transactions and settlements.
7. The periodic settlement in the NSE is as follows:
   (a) The trading period starts on **Wednesday** and ends on **Tuesday** of the next week.
   (b) All the transactions concluded in a particular trading period are settled during the next week.
   (c) At the end of a trading period it makes delivery statements for the members.
   (d) The securities are paid on every Monday following the trading period.
   (e) The pay out of the funds is on **Tuesday**.
   (f) The payout day for funds and securities takes place **on Wednesday**.
8. The settlement will be completed in eight days.
9. The clearing process is automated and the NSE set up a clearing house, known as **National Securities Clearing Corporation Ltd.** for managing the settlement of securities.
10. All the securities are handled by the NSCCL only.
11. The delivering members should bring the securities on the pay in the day to the **clearing house.**
12. The securities are distributed on the payout day to the members.

13. If the settlement is out of Mumbai, the clearing and settlement will be done by setting up a **Regional Clearing House.**
14. The Canara Bank is appointed as the clearing bank.
15. All the transactions will be passed through the clearing bank only.
16. All the transactions are effected through the **electronic fund transfer** system.
17. The clearing house makes short deliveries on **Tuesday** in turn. They will be auctioned on **Wednesday**.
18. On Thursday pay in for auction takes place and pay out on Friday.
19. All the bad deliveries are required to be reported by **Friday** to the clearing house.
20. Every Monday, the delivering member is required to rectify any problems.
21. The trading system specifies the turnover limits for its members in relation to their networth.
22. The NSE marks the market members position to maintain significant deposits on daily basis.
23. Margins are collected from the members if they reach beyond the limits.
24. The NSE provides prompt settlement process and assures cash settlement.

### Institutional Market Segment

The NSE provides some additional facilities for its institutional investors. The institutional market segment is categorised as **Institutional Lot Segment** and Trade for Trade Segment. Large volume trade takes place in Institutional lot segment. The trade for Trade Segment is meant to cater to the institutions which prefer this source as a means of minimising exposure risk. Institution lot contains in multiples of **1000 shares** irrespective the securities face value. The institutional investors can enter into the orders separately. The institutional lot trading period commences from Wednesday to Tuesday. A trading member may enter and monitor any security in this market. All the pay in and pay out of funds are effected on the same day, i.e., the subsequent Tuesday through the clearing house. All the transactions and settlements of the trades will be done through clearing house only.

The funds are passed to the **NSE clearing house** account the clearing bank on the settlement day and will be paid by the clearing bank on the same day.

The institutional market segment consists of two conditions in the settlement of securities, i.e. **Institutional lots and T.T. Segment**. The securities can be delivered in the institutional board lots 1000 shares and the receiving members has to accept such as good delivery. On conformation of the successful exchange of funds and securities, the custodians should report to the clearing house authorities. The delivered securities should be recorded on the name of the delivering member. The blank transfer forms are not allowed in this segment. The other condition is TT segment which differs in settlement. The transactions are settled on a **rolling** basis. The transactions are required to be confirmed by T+3 and will be settled on T+5. The delivery of shares are to be accepted by the receiving member. The settlement of the transactions are effected between institutions and custodians and it should be reported to the NSE. The custodians are more important in the settlement cycles.

All the transactions are handled by the NSE itself. It operates the **HELP LINE** services to help the members and provides a better quality of standard services to come out of embracing situation. The majority of the participants in the debt market **(90%)** are in Mumbai.

## Listing of Securities

All the Companies which have more than **Rs. 10 crores** of paid up capital can be listed on the NSE. A company can list its share both on a regular stock exchange and NSE. The same listing formalities will be followed as in case of regular stock exchange. The Company should make a listing agreement with NSE and should inform to the SEBI and Government.

The NSE is perceived to be more friendly investor than any other stock exchanges by most of the investors. The Indian stock market is ready for the next big leap derivatives which are the important constituents of the trading volumes on major exchanges across the world. In future, the trading volumes of a stock exchange will increasingly feed off each other in a symergistic relationship in cash and derivatives market. Investors who seek to build up positions in the cash market will be able to hedge them by using derivatives and those building up positions in derivatives will be able to do the reverse. By the turn of this decade **24 hours** stock exchanges will come into being. Investors in India can trade in blue-chip securities all over the world.

## REFERENCES

1. Hemandra Kothari, The rise of equity cult, *B.T. Anniversary Issue*, p. 64.
2. NSE: India's premier stock exchange, *Business Today Anniversary Issue*, 2001, p. 70.
3. Van Horne, *Fundamentals of Management*, p. 234, PHI, 1997.

# 5

# DERIVATIVES TRADING

## Introduction

The financial sector reforms are expected to give a boost to the economy by allocating the funds for productive investment and capital formation. The operational investments in the financial systems are expected to facilitate and expedite the process of market information. The Indian stock market is characterised by high price volatility. Speculation dealings are to be settled on cash basis. It is unavoidable and it is the drilling force. It is the oxygen to the stock market. In the present circumstances the stock markets do not have any risk hedge instruments which would allow the investors to manage and minimise the risk. In developed countries, there will be money market, capital market securities and a variety of other securities available for investment and trading. The other securities are known as "Derivatives". These have now become available for investment and trading. It originate in mathematics. It refers to available which has been derived from another variable. The amendments to the SCRA led to the introduction of derivative trading. It is recommended by L.C. Gupta Committee. They are treated as the risk management tools. They have no independent value. They can be sold in the cash market on normal delivery terms. It is the most cost effective device against the risk. It is a financial product which has been derived from another financial product or commodity. They are contracts written between two parties for easily marketable assets. They are also known as deferred payment instruments. Derivatives can be defined as "A derivative is a financial product which has been derived from another financial product or commodity". D.G. Gardener defined derivatives "A derived is a financial product which has been derived from market for another product". They are mostly secondary market instruments. They have little use in mobilising fresh capital by the companies. They are liquid and low transaction cost. There is a lot of demand in India for them. The authorities have taken various steps to introduce the derivatives. The SEBI approved derivatives trading in June 2000. The first instruments to be traded were index futures. This was followed by the options trading on the two indices in June 2001. Futures trading in individual stocks was permitted in **November 2001**. Within a month, after the launch, the NSE has achieved a record of sorts, the number of contracts are **11,135** on Dec. 14, 2001. It is the second highest in the world after **Spain's MEFF** and a head of hand on International Financial Futures Exchange. The growth in the derivative trading is presented below:

**Growth in Derivatives Trading**[1]

| *Period* | *Total Number of Contracts Traded* |
|---|---|
| June 2000 | 1191 |
| December 2000 | 9208 |
| January 2001 | 19141 |
| December 2001 | 413809 |
| **Period** | **Turnover** (Rs. in crores) |
| June 2000 | 35.25 |
| December 2000 | 237.02 |
| January 2001 | 471.22 |
| December 2001 | 8760.13 |
| **Period** | **Average Daily Turnover** (Rs. in crores) |
| June 2000 | 2.35 |
| December 2000 | 11.85 |
| January 2001 | 21.42 |
| December 2001 | 438.01 |

The derivative markets have been started in **UK, USA and Europe** in securities. In 1988 Japan has started its options and in 1993 Hongkong has had its first options contract. The rapid growth of derivatives was due to the need for hedging.

## Advantages of Derivative Markets

(a) They provide lower transaction costs.
(b) It increases the volume of transactions.
(c) It increases hedge for the investors.

(d) Increases liquidity for investors.
(e) It enhances the price discovery process.

**Functions of Derivatives**

The basic purpose of the derivative instruments is not to borrow or lend the funds but to transfer the price lists associated with the fluctuations in the assets values. The derivatives provide three important economic functions, **i.e. Risk management, price discovery and transactional efficiency**.

**Players in Derivatives**

There are three major players in the derivatives trading:

(a) Hedgers,
(b) Speculators, and
(c) Arbitrageurs.

(a) **Hedgers** means the part, which manages the risk. Hedgers try to protect themselves against the price changes in a commodity in which they have an interest.
(b) **Speculators** are the major players in the market, without whom the market probably would never exist.
(c) **Arbitrageurs** are specialised in making buying and selling in different markets at the same time. The profits are earned through the difference in prices between the two centres.

**Components of Derivatives**

Different varieties of derivatives are available in the market. These are also called as **Components of derivatives**. The different components of the derivative markets are presented below:

(a) Futures.
(b) Options.
(c) Swaps.
(d) Warrants.
(e) Convertibles.

(f) Credit derivatives.
(g) Swaptions.

## Concept of Futures

Futures are the agreements between two counter parties. They fix the terms of an exchange. They are highly standardised contracts. They are not securities. Future contracts provide the delivery of contracted assets. They are also known as **paper markets**. They are organised by Futures Exchanges. They are transferable legal agreements. The terms of the agreements are unchangeable during the life of the contract. The future trading is a kin to badla trading. It includes an interest component. It requires only margin deposit and not full payment immediately. The future contracts are on **stock indices** and not on individual stocks.

### *Definition of Future Contract*

The future contract is defined as "A contract for the delivery of a commodity, foreign currency or financial instrument at a specified price on a stipulated future date. Future contracts are traded on organised exchanges."[2]

> "A future contract is an agreement between a seller and buyer that calls for the seller to deliver to the buyer a specified quantity, grade of an identified commodity at a fixed time in the future and at a price agreed to when the contract is first entered into."

### *Characteristics of the Future Markets*

The main characteristics of the futures markets are presented below:

(a) The future trading unit is large and indivisible.
(b) The maturity period of the contract is not more than three months.
(c) The successful contract ratio of new contracts is about **25 per cent** in worldwide markets.
(d) The contracts are also useful to the farmers and intermediaries.

(e) The contracts are both commercial and non-commercial users of futures.
(f) The commercial users are to be a large extent intermediaries.
(g) The intermediaries belongs to long and short positions.
(h) The main use of the futures is to hedge the commercials.
(i) The non-commercial are almost entirely speculative positions.
(j) They are used in the underwriting of fixed income securities but not in equity underwriting.

### *Functions of Future Markets*

The major functions performed by future markets are presented below:

(a) They facilitate stock holding.
(b) They can reduce the risk.
(c) They fulfil the desire of the speculators.
(d) They provide financial facilities for the payment of margins and contract settlement.
(e) They perform as forward pricing function.

They rise of future trading depends upon the three important elements, they are risk, uncertainty and opportunism. Future trading is designed to increase the business efficiency. Various types of contracts are available in the market for commodities, and financial instruments. The different types of contracts are presented below:

(a) Ready delivery contract.
(b) Forward contract.

**Ready delivery contract** provides delivery of goods or instruments. The payment of price will be made either immediately or within **11 days** of the contract time. It leads to spot or cash transactions which takes place at current price of commodity. **Forward contract** is a contract for delivering the goods. These transactions are spot transactions. It is also known as specific delivery contract.

### Margin

Margin is the most important factor in futures market. Margin is an agreement made at no initial investment. Margin payments are used as a means of settling. The losses and gains on the contract gradually. They are paid frequently in small amounts relative to the size of the contract. In future market, the daily cash settlement plays an important role in maintaining the trading system. The futures market has a financial integrity and low default risk. The following illustration explains how the margin works. **For example,** if an investor who contacts with his broker on January 9, 2002 to buy two March 2002 gold futures contracts as the ABC commodity exchange. We suppose that the current futures price is Rs. 5,000 per 10 grams. Since the contract size is 100 grams. The investor has contracted to buy a total of 200 grams at this price. The broker requires the investor to deposit funds. It is termed as **Margin account**. The amount deposited at the time of the contract is known as the initial margin. We assume this as Rs. 2,500 per contract or **Rs.50,000** in total. At the end of each trading, the margin account is adjusted to reflect the investors gain (or) loss. Suppose by the end of January 9, 2002. The futures price has dropped from Rs. 5,000 to Rs. 4,900. The investor has a loss of 20 × 100 or Rs. 2,000. This is because of January 2002, gold which he contracted at Rs. 5,000, cannot be sold for Rs. 4,900. The balance in the marginale would be reduced from Rs. 2,000 to Rs. 48,000. Similarly, if the price of January 2002 gold rose to 5100 by the end of first day, the balance in the margin account would be increased from Rs. 2,000 to Rs. 52,000. A trade is first marked to marketd at the close of the day on which it takes place. It is thus marked to market at the close trading on each subsequent day.

The investor is entitled to withdraw any balance in the margin account in excess of the initial margin. The balance in the margin account never becomes negative. If the balance in the margin account falls below the maintenance margin, the investor receives a margin call and is required to adjust the initial margin level the next day.

### *Kinds of Futures*

The following are the different kinds of futures:

(a) Commodity Futures.
(b) Financial Futures.

**(a) Commodity futures** deals with trading in all domestic commodities future market. The value of commodity future generally depends upon the price movements of the market.

(b) **Financial futures** are the futures that are based on a financial investment or a financial index. Financial futures can be classified as:

1. Interest rate futures.
2. Currency futures.
3. Stock index futures.

1. ***Interest rate futures*** are written on the basis of interest rates or price indices of fixed interest securities.
2. ***Currency futures*** are both commercial and non-commercial users.
3. ***Stock index futures*** Stock index future contract means it is a contract based on stock indices. Stock index future is a speculation tool. It is an inexpensive and highly liquid asset in the market. It is a tool for expressing an opinion about the general situation of the market. These contracts are more useful to portfolio managers to alter the Risk-Return distribution in their stock portfolios. The institutional investors can enter the market immediately, by purchasing, the stock index contracts. A stock index futures contract is an obligation to deliver on the settlement date an amount of cash. No physical delivery of stocks is made to the buyers. In order to ensure that sufficient funds are available for the settlement; both buyers and sellers are required to put up a good faith deposit or margin. The margin is not down payment, and neither loans nor margin interests are involved. The contract is marked to the market daily and additional cash margin may be required depending upon the market movements. It is easy to see that the higher leverage afforded in the stock index futures market is an essential attractions to both buyers and sellers. For example, "Assume a contract is struck at 600 and the index moves up as high as 675 and down as low, 560 prior to expiration. During this time, funds are being debited and credited each day from buyer to seller". In stock index futures contract, everyday at the end of each trading session, each customer's position is marked to the latest settlement prices. Each customers account is credited/debited according to the price changes. If there is any change, the customer has to adjust the cash. Sometimes the customer account shows any excess amount, that amount

may be withdrawn by the customers. For example, we are dealing with a Sensex of 1800 contract, the original margin is Rs. 20,000 and the maintenance margin is Rs. 10,000. Assume, the contract is struck up with Sensex at 1800. The next day Sensex moves up to 1810. The buyer receives Rs. 18,000 from the seller's margin account [(1810 – 1800) × 1800] using the contract, if the Sensex from 1800 moves to 1780, the buyers owes the seller Rs. 36,000 [1800 – 1780] × 1800.

**Valuation of Stock Index Futures**

The valuation of the stock of index futures is very simple and easy. It can be explained with simple example: An investor wants to hold the BSE Sensex Scrip-30 for the next year. Then he collects dividends, and his principal value will increase up or down with the index. At some price for the futures index, the investor can get exactly the same return by investing in the Treasury bills and purchase a contract for future delivery of the index.

Return on index = Index price at expirations – Current index price + Dividends

$$= I_E - I_B + D$$

$I_E$ = Index price at expiration
$I_B$ = Current index price
D = Dividends

$$\text{Return on futures} = \frac{\text{Futures price}}{\text{Expration}} - \text{Current futures price} + \text{Interest}$$

$$= F_E - F_B + D$$

$F_E$ = Future price at expiration
$F_B$ = Current Future price
$R_F$ = Interest

Therefore, the following formula expresses the value of stock index future:

$$= F_B - F_B + (R_P + D)$$

$F_B$ = Current future price
$I_B$ = Current index price
$R_f$ = Interest
D = Dividend

The price of the index should be equal to the price of the futures at expiration.

## Stock Index Arbitrage

Arbitrage means buying and selling of a commodity in two different markets in order to get the profit from the price fluctuations from the two markets. **For example**, if the price of the gold in Mumbai is Rs. 5,500 per 10 gram and the same in Chennai is Rs. 5,600, therefore an opportunity exists to buy gold in Mumbai and sell in Chennai to earn a profit of Rs. 100 per 10 grams. Arbitrage makes market more efficient. Stock index arbitrage means buying a basket of stocks and selling the futures when mis-pricing occurs. It is not risky. It requires a large amount of capital in the futures contract. The most important part of the arbitrage play comes in the pricing of those contracts. In the pricing of futures, the index dividend return and return on alternative investments should be kept in mind. Market sentiment also plays an important role in future pricing. However, every stock index arbitrager has his own factors at that time like the amount of capital available, transaction costs, the rate of return available from the arbitrage.

The following are the different kinds of securities:

**(1) Futures on fixed income securities.**

**(2) Futures on short-term fixed income securities.**

**(3) Futures on long-term securities.**

### *(1) Futures on Fixed Income Securities*

The increasing rates of interest created a new phenomenon in the capital market. Treasury bills, bond notes, other credit instruments bear a resemblance to the fluctuations. The prices traditionally fluctuate in reaction to the several changes in many factors, i.e., war, depression, weather, inflation etc. Fixed income futures have become an integral part of financing and investment and transformed the whole process of interest rate risk management. The fixed income futures are used for increasing and reducing exposures to the risk of the changing interest rates.

### *(2) Futures on Short-Term Fixed Income Securities*

Treasury bills, certificates of deposit and Euro dollar futures include short-term fixed income futures. The treasury bill futures the CD's are not yet developed in India. The treasury bills are traded on a discount basis with the holder receiving the difference of the price paid and selling price or face value, as interest. The annual discount rate and yield a fixed income securities future can be calculated as follows:

$$\text{Annual Discount Rate} = \frac{(\text{Face Value} - \text{Price})}{\text{Face Value}} \Big/ \frac{\text{No. of days to maturity}}{360}$$

The formula for the yield

$$= \frac{(\text{Face Value} - \text{Price})}{\text{Price}} \Big/ \frac{\text{No. of days to maturity}}{365}$$

Treasury bill futures trading is done in terms of prices and yields. The use of prices allows the future to be put as the same price. Short-term rates would be motivated to participate in the treasury bills future market. The major users of the markets are banks, brokerage houses, and securities dealers. There are different types of treasury bill futures transactions. They are arbitrage, speculation or hedging activity. Dealing with the Government securities involves constantly buying and selling large amount of treasury bills. Dealers are in a position to analyse the treasury bills futures prices.

### *(3) Futures on Long-Term Securities*

These futures contracts are very popular in America. But in India, they are to be developed. Presently these contracts call for delivery of securities either issued or guaranteed by the Government. The following are the different types of securities under this category:

1. Treasury bond.
2. 10 years treasury note.
3. 5 years treasury note.
4. 91 days treasury bill.
5. Euro dollar time deposit.

### *Characteristics of the Long-Term Securities*

(1) Securities have the face value of $1,00,000.
(2) The maturity period will be more than 15 years.
(3) Bond futures markets are based on 8 per cent coupon rate.
(4) These securities markets have a very liquid market.
(5) Conversion factors adjusts the future price.
(6) Conversion factors are equal to the ratio of the price of a deliverable bond.
(7) The actual amount a future is based on the following formula:

$$\text{Actual amount} = \$1{,}00{,}000 \times \text{Settlement price of futures} \times \text{Conversion factor} + \text{Accrued Interest}$$

## Options

An option is a contract which involves the right to buy or sell the securities at the specified prices within a stated time. The option is a device for the gains from speculation. The option dealings are prohibited under the Securities Contract Regulation Act of 1956, "An option is a type of contract between two parties". The option is a derivative security used for the purpose of risk management in the investment market based on some security. The largest option period is 9 months but it can be for a shorter period of 30 to 90 days. The contract unit can be of 100 shares or stocks. The minimum trading unit can be fixed at 100 contracts. The options are created and traded by the investors. The companies which issue assets underlying them have responsibility in respect of their creation.

### *Characteristics of Options*

The following are the main characteristics of the options:

(1) The option holders do not receive any dividend or interest.
(2) The options yield only capital gains.
(3) The option holder can enjoy a tax advantage.
(4) Options are traded on O.I.C. in all recognised stock exchanges.
(5) The option holders can control their rights on underlying assets.
(6) An option creates the possibility of gaining a windfall profit.

(7) The option holder can enjoy a much wider risk-return combinations.
(8) Options can reduce the total portfolio transaction costs.
(9) Options enable the investors to gain a better returns with a limited amount of investment.

In options trading, exercise date means, the date on which the buyer actually exercises the option. It is the price at which the option holder can buy or sell the underlying asset. Exercise price is also called as "striking price". The options are mainly classified as:

(a) Call option.
(b) Put option.

*(a) Call Option*

A call option is the right to buy shares under a negotiable contract. It does not carry any obligation. The buyers have the right to receive the delivery of assets known as "call option".

*(b) Put Option*

In this option, the owner has the right to sell the underlying asset under a negotiable contract. The put option holder has the right to receive the payment by surrendering the asset.

The writer of an option is a stock broker member or a security dealer. The buyer of an option pays the price depending on the risk of the underlying security and he as an investor or a dealer or trades.

***Kinds of Options***

There are a wide variety of options available in the market. They are:

(a) commodity option,
(b) currency option,
(c) stock option,
(d) stock index option.

*(a) Commodity Option*

Commodity option means, it enables the farmers to trade as general commodities market movements. The trading is based upon the consumption goods. The price movement of the commodities will reflect in the worth of commodity option.

*(b) Currency Option*

The recent addition to the options markets has been the foreign currency exchange or currency options. It acts as a vehicle to protect against the adverse exchange rate fluctuations. They are contracts that confer the right to buy or sell the foreign currency at a specified price on some future date. The latest innovation in this context is the future options—a combination of future and options.

*(c) Stock Option*

A complex variety of options exist in the market stock option is one of the options. The stock options may be an individual stocks or on various stock price indices. The stock option requires the actual delivery of stock upon exercise. The stock option is costly to some extent when compared with the stock index option. It mostly involves the individual stock or group.

*(d) Stock Index Option*

Stock index option means, it enables the investors to trade on general stock market movements. The stock prices movement reflects in the stock index option prices. In stock index option the transactions are settled by the payment of cash. The amount of cash settlement is equal to the difference between the closing price of the index option price and the strike price of the options. The investment strategies with the index options are similar to those of individual stock options.

***Features of Option***

1. The option is exercisable only by the owner, namely the buyers of the option.
2. The owner has a limited liability.

3. The owners of the options have no voting rights and dividend rights.
4. The options have high degree of risk to the option writers.
5. The options involve buying counter positions by the option sellers.
6. Flexibility in investors needs.
7. No certificates are issued by the Company.
8. Options are popular because they allow the buyer profits from favourable movements in exchange rate.

A wide variety of options exist in the market. The following are the types of options:

(a) call option,
(b) put option,
(c) writing option,
(d) spread option,
(e) gale option, and
(f) double options.

*(a) Call Option*

A call option is the right to buy shares under a negotiable contract and it does not carry any obligator.

*(b) Put Option*

In the put option the owner has the right to sell the under laying asset under a negotiable contract.

*(c) Writing Option*

Options in writing are of two kinds:

1. covered option,
2. uncovered option.

Covered option means it is written against an owned stock position. Uncovered option may be written without owning the securities.

*(d) Spread Option*

It is a process which involves the simultaneous purchase and sale of different options of the same security. Spread options may be of two kinds:

(i) Vertical spread.
(ii) Horizontal spread.

***Vertical spread*** means purchase of two options with the same expiry date but with different striking prices.

***Horizontal spread*** means the striking price is the same but the expiry dates are different.

Options may be purchased or sold by placing an order with a broker. An innovative development eliminates the minating physical instrument. In option dealing, no certificate is issued. This facilitates the prompt settlement of transactions. In the absence of a certificate each transaction and associated money activities must be handled as a book keeping entry.

The option prices are the result of the interaction of a number of different forces. There are six fundamental factors which influence the value of an option:

(a) Current stock price (S).
(b) Striking price (K).
(c) Time to expiration (t).
(d) Stock volatility (stock prices fluctuation).
(e) Rates of interest.
(f) Cash dividends.

The striking price depends upon the current stock price and the expiration date. The higher the stock price, the higher the call value. The stock volatility is an important determinant in value of an option. If the volatility is higher in the stock market, then the stock will do either very well or very poorly. Therefore, the higher the volatility over the life time of a call, the higher its value relative to the stock. Another important determinant factor is "Interest Rates". The higher the interest rate, the lower the value of the striking price. A higher interest rate will have the same influence as a lower striking price. Higher interest rates end to imply higher call prices. Cash dividends also plays an important factor in the valuation of an option. The higher the cash dividend prior to the expiration, the higher the value of a put.

Option strategies may be for hedging, speculation or spreading purpose. Hedging in option involves the attempts to control the risk. Speculation in option requires the purchase or the sale of an option without any position in the underlying stock. Spreading requires the simultaneous purchase of one option and the sale of another. Spreading may be categorised as:

(a) bullish spread,
(b) bearish spread.

***Bullish spread*** involves in buying the more expensive option and selling the cheaper option. The spread will show a profit if the prices rise. The same reverse direction is applied to ***bearish spread***. In bearish spread, a profit is anticipated if the stock price declines. In the valuation of an option "The Black-Scholes model" is very important. Black and Scholes have developed a device which assumes that the share returns are normally distributed. Let us examine how the Black-Scholes model is useful in the valuation of an option.

*Black-Scholes Model*

Black and Scholes developed a formula for determining the value of an option. The model is very popular in the market and it is useful to the option holder to know the over price or under price of an asset. The model provides an excellent analysis in the valuation of a debt relation to the equity the equilibrium value of an option can be determined by the following assumptions:

(1) There is no dividend payment on shares.
(2) There is no interruption in market operations.
(3) There are no transaction costs.
(4) There are no taxes.
(5) The share prices are not volatile position.
(6) The interest rates are constant.
(7) The option is to be of European type.

The Black-Scholes formula is used for estimating the fair value of a call option:

$$V_c = P_s[Nd_1] - \frac{P_x}{e(RF)(T)}[Nd_2]$$

$$d_1 = \frac{I_n\left[\frac{P_s}{P_x}\right] + T\left[RF + \frac{\sigma^2}{2}\right]}{\sigma\sqrt{T}}$$

$$d_2 = \frac{I_n\left[\frac{P_s}{P_x}\right] + T\left[RF - \frac{\sigma^2}{2}\right]}{\sigma\sqrt{T}}$$

$$= d_1 - \sigma\sqrt{T}$$

$P_s$ = The exercise price of the cell.
e = 2.7183.
RF = Compound annual risk free rate.
$\sigma$ = The standard deviation of the continuously compounded annual rate of return on the share.
$P_s$ = The current price of the share.
$I_n$ = The natural log of the bracket number.
T = The time remaining to expiration on annual basis.
$Nd_1$, $Nd_2$ = The value of the cumulative normal distribution at $d_1$ and $d_2$.

After taking the dividends into consideration, the formula (Block-Scholes) should be as follows:

$$P_s' = P_s - \sum_{t=1}^{T} Dt/e^{RF \times t}$$

$P_s$ = The current price of the share.
$P_s'$ = Adjusted stock price.
$D_1$ = Declared/known cash dividend to be paid on day *t* from now.

## The Valuation of an European Model

The valuation of an European Model is as follows by incorporating the Black-Scholes call price

$$P_P = -P_s \, N - d_1 + \frac{P_x}{e^{RF \times T}} N - d_2 .$$

The following are the important factors in the portfolio analysis in relation to the Black-Scholes call price:

1. Delta.
2. Theta.
3. Gamma.
4. Vega.
5. Rho.

Deltas are the important by products of the Black-Scholes Models. Deltas provide more useful information to the investors who use options in the portfolios. Delta means a change in option premium expected from a small change in the strike price. Theta is used as an option for the rate of change in the value of a portfolio as all things remain constant. Theta is always negative for an option. Gamma is useful in the portfolio of an underlying assets. It is the rate of change in the portfolios delta with respect to the price of the underlying asset. Vega is an option of portfolio, which is the rate of change in the value of the portfolios with respect to the volatility of the underlying asset. The Rho is an option of portfolio which changes the value of a portfolio according to the interest rate. The Rho measures the sensitivity of the value of a portfolio to interest rates. The overall conclusions are that the Black-Scholes Model provides an excellent analysis to actual data and it serves as a useful valuation model.

**Portfolio Insurance**

Portfolio Insurance is a device to protect the basket value of different assets. It was developed in mid-1980s as one of the most popular uses of options. If an investor holds a highly diversified portfolio, he needs some protection from the risk. The portfolio insurance is a strategy that provides an alter to the amount of risk.

The three important factors in the portfolio insurance are:

(a) loss is restricted to a prescribed extent,
(b) the ratio of return on insured portfolio and uninsured portfolio,
(c) The amount of investments of portfolios are restricted to market index.

The portfolio insurance can be applied to two portfolios. The first portfolio may be assumed as the safe to the level of protection desired. This protection level is called as the floor and is the lowest value can have. The second portfolio having the difference between the total value of the portfolio and the floor is generally called as portfolio custion. The assets of this portfolio consists of risky assets. The actual amount of investment between risky and risk free assets is determined by changing market fluctuations. A change in the market fluctuations offers the best opportunities to show the dynamic nature of portfolio insurance, we can expect that the rise and fall of the market takes over a time gap enough for the investors to rebalance the position.

**Definition of Swaps**

According to A.K. Seth, "A swap is an agreement between two or more people of parties to exchange sets of cash flows over a period in future".

Swaps are agreements between two parties to exchange assets at pre-determined intervals. Swaps are generally customised transactions. The Swaps are innovative financing which reduces borrowing costs, and to increase control over interest rate risk and forex exposure. The Swap include both spot and forward transactions in a single agreement. Swaps are at the centre of the global financial revolution. Swaps are useful in avoiding the problem of unfavourable fluctuations in forex market. The corporates, commercial banks, institutional investors, individual investors are now using the Swaps more frequently. The following factors have been influed for the growth of swap market in India.

(a) Deregulation of financial policies.
(b) Growing global financial integration.
(c) Increasing volatility of interest and exchange rates.

The Swaps are associated with equity indices and physical commodities like oil and oil products. Swaps are concerned with exchange rates or interest rates. Swaps can penetrate savings in perfectly at free markets. Financial swaps are revolutionary especially for portfolio management. A swap which is coupled with an existing asset or liability can radically modify effective risk and return. Swaps have had a major macro economic impact forging the linkage between the Euro and domestic markets. The following are the various kinds of swaps available at present in the market:

1. Short date swaps.
2. Syndicated swaps.
3. Hi-tech swaps.
4. Draw down swaps.
5. Puttable swaps.
6. Extendible swaps.
7. Collateralised swaps.
8. Cross currency interest rate swap.
9. Amortising swaps.
10. Options on swaps.
11. Variable principle swap.
12. Non-US bank swaps.
13. Dollar swap.
14. Floating rate swaps.

**Short date swaps** means where the floating and fixed rates are of less than two years. The corporate sector finds its attractive to do a swap out of one month. **Syndicated swaps** means arrangement of swaps in a large way at a competitive environment. **Hi-tech swaps** means, they can give enormous value and flexibility in exposure, tax and earnings management. **Draw down swaps** means, it has planned under a pre-committed floating rate finance system. The swap mainly depends upon a completion of a project. **Puttable swap** requires to sell a swap in 3 years. **Extendible swap** is meant for the swap which is for 3 years it may be extendible to 5 years. **Collateralised swaps** will depend upon the major credit risks in stock market. **Cross currency** interest rate swaps combines all aspects of both currency and interest rate swaps. **Amortising swaps** eliminates the potential exposure of foreign interest rates and currency rise. **Options on swaps** are traded in a high uncertainity environment and in high volatile market. They are valuable and expensive. **Variable principle swaps** are tailored for the specific asset or liability of the counter party. **Non-US Bank swaps** deals with mainly of interest to non-US banks in managing their dollar books. **Dollar swaps** are ranging from two years to 15 years.

### Warrants

Warrant means a corporate created options to purchase a stated number of common shares at a specified price within a specified time. Warrants are attached to bonds/debentures and equity issues. Warrants generally have long-term maturities. Warrants help companies in raising fresh capital. Warrants can be detached and traded separately. The maturity period of warrants is 3 to 10 years. Perpetual warrants are available in abroad. Warrants can be traded on the exchanges or over the counters. Warrants are similar to call options with some differences. Warrants are issued by companies and options are created by investors. Warrants are issued for long-term basis but options expires to nine months. Options are standardised but warrants are not.

A warrant holder has no equity rights in the firm. He does not receive dividends and does not have voting rights. Warrants are issued with ratio determined both company shares as one warrant per one share. The difference between the actual price of a warrant and its minimum value is called as "premium". The warrant value depends upon the stock potential for rising the prices. A high dividend pay out may also have an adverse effect on the price of a warrant. Many investors purchase the warrants for speculative purpose only. Warrant market is a gambler's market. Warrants provide benefits both to the

(A) Corporate sector,
(B) Advantages to the investors,

### *(A) Corporate Sector*

The following are the benefits to corporate sectors:

1. Warrants facilitate to raise funds to the corporate sector.
2. There is no obligation to pay interest and repayment of principal.
3. Issues of warrants do not have flotation costs.

### *(B) Advantages to the Investors*

The following are the advantages to the investors:

(a) Low investment.
(b) Liquidity.
(c) Capital gains opportunity.

The following formula can be used to value the warrants:

$$P_w = f(P_o \cdot T_n \cdot P_e \cdot D_i \cdot F_e)$$

$P_w$ = market price of the warrant.
$P_o$ = option price of the equity price.
$P_e$ = current price of the equity share.
$T_n$ = duration of the issue.
$D_i$ = the ratio between shares at outstanding and warrants.
$F_e$ = the equity share price.

$$V = (P_c - P_o)N$$

V = the value of a warrant.
$P_c$ = current price of the equity share.
$P_o$ = option price of the equity share.
N = No. of shares may be purchased with one warrant.

**Convertible Debentures**

Convertible debentures are more popular. Because there are a hybrid securities. The debentures which may be converted into equity shares after a fixed date of time are called as convertible debentures. Until this period the convertible carriers an interest rate as usual. The investments are more attractive as compared to fixed deposits. Convertible debentures combines high rate of return with the profitability of capital appreciation and the liquidity of shares. The main features of convertible debentures are presented below:

**Salient Features**

(1) Conversion price.
(2) Conversion ratio.
(3) Quantum of conversion.
(4) Convertible value.
(5) Investment value.
(6) Timing of conversion.
(7) Premium.
(8) Market price.

***(1) Conversion Price***

The debentures are converted into equity shares at the end of a specific period. The ratio at which the convertible debentures are exchanged for equity shares is known as conversion price. Conversion ratio is calculated by dividing the face of a convertible debenture by its conversion price. For example, if the face value of a convertible debenture is Rs.100 and it is convertible into 2 equity shares of Rs. 50 each, the conversion price is Rs. 50 and the conversion ratio is 2. The face value of equity is Rs.10 and the remaining Rs. 40 is the premium. The debenture may be fully converted or partly be converted. It depends upon the terms of issue of debenture.

***(2) Conversion Ratio***

The conversion ratio means the number of equity shares are issued for each convertible bond. For example, if a company made a public issue of 15 per cent convertible bonds of Rs. 350 each for cash at par. Each bond face value is Rs. 350 and had a conversion price of Rs. 175 the conversion ratio is 2.

***(3) Quantum of Conversion***

The quantum amount of conversion will be based on same percentage of the face value of the debenture. The capital amount will be increased after the conversion amount transferred to capital account.

***(4) Convertible Value***

The conversion value is based on the right to receive equity. The convertible value of a debenture depends upon the conversion ratio and the market price of the share.

*Formula for conversion*

$$\text{Conversion ratio} = \frac{\text{Issue price}}{\text{Conversion price}}$$

***(5) Investment Value (a debenture)***

The value of debenture is influenced by two factors, such as debenture value and the potential of the equity shares if converted. The debenture value depends upon two components, the investment value and the conversion value. The investment value is the market price based on yield to maturity. Investment value can be assessed with a fair accurate by a competent security analyst. The potential earnings of a company depends upon market environment.

### *(6) Timing of Conversion*

The period during which the conversion option is exercisable is called as "timing of conversion". This period may vary from one year to five years. It is better than the timing of larger period conversion. The company can enjoy the benefits of "pre-tax and earnings dilution" during the larger period of timing of conversion.

### *(7) Premium*

If the market price of the convertible security is higher than its conversion value it is called as "premium". Some of the investors are risk averse. They can avoid the risk by purchasing a convertible debentures/bonds. Generally a bond will be at a premium over bond value. The amount of premium depends upon the market value and conversion value. But the amount of premium can vary from issue to issue. The following factors may influence the premium:

(a) lower transaction costs on convertible bonds,
(b) the amount of dividend,
(c) the duration of convertible bonds, and
(d) PFI are restricted to buy equity directly.

### *(8) Market Price*

Market price of a convertible bond depends upon two components, conversion value and investment value. The convertible bond is the combination of bond and willing to buy a company's equity shares. In the stock market, if the value share rises, then the value of convertible automatically rises. Even the value of equity share falls, the price of the conversion will not fall.

## Classification of Debentures

The convertibility debentures may be classified into three categories:

(1) Fully Convertible Debentures (FCD's).

(2) Non-Convertible Debentures (NCD's).
(3) Partly Convertible Debentures (PCD's).

Fully convertible debentures are the debentures which are converted into equity shares of the company on the expiry of specific period. Convertible debentures may or may not carry any interest. According to the SEBI guidelines, the conversion is to be made at (or) after 18 months from the date of allotment but before 36 months. The conversion is optional on the part of the debenture holders.

Non-convertible debentures do not confer any option on the holder to convert the debentures into equity shares. NCD's are redeemed at the expiry of a specific period. The debentures which never convertible called as NCD.

Partly convertible debentures means, the debentures for which the sum of the portion will be converted into equity share and the remaining portion will be lying as a debt in the company, at a specified date. But the debt portion will be redeemed at the expiry of certain period. The conversion should take place at or after 18 months. The conversion is optional at the discretion of debenture holders.

**Advantages of CD's to the Corporate Sector**

The following are the advantages to the corporate sector by issuing the convertible debentures:

1. Tax benefits will be available to the Company.
2. The companies are able to reduce its dependence on FIs and banks.
3. Funds are available at little cost.
4. Flexibility in maintenance of debt equity ratio.
5. There may be steady increase in capital after each conversion.
6. FCD's/PCD's became more popular at present.
7. These instruments have the quick mobilisation power.

**Advantages of CD's to the Investors**

The following are the advantages to the investors if they purchase the convertible debentures:

(1) The investors will get a fixed return till conversion.

(2) The debentures are listed in stock exchanges and enjoy a fair amount of liquidity.
(3) The investors will get 100 per cent security, because they are fully secured.
(4) On conversion, the investors can expect a hand some capital appreciation.

**Objectives of Convertible Debentures**

Convertible debentures are the best devices to get the utmost satisfaction of the shareholders by the Finance Manager of the Company. It should be issued by the companies when the actual pressure on funds requirement of the firm. The objectives of CD's are presented below:

(1) A gradual dilution of EPS may be applied through CD's.
(2) It is a tool of financing long-term assets.
(3) CD's are attractive during periods of dull market conditions.
(4) CD's can attract a low underwriting commission.
(5) Banks may be willing to lend more money on CD's than equity shares.
(6) The corporate sector can issue this instrument as a life boat/ or like a parachute.
(7) The companies can enjoy the advantages of debentures upto conversion time, afterwards they derive the advantages of equity share capital.

**Credit Derivatives**

Credit derivatives were developed in the USA. It is a new financial instrument, which is developed for reducing the credit risk. These derivatives are helpful to commercial banks, finance companies, to manage credit risk. Credit derivatives are an insurance against adverse changes in the quality of borrowers. The credit derivatives have been increasing exponentially. In market, 3 types of credit derivates are available. They are called as credit swaps, credit options, credit linked notes. Credit swaps are used by the Commercial Banks. Banks can swap the payment from the some of their loans for the payments from a different institution. It is also called as a loan portfolio swap credit options means the investors can reduce the default risk by taking an insurance policy against their credit amount. A credit linked note is another type of credit derivatives. It is a combination of a regular bond and a credit option. This note assures to make regular interest payments. It also promises to pay a large amount when the bond matures. The credit derivatives cannot only reduce the credit risk but also they expose the users of the new financial risks. Credit derivatives are privately negotiated financial contracts. Credit derivatives are well developed after 1992.

The derivatives business has undergone significant structural changes over the years. The derivatives trading has increased phenomenally. Derivatives increase risk not only for their issuers but also for the whole system.

**Swaptions**

The option on swaps is known as swaptions. The swaption holder has a right to enter into the swap contracts without any obligation on or before the expiry date. In a put swaption, the holder is entitled to receive a fixed interest. In call swaption, the holder will have to pay a fixed interest. The premium will be paid for obtaining the swaption.

**RBI Policy on Derivatives**

The Reserve Bank of India has liberalised the policy on derivatives in the Act of 1996. According to the guidelines issued by the RBI, the Commercial Banks can offer the hedge instruments to the corporates. They are presented below:

(a) Authorised dealers in Forex market can offer currency swaps, cross currency options and forward rate agreements.
(b) The financial derivatives can be offered to book the overseas transactions.
(c) Options will be allowed to sold to the customers by the authorised dealers only.
(d) The authorised dealers are required to get the final approval from the RBI.
(e) Corporate bodies have to maintain and furnish the reports to the RBI within a week.

**Summary**

The new economic policy aimed at correcting the imbalances and creating a more competitive environment to improve productivity and efficiency. In the new economic environment a series of structured changes were undertaken in financial sector to achieve the objective. The financial sector reforms encourage investors to invest in the capital market. The reforms are expected to give a boost to the economy by allocating the funds for productive purpose. The Indian stock market is characterised by high price volatile. Speculation is unavoidable and it is a driving force which builds up activity and ensures sustained interest for investors. Derivatives have now become available for investment and trading. Derivatives are contracts. They are written between two parties these are easily marketable assets. Derivatives are mostly secondary market instruments. They are quite liquid and have low transaction costs. The markets for derivatives are most likely to remain narrow and shallow. Different types of derivatives are available in the market, namely futures, options, swaps, warrants, convertible bonds, debentures, swaptions, etc. Futures means an agreement to exchange a standard quantity of an asset at a specified data in the future at a pre-determined price. Future contracts are transferable. They are traded in auction markets. There are many future contracts available. These are commodity futures, financial futures, stock index futures, interest rates future and currency futures. Option is a contract which involves the right to buy or sell securities at specified prices within a stated time. Option is a device to get profits from speculation. Options can be divided into commodity option, currency option, stock option, stock index option, options in future etc. For valuation of option Black and Scholes have developed a formula. The formula provides an excellent analysis. The deltas are important by-products of Black and Scholes. Portfolio insurance is a device to protect the value of the basket of different assets. Swaps are agreements between the parties to exchange assets at pre-determined intervals. Warrant is a corporate created option. A warrant holder has no equity rights in the firm. Convertible debentures are more popular now-a-days. It is a hybrid security. Convertible debentures may be categorised as fully convertible, partly convertible and non-convertible debentures. Credit derivatives were developed in USA. These are developed for reducing credit risk. Credit swaps are used by Commercial Banks.

Credit option will adjust the risk by insurance method. The options on swaps known as swaptions.

## Questions

### *Short Questions*

1. Explain the concept of Derivatives?
2. What are the advantages of derivatives market?
3. What do you mean by Futures?
4. Explain the meaning of Ready Delivery Contract?
5. What is forward contract?
6. Explain the concept of stock index future.
7. What are the characteristics of futures in long-term securities?
8. Explain the concept of options?
9. Explain the difference between put option and call option?
10. What do you mean by Delta?
11. Explain the concept of Theta?
12. What is Gamma?
13. Explain the meaning of Vega?
14. What do you mean by portfolio insurance?
15. Explain the concept of Swaps?
16. What is warrant?
17. What do you mean by credit derivatives?

### *Essay Questions*

1. What do you mean by derivatives? How far they are useful to our capital market?
2. What do you mean by option? Explain different kinds of options?
3. What is Black and Scholes theory? How is it useful?
4. What are the differences between hedging and portfolio insurance?
5. Explain the importance of futures.
6. What are convertible debentures? Explain the various features of them.
7. Explain the process of valuation of stock index futures.

8. What are the fundamental factors which influence the option price?
9. What do you mean by Swaps? Explain the various kinds of swaps?
10. Explain the concept of warrant? What are the advantages?
11. Explain the salient features of convertibles?

## REFERENCES

1. Derivatives—A new way to trade, *Business Today, Anniversary Issue*, 2002, p. 71.
2. Van Horne, *Fundamentals of Financial Management*, p. 691, PHI 1997.

# 6

# BOMBAY STOCK EXCHANGE (BSE)

## Introduction

The first stock exchange was set up in India under the name of **Native and Stock Brokers Association of Bombay** in 1875. It was established as a voluntary non-profit organisation. It is managed by an executive or the governing body. It is the oldest and has been recognised permanently. The other exchanges in India are renewed for every 5 years. Its business is not confined to **Mumbai** alone. There were 100 other cities in which it had set up business. It is a great surprise that the BSE membership fee in 1857 was just **Re. 1 (one rupee only)**. Now it commands at more than **Rs. 2 crores**. The BSE has introduced **online** trading system on 19.1.1995. It provides a quote derives automated trading facility to the investors.

The market indexes have always been of great importance in security analysis. People observing the stock market fluctuations through market indicators. The investors use the market index as a benchmark. The economists and statisticians also use the index to study the trend of growth patterns in the economy. The investors will use the various indexes for their analytical purpose. They also compute and compile the index numbers. The indexes are equal weighting approach or price weighted or value weighted approaches. All these methods are used in the calculation of index. The price weighted index is a simple air thematic average. The price weighted index is the concept of indexing which involves the comparison of currently computed averages with some base value. There are two forms of indexes they are **Paasche Index** and the **Laspeyres Index**. These two methods are used for determining the consumer price index. They measure the price inflation by taking the quantity as constant.

$$\text{Paasche price index} = \frac{\Sigma P_1 Q_1}{\Sigma P_0 Q_1} \times 100$$

$$\text{Laspeyres index} = \frac{\Sigma P_1Q_0}{\Sigma P_0Q_0} \times 100$$

$$\text{Fisher's ideal index} = \sqrt{\frac{\Sigma P_1Q_0}{\Sigma P_0Q_0} \times \frac{\Sigma P_1Q_1}{\Sigma P_0Q_1}} \times 100 .$$

The BSE started publishing a index number of equity prices from the **2nd January, 1986** with the base year 1978–79. It is known the BSE sensitive index. The equity shares of 30 companies have been selected on the basis of market activity with due representation to the major industries. The shares selected and the industrial group to which they belong are presented below:

**Components of Sensex**

| *S.No.* | *Name of the Company* | *Industry Group* |
|---|---|---|
| 1. | Hindusthan Lever Ltd. | FMCG |
| 2. | Reliance Industries | Synthetic Textiles |
| 3. | Infosys Technologies | Computers |
| 4. | I.T.C. | Tobacco, Hotels |
| 5. | Reliance Petroleum | Refinery |
| 6. | S.B.I. | Banking |
| 7. | HPCL | Petroleum |
| 8. | Ranbaxy | Pharmaceuticals |
| 9. | MTNL | Telecom |
| 10. | Satyam Computers | Computers |
| 11. | HCL Technology | Computers |
| 12. | Dr. Reddy Lab | Pharmaceuticals |
| 13. | Hero Honda | Automobile |
| 14. | Zee Telefilm | Entertainment |
| 15. | Cipla | Pharmaceuticals |
| 16. | Hindalco Industries | Aluminium |
| 17. | ICICI | Banking |
| 18. | Bajaj Auto | Automobiles |
| 19. | Nestle | FMCG |
| 20. | L&T | General Engineering |
| 21. | BHEL | Heavy Electricals |
| 22. | TISCO | Steel |
| 23. | Gujarath Ambuja Cements | Cements |
| 24. | TELCO | Automobiles |
| 25. | BSEC | Power |
| 26. | A.C.C. | Cement |
| 27. | Grasim Industries | Textiles |
| 28. | Glaxo Smithkline | FMCG |
| 29. | Castrol | Lubricants |
| 30. | Colgate Palmolive | FMCG |

The method of compilation of the Sensex is based on standard and poor. USA, the S&P500 is a value weighted index of 400 industrial stocks, **40** utility stocks, **20** transportation stocks and **40** financial stocks. The calculation of Sensex is computed as follows:

$$P_t = \frac{\Sigma P_{it}}{\Sigma P_{io}} \times \frac{\Sigma Q_{it}}{\Sigma Q_{io}} \times o$$

$P_{it}$ = Period of stock *i* in Period *t*;
$Q_{it}$ = Number of shares outstanding for stock *i* in Period *t*;
$P_{io}$ = Price of stock *i* in the base period *o*; and
$Q_{io}$ = Number of shares outstanding for stock in base period *o*; and the base period 1978–79 has been chosen.

The Sensex components are 30 companies from both specified and non-specified groups. The BSE has launched 13 more indices and some of these have taken some shine of the Sensex. But the index retains its gold standard reputation. The highest 6,150.69 is in intra trading on February 14, 2000. The lowest is 956.11 on January 25, 1991, but we cannot rather dwell on that.

The BSE has seen several changes. The number of companies listed on the BSE has grown from **197** in 1946 to **5,937** today. In 2000–01, the average daily volumes were **Rs. 4,775.8 crores** still the exchange has lost much of its former glory with creation of the NSE statement showing the average daily turnover.[1]

*(Rs. in crore)*

| *Year* | *Turnover (Average daily)* |
|---|---|
| 1989–90 | 134.80 |
| 1990–91 | 188.54 |
| 1991–92 | 332.50 |
| 1992–93 | 238.00 |
| 1993–94 | 387.78 |
| 1994–95 | 212.02 |
| 1995–96 | 215.79 |
| 1996–97 | 517.85 |
| 1997–98 | 851.00 |
| 1998–99 | 1283.95 |
| 1999–2000 | 2729.20 |
| 2000–2001 | 4775.77 |

**Statement Showing the Number of Companies Listed in BSE[2]**

| *Year* | *No. of Companies Listed* |
|---|---|
| 1988–89 | 2275 |
| 1989–90 | 2247 |
| 1990–91 | 2471 |
| 1991–92 | 2601 |
| 1993–Dec. | 3263 |
| 1994–Dec | 4413 |
| 1995–Dec. | 5399 |
| 1996–Dec. | 5999 |
| 1997–Dec. | 5843 |
| 1998–Dec. | 5860 |
| 1999–Dec. | 5863 |
| 2000–Dec. | 5937 |

The BSE Sensex can be compared with the NYSE Dow Jones. The Sensex movement is presented below:

**Statement Showing the Movement of Sensex[3]**

| *Year* | *Sensex Average* | *High for the Year* |
|---|---|---|
| 1986-87 | 570 | 659 |
| 1987–88 | 455 | 536 |
| 1988–89 | 613 | 719 |
| 1989–90 | 730 | 798 |
| 1990–91 | 1050 | 1559 |
| 1991–92 | 1845 | 4285 |
| 1992–93 | 2899 | 4286 |
| 1993–94 | 2895 | 4467 |
| 1994–95 | 3975 | 4631 |
| 1995–96 | 3289 | 3598 |
| 1996–97 | 3469 | 4069 |
| 1997–98 | 3812 | 4548 |
| 1998–99 | 3295 | 4281 |
| 1999–2000 | 4659 | 5934 |
| 2000–2001 | 4270 | 5542 |
| 2001– 2002 | – | 3742 |

**A Chronology of Major Stock Scams[4]**

(1) Mundhra Scandal, 1957.
(2) The Securities Scam, 1992.
(3) M.S. Shoes Scam, 1994.

(4) CRB Scam, 1997.
(5) Mehta's Second Coming, 1998.
(6) Vanishing Companies Scam, 1998.
(7) Plantations Companies Scam, 1999.
(8) Ketan Parekh Scam, 2001.

### *(1) Mundhra Scandal*

It was the media that first hinted there might be a scam involving the sale of shares to LIC. Feroz Gandhi sourced the confidential correspondence between the then Finance Minister, T.T. Krishnamachary and his Principal Finance Secretary and raised a question in Parliament on the sale of fraudulent shares to LIC by a Calcutta based Marwari businessman Haridas Mundhra. The then Prime Minister, Jawaharlal Nehru set up a one man Commission headed by Justice M.C. Chagla to investigate the matter when it became evident that there was *prima facie* case. Chagla concluded that Mundhra had sold a fictitious shares to LIC, thereby defrauding the insurance to the tune of Rs.1.25 crore. Mundhra was sentenced to 22 years in prison. The scam also forced the resignation of T.T. Krishnamachary.

### *(2) The Securities Scam, 1992*

The man who seemed to own the sobriquet big bull, and whose Toyota Lexus became the subject of reams of column in the media, leveraged a loophole in the country's banking system to Siphon funds from banks (using banker's receipts) and used the money to ramp up the price of shares. The scam was uncovered in April, 1992 and the Sensex came crashing down from a peak of 4467.32 on April 22, of that year to 3,896.90 on April, 28. It caused ripples in Parliament and the quantum of the money involved was placed in excess of Rs. 3,000 crores, but unlike Mundhra scam where Justice was swift, the judicial process related to the Mehta scam continued to drag on this day. Although the man's sudden demise on December 31, 2001, (he was 47) could change that. In a bizarre twist, a few months before Mehta's death, the CBI filed a case against his brother and him for allegedly selling the shares of their clients in their possession and later claiming that these very shares stolen from their offices when their properties wherein the court possession. Harshad Mehta also had another brush, albeit minor one, with stock market in fame, in 1998, but that's another story at the time of his death, ascribed to a cardiac arrest. Mehta had been in Jail for over 50 days over the missing shares issue. Intriguingly, one of the other people involved in scam, UTI's M.J. Pherwani also died abruptly due to a heart attack in 1992.

***(3) M.S. Shoes Scam, 1994***

Anyone who was enough in 1994 regarding the Pawan Sachdeva. For the record, it was the peak of the public issue led advertising the boom and the ads way created by the Delhi branch of Redfusion. Sachdeva, the promoter of M.S. Shoes allegedly used company funds to buy the shares (of his own company) and rig prices, prior to public issue. He is alleged to have colluded with official in the SEBI and SBI caps, which lead managed the issue, to dupe the public into investing his Rs. 699 crores public-cum-rights issue. Sachdeva was later acquitted.

***(4) CRB Scam, 1997***

Another scam forged by greed and discover through accident. Chain Roop Bhansali, a smart talking entrepreneur, created pyramid financial empire based on high cost financing. At it speaks his **Rs. 1,000 crores** financial conglomerate had in its ranks a mutual fund, a financial services company into fixed deposits, and a merchant bank. That Bhansali knew how to work the system became evident when he also managed to secure a provincial banking licence. Then his luck ran out. An executive in the SBI inadvertently discover that some interest warrants issued by Bhansali were not backed by cash. The bubble finally burst in May 1997, but by that time the investors had lost over Rs. 1,000 crores. This was among the retail scams in India and it was played out in smaller avatars, across the country especially in the south where financial services companies promised returns in excess of 20 per cent and decamped with the principal. Bhansali arrested for a few weeks and released later on bail.

***(5) Mehta's Second Coming, 1998***

The big bull returned to the bourses. This time he allegedly colluded with the promoters of **BPL, Videocon and Sterilite Industries** to rig the share prices of these companies. The inevitable collapse happened sooner that planned, Mehta orchestrated a cover up operation that included a high jinks efforts by officials of BSE to (illegally) open the trading system in the middle of the night to set things right, but the damage had been done. SEBI finally passed its ruling on the scam in 2001, banning the 3 companies concerned from tapping the market **BPL for 4 years, Videocon for 3 years and Sterilite for 2 years**. Mehta was debarred for life from dealing in securities. SEBI's order against Sterilite was later set aside Securities Appellate Tribunal (SAT) in October 2001.

### *(6) Vanishing Companies Scam, 1998*

A passing remarks heard by then Finance Minister Palaniappan Chidambaram resulted in a furore over what was a badly kept secret on Dalal Street. Chidambaram was told that 100 of companies had disappeared after raising moneys from the public. An informal scrutiny revealed that perhaps over 600 companies were missing. Chidambaram ordered a probe by SEBI. The SEBI probe conducted in May 1998 revealed that while many companies are not traded on the bourses at least 80 companies that had raised **Rs. 330.78 crores** were simply missing. Later that year, the Department of Company Affairs (DCA) was asked to probe and penalise these companies. DCA still investigating. Investigations continue to this day.

### *(7) Plantations Companies Scam, 1999*

It was an innovative a swindle as any effected in the world. Savvy entrepreneurs convinced gullible investors that given the right irrigation and fertiliser inputs, teak, strawberrises and anything else that could be grown would grow anywhere in the country. The promoters would afford to collect the money from the investors and not worry about retribution (Returns, for that matter). For, plantation companies fell under the purview of neither SEBI nor RBI. Indeed they did not even home under scope of the DCA by the time the Government decided to change things in 1999, enough investors had been gulled 653 companies between them, had raised **Rs. 2,563 crores** from investors. To date, not many investors have got their principals back, just another affirmation of the old saying about money not growing on trees.

### *(8) Ketan Parekh Scam, 2001*

Ketan Parekh *modus operandi* was not very different from Harshad Mehta. If Mehta used bankers receipts then Parekh used pay to others ramp up the prices of his favourite scrips (The K-10). Apart from money from the banking system Parekh also re-routed money from corporates like **HFCL (Rs. 425 crores), Zee (Rs. 340 crores)** to good effect. He was caught when pay orders issued by Madhavpura Mercantile Bank bounced. Although the total amount involved in the scam was just **Rs. 137 crores**, the impact was far greater. Apparently when a bear cartle sensed Parekh was in trouble, it stepped in and leveraged a dip in the NASDAQ to beat down stop prices. The resultant slump in the markets soon after Finance Minister Yashwant Sinha presented what he considered his best budget ever. Under pressure from the Government, SEBI investigated the scam and heads began to roll. Among them the entire management team of BSE, including its present Anand Rathi, C.S.F.B., First Global, in an indirect connection P.S. Subramaniyam, the Chairman of UTI. Evidently for the 18 months that P. Subramaniyam, Chairman of UTI. The trust had mirrored the actions of the bull capital? The result? When the market tanked, so did the NAV of its wholly cow, the U.S. 64.

## The History of Stock Markets in India[5]

A brief history of the rise of equity trading in India are presented below:

1. **July 9, 1875:** Native brokers from the Native Share and Stock Brokers Association in Mumbai. Membership fee is Re. 1/- and there are 318 members on the list.
2. **1899:** Bombay Stock Exchange acquires own premises.
3. **1921:** Clearing houses are established for settlement of trades as volumes increase.
4. **1923:** K.R.P. Shroff becomes the Honorary President of Bombay Stock Exchange.
5. **1925:** Bombay Securities Contract Act comes into force.
6. **1.12.1939:** Stock exchange building is acquired.
7. **1943:** Forward trading banned till 1946. Only ready to delivery and hand delivery contracts permitted.
8. **1956:** Securities Contract Regulation Act, drafted on the lines of BSCCA, comes into force.
9. **1957:** BSE becomes the first exchange in India to get permanent recognition.
10. **1964:** U.T.I. is born.

11. **1.4.1966:** K.R.P. Shroff retires and Shri Pheroze J. Jeejebhoy becomes Chairman.
12. **June 29, 1969:** Morarji Desai bans forward trading.
13. **1973:** Construction of P.J. Towers named after late Pheroze Jamshedji Jeejebhoy starts.
14. **2.1.1986:** BSE Sensex launched as the first stock market index with 1978–79 as the base year.
15. **November 1987:** SBI Mutual Fund launches Magnum regular income scheme.
16. **April 1988:** Securities and Exchange Board of India set up.
17. **January 1992:** SEBI given statutory powers.
18. **May 1992:** Harshad Mehta securities scam breaks.
19. **May 27, 1992:** Reliance is the first Indian company to make a GDR issue.
20. **May 30, 1992:** The Capital Issues Control Act, 1947 is repeated.
21. **September 1992:** FIIs are permitted to invest in Indian securities market.
22. **November 1992:** National Stock Exchange is born.
23. **November 1992:** Manmohan Singh, the then Finance Minister inaugurates OTCEI.
24. **October 30, 1993:** The first private sector mutual fund **Kothari Pioneer Mutual Fund** begins operations.
25. **1993:** SEBI bans badla trading on BSE.
26. **June 1994:** NSE commences operations in wholesale debt market segment.
27. **November 1994:** Capital market segment of NSE goes on stream trading in screen based for the first time in India.
28. **March 1995:** BSE Online Trading System **(BOLT)** replaces open outcry system.
29. **June 1995:** NSCCL India's first clearing corporation is set up.
30. **October 1995:** NSE overtakes the BSE as the largest stock exchange is terms of volume of trading.
31. **April 1996:** National Index for fifty shares is born.
32. **November 1996:** The National Securities Depository is created.
33. **February 1997:** SEBI releases norms for takeovers and acquisitions.

34. **May 1997:** BSE introduces screen based trading.
35. **November 1998:** SEBI gives recognition to integrated stock exchanges founded by 16 regional stock exchanges.
36. **February 1999:** Launch of automated lending and borrowing mechanism on NSE.
37. **March 11, 1999:** Infosys Technologies in the first company to list on NASDAQ through a public offering of American Depository Receipts.
38. **March 22, 1999:** Central Depository Services (India) promoted by BSE commences operations.
39. **September 1999:** ICICI is the first Indian Company to list on NYSE.
40. **October 11, 1999:** For the first time in BSE's history the Sensex closed above 5000 mark at 5031.78.
41. **January 2000:** BSE creates Z category of scrips in addition to A, $B_1$ and $B_2$ comprising scrips that breached or failed to comply with the list agreement.
42. **February 2000:** Internet trading commences on NSE on February 21, NSE records peak market capitalisation of **Rs. 1,194.282 crores**. On February 14, 2000, BSE Sensex hits an all time high off 6,150.
43. **April 10, 2000:** The Sensex is revamped to include Dr. Reddy's Lab., Reliance Petroleum, Satyam Computers, Zee Telefilms, replacing Indian Hotels, Tata Chemicals, Tata Power and IDBI.
44. **June, 2000:** BSE and NSE introduces derivative trading in the form of Index futures.
45. **July 9, 2000:** BSE turns 125 years.
46. **October 19, 2000:** Wipro lists on the NYSE.
47. **January 22, 2001:** Borrowing and Lending securities scheme launched on BSE to promote securities and Lending and borrowing activities.
48. **March 2001:** Ketan Parekh scam breaks. SEBI suspense all the brokers, directors of the BSE in relation to KP Scam on March 13.
49. **May 2001:** BSE advices compulsory Demat for B2 scrips.
50. **June 2001:** Index options start trading on NSE.
51. **July 2001:** A SEBI directive banks carry forward all major securities are moved to rolling settlement. Options of individual scrips start trading on NSE.

52. **Nov. 9, 2001:** BSE and NSE launch futures in individual stocks.

**REFERENCES**

1. Roshini Jayakar, BSE Then and Now: *B.T. Anniversary Issue*, 2000, p. 63.
2. *Ibid.*
3. Roshini Jayakar, The Sensex, *B.T. Anniversary Issue*, 2002, p. 69.
4. *Business Today, Anniversary Issue*, p. 66, 2000.
5. *Ibid.*, p. 62, 2002.

# 7

# OVER THE COUNTER EXCHANGE OF INDIA (OTC)

## Introduction

Over the Counter Exchange of India was established to fulfil the needs of the small companies. There is a strong need for the fully computerised, ringles, scripless, electronic stock exchange. The trading and settlement standards are in tune with the global standards that provide capital market access to the small companies. It provides these services to the investors and to the companies. The OCT is known as exchange without **floors and rings**. It is a market place where the transactions are executed by bids and offers through the computer device.

The OTC was set up in 1989 as a company, and registered under Section 25 of the Companies Act. The **Securities Contract Regulation Act, Section 4** recognises the OTC as a stock exchange. It is promoted by **UTI, ICICI, IFCI, LIC, GIC** SBI capital markets, IDBI, Can Bank the financial services.

The OTC is floor less exchange. All the activities are computerised. It allows the designated dealers to operate through their computers. All the quotations and transactions are recorded and processed in the OTC exchange. The dealers are scattered throughout the country and have the access to the central computers. The dealers are able to know the best bids and offers of the market makers in respect of each scrip. The interested dealer can place his order through the computer. The important documents in the OTC activities are—

(a) Counter Receipt.
(b) Sales Confirmation Slip.

If the deal is made, a counter receipt will be handed over to the buyer. The buyer should kept the CR carefully because it is a tradeable document. It is just like a share certificate. **The Sales Confirmation Slip** will be passed on to the seller if the deal materialises. The seller should preserve the certificate until the payment is made. The OTC allows only the securities of the lested companies. The listing agreement will be made on the basis of the following norms:

1. Companies with issued capital between **Rs. 30 lakhs to Rs. 25 crores.**
2. Companies which have already listed their securities on the stock exchanges are not eligible for listing in the OTC.
3. Closely held companies interested in listing.
4. Venture capital companies (20% shall be issued to the public).
5. NBFCs with paid up capital of **Rs.1 crore** are eligible for listing in the OTC.
6. The companies which are not listed in any other stock exchanges provided—
   (a) the Company should offer to the public at least **40 per cent** of the issued equity or Rs. 20 lakhs whichever is **higher** for the companies between the ranges **Rs. 30 lakh to Rs. 3 crores.**
   (b) for issues between Rs. 3 crore to Rs. 25 crores, the public offer should be 60 per cent.
   (c) the Company does not carry on the business of investment leasing, finance, hire purchase or amusement parks.

The promoters of the OTC are called as **Sponsor Members**. The sponsor members are entitled to make the listing agreements with the interested companies. They have full authority to admit a company for listing. The sponsor members will evaluate the companies performance before admitting a company. The sponsors will closely monitor the technological and financial viability of the proposed company. They also ensure that all the legal formalities have been compiled with. Finally, they will value the shares of the company in compliance the SEBI guidelines for the issue successfully. The sponsor member should act as market makes for at least 3 years and also to appoint an additional market makes for that scrip for a period of at least one year. Further SEBI relaxed the norms for listing on the OTC. Dave Committee have been appointed to review the works of the OTC to make recommendations.

# 8

# BROKERS

## Introduction

The most important financial intermediaries are the stock brokers. They play a very important role either in New Issue Market or Secondary Market. In the NIM, it is highly impossible to mobilise the share capital in Public Issues. Brokers will be constantly in touch with the investors. The investors are the regular customers to the brokers. In India **90 per cent** of the decisions are taken by the Investors on the advice of the brokers. The brokers influence the investors in buying and selling of the securities. In the Secondary Market, all the transactions will be executed through the brokers only. The investors are not allowed to enter into the stock exchange. Any transaction should be made through the members of the stock exchange only. The brokers know about the investors habits. They know the pulse of the investors. They will guide, advice, recommend and render services for the smooth functioning of the stock market.

Generally every Stock Exchange would run through its members. The member of a stock exchange is known as stock broker. The stock broker in a recognised stock exchange, buys and sells the securities on behalf of his clients. The person who wants to become a stock broker, is required to get a registration certificate from the SEBI. The SEBI is the most powerful organisation to control, regulate, monitor and guide the market from time to time. The SEBI is empowered to grant the registration certificates to the eligible brokers. The SEBI has the authority to improse conditions before granting the registration to a broker. A person who is granted the status of the broker by the SEBI must abide by the rules, regulations and byelaws. The stock broker is required to pay a prescribed fee to the SEBI. The stock brokers are responsible for the redressal of the investor's complaints. They should solve the problem within one month from the date of receipt of the complaint. They should inform the SEBI about the number of complaints received and solved by them. They should also bring into the notice of the SEBI regarding the nature of complaints received by them. In India the brokers are categorised into two:

**(1) Indian Brokers.**
**(2) Foreign Brokers.**

### (1) Indian Brokers

The stock brokers in India should move according to the guidelines issued by the SEBI from time to time. The SEBI guidelines are very important to the brokers. The SEBI has taken the monitoring function to prevent the malpractice in trading and to protect the rights of the investors. The function includes the submission of the report by the stock exchanges and registration of the brokers. The broad regulatory framework of the stock exchanges contain the major organisational reforms in respect of **stock brokers, sub-brokers, foreign brokers, custodial services, depository system and stock lending scheme**. The stock brokers have to fulfil the following legal formalities:

(a) Registration.
(b) Fee.
(c) Code of conduct.
(d) Capital adequacy norms.
(e) Sub-brokers.

A stock broker in a recognised stock exchange has to get the registration with the SEBI. The stock broker should apply to the SEBI through his recognised stock exchange. The stock exchange may forward the application with their comments to the SEBI regarding his candidature. On receipt of the application from the stock exchange, the SEBI will enquire into the matters regarding such broker. Before granting the registration the SEBI considers the factors such as membership in the recognised stock exchange, capability of the broker, his manpower, infrastructure facilities, his past experience, his discipline and suitability. The SEBI will grant the certificate of Registration to the stock broker, if he satisfies and fulfils all the norms. The selected broker should undergo some process to the registration certificate.

The selected broker has to pay the fee to the SEBI as the registration fee. The registration fee will be based on the annual turnover of the broker. The annual turnover means the quantum of sales and purchases of the securities received and receivable by the stock broker on his own account and as well as his clients account during any financial year. The grant of registration will be valid for **five years**. The registration fee should be paid by the broker. If his annual turnover is found to be **Rs. one crore**, then he should pay **Rs. 5,000**. If his turnover exceeds **Rs. one crore**, then he should pay **Rs. 5,000+1 per cent**. The turnover of the broker should be certified by the auditor of the concerned stock exchange. After the completion of 5 years also if the broker keep it in force he should pay **Rs. 5,000** for this purpose. If a stock broker fails to pay the fee within the specified period, he would be liable to pay the interest at **15 per cent** per annum for each month of delay. If the individual or firms are converted into a corporate body, then the fee would be exempted for the conversion period. The corporate body should pay the fee on the basis of turnover. The underwriting and collection of deposits will not be taken into consideration for the purpose of calculating the turnover. On execution of the orders, the brokers are charged with **1/4th** of the fee payable on the other items of the turnover. In case of turnover on accounts of the transactions in **PSU bonds, Mutual Funds, and Unit Trusts** the government securities are subjected to **1/10th** of the fee payable on the other items of the turnover. In case of the carry forward transactions from one settlement to another, two entries are made by the stock exchange. Therefore, **one entry** should be counted for the purpose of assessment of turnover.

Every worker who registers with the SEBI should abide by the code of conduct as presented below. The following formalities should be fulfilled by the stock broker for the smooth functioning of the stock market:

(a) Transparency.
(b) Service to the investors.
(c) General obligations.
(d) Inspection.
(e) Default.

Every stock broker has to maintain the best relations with the investors. The broker should maintain high standards of integrity, promptness and fairness. He should have adequate skills, care and intelligence to discharge his duties. The broker should be transparent at the price considerations in dealing with the investors. The broker should not involve in manipulative, fraudulent transactions or schemes and he should not spread rumours to make personal gains. The broker should be honest while dealing with his customer. His business mainly depends upon his degree of honesty. The investors should always think about the credibility of the broker before he commits his investment decisions. The broker or his colleagues should not create false market. He should not involve in excessive speculative activities. He has to abide by all the rules and regulations of the SEBI Act. The broker should follow the rules issued by the Government of India from time to time. The stock exchange can also issue the rules and directions to the brokers.

The fundamental duty of the broker is to provide better quality of services to the investors. The brokers should work to the utmost satisfaction of the investors. The broker must be in a position to provide any services related to the dealings in securities to the investors. The following duties should be provided to the investors by a registered broker:

(a) While dealing with the public, the broker must be transparent in all aspects.
(b) The broker should execute the orders faithfully in buying and selling of the securities.
(c) He should always provide the securities at the best available market place.
(d) The broker should not show the partiality between big and small investors.
(e) He should promptly inform his clients about the execution and non-execution of an order.
(f) The broker should issue a contract note to the client without any delay according to the specifications of the stock exchange.
(g) He should not reveal about the personal investment to his client to another investment. He should maintain confidentiality in this aspect.
(h) He should not encourage the sales or purchases of securities with the sole objective of earning the brokerage or commission.
(i) He should deal with the investor who defaults with another broker knowingly or unknowingly.

(j) The broker should not behave against the advantage of the investor. He should not create any conflict of interest between him and his client.
(k) The broker should not give investment advice to the investor unless he has reasonable grounds for believing the information.
(l) The stock broker should have the excellent trained staff with competent skills and outstanding abilities to render services to the clients with fairness and promptness.
(m) The stock broker should maintain a cordial relationship with other fellows.
(n) The stock brokers should cooperate with each other when the unmatched transactions arise.
(o) He should not wilfully and knowingly make bad deliveries.
(p) He should cooperate with other fellows in the replacement of documents in case of bad deliveries.
(q) The broker should cooperate with others in case of investor's rights, dividends, bank shares and another related to such securities.
(r) Every broker should cooperate with each other in the settlement of transactions.
(s) The stock broker can make wide publicity only with the permission from the stock exchange.
(t) Every stock broker should submit the annual report to the SEBI in a stipulated time.

A stock broker should not neglect or refuse the instructions of the SEBI.

The broker who is the member of the recognised stock exchange should submit the required returns to the stock exchange.

**General Obligations**

The stock broker is required to maintain the books and records as per the Act. Every registered broker should maintain the following books:

(a) sauda book,
(b) general ledger,
(c) client ledger,
(d) cash book,

(e) ledger,
(f) pass book,
(g) document register,
(h) register of accounts of sub-brokers,
(i) margin register,
(j) members agreement book,
(k) client's consent letters register,
(l) confirmation register,
(m) agreement register of sub-brokers.

All the above books should be maintained by every broker. The books and records must be preserved for every **five years**. The SEBI has the full authority to verify all the books which should be maintained by every broker. The SEBI is empowered to appoint an Inspection Committee. The Committee consists of one or two members to inspect the books of accounts, records and other documents of the stock broker. It should ensure that the broker maintains all the records as per the stipulated Act. The Committee may investigate whether the broker had fulfilled the Securities Regulation Act or not. It is empowered to look into the affairs of the investor's complaints. It should also verify about the complaints from other brokers and sub-brokers. The SEBI has the **suo-motu** to investigate the affairs of the investor's interest. In some situations, the SEBI can also appoint a qualified auditor to carry out investigation into the records of the brokers. After the submission of the report by the inspection committee, the SEBI can direct the broker to take effective measures. A stock broker who fails to take measures or recommendations will be punished as per the Act. He will be punished, if he violates the conditions or contravenes with any of the provisions of the SEBI Act, SCRA, byelaws and stock exchange regulations. The broker's licence will be cancelled or suspended for a specific period of time.

**Suspension**

The SEBI has the authority to suspend the registration of a broker on the following grounds:

(a) If the broker violates the SEBI provisions.
(b) Violation of conditions of the grant of registration.
(c) If the broker does not follow the code of conduct.

(d) If the broker involves in price rigging or cornerning.
(e) If the broker is guilty of misconduct, improper business or unprofessional conduct.
(f) If the broker fails to furnish any information required by the SEBI.
(g) If the broker fails to pay the annual fee.
(h) If the broker does not cooperate at the time of inspection.
(i) If the broker furnishes false or wrong information to the SEBI.
(j) If the broker fails to submit the periodical returns within the stipulated period of time.
(k) If the broker fails to resolve the investor's complaints or gives a satisfactory explanation to the SEBI.
(l) If the membership of a broker is suspended by the stock exchange, the SEBI also suspends the registration.

**Cancellation**

The SEBI has the authority to cancel the registration of any broker. It should indicate in writing about the defaults of the broker. It has the power to cancel the registration in case of repeated defaults. The registration of a broker can be cancelled on the following grounds:

(1) Violation of any provisions of takeover regulations and insider trading.
(2) Involves in a guilty offence or conviction for a criminal offence.
(3) Cancellation of membership by the recognised stock exchange.

The suspension or cancellation of registration of a member can be done only after a thorough enquiry by the Act. If the SEBI decides to cancel the registration of a broker or to suspend the registration, it must be published in at least two daily newspapers. After the publication, the broker is prohibited to buy and sell the securities in the market. If the broker dissatisfies with the SEBI orders, he can approach the **Securities Appellate Tribunal** for justice.

**Capital Adequacy Norms**

Every registered broker in India should meet the capital adequacy norms as per the Act. It contains two important components. They are presented below:

**(A) Minimum Capital.**
**(B) Additional Capital.**

### *(A) Minimum Capital*

Every broker who is a member in a recognised stock exchange should pay a minimum amount of deposit to the concerned stock exchange. The minimum amount of deposit depends upon the stock exchange status. A member in Mumbai Stock Exchange should deposit **Rs. 5 lakhs** in the stock exchange. The Calcutta Stock Exchange also requires a minimum amount of **Rs. Five lakhs** as deposit. The Delhi and Ahmedabad Stock Exchanges command **Rs. 3.5 lakhs** as deposit without relation to the turnover of the broker. The other regional stock exchanges require **Rs. 2.00 lakhs**. The deposit that is kept by the brokers in the stock exchange forms a part of the base. From the base capital, 25 per cent should be in cash with the stock exchange and another **25 per cent** should be in form of FDR with a bank, and the rest of the balance may be in the form of securities with **30 per cent** margin. The value of the securities will be reviewed by the stock exchange for every two months. If any amount shows the deficit, the member broker should bring some amount additionally to meet the capital adequacy norms.

### *(B) Additional Capital*

The additional capital brought by the member broker at any time should be together with the minimum base capital. It should not be less than **8 per cent** of the gross outstanding business in the exchange. The gross business turnover means the buying and selling of the securities. It also includes inter client business which does not arise on the floor of exchange. The gross outstanding business should not exceed **12.5 times** the base and additional capital requirements. If the outstanding business exceeds **10 times** the base and additional capital requirements, the broker should intimate about it to the stock exchange. If the gross business outstanding reaches **12.5 times**, the base and additional capital requirement, the broker should bring the additional capital. Until then, he will not be allowed for trading in the stock exchange. The member of the stock exchange should always fulfil the capital adequacy norms. The capital of a broker is computed by adding capital and reserves **minus** non-allowable assets. The non-allowable assets are **member's**

**card, bad deliveries, fixed assets, pledged securities, doubtful debts and advances, tangible assets and 30 per cent of marketable securities**. The brokers who do not submit their audited accounts should be liable to deposit the additional capital in the form of cash in the stock exchange. Every broker should submit the audited accounts quarterly indicating the net liquid capital with the member of the stock exchange. The stock exchanges are required to adjust with the margin requirements on daily basis to facilitate the working capital management of the member broker. Every broker should submit quarterly reports to the concerned stock exchange for meeting the capital adequacy norms. For this effect, he should submit an auditor's certificate to the exchange within one month of every quarter year **(ending, March 31, June 30, September 30 and December 31)**. Every broker should meet the requirements of the capital adequacy. If he fails to meet this norms, he deserves a **penalty** including fines and suspension from trading. The byelaws of the stock exchange indicates that if any broker fails to inform the stock exchange on reaching the prescribed limits, he is punishable accordingly. The transactions which are required to deliver within **48 hours** would be exempted from the capital adequacy requirements.

## Client and Broker

The transactions between the client and the broker should be regulated. Every broker should keep his own money and his client's money in separate accounts. The broker should not utilise his client's money for his own purpose. But however if the member has the lieu, set off, counter claim or otherwise against money standing to the credit of client's accounts..The broker should purchase the securities from the market only on receipt of **20 per cent margin** on the price of the security. The margin amount would be exempted for the purchase of shares meant for **FIIs, MFs and Financial Institutions**. The member should sell securities on behalf of his client only on receipt of **20 per cent margin** on the price of the securities. But the Mutual Funds, FIIs and FIs are exempted from this restriction.

Generally the member must issue the contract note to a client within **24 hours** for buying or selling a scrip. The broker can close a transaction, if the client fails to make the full payment for the execution of the contract within **two days** of cash shares. The time limit for the specified group shares is **seven days** within the delivery of contract note. If any loss arises in this transaction, it should be adjusted from the margin of the client. The same process will be applies for the sale of shares by the clients.

## Sub-brokers

The sub-broker is the agent of the stock broker. He acts on behalf of the stock broker. He assists the investors in buying and selling of the securities in the market. He himself is not a member of the stock exchange. He should get a registration certificate from the SEBI. The SEBI is empowered to grant the certificate of registration subjected to the following conditions:

(a) The fee should be payable by the sub-broker.
(b) Authorisation should be given in writing by a broker.
(c) The sub-broker should make adequate steps for the redressal of the investor's grievances.

The following process is required to act as a sub-broker under the provisions of the Act:

**(1) Registration of Sub-brokers.**
**(2) General obligations.**
**(3) The relation between Sub-broker and Broker.**
**(4) Regulatory authorities.**

### 1. *Registration of Sub-broker*

Every sub-broker should register with the SEBI. He should apply to the exchange for the registration in a prescribed form. He must submit the application along with the recommendation from the stock broker with whom he affiliates. He should also submit two references including his banker. On receipt of the application, the stock exchange should verify the information contained in it and also certify that the applicant is eligible for registration. The age of the sub-broker should not be less than **21 years**. He should not convict himself in any offence which involves fraud or dishonesty. He should at least pass **+2 standard or equivalent examination** from a recognised institution. The educational qualifications may be relaxed by the **SEBI** after considering the experience. The concerned stock exchange should forward the application to the SEBI within **30 days** from the date of receipt of the application.

## 2. *General Obligations*

Every sub-broker who registers with the SEBI should pay **Rs. 1,000** as annual fee for an initial period of **5 years**. After the completion of **5 years**, every sub-broker should pay **Rs. 500** as long as the registration is in force. The broker and sub-broker should make an agreement between them specifying the role of the sub-broker. The sub-broker should maintain all the books of account on par with the stock broker. The sub-broker should follow the code of conduct. The sub-broker should maintain high standard of integrity, fairness, transparency and skill. He should take care and diligence in all the business activities. He should behave smoothly with the general public and clients. Brokership mainly depends upon the characteristics of an individual. The investors and general public closely watch the affairs of the sub-broker's activities. The business is based on personal reputation, a strong belief in the public and confidence. He should faithfully execute the orders in buying and selling of the securities. He should make purchases to his clients at the best available market price and promptly inform the information about the execution and non-execution of the orders. The sub-broker should issue promptly to their clients:

(a) purchase/sale notes through the main broker,
(b) scrip-wise particulars purchase/sale, and
(c) client-wise particulars.

A sub-broker should maintain the confidentiality of the information about the clients. He should not disclose any information or make improper use of the details for his personal investments. He should not encourage, deal or execute either directly or indirectly with a defaulted person, another broker or sub-broker. He should not take the advantage while dealing with his clients. He should not encourage the investors with a view to earn brokerage or commission. He should not charge more than **one per cent, and one and a half per cent** of the value mentioned in the respective sale or purchase contract. He should not give a false information or mislead the clients. He should not recommend any particular scrip to his clients, unless there is a reasonable ground. He should have sufficient staff with high skill and they should be competent in their profession. The services should be fair, prompt and transparent to his clients. He should maintain friendly relations with other brokers. He should cooperate with others in finalisation of the unmatched transactions. He should provide his best services in locating the bad deliveries. He should protect the investor's interest regarding their right to dividends, bonus shares or any other related information. He should carry out his transactions with the stock broker more effectively and promptly. He should not show negligence in completing the transactions with the broker. The contract or agreement made between the broker and sub-broker would clearly specify the rights and obligations of both the parties. The sub-broker should not involve in the Advertising Campaign unless he gets the permission from the concerned stock exchange. He should not procure clients from his counterparts. He should comply with all other regulatory bodies. He should not indulge in any unfair practices, dishonest, or disorder wilfully and obstruct the business of the stock exchange. He should not involve in excessive speculation activities. The inspection and punishment process will be same on par with the broker status.

**2. Foreign Brokers**

The entry of the Foreign Institution Investors led to the emerge of the foreign brokers. The SEBI has taken an initiative step to encourage the **FII's**, a different set of guidelines issued by it. The guidelines issued by the SEBI are presented below:

**(a) Registration.**
**(b) Transactions.**
**(c) Market Operations.**

***(a) Registration***

Every foreign broker has to register with the SEBI. He has to disclose all the information regarding his abroad registration particulars in a stock exchange. He should also submit an undertaking that he will operate and assist only on behalf of the **registered FII's.** He should not deal with the securities on his own in India. The SEBI and the RBI accords approval to him to open a foreign currency denominated bank account and a rupee account with a designated bank branch. The foreign broker has to appoint a registered custodian on whose behalf he is going to place the order with a member of the Indian Stock Exchange.

### *(b) Transactions*

As per the approval of the SEBI and the RBI, the foreign broker should open an account in foreign currency denominated account. The amount of funds that he had brought to India should be deposited in this account. He is also entitled to pay an initial amount against the purchase contracts on behalf of the **registered FII's**. The rupee account will be credited with the brokerage or commission earned by him in India. The fulfilment of purchase contracts may also be paid from the Rupee account. The initial amount of payment would be reimbursed by the custodian of FII or by the designated bank. The brokerage or commission earned by the broker will repatriate to the foreign currency denominated account and subjects the payment of taxes. The earned commission may be convertible into foreign currency and it would be transferred to the native place of the foreign broker.

### *(c) Market Operations*

A foreign broker cannot deal in securities for his own purpose. He can operate only on behalf of **the FII's**. He can execute its order through a member of a recognised stock exchange. He has no freedom in the market and his position is strictly restricted. The other particulars need not be mentioned in placing a contract notes. The notes should be given to the custodian for the smooth functioning of the affairs. The payment for the purchases are made by the foreign broker from his rupee account. It should be credited to the rupee account of the **FIF** for the purpose of tax. The scrips which are purchased/sold should be delivered within **four hours** through the custodian. It has no freedom in repatriation of sale proceeds. Repatriation of surplus can be made only after the completion of such reconciliation. The custodians and the designated bank branches should submit their reports to the SEBI and the RBI. The custodian should send monthly returns to the SEBI and the RBI with full information about the transactions they made. The particulars should be regarding the volume of transactions, number of scrips purchased, date of receipt of the delivery etc. The SEBI has the authority to inspect the books of account of the foreign brokers. Any violation of the guidelines lead to severe punishment.

# 9

# DEPOSITORY SYSTEM

## Introduction

The industrial financial system has evolved in response to the emerging liberalised deregulated and globalised economic environment. The transformation is essentially focussed in a shift way from financial institutions to the capital market and related institutions. The growth of the capital market and the entry of FIIs revealed the gross inadequacies of the market infrastructure to support the volumes of securities trading in India. The existing and traditional methods are time consuming. The traditional methods of trading, clearing, settlement, transfer, registration and maintenance of records are to be replaced with the modern techniques and state of art. The latest technology may help the smooth functioning of the stock market. The rapid changes in the investor habits may lead to more exposure of the markets. The investors perception will be reflected in the **Sensex** movement. The Sensex is highly influenced by the GDP. The past behaviour of the **Sensex** and its link to the **GDP** provides a mathematical basis for the future expectation of the market. The Sensex for the year 1995–96 grew 27 per cent touching a high of **3598.37** and the GDP at **Rs. 10,73,300 crores** grew 7.3 per cent during the year. The market capitalisation of the BSE in 1995–96 was **43 per cent** of the GDP. The year also witnessed record investments of $3.05 billion by the FIIs. All these factors increased the systematic risks like credit risk, bad deliveries, long delayed deliveries counterfeit scrips, forged certificates, wrong signatures and stealing of shares. To overcome all these problems a new modern infrastructure has been created like emerging of computer recording of transactions, paperless trading and depositories. The technological revolution has created waves in the trading methods. Now-a-days the trading can be done with a click of mouse. Trading become a highly sophisticated execution of transactions without the physical presence in the exchange. The entry of **bulk buyers/FIIs** have changed the scenario of the trading. The stock market reforms cleared the way for the introduction of depository/custody in the securities. The system of trading is based on physical transfer and efficient functioning of the markets especially in the context of high volume of transactions.

**Problems**

Usually in the stock markets, the investors face many problems regarding the buying/selling of shares. The problems faced by the individual investors/institutional investors/foreign institutional investors are presented below:

(1) Delay in transfer of securities.
(2) Delay in getting the duplicate share certificate.
(3) Delay in getting the duplicate Debenture/Bond Certificate.
(4) Delay in the receipt of securities allotment order for all others.
(5) Delay in non-receipt of refund orders to non-allottees.
(6) The return of share certificate is common in the following situations such as **bad, delivery**:
    (a) in case of forged transfer deeds,
    (b) in case of false certificate,
    (c) on account of forged signature,
    (d) on account of mismatch of signature,
(7) Lack of infrastructure facilities to handle a bulk volume of transactions – inadequate banking and postal facilities.

To revamp all the problems, the Government of India took an initiative to introduce the scripless trading. The steps have been taken to bring actions in the securities which take place by a book entry method, without the physical delivery of securities. The ingredient of the scripless trading in the **dematerialisation** of the share certificates through the depositories. In this method all the certificates are surrendered to the issuer company. On the receipt of the certificates through the depository the issuer company can cancel the share certificates. The depository's name is entered in the register of members of the company. The name of the beneficial owner whose name is recorded with the depository is **deleted**. The Government has introduced the ordinance for the **Depositories** in September 1995. The ordinance was converted into Depositories Act, 1996. The depository system operates within the framework of the Depositories Act, 1996 and the SEBI regulations.

## Depositories Act

The objective of the Depositories Act is to provide the regulation of depositories in the securities market. The Depository Act discloses the following procedure:

- **(a) Certificate of commencement of business.**
- **(b) Obligations of depositories.**
- **(c) Enquiry and inspection.**
- **(d) Power of the SEBI.**
- **(e) Byelaws.**
- **(f) Amendments.**

If any individual company wants to act as a depository, a certificate from the SEBI is required. Every company should get a registration certificate from the SEBI. No company is allowed to act as a depository without the permission from the SEBI. The SEBI has empowered to grant the certificate to the concerned parties. When the interested party applies to the SEBI for the registration the SEBI will scrutiny the application before granting the certificate. The SEBI must satisfy that the depository has adequate infrastructure facilities. The depository should have the technical capabilities to prevent the manipulation of records. The depository should have the excellent facilities for the smooth functioning of the trading activity.

**The obligation of the depository** is to make an agreement with the Depository Participant (DP). The DP should have relation with an agent. Any investor can avail the services connected with the recording of allotment or transfer of securities. All the transactions should be recorded in a depository through a DP by surrendering the certificate to the issuer company in a prescribed manner. On receipt of the certificate from the DP, the issuer company would cancel the certificate and substitute in its records the name of the depository as a registered owner. The depository in turn would record the name of the person as the beneficial owner. Generally the investors indicate either to receive the certificate or hold them with a depository while they subscribe the shares. The public issue company should transmit the information to the depository regarding the full information about the allotment process and the names are to be recorded as the beneficial owners of the financial instrument. The securities which are at the disposal of the depository would be in dematerial position. The depository has the full authority to transfer the ownership on behalf of a beneficial power. But the depository would not have any voting rights in respect of the securities held. The beneficial owner has the rights and benefits regarding the financial instrument. The beneficial owner is also responsible for the liabilities effected from that financial instruments. The Companies Act indicates that every depository should maintain a register and an index of beneficial owners. The beneficial owner does have the right to pledge/hypothecation with the prior approval of the depository. Therefore, the depository should make adjustment entries in the records accordingly the entry made by the depository is the evidence for hypothecation. According to the byelaws of the depository, he should inform to the issuing company regarding the transfer of securities in the name of the beneficial owner at regular intervals. The issuer company also should provide the necessary information in respect of securities held by it. The beneficial has the option out of a depository. Then he has to inform the message to the depository. The depository in turn passes the message to the issuer company within 30 days. The issuer would issue the certificate of securities to the beneficial owner/ transfer on fulfilment of conditions and payment of fee as specified by the SEBI. The transactions which are recorded by the depository will be treated as evidence on par with Section 2 of the Banker's Book Evidence Act, 1891. The depository can recover any loss caused due to the behaviour of beneficial owner from the **DP only**.

All the depository transactions are monitored, directed, guided by the **SEBI**. The SEBI is the most powerful organisation to control the activities of the depositories. **The enquiry and inspections** of the depositories can be conducted by the SEBI with the interest of the public. The SEBI is empowered to call for the information or make an enquiry into the affairs of the **Issuer Company/beneficial owner and DP**. The SEBI also has the power to give appropriate directions for the welfare of the investors or to prevent the affairs in detrimental to the future of the investor or market. If any person dissatisfies with the SEBI orders, he may appeal to the **Security Appellate Tribunal**. Any person who violates the rules and regulations/byelaws is punishable with imprisonment for a term of **5 years** or with fine or with both. The SEBI can collect the information and assess the situation from time to time.

**The SEBI has** the full powers to make the regulations regarding the maintenance of records. The SEBI can issue a licence to the depository for the commencement of business. The SEBI can also make regulations in the following situations:

(a) for proper maintenance of records;
(b) prescribes the process for surrendering a security certificate;
(c) rights of depository;
(d) obligations of the depository;
(e) the process of creating pledge;
(f) the manner of hypothecation by the beneficial owner;
(g) fee payable for the issue of certificate of securities;
(h) rights and obligations of the issuer company, participants;
(i) the entry norms for the admission of scrips to the demat.

**Byelaws**

The Act empowers the SEBI to regulate the working affairs of the depository, DP and issuer company. The depository can make the byelaws in accordance with the provisions of the Act. The byelaws that are prepared by the depository should get the approval of the SEBI. The contents of the byelaws are presented below:

(a) The entry level norms for the admission of securities in depositories.
(b) The procedure for the removal of a security in the depository.
(c) The conditions for dealing the securities.
(d) The appointment produce for the DP.
(e) The process of dematerialisation of securities.
(f) The procedure of affairs of the transactions in a depository.
(g) The system for protecting the interest of participants.
(h) The manner for protecting the interest of a beneficial owner.
(i) The process of pledge in respect of securities held with a depository.
(j) The process of furnishing information to the SEBI.
(k) The manner of providing information to the issuer company.
(l) The auditing process reviewing and monitoring.
(m) The manner of internal control standards.
(n) The procedure for the settlement of any disputes between the parties.

(o) The rights and obligation of the depository.
(p) The rights and obligations of the DP.
(q) The procedure for the distribution of dividends to the beneficial owner.
(r) The manner for the distribution of interest to the beneficial owners.
(s) The procedure for the transmitting the information which is received from the issuing company to the beneficial owners regarding the dividend declaration, shareholders meetings and other matters.

The SEBI has the authority to direct a depository to make any byelaws or to amend or revoke any byelaws in writing. If any depository neglects or fails to comply with the orders/directions, it may make modifications or revoke the byelaws for the welfare of the investors. The Depository Act can be implemented by making some amendments to the **Securities Contract Act, Income Tax Act, SEBI Act, Indian Stamp Act, Companies Act and Benami Transactions Act**.

## SEBI Regulations

The SEBI has the authority to make regulations and control the affairs of the depository. The regulations of the SEBI are presented below:

**(A) Registration.**
**(B) Certificate of commencement of business.**
**(C) Depository Participation (DP).**
**(D) Rights of depository.**
**(E) Rights of depository participant/issuing company.**
**(F) Inspection.**
**(G) Default.**

### *(A) Registration*

Every depository must register with the SEBI. The SEBI has the power to grant the registration for the depositories. The interested firm should apply to the SEBI in a prescribed manner along with an application fee of **Rs. 50,000**. The application form should be accompanied with the draft byelaws of the proposed depository. The proposed depository may be established by an individual institution or combination of other institutions. Generally the following institutions may think about the set up of depository services:

(a) Commercial banks.
(b) Recognised stock exchanges.
(c) Developmental financial institutions.
(d) Foreign banks.
(e) Body corporate (Financial services organisation).
(f) A body corporate recognised by a Foreign Country for providing the custodial services.
(g) A recognised financial institution, which engages in the financial services outside India.

Every proposed depository company should satisfy the following conditions:

(a) Able to pay an annual fee of **Rs. 10,00,000** to the SEBI.
(b) Payment of registration fee of **Rs. 25,00,000** within 15 days.
(c) Compliance with the regulations of the SEBI, byelaws and Act.
(d) False information should not be furnished by the proposed depository.
(e) Amendments can be made to the byelaws from time to time as directed by the SEBI.
(f) Only depository services are allowed as per the law.
(g) Other than depository services are prohibited.
(h) The sponsor of the proposed depository should have at least **51 per cent** of the equity capital and the rest by the participants.
(i) The depository participants are allowed to invest up to **Five per cent of** the equity.
(j) No foreign entity will be allowed for more than **51 per cent** of the equity.
(k) The depository should redressal the grievances within 30 days from the complaint given by participants/beneficial owners and should inform the SEBI regarding the number of complaints registered and resolved.
(l) The depository should apply for the certificate of commencement of business within one year of registration.

### *(B) Certificate of Commencement of Business*

The proposed depository will submit the application form for the registration along with other required documents and fee. One year of time will be given to the depository for getting the certificate of commencement of business from the SEBI. Before granting the certificate of commencing the business, the SEBI would scrutinise all the contents relevant to the efficient and better functioning of the depository. The SEBI may consider the following factors while granting the certificate of commencement of business:

(a) The depository should have a financial soundness. It must have the networth of more than **Rs. 100 crores.**

(b) The byelaws of the depository must be compliance with the provisions and it should be approved by the SEBI.

(c) The depository services will depend upon the technical capability of the depository. The depository should take care of the automatic data processing systems.

(d) The data processing must be protested against the unauthorised access, dissemination of records, alteration, destruction, etc.

(e) The network of the depository system must be secured against any unauthorised access.

(f) The depository should provide a continuous electronic means of communication among the four parties, i.e., **the depository, depository participants, issuer company and issuers agent.**

(g) The depository should provide a better quality of network services on par with the world standards.

(h) The electronic access to the data storage sites, and to the premises is controlled, monitored and recorded.

(i) The depository should establish adequate procedures and provide arrangements for maintaining the backup facilities.

(j) The depository should provide the insurance arrangements for indemnifying the beneficial owners for any loss due to the negligence default by him.

(k) The SEBI should make a physical verification of the infrastructure facilities and systems provided by the depository.

(l) The certificate of commencement of the business should be in the interest of the investors.

### *(C) Depository Participant (DP)*

According to the SEBI Regulation and Depository Act every depository participant should apply to the SEBI for the grant of registration. The DP should pay a registration fee of **Rs. 5,000** along with the application form through a depository. The depository should certify and recommend the same by forwarding the form to the SEBI within **30 days**. On receipt of the application form from the depository, the SEBI considers the requirements of the DP. The DP must satisfy the anyone of the following categories:

(a) A public financial institution **(IDBI, IFCI, ICICI)**.
(b) A foreign bank.
(c) A bank.
(d) A State Government sponsored financial corporation **(SFC)**.
(e) A NBFC with same conditions.
(f) A financial consortium led by (a) to (d) organisation.
(g) A recognised stock exchange.
(h) A registered custodian.
(i) A clearing corporation
(j) A registered stock broker (the minimum networth of Rs. 50 lakhs).

On verification of the eligibility, the SEBI can grant the certificate and it may be intimated through the depository. The SEBI should satisfy that the DP has adequate infrastructure and systems. The registration will be made in the interest of the investors and the market. The SEBI permits the DP after subjecting it to the under-mentioned conditions:

(a) The DP should pay the registration fee of **Rs. 1.00 lakh** within 15 days.
(b) The DP should be in compliance with the provisions of the Depository Act.
(c) The DP must comply with the byelaws, agreements of the depository.
(d) The depository should hold a certificate of commencement of the business while permitting the DP.
(e) The DP should inform if any wrong information is found in any manner or if there is any change in such information.
(f) The DP has to pay an annual fee of **Rs. 1,000** to the SEBI.

(g) The grievances of the beneficial owner should be settled within **thirty days**.
(h) The depository should inform about the nature and number of the redressal of grievances.
(i) The validity period of the registration of the DP is **5 years**.
(j) The registration of the DP may be renewed for another five years on the payment of **Rs. 10.00 lakhs**.

### *(D) Rights of Depository*

The depository should comply with the SEBI regulations, depository act and byelaws. The depository act mentions the rights and obligations of the depository. The depository should state in the byelaws, eligible for the dematerialisation on the following elements (instruments):

(a) Scrips, bonds, shares, debentures or other marketable securities of any company.
(b) Units of mutual funds, commercial paper, certificate of deposits, venture capital funds, right issues, securities debt, unlisted securities and money market instruments.

The issuing company may make an agreement with the depository to dematerialise its securities. If the issuer company has appointed a registrar to issue the agreement, then it should be made among three parties, i.e., the depository, the DP and the registrar to the issue. The depository should be in a capable position to coordinate and reconcile the records of ownership of the securities with the issuer and the DP on a daily basis the depository should have an excellent means of electronic data transfer with all the ingredients. The depository should satisfy the SEBI regarding the efficient service of the transfer of securities. The depository should allow the participant to withdraw or transfer its accounts with the compliance of the law. The depository has an obligation to arrange the insurance facility to protect the interest of the beneficial owners. The depository has the obligation to maintain the integrity of the electronic which it holds. The depository should have the obligations to take all the precautionary approaches to secure the data safely. However, the depository should maintain the under-mentioned records:

(a) The particulars of the securities dematerialised and **rematerialised**.
(b) Particulars about the data of transfer of the securities.
(c) The details regarding the transferors and transferees.
(d) A register and index of the beneficial owners, the full details about their holdings at the end of every month.
(e) The correspondence made with the DP, issuers company and beneficial owners.
(f) Other records as specified by the SEBI from time to time.
(g) All the records must be maintained for at least five years.
(h) The depository should inform the SEBI where the documents are maintained.
(i) The depository should extend the cooperation to the involved parties in dematerialisation process for the prompt and accurate clear settlement of securities transactions and conduct of business affairs.
(j) The depository should not assignary work/task to any other person without the knowledge of the SEBI.

### *(E) Rights of DP*

The depository byelaw specified that every DP should make an agreement with the beneficial owner of the asset. The DP should open and maintain accounts for each beneficial owner. The transfer of securities should be registered by the DP taking the instructions from the beneficial owner. The process should be implemented in a specified manner by the byelaws of the depository. .The DP should keep the records of instructions from the beneficial owner and made entries in his account accordingly. The following obligations should be fulfilled by the DP:

1. The DP should maintain the statement of accounts with the beneficial owner and provide the statements to him.
2. The beneficial owner will be allowed to withdraw/transfer from his account as per the agreement.
3. The DP should provide continuous means of electronic communication to the beneficial owners.
4. The DP should have the capabilities to review, evaluate, control, systems and monitoring the internal accounting.

5. The DP should maintain the integrity of the data processing system.
6. The DP should ensure that the records are to be kept safely, not destroyed or not tampered and the records are available at a particular place.
7. He should maintain his records and reconcile with every depository on a daily basis.
8. He should submit periodic returns to the SEBI and to the depository in a specified format.
9. The following records are to be maintained by the DP:
   (a) Record of transactions with depositories and beneficial owners.
   (b) The full particulars of dematerialised/rematerialised on behalf of the clients.
   (c) The register of instructions received and executed.
   (d) The records of notice, entry and approvals.
10. The records should be preserved for 5 years.
11. The DP should not assign any work to any one without the approval of the SEBI.
12. All the records should be made available to the depository.

The issuing company should enter into an agreement with a depository. There is no need of agreement for the issue of government securities. The beneficial owners are required to submit the particulars of the security certificates for dematerialisation and surrender the certificates to the DP. The DP in turn forwards the same to the depository along with the agreement copy of the beneficial owner. The DP should maintain the records which contains all the information with the correspondence made to the depository. On receipt of the security certificate, the issuer company immediately cancel it and further entries will be made accordingly. The issuer company would maintain a record of certificates which has been dematerialised. The issuing company should take the following steps:

(a) The issuing company should make a reconciliation of the records which are materialised by the depository on a daily basis.
(b) If the Government is a issuer, it should also reconcile the records on a daily basis of the dematerialised securities.

(c) The issuer should make arrangements to continue the electronic means of communication with the depository.
(d) The issuer company must provide the information to the depository about the dematerialised securities, i.e., the details of book closure, record dates, annual general meetings, other meetings, dividends, interest, conversion methods, redemption of debentures, warrants, call money dates etc.
(e) The issuer company should provide any other information to the depository regarding the materialisation of securities.

### *(F) Inspection*

The SEBI has the full authority to undertake the inspection of books, documents, records etc., of a depository or DP or issuing company. The SEBI can enquire about the technical capabilities of the systems of the depository. The SEBI has the authority to investigate the affairs of the depository, DP and beneficial owner and issuing company. The inquiry will be conducted by the SEBI for the following purposes:

(1) To ensure the smooth functioning of the affairs as specified by the Law.
(2) To respond to the complaints from the investors.
(3) To look after for compliance of all the provisions **(SEBI Act, byelaw and Depository Act)**.
(4) To take the veto powers in the interest of the investors.

### *(G) Default*

The Inspection Committee will submit its report after the completion of the inspection to the SEBI. The SEBI may take an action in case of the default by either suspension of registration or cancellation of the depository or DP. The SEBI may suspend the registration on the following situations:

(a) any violation of the provisions of the SEBI, byelaws depository act and agreements;
(b) any failure to furnish the full information regarding the rules and regulations;

(c) if any violation of the SEBI directions and fails to pay the annual fee;
(d) during the SEBI inspection, any non-cooperation by the parties;
(e) furnishing of false information, misleading information.

The SEBI has the authority to cancel the registration of the depository/DP/issuing company/beneficial owner on the following grounds:

(a) repeated defaults,
(b) if any fraud or convict of an offence by any party.

## REFERENCES

### (I) Indian Edition

Avadhani, V.A., *Studies in Indian Financial System*, Jaico, Bombay, 1978.

Basu, S.K., *A survey of contemporary banking trends*, The Book Exchange, Calcutta, 1965.

Bhat, V.V. On Financial Innovations and Credit market Evolution, *EPW*, Nov. 2, 1985.

Bhatia, B., *New issue markets of India*, Vora, Bombay, 1976.

Bhatt, R.S., *UTI and MF: A study*, UTI ICM, Bombay, 1996.

Bhattacharya, S., Venture Capital Financing, *EPW*, 1989.

Bhole, L.M., *A perspective on financial restructuring in India in Atmanand*, Globalisation and Dimensions Management in India, Shipra, Delhi, 1997.

Cox, J.C. and Rubenstein, M., *Options markets*, PHI, 1985.

Ghosh, P.K. and Gupta, G.S., *Fundamentals of leasing and lease financing*, Vision Books, New Delhi, 1985.

Gupta, U.L., *Working of stock exchanges in India*, Thomspon Press, New Delhi, 1972.

Khan, M.Y., *Indian financial system*, Tata MacGraw Hill, New Delhi, 1996.

Mehatha, R.C., *Capital markets in India for planned growth*, Kitabghar, Gwalior, 1965.

Nadda, N.I., *Capital markets in India*, Bharati, Patna, 1965.

Sahadevan, K.G. and Thiripalaraju, M.I., *Mutual Funds*, PHI, New Delhi, 1997.

Verma, J.C., *A manual of merchant banking*, Bharat Law House, New Delhi, 1989.

World Bank, *The World Development Report*, Oxford University Press, New York, 1989.

**(II) Foreign Edition**


Bennigna, S.Z. and Sarig, O.H. *Corporate Finance: A Valuation Approach*, McGraw Hill, New York, 1997.

Benton, E.G., *Financial Intermediaries: An Introduction*, Houghton, Boston, 1976.

Cox. J.C. and Rubenstein, M., *Options Markets*, PHI, 1985.

Dougall, H.E. and H.E. Gaumitz, *Capital Markets and Institutions*, PHI, New Jersey, 1975.

Edminister R.O., *Financial Institutions and Markets*, McGraw Hill, New York,

Edwards, F.R. and Ma C.W., *Futures and Options*, McGraw Hill, New York, 1992.

Fama, E.F. *Foundation of Finance*, Basil Blackwell, Oxford, 1977.

Farrell, J.L., Jr., *Portfolio Management*, Second edition, McGraw Hill, New York, 1997.

Festermaker, J.V., *Readings in Financial Markets and Institutions*, Appleton, New York, 1969.

Finnerthy, J.D., *Financial Engineering in Corporate Finance: An Overview Financial Management*, Winter, 1988.

Goldsmith, R.W., *Financial Structure and Development*, Yale, London, 1969.

Goss., B.A. and Yamey, B.S., *The Economics of Futures Trading*, MacMillan, London, 1978.

Johnson, H.J., *Financial Institutions and Markets*, McGraw Hill, New York.

Jones, C.P., *Investments*, John Wiley and Son, New York, 1988.

Moore, B.J., *An Introduction to the Theory of Finance*, Allied, New York, 1968.

Ohlson, J.A., *The Theory of Financial Markets and Institutions*, North Holland, Amsterdam, 1987.

Peter, E.E., *Chaos and Order in Capital Markets*, John Wiley, 1991.

Smith, P.F., *Money and Financial Intermediation, the Theory and Structure of Financial Systems*, Prentice Hall, New Jersey, 1978.

Taylor, B and G.D. Moubray, *Strategic Planning for Financial Institutions, Bodley*, London, 1974.

Tobin, James on the efficiency on the financial system, Lloyds, *Bank Review*, 153, 1984.

Van Horne, J.C., *The Function Analysis of Capital Market Rates*, Prentice Hall, New Jersey, 1970.

Weller Paul, *The Theory of Futures Markets*, Blackwell, Oxford, 1992.

# UNIT IV

- Factoring and Forfaiting
- Insurance
- Credit Cards
- Housing Finance
- Hire Purchase
- Unit Trust of India
- Commercial Paper
- Electronic Commerce (E-Commerce)

# 1

# FACTORING AND FORFAITING

## Introduction

Factoring is a financial service. It is rendered by the specialised persons known as **Factors.** It is a fund based financial service. It provides resources to finance receivables as well as facilitates the collection of receivables. The factor deals in realising the book debts, bills receivables, manages sundry debts and sales registers of commercial and trading firms in the capacity of an agent for a commission. In this topic an attempt has been made to causes three different financial services. These are:

**(A) Factoring.**
**(B) Forfaiting.**
**(C) Bill Discounting.**

## (A) Factoring

Factoring helps in realisation of credit sales of trading firms. The factoring is used for short-term trade financing. The term factoring has been defined in various countries in different ways. According to the study group appointed by the **International Institute for the Unification of Private Law Rome.** Factoring has been defined as "Factoring means an arrangement between a factor and his client which includes at two services to be provided by the factor : Finance, Maintenance of accounts collection of debts, protection against credit risk."[1]

A factor is a financial institution which manages the collection of accounts receivables of the companies on their behalf and bears the credit risk associated with those accounts. Factoring means selling with or without recourse, the receivables by the firm to a factor. It is an accepted and fairly well-developed financial service in abroad. It covers both national and international business. In USA and UK these services are offered by the banks.

At present the business transactions take place partly on the basis of cash and on the basic of credit. The buyers usually do not have to pay cash on delivery of goods and services. The sellers allow the buyer same time period before they make payments for goods received. The sellers extend credit to the buyers for a particular period of time. This is known as **"trade credit"**. The interval time between receipt of cash and delivery of goods is known as **Net credit period.** The dues which arise during this process of credit sales are known as **"trade receivables"** from the point of view of seller and trade payables to the buyer. The volume of factoring assignment depends upon the turnover of credit sales. If the firm allows more credit transactions, the Quantum of work also increases. The high turnover of cash sales may reduces the work of factoring service. The seller may require promissory notes from buyers. The practices of extending credit may boost the sales, it has a cost also. Hence, the seller always to collect receivables as quickly as possible. Therefore, the seller may make their own internal arrangements to collect receivables or they may assign this task to a highly specialised collection agency. This agency is known as a "**factor**" in the business world. There are three parties in factor arrangements—**The factor, The client (seller) and the customer (buyer).** The arrangements are governed by a contract between the factor and the client. The contract between these two parties will be made for a particular period. The contract is normally renewed automatically. The contract can be cancelled only with a sufficient advance notice. The factoring is a routine assignment. All the customers are well informed that the seller account has been sold to the factor and they would send the payment directly to the factor. Therefore, the responsibility of the factor to collect the receivables on behalf of his client. For serving the receivables and bearing the risk, the factor charges a fee which in the form of a given percentage, (approximately **1 to 3%**). The factor in turn make the payment to his client which the amount is collected from the buyers. Sometimes the factor may make an advance payment, then the factor will charge an interest in addition to a fee.

### *Characteristics of Factoring*

The importance of factoring service is well recognised by the business community. It enables the traders to concentrate on sales and realisation of credit sales to minimise the risk of bad debts. The main characteristics of factoring are presented below:

(1) Handing over of accounts receivables in favour of factor.
(2) Framing the conditions when the non-payment from the customer.
(3) Fixing a certain percentage of commission to factor.
(4) Particulars regarding the limit of any overdraft.
(5) Assigning conditions and terms to handle accounts of different customers.

### *Advantages of Factoring*

Following are the advantages resulting from the factoring:

(a) It avoids bad debts.
(b) Improvement in liquidity.
(c) It eliminates trade discounts.
(d) It facilitates prompt payments and credits.
(e) It reduces the administrative cost substantially.
(f) It improves scope for operating language.
(g) It provides better credit discipline amongst customers.
(h) It reduces the working capital requirements.

### *Types of Factoring*

The factor can be classified into three categories:

**(1) Domestic Factoring.**
**(2) Export Factoring.**
**(3) Cross Border Factoring.**

#### *(1) Domestic Factoring*

In the domestic factoring three parties involved customer (buyer), client (seller/supplier) and factor (financial intermediary) are in the same country. Domestic factoring could be further divided into three categories. They are:

(a) **Disclosed factoring.**
(b) **Undisclosed factoring.**
(c) **Invoice discounting.**

In **Disclosed factoring** the name of the factor will be indicated in the invoice by the supplier or seller. The buyer is instructed to make payment to the concerned factor so named therein. Therefore, the supplier may continue to bear the risk for non-payment by the buyer. In such cases, the factor is said to have recourse to the principle. Normally the factor assume this risk under non-recourse arrangements. Under a recourse factoring arrangement the factor has recourse to the client (firm). If the debt turnouts to be irrecoverable. In other words, the factor does not assume risk associated with the receivables. In non-recourse factoring, the factor does not have the right of recourse. In other words, the factor should take the loss arising of irrecoverable receivables. For this purpose he is entitled to get compensation in the form of higher commission. The addition commission charged by him is known as "**Delcredere commission**" like in consignment business. Therefore, the factor is actively associated with process of grant of credit and the extension of line of credit to the customers of the client.

In **Undisclosed factoring** category, the name of the factor is not reveal in the invoice. But the factor maintains the sales ledger of the seller/supplier. The buyer do not know the factor name. The transactions are being made in the name of the supplier but control of money lies with the factor. The factor provides short-term finance against sales invoices. This type of factoring is followed by UK.

**Invoice discounting** factor refers that the factor discounts the invoices of the supplier at a pre-agreed credit limit providing finance to the seller. There can be many kinds of factoring. They are bill discounting factor and seller based factoring. **Bill discounting factor** means. It could be buyer based or selective discounting factor. **Seller based factoring** is in vogue in all developed nations. Seller does not maintain credit. He passes on after sale a copy each of invoice and delivery challan, buy-sell agreement and other related papers to the factor. The factor receives payment from the buyer on due dates. The factor remits the collected money to the seller after deducting his commission at the agreed rate. The seller closes his transactions after transmitting the papers to factor for recovery of the amount.

### *(2) Export Factoring*

Export factoring is related to the International trade. In this type of factoring the banks play an important role. The export company obtain finance from the banks by selling the export documents to it on a reasonable basis. The process of export factoring is almost similar to domestic factoring. The factor bank usually advances 75 per cent of the claims of the supplier exporter.

### *(3) Cross Border Factoring*

Export financing is also known as cross border factoring. There are usually four parties to a cross border factoring transaction. They are: (a) exporter **(client)**, (b) importer **(customer)**, (c) export factor and (d) import factor. It is called as two factor system. It is also called as international factoring. It results in two separate agreements. **(I)** The agreement between the exporter and the export factor. **(II)** The agreement between the export factor and import factor. Generally the export and the import factors belong to a formal chain of factors with well-defined rules governing the conduct of business. The import factor has knowledge of local conditions and provides help in realisation as well as reduction of commercial risk The import factor serves to solve the international barriers like language problem, legal formalities etc. The flow of documents and information between the parties involved in international factoring are presented below:

(a) The exporters sends the information to the export factor about the consignment to a importer.
(b) The export factor enquires the import factor about the credit worthiness of the importer.
(c) The import factor may submit the information about the reputation of the importer. If the exporter gets a satisfactory reports about the importer then he delivers the goods to the importer with the relevant invoice, bills of lading and other supporting documents.
(d) The export factor may check the sales ledger with the import factor.
(e) The import factor collects the payment from the importer and affects payment to the export factor as per the terms of assignment.

(f) Ultimately the export factor makes payment to the exporter upon assignment.

The international factoring is a non-recourse factoring deal. The exporters have 100 per cent protection against bad debt loss on credit approved sales. The factor becomes the sole debtor to the exporter once the goods have been shipped.

### *Mechanism of Factoring*

The credit sales generate the factoring business in business dealings. Realisation of credit sales is the basic function of factoring service. Once the sale transactions are completed the factor will come into the picture. The factor is the financial intermediary between seller and buyer. Various activities undertaken by three parties in a factoring transaction.

(1) The Buyer.
(2) The Seller.
(3) The Factor.

*(1) The Buyer*

(a) The buyer makes his purchases with the seller.
(b) The buyer receives delivery of goods with invoice.
(c) The seller will give instructions to make payment to the factor on due dates.
(d) The buyer makes payment to the factor in stipulated time or gets extension of time or in the case of default is subject to legal process at the disposal of factory.

*(2) The Seller*

(a) The seller enters into a memorandum of understanding with the buyer party.
(b) Seller sells goods to the buyer as per agreement.
(c) The seller transmits the invoice copy, delivery challan, agreement copy and instructions to pay the amount to the factor.

(d) Seller, receives 80 per cent or more payment in advance from the factor on selling the receivables from the buyer to him.
(e) The buyer remits the amount after deduction of his factor's service charges.

*(3) The Factor*

(a) Generally the factor is a financial intermediary.
(b) The factor enters into agreement with the seller.
(c) The factor, on receipt of copy of sale document from the seller, he makes payment to the seller of the 80 per cent of the price of the debt.
(d) The factor receives the money from the buyer on due dates and in turn the factor remits the money after usual deductions.
(e) The factor should also check the transactions and parties credit worthiness and their reputation.

### Legal Aspects of Factoring

The factoring is a financial services and it is based on contract between two parties. They are—(a) The seller, (b) The factor. Factoring contract is a general agreement regulated under the law of contract. There is no specific code to regulate this service in India. The legal relationship between a factor and a seller is influenced by the number of elements. The contents of a factoring agreement and legal obligations of the parties are explained below:

(a) The seller (client) gives an undertaking to sell his accounts receivables to the factor.
(b) The factor also agrees to purchase the receivables of the seller, subject to terms and conditions contained in the agreement.
(c) The seller assures that the receivables are undisputed, valid enforceable and recoverable.
(d) The seller should make transactions within the credit limits authorised by the factor.
(e) The seller should serve notices to all those customers whose receivables have been factored.
(f) The seller should provide copies of all invoices, credit notes to the factor.

(g) The factor in turn would remit the amount to the seller.

(h) The factor acquire the power of attorney to assign the debts.

(i) The period of time should be mentioned in the agreement.

(j) The legal status of a factor is that of an assignee.

(k) In some situations the buyer would directly pay the amount to the seller. Therefore, the seller should remit that amount to the factor.

(l) The agreement must provide freedom for the factor to act swiftly in his own name.

(m) The agreement should mention full details regarding the affairs.

(n) The factor has the power to inspect the sellers books and accounts and the period of the factoring arrangement will be specified in the agreement.

(o) The following elements are more important on the part of the factor:

    (i) The factor should verify the invoice and other evidence of delivery.

    (ii) The factor must verify with the sellers banker to ensure that there is no double financing.

    (iii) The factor interest will be protected by the Section 130 of the Transfer of Property Act.

### *Functions of a Factor*

The functions of a factor in general terms can be classified into five kinds:

(1) Administration of sales ledger.
(2) Collection of the receivables.
(3) Financing.
(4) Credit risk.
(5) Advisory services.

#### *(1) Administration of Sales Ledger*

After making an agreement between factor and seller, the factor has the authority to maintain clients sales ledger. If a business transaction arises, an invoice copy will be prepared in triplicate, one copy will be kept himself by the seller, another copy is sent by the seller to the buyer and a copy of the same is sent to the factor. The ledger is maintained as per the accounting process. The buyer account clearly reflects the various transaction. The factor should provide to the seller regarding his current status of his receivables on a fortnightly basis. The factor is also prepare a list on a customer-wise record of transaction.

*(2) Collection of Receivables*

Once the agreement had been made between factor and seller. The factor will undertake all the credit sales transactions on behalf of his client. The seller is free from the problems involved in collection. All the affairs will be handled by the factor. The factoring enables the seller to reduce the cost of collection by way of savings in time and efforts. The debtors are more responsive to the demands from a factor. The main function of the factor is collection of receivables.

*(3) Financing*

The factoring service provides a short-term finance to the seller. The seller is not only free from the bad debt but also enjoys immediate finance. When a factor purchases the book debt of a seller at a agreed price immediately the factor will pay 80 per cent of the transaction value. If the debt is in case of non-payment by the buyer the amount will be refundable to the factor.

*(4) Credit Risk*

Credit risk is one of the important functions of a factor. The factor will fix the credit horizons for approved customers in consultation with the seller. Therefore, the factor assumes the risk of default in payment by the customers. By assigning a task to the factor, the seller will get two benefits—

(a) factoring relieves the client of the collection work,
(b) the factor can provide first hand information about the financial standing and credit rating of individual customers and their track record of payments. The factor is able to advise the seller on the creditworthiness of potential customers, because he closely observe the financial activities of the buyer than the seller. The credit horizon of the buyer will be fixed by factor

on the past payment record basis. The past payment record sheet will reveal the financial behaviour of the buyer parties. The past record is the litmus test for granting the credit horizon to the buyer. So the assignment of the factoring is more useful and scientific way of approach to detect the bad debt. There are various approaches in granting the credit limits to the buyer party. According to one approach followed by the factor is on the basis of **monthly turnover.** For example, the approved limit for a customer is Rs. 10.00 lakhs and the average collection period is 60 days, sales upto **Rs. 5.00 lakhs** (10 × 30/60) per month will be automatically covered. The factors follows another approach to sanction the credit limits to another party. According to this approach, some factors provide periodic reports to the clients on customerwise outstanding and aging schedules to enable the clients to assess the extent of credit utilitisation before any major sale is made. The financial capability, credit worthiness of the buyer is assessed by the factors on the basis of information. The financial information is available from a number of sources such as **Credit Report Rating Bank References, Trade References, Financial Statements etc.** The analysis of financial statements can reveal the current ratio, quick ratio, net profit margin and returns on investment etc.

*(5) Advisory Services*

Factoring is being a highly specialised skilled talented work create the close relationship between a factor and a seller. By virtue of their specialised knowledge and experience in credit transactions maker them to provide a variety of incidental advisory services to the clients. They are able to provide the following services and advises to the seller party.

(a) The factor is able to know the customer's pulse of the seller product.
(b) They can expect the changes in marketing strategies of the different companies/suppliers.
(c) They are able to know the energing trends in the market and can guide the seller party also.

(d) The factor can also be helpful in auditing process of the seller party.

(e) The factor provide various other services at a charge.

## Factoring in India

Factoring services is not well developed in India. But this service is getting the attention of the Indian corporate sector. It is of recent origin. RBI had constituted in January 1988 a study group under the chairmanship of **Sri C.S. Kalyana Sundaram** to study the feasibility and mechanism of commencing factoring system in India. The study group submitted its report in January 1989. It had gone into its various functional formalities, implication and importance for promoting factoring in the country with the involvement of banks and NBFCs. The group had submitted its re commendations and were accepted by the RBI. Following the commendations of the working group, the Government has permitted the banks to enter this sector. The regulatory authorities permitted the banking companies to carry as factoring business. The statutory authorities allowed the banks to set up subsidiaries or invest in companies jointly with other banks. The RBI has issued the following guidelines:

(a) At present, the banks have no chance to enter into this segment directly. But they may invest in factoring companies with the permission of the RBI. They cannot act as promoters of such companies.

(b) The banks are permitted to set up separate subsidiaries/invest in factoring companies jointly with other banks which would require the prior approval of the RBI.

(c) A factoring subsidiary or joint venture factoring company is not allowed to invest in other companies or other factoring companies.

(d) The banks are not allowed to invest more than 10 per cent of the paid up capital and reserves of the bank.

## Recommendations of the Kalyana Sundaram Committee

The Kalyana Sundaram Group was constituted to examine the feasibility and mechanics of starting factoring services in India. The group was appointed by the RBI in 1989. A brief summary of the Kalyana Sundaram Committee are listed as follows:

(a) The group had suggested that there is a strong need to introduce factoring services in India which would be complimentary to the services provided by banks.
(b) The export factor service would be more useful to the exporter.
(c) The factoring service should offer their services to all industries and all sectors in the economy.
(d) At the infancy stage the factoring organisations may be promoted on a zonal basis.
(e) Factors cannot provide the services efficiently, effectively and economically without the support of computers and IT.
(f) The Central Government and RBI should initiate appropriate measures immediately for setting up specialised agencies for credit investigations.
(g) The development of factoring service depends upon the utilisation of **IT**.
(h) The RBI could consider allowing factoring organisations to raise funds from the **Discount and Finance House of India** and also from other approved financial institutions.
(i) The price for financing services would be around **16 per cent P.A.** and the aggregate price for all other services may not exceed **2.5 per cent** to **3 per cent** of the debts services.
(j) The subsidiaries or associates of banks are ideally suited for undertaking this business.
(k) Factoring activities could be taken up by the Small Industries Development Bank of India in association with one or more commercial banks.
(l) The banks branches should educate the business community about the benefits accruing therefrom.
(m) The price for financing services would be around 16 per cent p.a. and the aggregate price for all other services may not exceed 2.5 per cent to 3 per cent of the debts services.
(n) In the beginning the, entry should be restricted to select promoters/institutions with good track record in **financial services** and competent management should be permitted to enter into this new field.

The RBI initially suggested the factoring services on zonal/regional basis covering the entire India with one bank concentrating in a single zone at a time. It also recommended factoring services through subsidiaries of nationalised banks. The RBI identified the following banks to concentrate on zonal basis in their respective territories.

**(1) State Bank of India (Western Region).**
**(2) Canara Bank (Southern Region).**
**(3) Punjab National Bank (Northern Region).**
**(4) Allahabad Bank (Eastern Zoan).**

Therefore, the first two banks sponsored factoring services.

*(1) SBI Factors and Commercials Services Ltd.*

SBI FACS was promoted by a group of Commercial Banks. The SBI, UBI and SIDBI were participated jointly to commence the operations in March 1991. It has a paid up capital of Rs. 25 crores. It has become an associate member of the Factors chain International based in Amsterdam. It has contemplated to undertake collection and credit services designed to improve cash flow of business concerns by timely realisation of debts. It takes the responsibility of collection of debts due from customers of the seller. It will also undertake the maintenance of clients sales ledger by using the computerised system, monthly sales analysis, invoice analysis and customers payment reports will be provided to clients. It extends its services to all forms of business organisations engaged in manufacturing and trading.

*(2) Canara Bank Factors Ltd.*

Canara Bank Factor Ltd., was incorporated in August 1991 as a subsidiary of Canara Bank. It has been operating the business in southern zone. It has paid up capital of **Rs. 10 crores**. The paid up capital was contributed by Canara Bank, Andhra Bank, and SIDBI. They were contributed the paid up capital in **60 : 20 : 20** respectively.

***Problems in Factoring***

The factoring service in India is not well developed. The growth is relatively limited. The following problems have been faced by the factoring in India:

(a) The factoring in India has limited presence in the market. Though the SBI and Canara Banks-initiated measures for factoring no progress has been made.

(b) The factoring services requires payment of stamp duty which is as higher as 15 per cent of the amount exceeding Rs. 2.00 lakhs. It increases the operations cost of factoring services. Therefore, there is a strong need of waiving of stamp-duty on assignment of debt factors.

(c) The factors have to collect the credit information from their own sources for credit evaluation of clients. They do not have access to any authentic common source of information. The establishment of credit information agency is required.

(d) There is a strong need that the factor should be allowed to purchase book debts without requiring disclaimer certificate from banks. Every factor is required to get a disclaimer certificate from the banks to purchase the book debts of a client.

### (B) Forfaiting

Forfaiting is a kind of financing of receivables belonging to international trade. In this system all risks and collection problems are fully Forfaiters responsibility. The Forefaiter should take the risk in case of non-collection of a book debt. Forfitting is backed by bank guarantee. The salient features of forfaiting are presented below:

(1) It is commercial contract between exporter or importer.

(2) It involves delivery of goods from exporter to importer.

(3) It is delivery of bills of exchange by exporter to importer.

(4) Payment of bills by importers bank to forfaiter.

(5) Cash payment by forfaiter to exporter of the value of bills less discount.

(6) The discount rates are charged as a percentage over the **Euro market interest rates.**

### (C) Bills Discounting

Bill discounting is a source of short-term trade finance to the business community. It is fund based financial activity. It emerged as a profitable business to the **Finance Companies.** At present its importance declined due to the restrictions imposed by the **RBI.** It is used as a medium of financing the current trade. It should not be used for financing capital nature aspects. The bills are negotiable money market instruments. These bills are bought by the financial intermediaries at a discount before their maternity. The Bills are discounted by the third party. According to the Indian Negotiable Instruments Act, 1881. The bills can be defined as "The bill of exchange is an instrument in writing containing an unconditional order signed by the maker, directing a certain person to pay a certain sum of money only to, or to the order of, a certain person or the bearer of that instrument."[2]

The Discount houses play an important role in the system of banking. Bill discounting is a source of short-term trade finance. It is also known as acceptance credit.

### *Evolution of Bill Discounting Scheme in India*

The Indian Central Banking Enquiry Committee had recommended in 1931 for the establishment of a market in commercial bills for effecting improvement in the monetary system. The RBI introduced the Market scheme on January 16, 1952. The main features of the scheme are presented below:

(1) The RBI Act, Section 17(4)(c) permits the RBI to make advances to scheduled banks against the security of issuance of promissory notes. Therefore, the RBI announced a scheme for bills market.

(2) The Scheduled Banks were required to convert a portion of the demand promissory notes, obtained by them from their constituents in respect of loans/overdrafts and cash credits granted to them, into usance promissory notes maturing within 90 days to be able to avail of refinance under the above scheme.

(3) The existing loan, cash credit or overdraft accounts were required to be split up into two parts. They are : one part was to remain covered by the demand promissory notes, in this account further withdrawals or repayments were as usual being permitted. The other part which would represent the minimum requirement of the borrower during the next three months would be converted into usance promissory notes maturing within **90 days**.

(4) The procedure did not bring any change in offering same facilities as before by banks to their constituents.

(5) The amount advanced by the RBI was not exceeding the amount sent by the Scheduled Banks to the respective borrowers.

(6) The Scheduled Bank applying for accommodation had to certify that the paper presented by it as co-collateral arose out of *bona fide* commercial transactions and that the party was creditworthy.

(7) According to banks under this scheme in the initial stages were made at 1.5 per cent below the bank rate. The concessional rate of interest was withdrawn in two stages.

(8) The RBI had accepted to bear the cost of the stamp duty to the extent of **50 per cent.**

***Types of Bills***

There are various types of bills in practice. They can be classified on the basis of various factors. Some of these bills are presented:

**(1) Demand bills.**
**(2) Usance bill.**
**(3) Documentary bills.**
**(4) D/A bills.**
**(5) D/P bills.**
**(6) Clean bills.**
**(7) Creation of B/E.**

(1) *Demand Bills*: The Demand bill is payable immediately on presentation or at sight to the drawee. A bill may or may not contain time of payment. It is also known as Demand bills.

(2) *Usance Bill*: The usance bill is also known as Time bill. A bill of exchange and a promissory note may be payable either on demand or after a fixed time. It is payable on demand when:

(i) It is expressed to be payable on demand or at sight or on presentment.

(ii) No time for payment is specified in it. A bill of exchange might be payable at a fixed period after its date or after sight or after an event which is certain to happen. The event must be certain to happen otherwise the bill will not be valid.

(3) *Documentary Bills*: If the drawer of a bill of exchange encloses with it a document of title to goods or any other document it is called a

documentary bill. These document include the invoices and other documents of title such as RR, LR and bills of lading issued by custom officials. The documentary bills further be classified as **D/A** and **D/P bills.**

(4) *Documents Against Bills*: D/A bills means the documentary evidence along with the bill of exchange is deliverable against acceptance by the drawee. Therefore, the documentary becomes a clean bill after delivery of the documents.

(5) *Documents Against Payment Bills*: D/P bill has been accepted by the drawee, the documents of title will be held by the Bank or the finance company till the maturity of the bill of exchange.

(6) *Clean Bills*: There is no enclosure of the bill is known as clean bill. Because, the interest rate charged on such bills is higher than the rate charged on documentary bills.

(7) *Bills of Exchange*: In general business, when a seller sells goods to a buyer, the buyer usually pay the sum immediately. But today the market transactions are based on credit and the buyer may be allowed to pay afterwards. Thus the bill of exchange arises between buyer and seller parties. The seller draws a bill on the name of the buyer. The seller is called the drawer of the bill, and the buyer is known as the drawee. The seller sends the bill to the buyer who acknowledges his responsibility for the payment of the amount on the terms mentioned on the bill by writing his acceptance on the bill.

### *Advantages*

The advantages of bill discounting to investors and bank and finance companies. The bill of exchange is very popular among the business community and banking sectors. The investors are benefited with the bills of exchange. It is the short-term sources of finance to them. The business of the bill exchange is not a lending business and therefore no tax at source is deducted. The bill discounting rates are better than the rates of **Inter Corporate Deposits.** The banking sector has also getting benefits regarding the bill business. The amount of investment made in this segment is safe. Because the bills of exchange is a negotiable instrument and there will be a chance to enforce the claim easily. The bill of exchange is a liquid asset and the banker knows the advance date of maturity. Therefore, the banker can divert his idle fund towards bill of exchange which yields better returns. The bills of exchange shows highest yield than in other loans and advances.

**Consumer Finance**

Consumer finance is related to asset based financing activity. It offers finance facility to the individuals to acquire durable consumer goods. In this system, the individual consumer pays some amount as down payment at the time of the delivery of the asset and pays the balance with interest over a specified period of time. At present it has emerged as an important asset based financial service in India. The consumer finance have been developed in India by Commercial Banks, Multinational Banks, Foreign Banks, Finance Companies etc. These institutions provide finance to purchase cars, scooters, home appliances, washing machines, PCs, cooking ranges, food processors, CTVs, VCRs etc. In India there is no statutory organ to regulate consumer credit.

The consumer finance depend upon the nature of transaction, type of product, method of financing, mode of payment, repayment period, the interest rate and security. The consumer financing in India can be classified into three kinds. They are: (a) Hire Purchase, (b) Credit sale and (c) Conditional sale. According to the HP system, the customer has the option to buy the assets. The buyer may not exercise the option and return the goods according to the terms of the agreement. **Credit sale** is another method of consumer financing in India. In this method, the title of the asset is transferred to the customer on payment of the first instalment. The conditional sale method indicates that the title of the asset is not transferred to the customer until the total purchase price including the credit charge is paid. The customer have no to terminate the agreement before the payment of the full price.

The Repayment period ranges between **12–60** monthly instalments. The rate of interest is usually at a **flat rate**. The mode of payment consists of two groups (a) down payment schemes (b) deposit linked schemes. The amount of down payment will be between **20 per cent or 25 per cent** of the cost. The deposit linked scheme requires down payment between **15 per cent to 25 per cent** of the amount of financed. There are same companies are offering **zero interest** scheme to buy the products. Generally the assets are in the form of a first charge on the asset. The consumer have no chance to sell or pledge or hypothecate the asset under any circumstances.

## REFERENCES

1. M.Y. Khan, *Financial Services*, p. 753, Tata McGraw, 1997.
2. *Ibid*. p. 833.

# 2

# INSURANCE

## Introduction

Financial services is an essential segment of financial system. Financial system in India has made commendable progress in extending its geographic spread and functional reach. The specialised financial institutions emerged in the Indians financial system to cater to the financial needs of the industrial sector. The Insurance companies also played a prominent role in resource mobilisation and directing investments in productive areas.

Insurance companies invest the savings of their policy holders. The policy holders will pay the amount to the insurance company in the form of **premium.** Insurance is just a contract between two parties. The Insurance company undertakes in consideration of a sum of money to make good the loss suffered by the party against a specified risk. There are two parties in an insurance contract: (a) insurer, (b) Insured/ beneficiary. The insurer is known as Insurance Company. The insured means a person/party who to undertake an agreement with an insurer. The terms of the contract will be laid down in a document. The document is known as **policy**. The property which is insured is the subject matter of insurance. The property may be insured against loss arising from uncertain events.

The insurance companies collect and invest large amounts of premium. They offer financial protection to the investors, and channelising the funds to the Government. They are working long-term basis. They offer policies for more than 10 years. Liquidity is not a problem to the insurance companies. They involve in the long-term investment activities. The rate of return is very low on the policies. The investments of insurance companies have been largely in government bonds, corporate bonds, mortgages and local self-government bonds.

Insurance companies are active in **life, health and general**. The insurance companies began to operate the pension schemes and mutual funds. Pension business is a specialised form of life assurance. Life insurance covers a specified period of life of a person. General insurance covers losses caused by fire, accident and marine adventures. The life insurance is different from general insurance. In life insurance the insurer has a fixed obligation to compensate the insured. In the case of general insurance the event insured against may not happen and company does not necessarily have to always to compensate the party to the contract. Insurance organisations in India provide finance to the industries. The insurance organisation in India comprise two state owned monolithic institutions, namely

**(A) Life Insurance Corporate of India.**
**(B) General Insurance Corporation of India.**

## (A) Life Insurance Corporate of India (LIC)

The LIC is one of the most important financial intermediaries in India. In 1956 the LIC was set up and the insurance business have been nationalised. Till 1956 the insurance business was mixed and decentralised. There were 245 companies on the one of nationalisation with different ages and sizes. The objectives of the LIC are :

(a) to provide insurance facilities to the masses at reasonable cost;
(b) to increase savings habits among the public;
(c) to channelise the small savings towards industrial sector;
(d) to maximise the benefits to the policy holders;
(e) to act as trustees of the policy holders;
(f) to protect the policy holders individual and collective interests;
(g) to introduce innovative schemes to meet the changing life insurance needs of the community;
(h) to ensure efficient and courteous service to the insured public; and
(i) to provide job satisfaction to the employees.

A large number of insurance policies have been introduced by the LIC. The LIC as diversified its activities by establishing

**(A) LIC Housing Finance Ltd.**
**(B) LIC Mutual Fund.**

**(C) LIC International.**
**(D) Jewan Bima Sahayoga Asset Management Corporation.**

LIC insurance policies make a very flexible financial instrument. The value of a policy is the present value of a lump sum or a future stream of income less the value of future premiums. It offers various schemes, policies and plans to the investors. The following are various categories of the schemes which are offered by the LIC:

(a) **Individual insurance.**
(b) **Group insurance.**
(c) **Group gratuity.**
(d) **Group superannuation.**
(e) **Non-medical insurance.**
(f) **Salary saving insurance.**
(g) **Annuities.**
(h) **Other schemes.**

The funds collected through the sale of various policies are invested in a variety of income generating financial assets. The fund will be built up out of the excess of premiums and investment income over claim and expenses. The life fund is evaluated from time to time. The valuation of life fund is being based on the method of discounting future income and expenditure. A life fund will be known as surplus when the value of fund is greater than the present value of future liabilities. This surplus amount will be distributed partially to all policy holders who are eligible according to the various schemes norms. The remaining surplus amount will be added to the Reserve account. The LIC will distribute surplus to policy holders in three kinds: (a) in the form of cash, (b) as a reduction in premium and (c) as an addition to the value of the policy. The LIC will distribute the surplus amount by adding the bonus to the value of policy then the policy is known as "**Revisionary bonus**". The revisionary bonus will be calculated on the basis of original sum assured. The Surplus can be categorised in two kinds **(a) Revenue surplus and (b) Capital surplus**. Revenue surplus means it is an excess of future income over future outgoings. **Capital surplus** means, it will be arised when the value of the fund is balanced by the values of the various assets of the life fund as recorded in the balance sheet.

The insurance policies are divided into life insurance and general insurance. The main features of the important life insurance policies are presented below:

**(a) Whole life policy.**
**(b) Endowment policy.**
**(c) Joint life policy.**
**(d) Annuities.**
**(e) Sinking fund policies.**
**(f) Janatha policy.**
**(g) Limited payment life policy.**
**(h) Double accident indemnity policy.**
**(i) Convertible whole life policy.**

**(a)** ***Whole Life Policy*** is the cheapest form of policy. The premium on this policy should be paid throughout the life of the assured person. The sum assured is payable only after the death of the person.

**(b)** ***Endowment Policy*** is the most popular form of life assurance. Under this policy, the insured amount is payable either at the end of a specified number of years or upon the death of the insured person which ever is earlier. The minimum amount for which a policy is issued under this plan is Rs. **1000**. This policy is useful for the marriage of children or for the education of children when they reach a certain age.

**(c)** ***Joint Life Policy*** is suitable for partnership firms. The policy money becomes payable either on maturity of the policy or the death of any of the persons jointly insured.

**(d)** ***Annuities*** is suitable for self-employed and petty businessman. The policy holder is required to pay the premium in regular instalments over a certain period or he may deposit a lump sum amount. After the assured reaches a certain age. The insurer pay back the money by monthly, quarterly, half yearly or yearly instalments.

**(e)** ***Sinking Fund Policies*** are more useful to the big business firms and companies. They make use of this policy for redemption of debentures, or replacement of assets or repayment of loans. The premium amount shall be paid by the companies by annually. After the completion of specified period the company gets the sum assured.

**(f)** ***Janatha Policy*** will be issued for a period of 10, 15 or 24 years with the condition that the policy should mature before the assured reaches 60 years of age. The policy can be taken by a person only before the age of 45. The amount of premium can be only Rs. 1000

There is no need of formality of medical examination if the person is below 35 years.

**(g)** ***Limited Payment Life Policy*** is similar to the whole life policy. Because the policy amount is payable only after the death of the assured. The premium amount shall be paid for a certain number of years or until the death of the person if it occurs within that period.

**(h)** ***Double Accident Indemnity Policy*** offers double amount of the policy to his survivors, if the assured dies of an accident.

**(i)** ***Convertible Whole Life Policy*** facilitate the assured an option to convert the policy into an endowment policy. The rate of premium is low at initially. After sometime the assured persons has the right to convert into endowment policy.

**New Jeevan Shree Policy** is an endowment policy with a term of minimum of 5 years and maximum of 25 years. The Jeevan Shree has undergone a sea change after it was scrapped from **31st January 2001,** and getting relaunched in the first week of March 2001, with the era of guaranteed returns getting phased out, the new Jeevan Shree scheme has guaranteed additions pegged at Rs. 70 per thousand sum assured per annum at the end of each policy year against the earlier Rs. 75 per thousand sum assured per annum. The provision for loyalty addition for policies, which were inforce on the date of death or on maturity, has also got scaled down and now no loyalty addition would be payable during the first four policy years. Loyalty addition is generally pegged at 5 per cent of sum assured in the new version of Jeevan Shree.

**Jeevan Surabhi** is the scheme, where the premiums are payable for a limited period. It allows for a periodic increase in insurance cover besides the free risk coverage even during the non-premium paying period. It is available with premium payment terms of 12, 15 and 18 years, and policy terms of 15, 20 and 25 years. And money back is allowed at intervals of 4 or 5 years as per the policy term.

**The Money Back Policy** with bonus, 20 years, this policy provides a life cover during the term of the policy along with the maturity benefits paid in instalments by way of survival benefits.

**The Money Back Policy** with 25 years besides providing life cover during the term of the policy, the maturity benefits are paid in instalments by way of survival benefits.

**Bima Kiran** is a low cost insurance policy to suit young man and women. The policy offers more vileges than other schemes. It covers risk and other attractive features are like **"in built accident", "loyalty addition", "free insurance cover after maturity".** It is low cost scheme at an affordable level to enable to maximise the risk cover with a minimum amount. If the premium amounts are paid regularly the following benefits for basic sum assured of Rs. 1000 are assured.

**(a) Death cover, (b) Accident benefit, (C) On disability due to accident.** On survival of the term, a minimum free cover (without accident benefit) is available for a period of 10 years at different situations.

**Jeevan Kishore** is a policy which provides gift to children for their secure future. Under this policy, parents or legal guardians can provide a gift to children. Children both made and female between the ages of 1 and 12 are eligible for this scheme. The risk commences either two years after the date of the commencement of the policy or after the completion of 7 years of age of the children whichever is later. However, the date of commens of risk cannot in any case, go beyond the policy after the completion of 12 years of age. The policy is eligible for bonus from the waiting period also.

**Children Money Back Policies** are more useful for education, and career of children. Under this scheme, the children's upto 10 years of age are eligible to be proposed for insurance by parents/guardians. The policy can also be gifted to the children by any person. The risk commences two years from the date of the policy or from the policy immediately following the completion of 7 years of age whichever is later. In the event of death during the term of the policy before maturity assured sum becomes payable together with guaranteed addition. The policy issued only in multiple of Rs. 25,000 subject to a minimum of Rs. 25,000 and maximum of Rs. 5.00 lakhs.

## LIC's Investment Pattern

The Insurance Act, Section **27** laid down the investment pattern of the LIC, as follows :

| | | |
|---|---|---|
| (a) | In Central Government securities not less then | 20% |
| (b) | In State Government securities including Central Govt. securities | 40% |
| (c) | Socially oriented sectors as indicated by GOI from time to time | 50% |

## Forms of Financing

The LIC facilitates funds to the corporate enterprises in the following kinds:

(a) direct lending to industry;
(b) subscription to shares and bonds of development financial institutions; and
(c) purchase of securities.

**(B) General Insurance Corporation of India (GIC)**

The General Insurance Corporation was registered as a private company under the Companies Act, 1956. It was formed as Government Company under Section 9 of the General Insurance (Nationalisation) Act, 1972. It has four subsidiaries. The subsidiary companies have acquired considerable experience expertise and financial strength. They have established reasonable standards of conduct of business. The four subsidiary companies are:

**(1) National Insurance Company, Kolkata.**
**(2) The New India Assurance Company, Mumbai.**
**(3) The Oriental Fire and Insurance Company, New Delhi.**
**(4) The United India Fire and General Insurance Company, Chennai.**

The GIC share capital at present stands at **Rs. 107.5 crores**. There is a proposal to raise the capital to Rs. 200 crores. The Government of India had 50 per cent of share capital and the remaining being held by public including employees. GIC holds 100 per cent equity of its subsidiary companies. The each subsidiary company had a share capital of Rs. 40 crores. The capital of each subsidiary company should be raised to Rs. 100 crores with the Central Government holding 50 per cent and the remaining proportion lies with the public and employees of the respective companies. There are at present 1124 divisional offices in the four subsidiaries through-out the country. The divisional officer supervises 3151 branches only. On an average one divisional office is looking the affairs of the three branch offices. Therefore, they are over staffed and need to reorganise their work in order to use the available man power in an optimal manner. The financial authority of various branches should be reviewed in the light of the functions assigned to them.

The GIC was given charge of the overall control, superintendence and policy making for smooth operation of the general insurance business. At present the direct business is done mostly by the subsidiaries of the GIC. The premium income of the GIC is obtained through the obligatory reinsurance premium on a sharing basis from its subsidiaries on their direct business. The GIC's direct business is only in the form of aviation insurance. The general insurance business is classified as follows:

**(A) Marine Insurance.**
**(B) Fire Insurance.**
**(C) Miscellaneous.**

### *(A) Marine Insurance*

Marine Insurance relates to ships and cargoes. A contract of marine insurance is a contract under which the insurer indemnifies the insured against marine losses. The losses relating to marine adventure or to navigation or business on the sea. There are many types of policies available in India which are presented below:

**(a) Voyage policy.**
**(b) Time policy.**
**(c) Mixed policy.**
**(d) Value policy.**
**(e) Floating policy.**

**(a)** ***Voyage Policy*** is the most popular policy in marine insurance. It insures the subject "at and from" or from one place to another place. The first policy covers the subject matter both while the ship is at the port of departure and also from the time of the sailing of the ship. The next policy covers only when the ship sails from the port.

**(b)** ***Time Policy*** is framing the time limit for a subject matter. The subject matter is insured for a specified time not exceeding a year. Sometimes the policy period comes to an end while the ship is till away from its destination. The ship should be taken care of by a **Continuous clause.**

**(c)** ***Mixed Policy*** is a combined policy of voyage and time. It covers the risk for a particular voyage to a specified period for example, from Chennai to Singapore for 6 months.

**(d)** ***Value Policy*** specifies the accepted value of the subject matter.

**(e)** ***Floating Policy*** mentions the amount for which the policy is being taken out. All the particulars regarding ship, goods and destination will be specified later.

The GIC fulfil the needs of industrial, manufacturing, commercial, services household and agricultural sectors through a wide range of innovative products. The GIC also underwrites a very vast and diversified portfolio of general business. It has been promoting personal insurance cover in the field of live stock, poultry, horticulture, pump sets pisciculture, sericulture and personal accidents. GIC has introduced innovative new policies like Mediclaim, Nuclear insurance pool, hut insurance, householder's comprehensive policy professional indemnity Insurance, insurance for members of stock exchange, etc.

### *(B) Fire Insurance*

Fire insurance means, it is a contract where the insurer accepts in consideration of the premium to pay the loss or damage caused by fire accident during the specified period. If in the case of loss, the assured party can claim from the company, the actual amount of loss or the maximum amount indicated in the contract, whichever is less. The following are the important fire insurance policies presented below:

**(a) Floating policy.**
**(b) Replacement policy.**
**(c) Specific Policy.**
**(d) Valued policy.**
**(e) Comprehensive policy.**

**(a)** ***Floating Policy*** covers property which are lying at various locations against loss by fire. For example, the goods placed in two godowns at various locations will be covered.

**(b)** ***Replacement Policy*** involves no cash payment. The insurer only agrees to pay the cost of replacement of the property damaged or destroyed by the fire. It avoids the mischiefs made by the assured.

**(c)** ***Specific Policy*** covers the loss suffered by the assured is covered only upto a specific amount which is less than the real value of the property.

**(d)** ***Valued Policy*** covers to pay a fixed sum of money irrespective of the amount of loss to the insured. Under this policy no profit can be made out of any loss.

**(e)** ***Comprehensive Policy*** covers losses arising from any type of risks such as **fire, theft, burglary, third party risks etc.** It is known as all in one policy. It covers loss of profits for the period during which the business affairs are suspended due to fire occurrence.

**Regulatory Framework**

The GIC business is basically cyclic in nature and the investment policy of the GIC and its subsidiaries is defined in the Insurance Act, 1938. The Government of India has the powers to issue guidelines from time to time. Under Section 27B of the Insurance Act, 1938 regulate the investment of the funds of the GIC and its subsidiaries. They are required to invest in the following manner:

(a) Approved securities.
(b) Approved investments.

The following financial instruments are categorised as approved securities by the Insurance Act, 1938.

1. Central/State Government securities.
2. Any securities guaranteed by either Central or State Government.
3. Debentures or securities issued by local self-government.
4. Statutory company shares guaranteed by Central/State Government.
5. Other securities (approved securities).

The following financial instruments are classified as approved investments by the Act as follows:

1. FDRs with scheduled banks or co-operative societies.
2. Shares of any company which have been guaranteed by another company.
3. Debentures issued by any Municipality.
4. Debentures issued by a first charge on the assets of any company which has paid the interest in full or the preceding three years.

The Insurance Companies invest not more than 25 per cent of their assets in other approved securities and investments with the consent of the Board of Directors. The restrictions are:

(a) not to invest in the shares or debentures of a private company.
(b) not to invest in any one company more than 10 per cent of the assets.

(c) 10 per cent of the prescribed share capital and debentures of the company (2% in case of banking or investment company).

**Objectives of the Investment Policy**

The objectives of the insurance companies are presented below:

(a) to meet the needs of the national priorities,
(b) safety and security of the share capital,
(c) adequate liquidity,
(d) protection against inflation,
(e) providing better returns, and
(f) marketability.

The deployment of funds in approved investments signifies the participation of GIC in national development and industrial growth. Some portion of the funds of the insurance companies have to be kept in fixed deposits. These financial instruments offer liquidity. The advantages of investments in equities are:

(a) participation in national priorities,
(b) capital appreciation,
(c) attractive net yields,
(d) protection against inflation, and
(e) dividend income enjoys inter-corporate tax relief.

The Insurance Companies also undertake the underwriting of the new issues of existing or new companies. The process should be taken care for maximisation of the investment income. The following factors should be observed while making an investment decision:

(a) The nature of the industry.
(b) The potential growth of the industry.
(c) The history of the promoters.
(d) Gestation period of the project.
(e) Buy back period of the project.
(f) Locational advantage of the Unit.
(g) Government policy.

(h) Financial feasibility of the project.
(i) Commercial viability.

The GIC and its subsidiaries invest in the following categories:

(A) The Government Securities.
(B) Term loans to Companies.
(C) Bill Rediscounting schemes.
(D) Others (loans to HUDCO/DDA/Housing/PSUs).

It also providing financial assistance in the following ways:

(1) Direct assistance.
(2) Purpose-wise assistance.
(3) Sector-wise assistance.

The GIC provides financial assistance directly to the corporate sector. It finances industry by granting loans and by underwriting the shares. It has also make direct subscription to the shares of the corporate sector.

It provides financial assistance **on Purpose-wise** basis. It renders assistance in four purposes.

(1) for new projects,
(2) for diversification and expanssion,
(3) for modernisation of the plant and rehabilitation purpose, and
(4) supplementary finance.

The GIC's focus was on the financial needs of the concerns already assisted rather than going in for new projects to improve its return on investments.

The GIC, is an investment institution, which tries to maximise its returns on investment. It provides maximum assistance to private sector. The private sector accounts for bulk of GIC's investments. The share of public sector has shown wide variation. The public sector is heavily funded by LIC and the private sector funded by GIC.

## Malhotra Committee

As a part of reforms of the insurance sector. The Malhotra Committee has suggested a comprehensive framework covering the life and general insurance. The major elements of the recommended framework has been presented below:

**(A) Insurance Intermediaries.**
**(B) Insurance Surveyors.**
**(C) Product Pricing.**
**(D) Investment Issues.**
**(E) Restructuring.**
**(F) Liberalisation.**
**(G) Rural Insurance.**
**(H) Regulation.**

***(A) Insurance Intermediaries***

The Malhotra Committee has made recommendations relating to the insurance intermediaries are submitted below:

(a) It has been suggested that the marketing divisions of the insurance organisations should be thoroughly reviewed in order to increase the marketing skills of the organisations.
(b) The development officers will play an important role in the insurance business. Therefore, the role of development officers should be viewed seriously.
(c) The development officers selection should be done properly and they should be encouraged to take up marketing related functions.
(d) For marketing of insurance products in rural areas a system of supervisory agents should be developed. The supervisory agents should be posted in the villages on commission basis.
(e) The insurance organisations should concentrate as direct business without the intervention of the development officers.
(f) The insurance organisations must encourage professionalism among agents to become more competent.
(g) The system of brokers should be introduced by the insurance organisations to improve professionalism and customer service.
(h) There is a strong need to periodically review the service terms and conditions and benefits of development officers.
(i) The incentive system should encompass the following anyone incentive scheme should be followed:

(i) targeted portfolio as laid down by each branch,
(ii) quality of business should be judged,
(iii) the amount of incentive should be reasonable, and
(iv) growth of the business over the previous year of an order of 20 per cent or Rs. 3,00,000 whichever is lower.

(j) In backward areas the insurance policies can be sold through institutional agents such as : voluntary agencies with proven track record of social service and cooperative societies may be considered.

***(B) Insurance Surveyors***

The Controller of Insurance has been conducting the examinations for granting the surveyorship. This system should be changed, because it has not served any useful purpose. The Insurance Companies should appoint a right surveyor to the right job. There is a strong need to set-up an institutional professional surveyors organisation. The institution should be a self-financed organisation. The cost of establishment of the institution could be substantial and the insurance industry may provide financial and other promotional support. The insurance industry may be represented on the governing body of the institution for the initial **5 to 7** years period. The institution should have the overall responsibility regarding surveyor's membership like code of conduct, unprofessional conduct of its members, disqualification from membership. The prospective surveyor should pass an examination to be conducted by the institution and thereafter to work as an apprentice for two years. The prospective surveyor may be kept at the disposal of a senior surveyor. The Insurance Companies should take some remedial actions to avoid malpractice's and eventualities.

***(C) Product Pricing***

The LIC should publish a revised mortality table based on recent experience. The revisions should be made for every ten years. The Insurance Companies should provide intensive training to their workforce. LIC should immediately review the system of product pricing. The renewal cost should be brought down. Therefore, the Insurance Companies should improve the productivity of its employees and streamline its systems and procedure. The cost of production of a product shall be reduced substantially by introducing computers in the organisation. Computerisation of its entire range of operations is very crucial for controlling costs and improving customer, service.

### *(D) Investment Issues*

The premium amount collected by the Insurance Companies should invest judiciously with the combined objectivities of liquidity, maximisation of yield and safety. The Insurance Companies are required to generate reserves for claims that may arise in future. The Return on Investment from insurance funds will influence substantially on premium rates and bonuses. Therefore, the insurers should maintain at all times, a prescribed minimum level of solvency as a protection to the policy holders interest. The investments of insurance funds is regulated. Investment of funds by insurance organisations are regulated in India under Section 27(A) and 27(B). The Malhotra Committee has recommended reductions in the extent of investments by Insurance Companies.

### *(E) Restructuring*

There has been a tremendous changes in the insurance industry. A close observation reveal that the entire insurance industry must be restructured in order to meet the present situation. The restructure of the industry will definitely enhance the profitability. Therefore, the following insurance institutions must be restructured to meet the market requirements.

**(1) Life Insurance Industry.**
**(2) General Insurance Corporation.**

#### *(1) Life Insurance Industry*

The Life Insurance industry having a vast scope for furthering growth of the business. According to the present situation, the entire branch operations must be revamped to meet the changing needs of the policy holders. The delegation of policy servicing responsibilities to the branches has been considerable to some extent but there is still dissatisfaction among policy holders. The delegation of authority and system of supervision are inadequate. The decision making power has slowed down. The present structure of LIC does not provide sufficient assurance. In this situation the **Malhotra Committee** has made a number of recommendations which are presented below. The Central office should basically work for a limited extent in order to make more effective efforts. The Central office should concentrate as **policy formulation, product development and pricing, personnel policies, accounts, investments and systems development.** The Central office should be filled with highly specialised, dedicated competent personnel and professionalised. At present it has been over staffed. There should be structural changes in between zonal office and head office. The Committee further recommended that the delegation of financial, administrative and operational to the zonal offices should be made effectively. There should be completely restructure of the entire life insurance organisation.

*(2) General Insurance Corporation*

The GIC has four subsidiary companies. The subsidiaries have acquired considerable experience, expertise and financial strength established reasonable standards of conduct of business. The GIC structure should be revamped and its subsidiaries also be restructured. In a competitive environment the cost would be crucial to the success. Therefore, these organisations need to reduce the cost of operating expenses substantially. There are at present 1124 divisional offices to supervise 3151 branches. Therefore, it is very clear that these organisations were overstaffed. It ultimately push the insurance product price. The additional staff should be posted to branch offices to enhance the productivity per employee and reduce the cost of expenditure. Therefore the financial authority of various branches should be reviewed in the changing circumstances. The computerisation is most important for GIC where the customer requires prompt service. All the four subsidiary companies must go for comprehensive computerisation for handling the business at all levels. The provisions of the Insurance Act, 1938 should apply to GIC and the four subsidiary companies.

***(F) Liberalisation***

According to the liberalisation policy of the government, it was decided that the private sector may also invited to enter into the insurance segment. The entry of the private insurance companies have created a competition to the public sector institutions. The competition may offer lower prices to the policy holders. It creates efficiency and professionalism among employees. The work culture may be introduced among the workforce. It may tap the untapped new lines of business. Private insurance companies should be allowed. But mushrooming of of small companies has to be avoided. No single company should be allowed to both life and general insurance business. The number of new entrants should be controlled. The rules must be rigid in case of new entrants. The minimum paid up capital should be **Rs. 100 crores**. But a lower amount of paid up capital may be fixed to the state level cooperative institutions which are taking up insurance business. The promoters quota should not exceed **40 per cent** of the total paid up capital. The individuals should not be permitted to hold more than 1 per cent of the equity. In the private insurance companies, promoters should hold at all times not less than **26 per cent** of the paid up capital. The foreign companies should enter the insurance business with Indian partner as Joint venture. In view of the entry of more players in the insurance business, the regulation of the industry must be strengthened. All the insurance companies must maintain adequate solvency at all times. The investment norms must be followed by all insurance companies as laid down by the Government from time to time. They do not invest in any affiliate of the promoters. The new entrants in general insurance would have to observe the tariff regulations in force. The following private sector organisations have been entered the insurance segment.

1. **ING Vyshya.**
2. **Max Newyork Life.**
3. **Birla Sun life.**
4. **Tata AIG.**
5. **ICICI Prudential.**
6. **SBI Life Insurance.**
7. **HDFC Standard Life.**
8. **OM Kotak.**
9. **Allianz Bajaj.**
10. **AIG.**
11. **Royal Sundaram Alliance.**

***(G) Rural Insurance***

This is the neglected segment of the insurance market. There is a strong need to concentrate in rural areas for spreading non-traditional insurance business. For widening the network, whenever possible to involve, the Panchayat Samithis, cooperative societies and non-governmental organisations etc., in the insurance market. Special attention should be paid for self-employed women. The new entrants may be required to undertake a specified proportion of their business as rural non-traditional business. Non-performance may be subjected to a penal assessment by the **Insurance Regulatory Authority.** The cooperative institutions may be encouraged to transact the general insurance business.

### *(H) Regulation*

Insurance companies sell promise to indemnify the insured for a happening of specified events. Before the nationalisation of LIC and GIC, they were regulated under the provisions of the Insurance Act, 1938. The Insurance Act was administered by the controller of Insurance.

Following the recommendations of the **Malhotra Committee**, the Government of India approved the setting up of the IRA. The Ministry of Finance has the overall responsibility to regulate the insurance sector in place of the Controller of Insurance. It had been assigned legal and comprehensive legislation work on the pattern of the SEBI.

### Salient Features of Interim IRA

The salient features of the interim IRA are presented below:

The IRA is headed by a chairman appointed by the Government of India. The Chairman is of the status of an Additional Secretary to the Central Government. The Chairman is the ex-offico controller of insurance. He is enjoying the powers as par with the COI. The maximum number of members in IRA were **seven**. From the members, Three shall serve full time. They shall be nominated by the Central Government. The persons are having experience and indepth knowledge in life insurance, general insurance, finance, economic legal and other matters. The Chairman and the Members would hold office until the pleasure of Central Government. The rules and regulations may be determined by the Government of India from time to time. The Chairman would have appropriate powers to discharge the functions more effectively. The Government would provide assistance for smooth functioning of the IRA. The IRA is free to determine its own procedures. It has powers to call for records, returns, notes data or any other relevant material. The Government has the power to ask information on various aspects of insurance business. It is required to submit periodical report to the Government of India. The Government could assign additional Non-statutory functions as may be considered necessary in order to promote and ensure the growth of the industry.

## Insurance Regulatory and Development Authority Act, 1999, (IRDA)

The IRDA was enacted in 1999 to protect the interest of the policy holders. It was enacted to regulate, promote and ensure orderly growth of the insurance industry. The IRA would consists of a chairperson and maximum number of members were 9. These members and chairman is to be appointed by Central Government. The five members of the team would be full time members. The members of the IRA shall have integrity, ability and standing with adequate knowledge, experience of life insurance, general insurance, actuarial service, finance, law, accountancy, business administration etc.

### Powers and Functions

The powers and functions of IRA are presented below:

(a) Licencing authority.
(b) Settlement machinery.
(c) Maintaining professional code of conduct.
(d) Statutory powers.
(e) Promoting and regulating the insurance organisations.
(f) Control and regulation of the terms, rates and conditions.
(g) Designing the books of accounts of the insurance industry.
(h) Supervising the functioning of Tariff Advisory Committee.
(i) Any other powers as may be assigned by the Government.

# 3

# CREDIT CARDS

## Introduction

The economic development of society and the socio-cultural changes had lead to the spectacular growth of service industry. The technological advances have increased the integration and efficiency of the financial system. After the basic needs were fulfilled, like food, shelter and clothing. There was a tremendous demand for improved satisfaction and it leads to a proliferation of variations in the same product. Increasing affluence combined with increasing complexity of life has led to the phenomenon of **Credit Cards**. They provide convenience and safety in the purchasing process. It is generally known as "**Plastic Money**". The credit cards are made of plastic is widely used by the consumers all around the globe. The changes in consumer behaviour and tastes led to the tremendous growth of credit cards. Credit card is a card which enables the consumers to purchase products or services without paying immediately. This credit concept is based on the principle of "**Buy now pay later**". Credit Card is a document that can be used for purchase of goods and services all over the globe.

The world's first credit card was issued by **Mobil in** 1940. This card was initially issued by the Company to give specialised services to its regular customers. It helped to boost sales and increase the customer base. After the tremendous success of Mobil Card various organisations began to think about the use of cards in different segments of the business. The **Diners Club, American Express and Carte Blanche** Cards have emerged. The credit cards were popularly known in **USA**. During the Second World War US saw the growth of the Credit Cards. The first bank card was issued by **Fanklin National Bank, USA** in the year 1952. In 1960, the Credit Card operating system was developed by **Bank of America, USA**. An international bank card system known as "**VISA**" International was established. Another international bank card system called "**Master Card**" was established. At present the market is dominated by the VISA and Master Card. In the year 1966 this system was launched by **Barclays Bank, UK and** the named as Barclay Card. The Access Card was launched in the year 1962 in UK by a Consortium of Banks. **The EURO CARD** was introduced in most of the West European Countries. In the year 1988, the **first woman** card was launched **"My Card"** by International Bank of Asia in Hong Kong. There was tremendous demand for that card. The another card was introduced as **"Ladys Card"** in Malaysia. In 1990, Green Card was launched in **UK and Europe**.

The credit cards are made of plastic. It is widely used by the consumers all around the globe in the **digital economy**. The card identifies its owner. The owner of the card is entitled to purchase the goods without cash. It provide purchase services without money and be eligible to get credit from a number of merchant establishments. The issuer of the card issues credit cards depending on the credibility of the customers. The card issuer enters into a tie up with different merchant vendors located indifferent geographical places in various fields of business activities. The card issuer will put up a credit limit for its card holders and a ceiling limit for each vendor. The card offers the card holders an opportunity to buy air, rail tickets and stay at hotels for payments. The card holder need only to present the card at the cash counter and has to sign some firms. The credit cards can be considered as a substitute for cash and cheques. The cards are not accepted by all the merchant vendors.

## Process of Credit Card Business Cycle

Credit Cards facilitate its holder to make purchases at various designated merchant establishments. The establishments like travel agencies. Star Hotels, Departmental stores will accept all valid cards in lieu of cash payments. The Card holder can avoid the risk of carrying cash. The following steps are involved in the process of a transaction.

***Step I:*** A card holder purchases goods and present the credit card to the designated merchant establishment.

***Step II:*** The retail vendor verifies the number on the card against the **hot list** provided to him by the Bank.

***Step III:*** The card holder is required to sign on the voucher and the signature has to tally with the one on the credit card.

***Step IV:*** The Retailer has to present the sales vouchers to the bank for reimbursement for the customers purchases. The bank also charges commission from the retailer.

***Step V:*** The bank will make payment to the Retailer on behalf of the card holder.

***Step VI:*** After completion of the process. The bank sends the bill to the card holder and received the money.

## Benefits of Credit Cards

The benefits of credit cards may be classified into two categories:

**(A) Benefits to the card holders.**
**(B) Benefits to the issuers.**

### *(A) Benefits to the Card Holders*

There are so many benefits to the card holders for using the cards:

1. The card holder need not carry cash at all times.
2. The card holder will be covered by free insurance.
3. The card can be used as identification card in some situations.
4. The issues of card offers rewards and gifts to the card holder.
5. The card holders can avail special counters for Air and Travel reservations.
6. The card holders can get complimentary Magazines. For example, diners club provide **"signature"** magazine to card holders.
7. Family members of the card holder can avail this facility.
8. The card holder can enjoy free credit upto 30 to 45 days.
9. If the credit card is lost/stolen the liability is limited to a maximum of one thousand rupees.
10. Some credit holders will get free services such as confirmed ticket booking and hotel reservations.
11. Some card holders will get benefit from the world-wide network, for example, Master Card, Amexp, Visa.

### *(B) Benefits to the Issuers*

There are also advantages to credit issuers. Such advantages are presented below:

1. This business offers higher profits.
2. The issuers can also improve their name and image by serving large number of credit card holder base.
3. This business is an additional activity in the banking sector to enhance their profitability.

**Privileges/Additional Facilities**

The credit cards besides providing credit facility, the issuer extend some additional facilities/privileges to attract more customers. These facilities and services are presented below:

**(a) Incidental expenses.**
**(b) Instalment cash withdrawal.**
**(c) 24 × 7 × 365 customer service.**
**(d) Free insurance .**
**(e) Buy anything on credit card.**
**(f) Joint credit card and ATM facility.**
**(g) Hotel discount facility.**
**(h) Fuel facility at petrol pumps.**
**(i) Purchase protection.**

**(a) Incidental Expenses:** The credit card holders can use their cards to pay for incidental expenses. They have to do is to call the issuer bank and instruct it to make payment like telephone bills, electricity bills, payment to mutual funds, public issues etc.

**(b) Instant Cash Withdrawal:** Some issuers allows their credit card holder to withdraw instant cash upto **60 per cent** of his credit line from **ATMs** (Any Time Money) in all metros. The card holders can also draw cash in case of medical emergencies for meeting expenses on treatment at other than their home town. This emergency medical advance facility is available with all Indian and foreign banks.

**(c) 24 × 7 × 365 Customer Service:** The technology adopted by the banking sector makes more comfortable life to the customers. The revolutionary phone banking service ensures that the banks are just a phone call away to assist the card holders around the clock. Foreign Banks provide a world class service to card holders. A credit card holder can call **"Citiphone banking"** and ask for temporary credit line any time.

**(d) Free insurance:** Some of the issuers, insures the card holder at free of cost for a particular sum. **Citibank** offer a complimentary personal accident insurance. The Bank of Baroda card extends insurance protection to card holders spouse also.

**(e) Buy Anything on Credit Card:** The Credit Cards are well accepted by the Public. The card can be used for all occasions and seasons. The Cards also useful for purchasing essential commodities like groceries, fuel, auto accessories and cosmetics. The Cards are useful even passing customs duties and hospital bills. We can purchase every thing, anywhere at any time under the sum at designated locations.

**(f) Joint Credit Card and ATM Facility:** Indian Banks and Foreign Banks have introduced a Joint Card. The Joint Card holder can access his accounts with the bank through **ATMs.**

**(g) Hotel Discount Facility:** The credit holders are entitled to get discounts at all leading hotels and clubs. The card holders are eligible to avail the facilities as per the schemes which were offered by the hotels, travel agencies and on air tickets. Even the consumer products are also available in this method.

**(h) Fuel Facility at Petrol Pumps:** The BOB, Citibank, Standard Chartered Cards are accepted at all Bharat Petroleum outlets. This is very convenient for card holders at all leading metro cities.

**(i) Purchase Protection:** The Credit Card facility protects the purchases against damage or loss due to fire and theft. For compensation the card holder can claim the value of the product damaged or lost from **The New India Assurance Company**. This protection is available for a limited period from the date of purchase of the product on the credit card.

Some of these facilities are exclusive offers, airport lounges, special hospital facilities, special travel services.

## Types of Credit Cards

The Credit Card system is becoming very popular in India and abroad. The system facilitate a wide range of products and services. The growth of service sector depend on the pulse of the customer. The needs of the customers are taken care off by different card issuers. The credit cards can be classified into 4 basic types based on the issuers : **Travel and entertainment card, Bank card, Retail card, Fuel card**. There are many types of cards which are popular in India and abroad. These cards can also be classified as follows:

**(1) Based on Geographical territory.**
**(2) Based on Franchise.**
**(3) Based on Status.**
**(4) Based on User.**
**(5) Based on Credit Recovery.**

### *(1) Based on Geographical Territory*

Under this category, the credit cards can be categorical as **Domestic card and International cards.** The domestic cards are generally available from most of the banks. These cards will be valid in India and Nepal only. All the transactions will be rupees only. **International cards** will be issued to persons who travel foreign countries frequently. These card holders make purchases in Dollars. These cards are subject to the rules and regulations of the RBI. These cards will be honoured in throughout the world except in India and Nepal.

### *(2) Based on Franchise*

The credit cards can be classified based on the Tie-up. They are **Visa card, Master card, proprietary card and tie-up card.** Visa Card can be issued by any bank which is having tie-up with VISA international USA. The card holder can avail the facilities of Visa network for their Transitions. **Master card** is a brand name for another type of credit card. The issuer of the card has to obtain permission from the Master card corporation of USA. It will be honoured in the master card network **Proprietary card** will be issued by the issuer bank on their own brand name. These cards will be issued by Banks in addition to their other tie-up cards. **Tie-up cards** are issued by a Bank having a collaboration with domestic card brands for example: **IOB has tie-up with cancard.** They give credit to customers on similar lines as the original card issuers.

### *(3) Based on Status*

This type of credit cards will be further classified as **Standard cards, Business card and Gold card**. The Standard cards is a normal card generally issued by all issuing banks. The card holder is offered a limited privileges when compared to the other cards. These cards are issued by some banks under the brand name of **"classic"** card. Business card is meant for tax consultants, chartered accountants, small firms, solicitors and executives etc. These cards are very useful for their business trips more and more convenient. The business card facilitates more privileges than the **standard card.** Some banks are issuing these cards in the brand name of **"Executive"**. The gold card is another type of card which has got a high value for the elite. The **gold card** offers some additional benefits and facilities to the card holders. These cards provide more credit limits and more cash advance while comparing with other cards.

### *(4) Based on User*

Under this category the credit cards are further classified as **Individual cards and Corporate cards**. The individual cards are issued to individual persons. All the brands of cards will be given to individual **Corporate cards** are issued to corporate companies and business firms only. The Corporate cards are issued on the name of the Company. The cards will be utilised by the executives and top officials the firms. The bills will be paid by the Company to the banks.

### *(5) Based on Credit Recovery*

These type of cards are again classified into two categories. They are **Revolving credit type card and charge card**. The revolving credit card is generally based on the revolving credit principle. According to this scheme, the card holder has to pay a percentage of the outstanding credit for every month. The interest is charged on the outstanding amount. The interest rate is more than **30 per cent P.A. Charge card** is a convenient instrument. It is not a credit instrument. The issuer gives a consolidated bill for every month to the card holder. The card holder shall pay the bills on presentation of the consolidated bills. Therefore, there are no **interest charges** on this use of cards.

## Credit Cards in India

The first credit card in India was **Diners club card** in the year 1964. Andhra Bank and Central Bank were the first to launch credit cards among the Commercial Banks. The Andhra Bank introduced the card in the year 1981 under the brand name of **"VISA classic"** followed by Central Bank of India in collaboration with **Master Card Corporation** in 1981. The other banks Canara Bank, Bank of India and Bank of Baroda introduced credit cards in India. The foreign banks such as **Citi Bank, Standard Chartered Bank, ANZ Grindlays Bank, Bank of America and American Express Bank** have also introduced cards in India through their branches in India. There are number of banks being credit cards are offering such as Corporation Bank, Karur Vayshya Bank, State Bank of India, Bank of Maharashtra, Vijaya Bank and South Indian Bank. In India almost all the credit cards issued by the banks are the franchisees of original Master Card Visa Corporation of USA. SBI is the third largest issuer of credit cards after Citi Bank and Standard Chartered Bank. Standard Chartered Bank has recently launched a woman's international card **Diva.** The card can be used by a woman to purchase tickets for movies, plays, shows and also planning for special parties. The card can also be used for pest control, home appliance repair, gifting like cakes and flowers, emergency services such as doctors and towing services. The card offers free and comprehensive insurance packages for the card holders and the family. These include accident insurance cover for self and spouse, children, education allowance and medical and purchase protection insurance.

India has 5.3 million credit cards[1] and 6.5 lakh debit cards. The average spend on a credit card, at Rs. 22,000 a year. The following data will reveal the development of credit cards in India.

**The Credit Card Ledger**

| *Year* | *No. of Cards (in millions)* | *Amount (Spending) (Rs. in crores)* |
|---|---|---|
| 1995 | 1.9 | 1700 |
| 1996 | 2.5 | 2500 |
| 1997 | 3.1 | 3650 |
| 1998 | 3.5 | 4700 |
| 1999 | 4.2 | 6500 |
| 2000 | 4.9 | 8500 |
| 2001 | 5.3 | 10500 |

**Market Share Credit Cards (upto 31.3.2001)**

| | *Name of the Card* | *Percentage of Market Share* |
|---|---|---|
| 1. | Citi Bank | 29 |
| 2. | Standard Chartered Bank | 25 |
| 3. | SBI-GE | 12 |
| 4. | HSBC | 10 |
| 5. | Amex | 6 |
| 6. | ICICI | 5 |
| 7. | Others | 13 |

## Modern Trends in the Payment Business

Information technology has made decisive in roads in all walks of life. It is being used extensively for ease of operations, communication, record keeping and for obtaining the better result from the system in which it is put to use. The new technologies in the payment business resulted in shaping future of money. As a result of this new type of cards and payment systems came into existence. The following are the latest instruments in the financial services sector:

**(A) Debit card.**
**(B) Chip card.**
**(C) Smart card.**
**(D) Electronic commerce.**
**(E) Co-branded card.**

**Debit Card** is the innovative instrument in the financial services sector. It is the most convenient method of payment to the merchant establishment. It needs involvement of many banks. The card holder will present the card on completion of his purchases at the merchant establishment on production of a debit card. The card details are fed through a terminal at the merchant establishment. The card holder is asked to key in his pin code which is allotted by the card issuer. On completion of the transaction. The amount is immediately debited from the card holder's account and transferred to the account of merchant establishment. No over drawing is allowed in the case of debit card.

**Chip Card** is a plastic and with a micro chip. It can be used on existing products like debit and credit card. It is also known as stored value cards. The transactions are effected by inserting the card in a pin pad and the value of transaction amount reduces accordingly. These cards are reloadable and disposable. It avoids the trouble of carrying cash. The chip card also scores over the magnetic card and it can retain 50–60 of the latest transactions which can be produced on demand.

**Smart Card** is in a credit card sized piece of plastic. It is a tiny integrated circuit chip card. It allows the greater amount of information than a magnetic strip card. These cards are more popular in telecom industry. The use of this card is electronic purse application. It is reloadable, high secure smart cards function as digital cash for in store and even in home or on the road transactions. It offers convenience, cost and security benefits to customers merchants, and banks. These cards reduce frauds.

**Electronic Commerce** is popularly known as **E-com.** It is simply a term of buying, selling ordering and delivering goods over the **Internet.** It will provide better communication between suppliers, brokers, sub-brokers, customers, end users and manufacturers. It is an inexpensive medium that reaches an attractive targeted persons. It consists of such technologies as **E-mail, E-fund transfer, E-data inter change, E-bulletin boards.** The customer on the internet searches the web for a particular product of interest. The search engine contains a list with a number of potential vendors who will deal with that product. The customer selects a vendor by browsing. The customer is required to fill the order form and submits it to the vendor. The data is then transmitted to the vendor after encryption for security. The order is then processed by the vendor. The vendor sends the data to an independent authentication centre where the identities of the buyer and vendor are checked. After verification of data, it is then transmitted to the vendor to despatch the goods to the buyer and settling the bill either with the bank or a Credit Card Company.

**Co-branded Cards** are more popular in the credit card industry world over during the five years. **The Times Card**, a co-branded card is the first card in the Assam sub-continent. This is a co-branded card of Times of India group with **Citibank and Master Card.** These cards are more popular in U.S. The consumers are pragmatic and value driven. Co-branding is an association between a well established two groups.

## ATM

ATM is becoming more popular in banking industry. It is known as **"Any Time Money"**. It is also called as **"Automated Teller Machine"**. The need for increasing network capacity in banking sector requires **"Asynchronous Transfer Mode"**. The potential of ATM is its ability to carry many kinds of traffic over the same network link. ATM also provides each application with the appropriate speed and control while making the best use of network capacity. ATM has many benefits like increased security, better possibilities for sharing bandwidth.

Three years ago, HDFC Bank and ICICI Bank began rolling out their networks, ATMs were just a novelty. Today the number of ATMs have swelled to **5400**. The Commercial Banks prefer to share their network with competitors, rather than take on the burden of continually building their network. The banks are installing ATMs because of its cost effective. An ATM costs around **Rs. 8–14 lakhs**. The annual maintenance varies between **Rs. 12 to 20 lakhs** per **year**. Now an ATM is profitable if **50–100** transactions are done per day on it. If it does **260–270**, the bank recovers its investment within a year. The foreign banks have used ATMs as an acquisition strategy. The public sector banks use this as retention strategy. Today the four private sector banks (**HDFC Bank, ICICI Bank, UTI Bank, IDBI Bank**) together account for over 50 per cent of the ATMs in India. The following table will reveal about the Network facilities of the banking sector, (**during the year 2001–02)**:

**Growth in ATM Network (2001–02)**

| | | |
|---|---|---|
| 1. | SBI | **764** |
| 2. | ICICI Bank | **495** |
| 3. | HDFC Bank | **272** |
| 4. | UTI Bank | **188** |
| 5. | IDBI Bank | **148** |

**ATM Network (upto May 02)[2]**

| | | |
|---|---|---|
| 1. | ICICI Bank | **1005** |
| 2. | IDBI Bank | **225** |
| 3. | HDFC Bank | **479** |
| 4. | UTI Bank | **491** |
| 5. | SBI | **1070** |

SBI has the largest ATM network in the country covering 370 towns. UTI Bank claims that over **90 per cent** of cash withdrawals now occur through ATMs.

## REFERENCES

1. Plastic Power, *Business Today*, *Anniversary Issue*, 2002, p. 88.
2. Retail Banking, *Business World*, p. 23, 27.5.2002.

# 4

# HOUSING FINANCE

Shelter is one of the basic human need of the society. It is associated with socio-economic development of a country. India has a great need and tremendous scope for the vast development of Housing sector. But the housing sector in India was completely neglected in the past. However, it is hoped that there would be some improvement in the future. Housing is a sunrise industry. There is a substantial gap between demand and supply. In **1988**, the National Housing Policy was announced by the Government of India and the housing was given top priority. The policy reflected that the housing activity is a productive investment and it is developmental factor. The housing sector creates a substantial employment opportunities. The housing sector was in unorganised area until 1988.

## Institutional Framework

National Housing Bank was set up in July 1988. It was marked the new era in housing finance as a new fund based financial service in the country. It is an apex level body and as a wholly owned subsidiary of the RBI. A large number of financial institutions, companies entered in this field. The NHB was set up under the separate NHB Act 1987. Various nationalised banks also set up housing finance companies as their subsidiaries. It is the principal agency to promote housing finance institutions at the regional and local levels and to provide financial support to such institutions. The housing finance industry can broadly be classified into two categories, namely organised and unorganised sector. The organised sector comprises of various public and private sector institutions normal finances, more than **30 per cent** of the total funds required in the housing industry. On the other hand the unorganised sector comprising of household savings disposal of existing property, borrowing from friends, relatives and money lenders etc., meets more than 60 per cent funds requirement of this industry.

**Objectives and Business**

The major objectives of the National Housing Bank are presented below:

(a) It is involved in promotion, establishment of housing financial institutions in the country.
(b) It arranges funds to housing finance institutions and scheduled banks.
(c) It provides funds to any authority established by any Central or State Act and engaged in slum clearance.
(d) To guarantee the financial obligations of housing finance institutions.
(e) It also underwrite the issue of stocks, shares, bonds, debentures and securities of every housing finance institution.
(f) It acts as agent of the Central and State Governments.
(g) It coordinate with other financial institutions in the discharge of overall functions.
(h) It formulate schemes for the economically weaker sections of the society.
(i) It organise training programmes and seminar symposia on matters relating housing.
(j) It provide guidelines to the housing finance institutions.
(k) It provides technical and administrative assistance to housing finance institutions.
(l) It formulate schemes for mobilisation of resources.
(m) It undertake research and surveys on construction techniques and other studies relating to housing.
(n) It acts as agent of the RBI in housing related activities.
(o) It has the powers to acquire rights of any housing finance institution.
(p) It has the power to access to all necessary records of any housing finance institution.
(q) It has the power to inspect any housing finance institution as directed by the RBI.
(r) It has the power to collect credit information from the housing finance institutions.
(s) It has the powers to provide advisory services to government, local bodies and other agencies connected with housing activities.

(t) It has power to borrow foreign currency with the prior approval of the RBI.

## Housing Finance Scheme

The institutional framework of housing finance and various institutions provide financial assistance to the needy persons. The salient features of some of the important and popular schemes in this regard has been presented below:

**(1) Home loan account scheme of NHB.**
**(2) HDFC schemes for individual finance.**
**(3) LIC housing scheme.**
**(4) GIC housing finance.**
**(5) Canfin homes scheme.**
**(6) SBI home finance scheme.**
**(7) Commercial bank schemes.**
**(8) Schemes of HUDCO.**
**(9) Schemes of state housing finance societies.**

### (1) Home Loan Account of NHB

The scheme initiated by NHB. The objective of the scheme is to encourage individuals to save the money especially for housing. The scheme is operated through all branches of the Scheduled Banks. The features of the scheme is presented below:

(a) Any citizen of India who is not owning in his or her name, a house/flat/apartment is eligible to become a member under this scheme. An eligible individual is allowed to open an account for himself and one account each in the names of minor children.
(b) The individual under this scheme is required to start a saving of minimum amount per month. The individual is eligible to avail the loan facility under this scheme, after the accumulation of 5 years savings. The individual can continue to save under the scheme as long as he wishes. There is no upper limit on the amount to be saved under the scheme.
(c) The individual is entitled for interest on the deposit made by him. The interest will be calculated on monthly product basis.

(d) If the individual fails to deposit for a continuous period for 12 months, the original date of opening the home loan account is shifted forward by the period of default. The account will be extended to further 5 years. In case of discontinuance the balance in the account along with the interest would be paid after 5 years from the date of opening the account subject to tax.

(e) Under this scheme the individual can be withdrawn only for constructing a house or a flat only after the expiry of 5 years. The amount can be withdrawn even if he does not avail of loan facility.

(f) The account holder is eligible for housing loan on the completion of the saving period. The quantum of the loan is based upon the built up area.

(g) The rate of interest payable by the borrower would depend upon the time period and quantum of the amount which has taken by him.

(h) The scheme cannot be used for acquisition of more than one house by the account holder. The house or flat acquired under this scheme cannot be sold for five years after completion or till the entire loan is repaid, whichever is later. The savings instalments under this scheme provide a tax rebate under Section 88A of the Income Tax Act. The tax rebate is also available on the payment of instalments of loan taken under this scheme.

(i) This scheme was started by NHB on 1-7-1988. It is implemented by more than 28 public sector banks, other banks, state cooperative banks and scheduled urban cooperative banks.

***Regulation of Deposits by NHB***

The National Housing Bank Act, 1987 contains the provision that no finance company can raise the deposits from the public. The NHB is empowered to prohibit the issue of advertisement to solicit deposits from public by housing finance companies. The NHB is empowered to call the information from HFCs. The information may relate to the amount of deposits, purpose and periods of deposits rate of interest and other terms and conditions. The HFCs should respond to the queries whichever made by the NHB. It is a statutory body to collect the information, regulate the deposits, monitor the activities of housing finance companies. The NHB has the powers to conduct an inspection by its officers to housing finance companies for verification and correctness of information.

***Share Capital***

The NHB share capital is fully subscribed by the RBI. The equity is Rs. 100 crores and it has been receiving an equity of Rs. 50 crores each year till 1992: Therefore, the capital stood at Rs. 250 crores. The RBI recently released an additional equity of Rs. 50 crores. Thus the total share capital now stands at **Rs. 300 crores.** NHB was permitted by the Government to mobilise savings of households. The Government was permitted NHB to issue capital gains bonds having a maturity period of 3 years and carrying an interest of 9 per cent per annum. The NHB had another source of funds which are guaranteed by the Central Government. The Central Government guaranteed the principal amount and the interest. These bonds quality as approved securities for maintaining of SLR purpose by the banking institutions. The NHB is also received external finance from international agencies.

***Refinancing***

The RBI is ultimate authority in the aspects of housing finance sector. The various refinance schemes are operated by the NHB in the following categories:

(a) Scheduled Commercial Banks.
(b) Scheduled State Cooperative Banks.
(c) Scheduled Urban Cooperative Banks.
(d) Cooperative Housing Finance Societies.
(e) Select House Financing Companies.

The refinancing facility will be provided to the above organisations by the NHB. The annual limits are fixed which are based on various parameters such as average refinance drawn during the previous year. The refinance made available to any housing finance companies is not to be more than 60 per cent of its outstanding housing loans at any point of time. Any housing finance company fails to pay the dues over three months exceed 5 per cent of the aggregate demand for that year, are in eligible to draw further refinance.

### *NHB Guidelines*

NHB is to promote a sound, healthy, viable and cost effective housing finance institutions. The NHB is the supreme authority to issue guidelines for the housing finance companies in India. The housing finance companies must conform to these regulations to be eligible for support from the NHB. Presently it provides refinance facility to all the eligible HFCs. The important and guidelines are briefly presented below:

**(1) Registering Authority.**
**(2) Lending Norms.**

#### *(1) Registering Authority*

The NHB has the powers to regulate the housing finance companies. It has the authority to grant the registration for up coming entities. It supervise the housing finance industry. The criteria for registration of a housing finance company as presented below.

**(a) Share Capital Provision.**
**(b) Activity Provision.**
**(c) Loan Norms.**
**(d) Prudential Norms.**

#### *(a) Share Capital Norms*

Every housing finance company should fulfil the statutory conditions before getting the certificate of registration. The housing finance company should have a minimum capital of **Rs. 3 crores**. The promoters contribution to the share capital should be followed by SEBI directions which are issued from time to time. At present, the promoter should contribute 25 per cent of post issue capital upto **Rs. 100 crores**. If the post issue capital exceeded Rs. 100 crores, the promoter shall contribute **20 per cent** of the post issue capital. Therefore, the housing finance company must offer at least **25 per cent** of equity capital to the public. Then the housing finance company scrip may be listed in stock exchange. According to the NHB norms, the HFC should list shares on at least one stock exchange. The NHB has the authority to give exemption for offering shares to the public by the following institutions:

**(a) Companies promoted by the Government.**
**(b) Scheduled Commercial Banks.**
**(c) Public Financial Institutions.**
**(d) Development Financial Institutions.**

The NHB can participate in the share capital of HFCs to the extent of **20 per cent** of their paid up capital. It wili depends upon the discretion of the NHB and on the merits of HFC.

*(b) Activity Provisions*

Every registered HFC is eligible to refinance and other support from NHB. The objective of the financial assistance is to provide long-term finance for construction or purchase of houses for residential purposes. The NHB has the discretionary powers to relax conditions in case of HFCs promoted by Scheduled Banks, government and public financial institutions. The NHB has the powers to direct the HFCs as follows:

(a) The names of the HFCs should not resemble the name of any relative company or construction company with which the promoters of the HFCs may be associated.
(b) The HFCs should not be subsidiaries of any construction company.
(c) Top level management of the HFC should not hold similar status in an construction companies which are associated with the promoters of the HFCs.
(d) The HFCs should involve at least 75 per cent of its financial activities has to be made for housing finance sector.

The NHB has powers to nominate two directors on the board of the HFCs, if the HFCs share capital is not contributed by any scheduled bank, public financial institutions and corporate groups. In the case of the HFCs to whose capital is contributed by banks financial institution. NHB and government their nominees will be represented on the board of HFCs. The appointment of the chief executive of the HFCs is subject to the approval of NHB.

*(c) Loan Norms*

The NHB has been established for providing financial assistance to the housing sector. The NHB guidelines in this regard has been presented below:

(a) The HFCs have been directed to provide financial assistance to the individual households.
(b) The NHB provides financial assistance by way of refinance to HFCs.
(c) The refinance facility is eligible to HFCs to the extent of **60** per cent in respect of housing loans, upto **Rs. 5.00 lakhs** for acquisition of new house.
(d) The refinance facility is also available to upgradation of the property to the extent of **Rs. 30,000** including major repairs.
(e) The refinance for loans for new houses exceeding **Rs. 3.00 lakhs** and upto **Rs. 5.00 lakhs** are subject to restriction of **40** per cent of total refinance from NHB during a particular financial year. The rates for NHB refinance schemes are fluctuated from time to time.
(f) The NHB prescribes the lending rates by HFCs from time to time.
(g) The NHB has directed the HFCs to keep the administrative as low as possible. It has imposed a ceiling on such costs of **1.5 per cent** of the outstanding loan.
(h) NHB has imposed ceiling on front end charges is **2 per cent** of the loan amount. It includes registration fee, processing fee, administrative fee, technical inspection expenses but **excludes** stamp duty and document registration charges.
(i) The NHB has the power to get the quarterly returns from the HFCs.
(j) The quarterly returns should include full information as required by the NHB.

*(d) Prudential Norms*

The NHB has introduced for the HFCs regarding capital adequacy ratio. The ratio is based on risk weightage of different types of assets and liabilities. The prudential norms for various aspects of the accounting procedure. The HFCs were required to fulfil a minimum capital adequacy norms as indicated by NHB from time to time. The HFCs should not invest more than 25 per cent of owned funds in shares and debentures of another company. All HFCs should obtain credit rating of their deposits by any of the rating agencies such as **CRISIL,**

**ICRA and CARE**. The rating should be obtained once in a year. The copy of the rating should be sent to NHB.

### *Taxation of HFCs*

The Government of India facilitates some tax concessions to the HFCS in order to encourage the construction industry. The tax concessions are announced by the Government in budget programme. The concessions are prescribed and liable to change from time to time.

The HFCs are allowed to create a special reserve fund which cannot exceed **40 per cent** of the total income. This amount of reserve is allowed as a deduction in computation of taxable income of the HFCS. The HFCs are liable to pay tax under the head of **profit and gains of business or profession.** The shareholders who receives dividend on shares of HFCs qualify for a deduction under Section **80L** of the Income Tax Act along with other eligible deduction. Any investor who deposits with HFCs are exempted from wealth tax under Section 5(1) (xxvii) of the Wealth Tax Act within overall ceiling of **Rs. 15 lakhs**. The subscription to notified deposit schemes of HFCs is eligible for tax rebate under Section 88 of the Income Tax Act. the borrower from HFCs are eligible for a tax rebate on payment of his principal amount. The interest on housing loan is deductible expense under Section 24 of the Act, income from house property. Investment in new equity of HFCS is eligible for a tax rebate under Section **80-A** of the Income Tax Act. Investments in bonds issued by the HFCs are eligible to qualify under Section **11(5)** of the Income Tax Act. The subscription to notified deposit schemes of HFCs is eligible under Section **88** of the Income Tax Act.

### (2) HDFC Schemes

Housing Development Finance Corporation Ltd. is a leading private sector housing finance company in India. The lead player in the HFC category covers 50 per cent of the total disbursements made by the Housing Finance Industry. It was set up in 1977 by the ICICI. It lends mainly for new residential housing finance to individuals, group of persons and members of the cooperative societies. It offers two schemes to the individual borrowers. They are presented below:

- **(a) Home Saving Plan.**
- **(b) Home Loans.**

Home saving plan is designed to provide housing loan on the basis of savings of the borrower. According to this scheme rules, the individual is required to made accumulated savings before getting loan amount from HDFC. The scheme is open to individual and individuals jointly with a child and spouse. The individual should contribute minimum savings period 25 months. The individual can save up to a period of 7 years. The maximum amount of loan would be **85 per cent** of the cost of the property, the remaining should be financed from the borrowers savings. The maximum repayment is over a 15-year period. The repayment does not ordinarily extend beyond the age of retirement or 65 years of age of the borrower whichever is earlier. The interest rates are fixed from time to time. The HDFC provides financial assistance to individuals for housing purposes for the following situations:

(a) buying or constructing houses,
(b) extension or improvement of existing houses,
(c) independent bungalow/row house, and
(d) acquiring a self-contained flat from the cooperative society or apartment owners association.

The individual is eligible to get a maximum loan to an extent of **Rs. 25 lakhs**. It charges the borrowers **0.8** per cent of the loan applied for as processing fee and **1 per cent** of the loan sanctioned as administrative fee.

Besides above stated schemes, it also issued various other housing loan facilities for individuals cooperative societies, companies etc. The amount of loan and rate of interest will be charged according to the rules and regulations notified from time to time.

The sources of fund for HDFC are from deposits mobilised through various schemes, long-term funds from commercial banks, domestic financial institutions, USAID, ADB etc.

### (3) LIC Housing Schemes

LIC Housing Finance Ltd., was incorporated in July 1989 by the LIC. The promoters of the LICHF are ICICI, UTI and IFCI. The Company is the largest housing finance company in terms of market share next to HDFC. It has a wide network more than 2000 branches and 65 area offices of LIC and also access to more than half a million agents in the country. It provides major finance to individuals ranging upto 90 per cent and remaining to others. The following are the important features in general of all the schemes are presented below:

(a) All LIC policy holders and a person who does not own a house are eligible for getting house loan.
(b) The loans will be sanctioned for construction extension of house or for purchase of constructed house/flat or house or flat under construction. The quantum of loan can be sanctioned **80 per cent** of the cost of property.
(c) Generally the repayment period is within 20 years or superannuation or on completing 65 years, which is earlier.
(d) The security for the house loan is the mortgage of the property. The policy is also use as collateral security.
(e) The repayment can be made through various options. The popular method is **Equated Monthly Instalments (EMI)**.
(f) It enjoys cheap funds from its parent company.

### (4) GIC Housing Finance

The GIC Housing Finance Ltd., was set up in December 1989 by the GIC as its subsidiary company. The co-promoters were National Insurance Company Ltd., The Oriental Insurance Co. Ltd., The New India Assurance Company Ltd., and The United India Insurance Company Ltd. It started its operations and is extending now its services all over the country through its various branches. It offered various schemes for house financing. It started a popular scheme **"GIC Apna Ghar Yojana Scheme"**. The important features of the scheme is presented below:

(a) The person must be in permanent service or engaged in profession or business is eligible to avail this scheme.
(b) The quantum of loan can be sanctioned upto **80 per cent** of the cost of the property. The amount will be liable to change from time to time.
(c) The loan will be sanctioned on the basis of applicants income, age, qualification, no. of dependents, stability and continuity of the income, repayment capacity, property value etc.
(d) The repayment of loan period normally ranges between 5 to 20 years.

(e) The Interest rates will be changed from time to time and depend upon the size of loans.

(f) The property financed under this scheme will be fully insured against the risks of fire.

(g) The borrower of the loan will be covered in **Group Accidental death insurance scheme** to the extent of the loan outstanding and will be in force throughout the period of the loan until final repayment of the same.

(h) Amount of loan will collected through in **Equivated Monthly Instalments**. The EMI is comprising of the principal amount as well as interest thereon calculated on monthly basis.

**(5) Canfin Homes Ltd.**

The Canfin Homes Ltd., is sponsored by the Canara Bank in **1988.** It has initiated various schemes for financing the houses like home loan scheme for purchase of house or flat, and scheme for repairs and extension. This company also operate the home loan account scheme of the NHB. The salient features of the housing finance are presented below:

(a) The individuals who do not own houses of their own are eligible for house loan.

(b) The house under consideration must be in the name of the applicant.

(c) The loan facility is also available for purchase of apartments/ flats from apartment owners association.

(d) In this scheme, the loans are available for purchase of constructed houses and it should not be more than 7 years old.

(e) The scheme is not applicable for providing loans to purchase/ construction of Industrial or Commercial properties.

(f) The quantum of loan depends upon the several factors. The cost of construction debt servicing capacity, the applicants age, qualification, terms of loan number of dependent, stability of income.

(g) The repayment of loan period is generally from 7 years to 20 years.

(h) The loan will be secured against the first mortgage of the property to be financed.

(i) The company has the right to change the rate of interest depending upon the market conditions or on the basis of NHB guidelines.

(j) The repayment of loan, the company has offered various schemes as **EMI**, Graduated Repayments instalment scheme, Decreasing repayment instalment scheme, Half yearly repayment scheme etc.

(k) The amount of EMI will depend upon the amount of loan, applicable rate of interest, tenure of the loan period etc. The Graduated repayment scheme is offered to those who have good opportunity for income growth over a period of time. The half yearly instalment scheme is applicable to agriculturists who depends on seasonal farm income.

(l) The equated monthly instalment is calculated with the following formula. The monthly instalment consists of the principal repayment and the interest on outstanding principal.

$$\text{EMI} = \frac{\text{Amount of funds borrowed}}{\text{PV of an activity of Rupee per month}}.$$

The interest rate and the amount of monthly mortgage payment is fixed for the entire term of the loan.

The Canfin Homes Ltd., offered a special concession of **0.25 per cent** in interest rates. No processing fee, total fee of 0.50 per cent. On the spot in principle sanction. All these offers were available before 31.3.2002.

It offers loans to salaried persons and business people including **NRIs**. The loans are sanctioned to the extent of **Rs. 50.00 lakhs** for purchase/construction of house/flat and even for taking over loans from other banks/institutions. It also offers loans upto **Rs. 7.50 lakhs** for repairs/renovations of existing flats/houses.

**The EMI Chart for Rs. 1 Lakh**

| *Loan Amount* | *Rate of Interest* | *EMI Amount* | | |
|---|---|---|---|---|
| | | *10 years* | *15 years* | *20 years* |
| 1. Upto Rs. 10.00 lakhs | 11.5% | 1400 | 1161 | 1059 |
| 2. Over Rs. 10.00 lakhs | 12.0% | 1428 | 1193 | 1093 |

The prospective applicant can be contacted the branches of the company for availing the loan facility.

### (6) SBI Home Finance Scheme

The SBI Home Finance was established in 1988. It is the subsidiary of the SBI. The aim of the Company is to provide financial assistance for housing in India. It provides various housing finance schemes to individuals, corporate members, promoters and developers. The following are salient features of various scheme promoted by the company:

**(A) Scheme for Individuals.**
**(B) Scheme for Promoters and Developers.**
**(C) Scheme for Corporate Bodies.**

#### *(A) Scheme for Individuals*

It grants the house loans to individuals for purchase of house, construction of house, repairs renovation, extension and alteration of the existing houses. The maxim amount of loan is liable to change from time to time. The repayment period ranges from 5 to 20 years. The loan amount should be completed before retirement of the borrower or 65 years of age which ever is earlier. The repayment of the loan is flexible and usually through equated monthly instalmants consisting of principal and interest. The rates of interest are subject to changes from time to time. At present the rate of interest charged by the SBI Home is **11 per cent.** The loans are secured by mortgage of property to be financed on first charge. Sometimes suitable collateral security is also required by the company.

#### *(B) Scheme for Promoters and Developers*

The company provides housing finance to the promoters and developers of the real estate sector. The loans will be sanctioned for construction of residential housing projects. These loans are additional to their own sources of finance. The quantum of loan amount will be different from time to time keeping in view of the market conditions. The rate of interest charged for such loan is based on the basis of the size of loans. The borrower is required to provide personal security and collateral security in addition mortgage of the property.

### *(C) Scheme for Corporate Bodies*

It offers various schemes under this category. It has offered three different schemes for housing loans to the corporate bodies. They are categorized as follows:

(a) According to this scheme, it offers loans for construction of quarters for the corporate employees.
(b) This scheme facilitates lending to the corporate employees for their own houses.
(c) Under this scheme, the SBIHF provides the loans to the nominated employees of the company.

The maximum and minimum amount of the loan will be different from time to time. Generally 85 per cent of the property cost will be sanctioned including the land cost. The period of repayment loan is ranged from 10 years to 20 years depending upon the category of the scheme. The rate of interest is the same as applicable in individual loan scheme. The rate of interest is based on the size of loan, repayment period, cost of housing and prevailing market conditions. The loans are payable usually as EMI.

### (7) Commercial Bank Schemes

The RBI has issued directions to all the Scheduled Commercial Banks to provide housing finance schemes in the country to boost the construction industry. As per the directions of the RBI every year the commercial banks are required to allocate **1.5 per cent** of their investment deposits for disbursing housing finance. The Commercial Banks provide housing loans to individuals, institutions and public agencies.

The scheme for sanction of housing finance to the individuals have been classified into four categories such as: (a) belonging to economically weaker sections, (b) buying flats from state housing board/trusts/ cooperative societies/private builders, (c) those owning land, and (d) belonging to SC/ST who have been allotted land by the Government.

The rates of interest vary as per category of individuals, presently the Commercial Banks charge from **11 per cent** to **12 per cent** per annum depending upon the category of loan and size of loan. The quantum of loan is determined on the basis of two elements; income of the borrower and the cost of property.

The Commercial Banks are providing term loans to various public and private institutions involved in house finance in the country. These housing finance companies can avail term loans from the banks. The guidelines will be issued by the RBI from time to time subject to other terms and conditions.

The banks also provide loans to the **builders** for various purposes like development of land, construction of house/flats under the refinance scheme of NHB. These loans will be sanctioned to the builders subject to the terms and conditions as laid down by NHB and RBI.

## (8) Scheme of Housing and Urban Development Corporation (HUDCO)

It is the most important organisations in housing finance area. It was established in April 1970. It is fully owned by the Government of India. The objectives of the HUDCO is presented below:

(a) to provide loans for construction of houses,
(b) to promote housing and urban development programme in India,
(c) to provide finance to the material industries,
(d) to finance or undertake the setting up of new satellite towns,
(e) allocation of funds received from the Government of India for housing and urban development purpose, and
(f) It provides financial assistance by way of subscribing the debentures and bonds of the Development authorities, State Housing Boards and improvement trusts.

The HUDCO provides shelter to the masses specifically to economic weaker sections and low income group. It is fully involved in providing financial assistance to rural areas and urban sector. It was established with an equity share capital of **Rs. 2 crores.** The present paid up share capital is **Rs. 298 crores**. It has authorised share capital of **Rs. 385 crores**. It mobilises resources from other fellow agencies like UTI, GIC, LIC, commercial banks and international finance agencies. It has the plans in future for the expansion of urban infrastructure, lending, retail financing, technology transfer initiatives and in house research.

## (9) Scheme of State Housing Finance Societies

The State Housing Finance Societies plays an important role in housing finance sector. These societies provide loans to the **primary cooperative housing societies**. These societies have been formed for construction of residential houses purchase of land, additions/extensions or improvements to existing houses. The share capital of these societies are contributed by Government and cooperative institutions. The quantum of loans varies between 65 to 80 per cent of the house cost and repayment period ranges between 15 to 25 years. The rate of interest charged is normally linked with the bank rate. The loans are recovered through EMIs.

# 5

# HIRE PURCHASE

## Introduction

Hire purchase has emerged as a source of equipment financing in recent years. It involves the purchase of an asset by the **Hirer**, will pay in equal periodic instalments spread over a length of time. It has emerged as a supplementary source of intermediate to long-term finance. The Hire Purchase schemes are provided by **NBFC, FIs,** and other organisations. In this business, the lender is the legal owner of the assets financed. The title of the asset lies with the owner/**lender** and right to economic use of the asset is with the Hirer. The Hirer enjoys the physical use of the asset without title. An agreement will be made between two parties for this effect, they are **Lender** and **Hirer**. The goods are let on hire basis with an option to the hirer to purchase the asset under the following conditions:

(1) The hirer should pay the amount in instalments over a specific period.
(2) The asset will be delivered to the hirer at the time of entering into the contract.
(3) The instalment amount is treated as hire charges.
(4) If any default is made in payment of any instalment, the lender will take away the asset.

Hire purchase credit is available in India for a wide range of products and services. The products like Machinery equipment, Industrial sheds, Sewing Machines, TV sets, refrigerators, automobiles, and other capital goods are financed with the help of such credit. A large part of instalment credit in India is given for the purchase of commercial vehicles.

**Hire Purchase Agreement**

The Hire Purchase Act, 1972 which came into force on 1.9.1973, has defined a hire purchase agreement as "an agreement under which goods are let on hire and under which the hirer has an option to purchase them in accordance with the terms of the agreement and includes an agreement under which—

(i) possession of goods is delivered by the owner thereof to a person on condition that such person pays the agreed amount in periodical instalments;
(ii) the property in the goods is to pass to such person on the payment of the last of such instalments; and
(iii) such person has a right to terminate the agreement at any time before the property so passes."[1]

According to Section 3 of the Hire Purchase Act, it is compulsory that hire purchase agreement should be in writing and signed by the parties concerned. It must state the following:

(a) the HP price of the goods to which the agreement relates:
(b) the cash price of the goods, that is to say, the price at which the goods, may be purchased by the hirer for cash;
(c) the date on which the agreement shall be deemed to have commenced;
(d) the number of instalments by which the hire purchase price is to be paid, the amount of each of those instalments and the date, or the mode of determining the date upon which it is payable and the person to whom and the place where it is payable; and
(e) the goods to which the agreement relates in a manner sufficient to identify them.

The Act has also defined various terms relating to prices. These are the following:

(1) "cash price instalment" means an amount which bears to the net cash price the same proportion as the amount of the hire purchase instalment bears to the total amount of HP prices:

(2) "deposit" means any sum payable by the hirer under the hire purchase agreement by way of deposit or other initial payment or credited or to be credited to him under the agreement on account of any such deposit or payment, whether that sum is to be or has been discharged by payment of money or by transfer or delivery of goods or by any other means.

(3) net cash price in relation to goods comprised in a HP agreement, means the cash price of such goods as required to be specified in the HP agreement less any deposit as defined in clause (i).

(4) "net hire purchases" means the difference between the net HP price and the net cash price of such goods.

(5) "net HP price" means the total amount of HP price of the goods as required to be specified in the HP agreement, less–

   (a) any amount which is payable to cover the expenses of delivering the goods or any of them to or to the order of the hirer and which is specified in the agreement as included in the HP price;

   (b) any amount which is payable to cover registration or other fees under any law in respect of the goods or the agreement or both and which is specified in the agreement as included in the HP price; and

   (c) any amount which is payable for insurance in respect of the goods and which is specified in the agreement as included in the HP price.

**Regulation Framework**

The Hire Purchase Act was passed in 1972. The Act was amended and the new bill was introduced in 1989. But the Act has not been enforced till now. There is no specific legislation dealing with HP transactions in India. The Act governs the hire purchase transactions if the general law does not exist. The Act contains the provisions for regulating.

**(A) The format of HP agreement.**
**(B) Warrant and the conditions within the HP agreement.**
**(C) Ceiling on HP charges.**
**(D) Rights and obligations of the hirer and owner.**

### *(A) Format of HP Agreement*

The agreement should be made between Hirer and Lendor and signed by both the parties to it. But there is no prescribed proforma for a HP agreement. The agreement involves a guarantee, it must be signed by the surety also. A hire purchase agreement must contain the following particulars:

(a) The HP price of the goods.
(b) The cash price of the goods.
(c) The date of commencement of the agreement.
(d) The number of instalments to be paid.
(e) The description of the goods.

### *(B) Warrants*

A Hire Purchase agreement has the following implied warranties:

The owner takes a warranty that the hirer shall have and enjoy quiet possession of the goods. The goods are warranted as free from any charge or encumbrance in favour of third party at the time the property in the goods is to pass. Thus where the goods are already pledged or hypothecated and the owner enters into a HP agreement, it amounts to a breach of warranty.

The following conditions are implied in the HP agreement, that—

(1) the owner has the right to sell the goods at the time the property is to pass to the hirer;
(2) the goods are of merchantable quality;
(3) the goods are fit for the hirer's purpose;
(4) the goods correspond with the sample; and
(5) the goods correspond with the description.

### *(C) Ceiling on HP Charges*

A restriction on HP charges is imposed in order to prevent exploitation. According to this clause, the net HP charges must not exceed statutory charges. Statutory charges are calculated as : Net HP charges represents the difference between the net HP price and the net cash price. The property in the goods under a HP agreement passes to the hirer only on the completion of the purchase, in the manner laid down in the agreement.

### *(D) Rights and Obligations of the Hirer and Owner*

The owner has the rights in HP agreements on the following aspects:

(a) Right to terminate agreement.
(b) Obligations of owner.

The owner has the right to terminate the agreement in various situations. If the hirer fails to make payment of more than one hire instalment, the owner may terminate the agreement. The owner should send a notice to this effect in writing. The notice should not be of less than one week.

The second situation indicates that the hirer makes any unauthorised use of the goods or breaks an express condition of the agreement. Then the owner terminates the agreement after giving the hirer a notice in writing.

The owner has the rights on termination of an agreement to retain hire, to forfeit initial deposit, to enter the premise and seized goods. However, where the agreement has been terminated by the hirer. The owner cannot seize the protected goods without the intervention of the court.

The owner has the following obligations:

(1) to supply, free of cost, a true copy of the agreement, signed by him, to the hirer immediately after execution of the agreement,
(2) to supply on demand, a copy of the agreement to the surety,
(3) to supply on demand by the hirer, the following information:

   (a) the amount paid by or on behalf of the hire;
   (b) the amount due and unpaid; and
   (c) the amount which to become payable.

The Hirer has the following rights:

(a) The hirer has a right to purchase the goods under the agreement, at any time during the continuance of the agreement, by giving to the owner at least 14 days notice of his intention to do so. For making the purchase the hirer has to pay to the owner, the balance of HP price after deducting a rebate, calculated as follows:

$$\text{Rebate} = \frac{2}{3} \times \frac{\text{Balance of HP price not yet due}}{\text{HP price}} \times \text{HP} - \text{CP}$$

CP = Cash price.

The hirer has the right to terminate the agreement at any time before the final HP instalment falls due. For this purpose the hirer has to give to the owner at least 14 days notice of his intention to terminate the agreement. The hirer is required to pay an additional sum on account of such termination subject to conditions.

The hirer is required to pay several hire purchase instalments to the owner. But sometimes the hirer may become due, the owner gets the right to apply the payment to the agreements in the order of their time.

The hirer has the right to assign his right, title and interest under the agreement with the consent of the owner. If the owner unreasonably withholds his consent, the hirer may make assignment without his consent.

The hirer must pay the HP instalment in accordance with the agreement and also comply with the terms of the agreement. The hirer is required to take as much care of the goods as a person of common man. The hirer must not use the goods for any purpose not authorised in the agreement, otherwise he is liable for any loss or damage to the goods.

If the owner of the asset asks the hirer about the whereabouts of the goods, the hirer must inform the owner where the goods are at the time he is given or posting the information. The hirer must inform the owner within **14 days.** If he fails to do so without reasonable cause, he is punishable with fine up to **Rs. 200**.

In India, the HP transactions are governed by the Provisions of the **Indian Contract Act** and the **Sale of Goods Act**. The HP transactions has two aspects:

**(1) an aspect of the Contract Act,**
**(2) an aspect of the sale of Goods Act.**

*(1) Provisions of Contract Act*

The law of contract applies to all types of contracts including hire purchase. The main features of the HP provisions of the law of contracts are briefly presented below:

A contract is an agreement enforceable by law. The essential elements of a valid contract are:

A contract is an agreement with an intention to create legal obligation. The offer and acceptance signify willingness on the part of the offer and the offeree to be bound by the proposal to enter into an agreement. A contract requires lawful consideration. A consideration must not be illegal, fraudulent opposed to the public policy. The parties to a contract must be of 18 years of age of sound mind, and not disqualified by any law to enter into a contract. The consent of the parties to a contract must be free. The agreement should not be void under any Act. Such agreements cannot be legally enforced. A contract may be discharged in any of the following ways:

(a) By performance.
(b) By frustration.
(c) By Mutual agreement.
(d) By operation of law.
(e) By remission.

The non-performance of a contract leads to a breach of contract. When a breach of contract arises, the other party may put an end to the contract on account of breach by the first party. The consequences of breach of contract are borne by the party at whose instance the breach had resulted causing suffering to the other party. The remedies available to the aggrieved party are as follows:

(a) Compensation/Damages.
(b) Specific performance.

Damages means monetary compensation for the loss suffered by the injured party. The damages can be categorised into two kinds, (a) ordinary damages and (b) special damages. Ordinary damages are recoverable for the loss arising natural in the usual course of things from the breach itself. Special damages are allowed for loss arising on account of unusual circumstances affecting the injured party provide such special circumstances were known to the defaulting party and the possibility of such special loss was within his contemplation. If the amount of damages for breach are stipulated in the contract, the said amount is payable by the party guilty of the breach irrespective of whether loss has been or has not been actually caused. Such damages are in the nature of penalty and are called as liquidated damages.

If the loss suffered by breach of contract cannot be compensated by damages or where the quantum of damages cannot be ascertained, the aggrieved party may approach the court for the grant of a decree for specific performance of the contract.

### *(2) Sale of Goods Act*

In a contract of HP, the element of sale is inherent as the hirer always has the option to buy the movable asset by making regular payment of hire charges and the asset passes to him on payment of the last instalment. The provisions of the Sales of Goods Act apply to HP contracts.

A contract of sales of goods is a contract in which the property is transferred from the seller to the buyer. The seller transfers the property in goods to the buyer for a price. If the transfer of property in the goods is to take place at a future time is known as agreement to sell. A contract of sale is constituted of the following elements:

(a) There must be two parties, the buyer and the seller.
(b) The goods must be transferred from the seller to the buyer.
(c) Price is known as money consideration.
(d) The title must be transferred from the seller to the buyer.
(e) Essentials of a valid contract under the Indian Contract Act.

The sources of HP finance are many. There are hire purchase finance companies. These companies are either public or private limited companies or partnership firms. These institutions are well organised and developed in South India. At present there are too many small companies involved in HP Finance business and the quality of services rendered by them could be improved through consolidation. These companies could get the funds from the public deposits and other borrowings. These companies may also be borrowed from the banks and other institutions. The other suppliers of HP finance are retail and wholesale traders, Commercial Banks, IDBI, ICICI, NSIC, SFCs and others. The banks also have increased their business in the field of instalment credit and consumer loans.

## REFERENCE

1. Shukla and Grewal, *Advanced Accounts*, p. 555.

# 6

# UNIT TRUST OF INDIA

## Introduction

The objective of the Unit Trust is to stimulate and pool the savings of the middle and low income groups and to enable them to share the benefits and prosperity of the rapidly growing industrialisation of the nation. The UTI was set up in 1964 as a public sector financial institution by the Government of India. The basic objective of the UTI was to encourage and mobilise savings of the community through the sale of Units. It channelise the savings into corporate investments with a view to maximising yield and capital appreciation. For achieving these objectives, the UTI is authorised to carry on and transact a number of business activities in the financial markets.

The initial capital of **Rs. 5 crores** was subscribed fully by the RBI, LIC, SBI, scheduled banks and other financial institutions. The RBI, LIC and the SBI are not permitted to transfer their share capital to other institutions. The UTI was delinked from the RBI with effect from 1.2.1976. The RBI share capital was transferred to IDBI. Therefore, the UTI became an associate institution of the IDBI. As per the Depak Parekh Committee recommendations, the UTI had mobilised additional permanent capital to the extent of **Rs. 500 crores** during the year 1999.

The UTI has empowered to carry on the following limited business activities:

(a) Sale and purchase of units as a saving instrument.
(b) Invest in securities.
(c) Deposit money with the banks.
(d) Propose and implement different types of schemes and financial plans.

The UTI Act had been amended in 1985 to expand its business activities and diversification to enable it to perform its basic objective more effectively. The UTI has empowered to involve in the following activities at present:

(a) Purchase and sale of units.
(b) Involving in bills of exchange business segment.
(c) Grants loans and advances.
(d) Investment in RBI issued securities or special papers.
(e) Formulation of unit schemes in collaboration with the insurance companies.
(f) Involving in immovable property transactions.
(g) Rendering financial and other assistance to any person for the acquisition of immovable property.
(h) Rendering merchant banking and investment advisory services on fee basis.
(i) Portfolio Management services to NRIs.
(j) Buy/Sale of foreign exchange transactions.
(k) Entering into business as per the guidelines of the Central Government.

## Management

The management of the business the UTI are vested in the Board of Trustees. The Board of Trustees consisted of eleven members. At present the chairman is appointed by the Government of India in consultation with IDBI. The Executive Trustee is appointed by the **IDBI**. The RBI has power to nominate one trustee and the other trustees are nominated by the IDBI. The UTI's management pattern combines the trustees and management of the mutual fund. The custody of securities with well recognised parties for safety of the funds of the investors. The UTI constituted three AMCs in consultation with the SEBI. The AMCs were established to look after the business of US–64, equity schemes, and fixed income schemes respectively.

## Tax Benefits

UTI facilitates tax exemptions and concessions to its unit holders. The tax benefits also available to UTI itself. The UTI is exempted under

Section 32 of the UTI Act, 1963 from the payment of taxes on income, profit and capital gains. It is also exempted from any deduction of tax at source. Some special benefits are offered to individuals, residents and NRIs. The unit holders enjoy a variety of tax benefits from their investments in units. The tax concessions to different categories of unit holders are available under the Income Tax Act from time to time. The following exemptions are available to the unit holders:

(a) 80–L of the Income Tax Act provides exemption to resident individuals.
(b) 88–ULIP–20 per cent of provident contribution rebate is available.
(c) Tax rebate available to Equity Linked Savings Scheme ELSS.
(d) Under Section 194k from the assessment year 1995–96, a 20 per cent deduction would be made for corporates and 15 per cent for others.
(e) Under Section 11 of the Act, the income of charitable and religious trusts in any year is totally exempted from income tax.
(f) Under Section 19(21), investment by scientific research associations enjoy exemption from tax if the funds are invested in units.
(g) The tax rebate to mutual funds under Sections 54E and 54EB.
(h) Investment in unit qualifies for total exemption from wealth tax both for resident and non-resident individual companies.

# 7

# COMMERCIAL PAPER

## Introduction

Commercial paper is one of the money market instrument. It is quite a new financial instrument in the Indian Money Market. It is a form of usance promissory note. It can be negotiable by endorsement and delivery. It may be issued even at discount. The legal formalities are prescribed by the RBI. It can be issued by a non-banking company for raising funds for short-term period. It can be issued for the requirement of working capital. It can be issued by mostly leading, reputed, credit worthy and highly rated large corporations. The Commercial Paper is also known as **"Industrial paper, Finance paper or Corporate paper"**. The CPs are issued in domestic as well as international financial markets. In international financial market it is called as **"Euro Commercial Paper"**. The CPs are unsecured. They are like treasury bills. CPs are close competitors of treasury bills. They have a buyback facility. They are usually issued in a bearer form. The issue of CPs are mostly in large denominations. They will be issued through banks or merchant banks or brokers in the open market. Sometimes they may be sold through direct placement with the lenders. They are primarily issued by the public utilities, bank-holding companies, insurance companies, transportation companies and finance companies. The CPs are purchased by the banks, NBFs and liquid business concerns. The CPs have a very flexible maturity. They are regarded as highly safe and liquid instruments. The CPs are to be one of the highest quality financial instrument from the private sector. They are a cheaper sources of finance than bank loans. They are mostly issued by the companies to meet current finance and seasonal needs of the company. They are issued for a minimum period of three months and maximum of 6 months. In USA, the maturity period of CP cannot be more than 270 days. In UK between 7 to 364 days, in France 10 days to 7 years, in Canada 30 to 365 days, in Australia 185 days

**Features of the CPs**

The following are the salient features of the commercial paper programme:

1. It is transferable by endorsement and delivery.
2. The minimum size of issue shall be Rs. 25 lakhs.
3. It is an unsecured promissory note.
4. The current ratio of the issuer company should not be less than 1.33:1.
5. The minimum credit rating from CRISIL shall be $P_2$ or $A_2$ from ICRA.
6. The tangible net worth shall be Rs. 5 crores.
7. It can also be issued to NRIs.
8. It can be issued to either discount or face value.
9. The issues company should be classified under the head, Health Code No. 1 status by financing banks.

**Issue Procedure**

The CP has to be issued in the proforma which is prescribed by the RBI is presented below:

1. The issuing company must get the credit rating from CRISIL. The rating status should be $P_1$.
2. The company shall submit the application in the prescribed form along with credit rating certificate to its banker.
3. The banker scrutinises the form, if the company is eligible to issue CPs. It shall forward the application to RBI along with rating certificate within one week.
4. The RBI on being satisfied may approve the issue.
5. The company shall make arrangements to privately CPs and complete the issue within a period of two months from the date of approval of the RBI.
6. The bankers will collect the amount from the investors through crossed account payee cheques.
7. The banker will reduce the working capital limits by the amount of the size of the CPs issued.
8. After the completion of the issue, the company should in form to the RBI within three days.
9. The issue expenses should be borne by the company.

**Indian Context**

The Vaghul Committee had been appointed in 1987 to study the CPs market. The Committee submitted its suggestions and recommendations to the RBI. Subsequently the RBI announced in March 1989 to introduce a particular scheme for commercial papers segment. According to scheme, certain corporates could issue CPs from the Indian Money Market. The RBI had issued guidelines to issue CPs which came into effect from 1.1.1990. These guidelines are applicable to All NBFCs and Non-Finance Companies. The companies governed by FERA 1973 have been accorded general permission by the RBI to issue CPs. The **Vaghul Committee** suggested the following recommendations:

(a) CPs must sold directly by the issuer to investors.
(b) The maturity period could be 5 days and over but not exceeding 6 months.
(c) The issuing company should have a net worth of Rs. 5 crores.
(d) The issuing company scrip should be listed on the stock exchange.
(e) The minimum denomination of notes could be Rs. 5 lakhs.
(f) The minimum amount of issue could be Rs. 1 crore.
(g) The issuing company would need to obtain every six months a credit rating from a credit rating agency. Companies with only a minimum of a rating would be permitted to enter the market.
(h) The interest rate on CP would be market determined.
(i) The issue expenses should not exceed a total of **1 per cent** of the amount raised.
(j) The RBI would authorise the programme size of a company and the timing of issues.
(k) The instrument should not be subject to stamp duty at the time of issue and there should not be any tax deduction at source.
(l) The paper should be freely transferable by endorsement and delivery and there should be no stamp fee on such transfers.
(m) The legislative amendments would be required from time to time.

Any person, bank, company and other registered incorporated bodies as well as unincorporated bodies can invest in CPs. The CPs may be issued on a single date or on different dates within a period of two weeks from the date of approval of the issue by the RBI. The banks are permitted to either undertake or to co-accept the issue of cps. The success of CPs depends on the emergence and growth of the secondary market for them. The disadvantage regarding issue of CPs are presented below:

1. The obtaining credit rating, every time a company wants to issue CPs, is prove restrictive, time consuming and costly.
2. The borrowers will lose a portion of their working capital limits with banks once they issue.
3. It is not an additional finance but it is just a substitute for bank finance.
4. Investment is CPs is technically unsecured and more risky than bank deposits.
5. The quantum of CPs issues is limited to only 20 per cent of working capital needs.

# 8

# ELECTRONIC COMMERCE (E-Commerce)

## Introduction

Information technology has emerged in the world affecting the average man's personal social and public life in all aspects. It is an outcome of the advanced in telecommunication and computer technology. It helps to optimise the use of scarce resources through intelligent information system. It has made decisive in roads in all walks of life in corporate/ Government offices, showrooms, banking, hotels, hospitals, factories, airports, railways stations, education communications, entertainment, scientific in laboratories, defence, navigation, archaeological survey and tourism. It has been used extensively in operations of routine activities like record keeping, communications and for obtaining higher productivity from the system.

It replaced old, out-dated methods and allows to handle big and complex data within a short period of time. The distance and access is no barrier for information. It has influenced the work culture in organisations and lifestyle of corporate sector. The offices are becoming as paperless offices. Therefore, it is considered fifth element on the earth. They are men, machines, IT, material and money.

Information is a product of data processing. The quality of information depends upon many factors. The information can easily and quickly accessible through the online access system. The processing of data for the information processing is allowed only after a thorough validation of transactions and the contents.

The term electronic commerce is becoming more popular in the **digital economy**. It is one of the business transaction in the trade world.

Electronic Commerce can be defined as "the use of electronic transmission medium to engage in the exchange, including buying and selling of products and services requiring transportation, either physically or digitally from location to location."[1]

It involves all transactions. It requires the digital transmission of transactions. The transactions are settled through electronic devices or digital mechanism. It allows a market place to exist where buyers and sellers can meet and transact with each other. The development of the E-commerce will depend upon the elements, the Internet and Website. The internet activity demonstrates the E-commerce that can provide substantial, tangible benefits to a firm when implemented properly.

**Benefits of E-commerce**

The following benefits are available through E-commerce:

1. It reduces lower selling and marketing costs.
2. It reduces purchase order processing cost.
3. It is more affordable than tradition system.
4. It can reach a more geographically dispersed location.
5. It reduces in inventories.
6. It facilitates better customer service.
7. It increases the volume of business.
8. It reduces substantial cost of production.

Internet allows firms to reach many customers in a very low cost fashion. The modern business enterprises are shifting their sales and marketing functions to electronic processes. This transformation stage allows the firm to either reduce their overhead costs or better utilisation of its human resources. Consumers are also reap benefits by using the internet. The following benefits are available to the customers.

(a) It reduces time from shopping.
(b) It facilitates a wide choice of vendors and products.
(c) It provides vast amount of information that can be accessed on demand.
(d) It arranges the goods at more competitive prices.

The customer have an increased choice of vendors. The E-commerce provides top international famous brands at the disposal of a common man. The customers have a greater choice of services which are available from global Internet companies. Information is buying power to consumers. A greater access to a wide information, enhances the sales volume of the business. The Internet is a network of networks. The internet came out in 1969 as a joint project between The **Defence Advanced Research Projects Agency** and a university. The switch theory is the most important element in the internet. This theory was first developed by **Leonard Keinrock** at Mitchigan Institute of Technology. The some packet switching theory is still the basis of today's data transfer methods. The electronic mail was introduced in **1972**. The internet was used for commercial sector in 1980. The world-wide web was born less than a decade ago and it has yet to reach anywhere close to its full business potential. It incorporates the use of hyper text links, software portability, network and socket programming.

The E-commerce is not a just technology it is a way of conducting business that has the potential to impact every aspect of the firm's value chain E-commerce strategies need to be formulated to achieve the overall business goals. The environmental changes may cause a business to rethink or adjust its missions and goals. The environmental changes may be business trends, once the trends are identified, the specific objectives may be framed.

## The Impact of E-commerce on the Value Chain

The firms engaging in E-commerce may share information with their customers and suppliers at many stages of the value chain. The customer oriented value chain able the customer to access the suppliers information system. A customer can access to the firms inventory data such as price, quantity and availability before making transactions. Therefore, the customer is able to get product specifications in electronically. The actual sales deal may be placed electronically. The seller/supplier will deliver the goods according to the customer's desire. The customer can also check the delivery status of orders placed with the supplier.

Internet strategy of business is the basic strategy of a business concern. A model developed by Albert Angehrn is known as "**ICDT**" Information, Communication, Transaction and Distribution. The Angehrn's model is based on four virtual spaces. They are presented below:

**(a) Virtual Information Space (VIS).**
**(b) Virtual Distribution Space (VDS).**
**(c) Virtual Transaction Space (VTS).**
**(d) Virtual Communication Space (VCS).**

The ***VIS*** provides a firm displays information about their products, brands and services. The displayed information must be accurate and current. The displayed information is accessible to authorised users. The site should be accessible at any time without long wait times.

The ***Virtual Distribution Space*** is used to deliver the product or services purchased by the consumer. The products must be delivered according to the specifications given by the customer. The products being delivered must be digital or the services through online broker. The delivery of products and services to approved customers only.

The ***Virtual Transaction Space*** is used to execute sales orders. This space provide data security. Therefore, all companies have been reluctant to enter this space. This VTS provide security over data, accuracy and integrity of processing methods reliability of vendor, reputability of trading partner and privacy concerns by customers.

The ***Virtual Communication Space*** is useful in relationship building, negotiation and exchange of ideas. This space is just like a forum, chat rooms and virtual communities. The Angehrn model is useful for determining the long and short-term achievement of a firms business strategy.

The another electronic model was developed by Peter Fingar. This model is known as **"Three pillars of electronic commerce"**. It builds on traditional market space and utilises electronic mechanisms. This model is based on the following pillars:

**(a) Electronic information.**
**(b) Electronic relationships.**
**(c) Electronic transactions.**

The **Electronic Information** is the first pillar in this model. Constructing an electronic information pillar is easy. The word processing software packages can easily convert documents into a web-readable format. The construction of the electronic information pillar should not be conducted in a shoddy fashion.

The **Electronic Relationship** is the second pillar. This pillar is about building a site that has the feeling of being a port of entry into a community. This site needs to have a certain features. It must be innovative, add value, provide information and interaction.

The third pillar is the **Electronic Transaction** pillar. This pillar provides security of data transaction. This pillar is similar to Angern's virtual transaction space.

## E-Commerce Security

The security of data transmitted over the internet is an impediment of the growth of electronic commerce. The web based companies sales have been declined due to the greater information losses, theft of data, and lost revenues due to security breaches. To overcome this problem, the companies are showing interest to install the Enterprise Resource Planning system.

The corporate sector is concerned about security and they are installing **Fire walls**. It is the answer to security solutions. Firewall provide a means to control connections between a company's private network and the internet. Many organisations want to increase protection from the threats. Therefore, the fire walls are considered by orgnaisations to be a very important security device. Fire wall is a system or group of systems that enforces an access control policy between two networks. Fire walls should be used as a component of enterprises security. It is not as the only solution and also provide a robust set of controls. They are not fool proof.

## E-Commerce and Role of Third Party

Electronic Commerce creates new risks to the corporate sector and consumers. It also creates a number of new opportunities for the third parties. In traditional business models, certified public accountant has been regarded as independent third party. Accountants are best known for opining on the accuracy of financial statements. The CPAs conduct an indepth review of the financial statements and projections. They perform a vital function.

The current security solutions are not perfect and must continue to evolve at any given point in time cost effective solutions can be identified. The level of production that is provided called data security. The desire by consumers to receive a signal indicating that

(a) Website is reputable.
(b) Private information is securely transmitted.
(c) The Private information is securely stored electronically.

## Regulatory Environment

The growing demand for internet leads to a close scrutiny by the Government agencies, consumer groups and business coalitions. The law makers should intervene, impose and enforce the laws of the land to this internet sector. Each country has three categories of internet users to serve:

(a) Government and law enforcement agencies.
(b) Businesses.
(c) Private citizens.

The primary issues faced by these three groups are:

(a) encryption.
(b) privacy rights of citizens,
(c) domain name disputes,
(d) tax policies,
(e) electronic agreement, and
(f) libel law and the responsibility of ISP.

The internet is global and involves a multitude of very different cultures and government that clash on most of these issues and the legal environment of the internet can appear unthretable. Government world-wide are issuing internet legislation and industry consortiums are proposing self-regulatory programmes.

**Cryptography** is a method of mathematical encoding used to transform messages into an unreadable format in an effort to maintain confidentiality of data. The constant evolution describes the necessary environment in which security solutions exist. In older to conduct e-commerce on the internet the messages must be electronically transmitted in some manner. Therefore, Digital Government needs Digital guidelines, the US Government is moving towards the use of digital data transmission and storage. Several important security services are required to ensure reliable trustworthy electronic transmission of business messages. The primary security services are divided into five categories.

(a) Confidentiality.
(b) Integrity.

(c) Authentication.
(d) Authorisation.
(e) Non-repudiation.

These security issues are not new concepts to business managers, the recent challenge has been to update security measures for internet based e-commerce.

The Internet is built on the concept of hyper text links. It is an item such as text or an image which has the address or location of another web page attached to it when a user clicks on the hyper text link. They are instantly transported to the attached location and the associated web page is automatically loaded.

E-commerce applications will have a corporate presence site from which it may collect data about its visitors and or conduct business transactions must be designed with the following international laws of each country from which is visitor resides.

(a) Taxation.
(b) Privacy.
(c) Intellectual property.
(d) Cryptography.
(e) Digital signature.
(f) Acceptable business practices.

**Financial EDI**

The Financial EDI can be defined as "The electronic exchange of payments, payment related information or financially related documents in standard formats between business partners."

Financial EDI is a key distinguishing feature between partially and fully integrated EDI systems. In partially integrated EDI systems, the payment and related information may be produced in hard copy form and sent through postal system. Fully integrated EDI system encompass financial EDI and both payment and remittance information is transferred electronically. Large institutions use financial EDI and the dollar amounts transferred electronically amount to more than cheque and cash transactions combined. The financial institutions change their customers payments and remittance information over a network called the **Automated clearing house**. This type of payments include the following transactions:

(a) Business to business payments.
(b) Government payment to contractor.
(c) Direct deposit payroll checks.
(d) Pensions and social security checks.
(e) Automatic payment of mortgages.
(f) Payment of utility bills and car loans.

The financial EDI is in a high growth phase and significant enhancements to the infrastructure over in forthcoming years is expected.

**Internet Trading Relationships**

The E-commerce websites fall into one of the three categories according to their internet trading relationships. They are presented below:

(1) *Consumer to Business:* The Internet opened up for commercial activity in 1992. This service have seen a phenomenal growth in the online store fronts selling goods directly to consumers. The consumers to have benefited from low prices, wider selections, purchase locations etc. This service reduce cycle time eliminating in efficiencies and lowering costs. In this consumer who make purchases at the site unknowingly initiate a chain reaction of events that flow across the company's internal database. The customers data will be recorded and a purchase order specifications will be executed. The purchase order is then sent to vide area network. The VAN is eventually routed to the proper trading partner. This process occurs in a matter of seconds. It requires no paper and no human intervention.

(2) *Business to Business:* It involves the relationship between two companies through the mode of internet. AB to B consists a number of buyers, sellers and intermediaries. Extra net is a secured business network of several co-operating organisations operated through VAN. The B to B saves the customer real time, minimise the labour cost for seller. It reduces costs, increased profit margins and higher customer satisfaction. It enables trading partners, suppliers and customers with common interests to form a tight business relationships.

(3) *Government to Citizen:* It is the best device to transmit the communication to the public. The Federal Government is using the internet to reach its citizens for a variety of information. The US postal service sells stamps online, allow address changes to be filled, missing postal money orders to be filed. The US Government allows tax payers to down load forms and to file their returns electronically.

The EDI Internet systems are capable of providing the following benefits:

(a) Universal connectivity.
(b) Lower entry cost.
(c) Sharing of information.
(d) Tracking of market data.

The internet and e-commerce offers endless possibilities and opportunities to businesses of all sizes as well as convenience to consumers. These benefits include some risks to merchant and consumers.

**Internet** is the private networking technology for intra company telecommunications. Risks may be solely at the enterprise level if intranets are in place at present. There are different types and levels of risks faced by parties engaging in electronic business transactions. There are three major different players involved in e-commerce on the internet.

## Internet Associated Risks

**Risk** may be defined as the possibility of loss or injury. It can also be defined as "someone or something that creates or suggests a hazard". Losses on the electronic frontier may arise in different ways. The data may be stolen, destroyed corrupted misused, altered or falsely generated. The risk is associated with the possibility of loss of confidential data or the destruction, generation or use of data or programmes that physically, mentally or financially norms another party as well as the possibility of harm to hardware.

**Threat** can be defined as "Anyone with the capability, technology, opportunity and intent to do harm. Potential threats can be foreign or domestic, internal or external, state sponsored or a single rogue element. Terrorists, insiders disgruntled employers and hackers are included in this profile."[2]

The number of external attacks is growing because of the increased use of the internet. The threats from insiders have not decreased and designers of systems need to adequately ensure that controls are in place to prevent dangers from both internal and external threats. The most common breaches involved in probing the system, internal documents, e-mail messages, introducing a virus and compromising trade secrets. At present the computer networks were attacked and penetrated by external perpetrators, the attacks are at a minimum considered to be a multimillion dollar nuisance. The companies currently connected to the internet need to identify and manage the risks associated with internet connections. Threats to business transactions data between trading partners are important. The following are the internet associated risk:

**(A) Risks to customers.**
**(B) Risks to sellers.**

### *(A) Risks to Customers*

The customers are not willing to make purchases through internet by Credit Cards. Because they feel insecurity about the theft of credit card information by internet hackers. There are some false websites are set up for the purpose of stealing visitor's IDs and password, stealing credit card information, spying on a visitor's hard drive and uploading files from the visitors hard drive.

The customer who transact the deals through internet shall pay with credit cards. Cyber cash payments methods are another popular alternative. This credit card information is stored by the selling agents ISPs. The hackers are breaking into selling agents and the ISP's systems and obtaining the customers credit card data.

The privacy on the internet is another important factor in Risk. The issue of privacy on the internet is of concern to many people. Cookies were designed to allow web servers to operate more efficiently. It provides a better response time to repeat visitors to their sites and more accurate track different visitors visit a site. The use of cookies, has become a very controversial topic.

### *(B) Risk to Sellers*

The sellers also face risk due to internet trading. The following types of risks involved by the sellers:

- **(a) Customer impersonation.**
- **(b) Denial of service attacks.**
- **(c) Data theft.**

#### *(a) Customer Impersonation*

The seller has no oral contacts with the customer. There is no interaction between two parties buyer and seller in the internet trading. Sometimes the seller is unable to identify his customers. Sometime the false customers also create problems. The customer can order goods and services for a variety of reasons. The customer may be to obtain a free service or product with a false credit card number. Some customers may be placed order with no intention to receive or to pay. This kind of risk more troubles as to a business concern. The customer intention is purely malicious. He has no intention to take the delivery of the goods. These false ordering techniques may be conducted for a number of reasons:

- (1) satisfaction to the hacker,
- (2) to hurt corporate profit by a competitor,
- (3) to hurt corporate profit by former employees.

#### *(b) Denial of Service Attacks*

A denial of service attack is used by an individual to destroy, shut down or degrade a computer or network recourse. The goal of attack is to flood the communication ports and memory buffers of the targeted site to prevent the receipt of legitimate messages and the service of legitimate requests for connections. These attacks are on the rise as methods and programme code for conducting such acts are publicly available on hacker websites. These attacks are extremely hard to present.

**Data theft** is another risk involved in the internet transactions. The important data will be kept under physical lock and key. The data files that are stored digitally and concerned to public telecommunications lines can potentially be accessed by an unauthorised user without the perpetrator ever having to leave the comfort of home.

The following techniques are used to break the data in computer down time or data loss.

**(a) Viruses.**
**(b) Trojan Horses.**
**(c) Hoaxes.**
**(d) Buffer over flows.**

The increasing in tremendous use of E-mail and down loaded data and programs from the internet virus infections are arised. The computer virus and that infections have increased exponentially during the last 5 years. For example, for every one million pcs, 28000 are victims of infection. A virus is malicious programming and it possess the following characters:

(1) It replicates itself in some form.
(2) It is incorporated into program code.
(3) It performs unrequested.

**Virus** detection programmes, knowns as anti-virus programmes, can help detect known viruses and sometimes clean them from the drive without any damage being inflicted. The implementation of good security measures against various forms of viruses is important. Virus scanning software packages can only scan for know virsus. The most virus scanning software packages have frequent updates to their packages to include newly found viruses.

**Trojan Horse** is like a virus and it can unknowingly infiltrate a computer system. It do not replicate. They sneak into the system by attaching themselves to what appears to be a legitimate programme or file. It can enter into any system and erase the hard drive. The program does not attempt to replicate itself from disk to disk or platformme to platform. It sneaks into the system as a legitimate software offer and perform its damage, erasing the hard drive. They are more difficult to detect by virus scanning software.

**Hoaxes** are false alarms about virsuses sent out *via* e-mail. The investigation about the hoaxes is very costly. The hoaxes do not infect systems.

Hackers may cause **buffer overflows** by exploiting known or suspected holes in the resources handling section of operating systems. The perpetrator basically crashes the system.

## E-Commerce Payment Mechanism

The basic payment process for traditional business are cash, cheque, credit cards, debit cards and electronic fund transfers. Many different e-commerce payment mechanism are emerging and consumers will ultimately decide which form of payment they prefer. The payment mechanism now operates through credit cards, magnetic strip cards, smart cards, debit cards and e-cash. Some of these are not being used for internet applications. They are being marketed and used as alternatives to carrying physical cash. Further a protocol, secure Electronic Transaction was designed with secure data transmission as its basic objective. The set protocol was developed jointly by Master Card and Visa with the goal of providing a secure payment environment for the transmission of credit card data.

More and more payment options are becoming available to both business and consumers. Many of these options are presented below:

**(A) Smart Cards.**
**(B) Electronic Cheque.**
**(C) Magnetic Strip Cards.**
**(D) Electronic Cash.**

### *(A) Smart Cards*

Smart card is a little plastic card. It is just like a credit card but it contains a micro-processor and a storage unit. This card is developed with latest technology and it is a innovation that overcomes all limitations. They are more expensive. The stored data is not exposed to physical damage. These cards can store at least 100 times more data than magnetic strip cards. They are more popular in Europe. They are categorised in two kinds; memory smart cards and intelligent smart cards. **Memory card** contains less information and processing capabilities, they are used to record a monetary or unit value for a specific amount. **Intelligent cards** contains more information and process' a wider variety of information components than a memory smart card. This card also have greater processing capabilities for programmed decision making for various applications. **The electronic purse** is used to refer to monetary value, that is loaded on to the smart cards micro processor and that can be used by consumer for purchase. The Merchants who are accepting the cards, must have a smart card reader. The smart card readers are compatible with magnetic strip card readers. The smart card technology may be used in either an online or offline mode as with magnetic strip cards. **Offline** card technology can be used in underdeveloped countries. The functioning of offline smart cards as presented below:

***Step I*:** Smart card holder inserts card into machine and down loads money from bank as to the microprocessor on the card.

***Step II*:** The consumer pays for merchandise/service by inserting smart card into merchant's smart card reader.

***Step III*:** The merchant's smart card reader records the transaction.

***Step IV*:** At the end of the day, the merchant inserts a smart card to receive download of the day's sales.

***Step V*:** Take to bank for credit for day's sale for cash.

Smart cards used in place of cash have the advantage of providing an electronic record for purchases and the ability to printout transaction data which can serve as receipts.

The smart card holder inserts his card into smart card reader enter a valid password and the amount of the purchase is deducted from the balance on the card. The card reader computes a running total of the sales amounts deducted from the customers. The smart card can be taken to the bank for immediate cash payment. If the merchant has a networked personal computer and banking software then it may insert the smart card and transfer the amount on the smart card directly into a bank account. The telephone manufacturers are introducing smart card phones that can be used for a variety of purposes. The phones can be used to :

(a) pay for items purchased over the phone,
(b) download money from bank accounts to a smart card,
(c) transfer balances between accounts, and
(d) check bank balances.

### *(B) Electronic Cheque*

Another mode for internet payments is the electronic cheque. In this method, the payor instructs its bank to pay a specific amount to another party, the payee. The financial EDI systems have performed this function for years using private communication circuits such as value Added Network. The new generation of electronic cheques provides the following functions:

(1) present the bill to the payor,
(2) allow the payer to initiate payment of the invoice,
(3) provide remittance information,
(4) allow the payer to initiate automatic payment authorisation,
(5) interface with financial management software, and
(6) allow payments to be made at first time.

Electronic payment system involves two parties payor and payee. An electronic bill contains the same information as a hard copy bill transported to the payor through the postal system. An electronic bill does not have to be received, a payor or can make payments for bills received through the postal system.

Most electronic cheque systems can accommodate situations where the payee does not have account at a financial institution, therefore many electronic cheque service providers will produce a hard copy check for these types of payments. Electronic payment of bills is expected to increase substantially over the forthcoming years

### *(C) Magnetic Strip Card*

A magnetic strip card is a small plastic card. These cards are widely used for applications such as bank credit/debit cards, telephone cards, employee identification card, vending machines and copy machines. These cards are used as an electronic purse. It allows the card holder to use the card to purchase goods or services. These cards support a form of e-commerce pre-paid phone cards have become very popular worldwide. Magnetic strip cards have been used for well over a decade to educational sector. The cards have one magnetic strip on them that contains two or three tracks of information. The encoding of this information is usually done in specifications of ISO 7810, 7811, 7813. The magnetic strip card readers are necessary to both read and encode the cards. These cards are three types:

(a) **Online magnetic strip cards.**
(b) **Offline magnetic strip cards.**
(c) **Hybrid cards.**

**Online magnetic strip cards** are used to read customer information from the strip. The information is then used to access information about the card holder from a central computer. These types of cards are commonly used for credit cards, debit cards, library cards. The **offline magnetic strip cards** actually store information that can be interpreted by the card reader and altered. Vending machines and telephone cards are using this technology to store the amount of money or call the units to the card. The magnetic strip cards that are combined with smart card technology are called **hybrid cards**. Recently the Government of Andhra Pradesh and Karnataka is thinking seriously about to adopt this technology towards power sector. The electric consumption of a consumer can be recorded with this technology. The value of the amount will be recorded in the card in advance and the consumption of power will deduct the balance amount. The remaining amount of power will be displayed. Therefore, the consumer will take precautions for his future consumption of power. These power cards are based on **"cellphone—prepaid card system"**. After the amount of money stored is exhausted, then automatically the power supply will be discontinued. Therefore, the customer should go for another power card. It reduces the theft of the power and also useful to the Government to avoid the bad debts. This process will reduce the power cost substantially, because theft will be detected and the power cost becomes cheaper. Therefore, the Government can provide the power at lowest prices in order to make the citizens more happy.

### *(D) Electronic Cash*

Electronic cash is used to refer to a prepaid, stored monetary value. The stored value can be used for electronic purchases. The payment mechanisms can be categoried as forms of electronic cash. **Electronic cash** is a form of stored value. The stored value can easily exchangeable in an electronic format. The electronic cash makes the entire system challenging to implement, especially when no physical storage device that can be inserted into a reader is available. The electronic cash needs to be verified as authentic.

The electronic payment mechanisms are the key element factor of the revenue and expenditure cycles of businesses. This is the development stage of new and improved payment technologies made possible by the internet infrastructure. The related security issues must be clearly understood, as well as the use of these devices to help business operate efficiently as they can provide latest technology.

## REFERENCES

1. Greenstein, *E-commerce*, TMH, p. 2, 2000.
2. Greenstein, *E-commerce*, TMH, p. 133, 2000.

# INDEX